THE
UNCERTAIN
PHOENIX

THE UNCERTAIN PHOENIX

Adventures Toward a Post-Cultural Sensibility

DAVID L. HALL

New York

FORDHAM UNIVERSITY PRESS

1982

Printed in the United States of America

For
DEBRA
Many . . . and One

ACKNOWLEDGMENTS

This work was conceived and written in a variety of contrasting locations. In addition to the athenaea at Austin, Berkeley, Boston, Chicago, New Haven, and New York, the desert spaces of Arizona, Nevada, and Texas, the mountains of northern New Mexico, and the beaches and tropical forests of the Yucatán Peninsula witnessed the writing of portions of this essay. The quality of the ambience, as well as the graciousness of the people encountered in these various locations, certainly contributed to the pleasure of writing this volume.

I am grateful to the Society for Philosophy of Creativity, The International Society for Chinese Philosophy, the Process and Praxis Group, The Society for Asian and Comparative Philosophy, and the Utopian Studies Society for providing me opportunities to try out many of my stranger ideas. I certainly appreciate the generosity of the University of Texas at El Paso Research Committee for underwriting much of the travel and research costs associated with this project.

Of all the individuals who have aided in the completion of the book, three must be given special notice: Robert Neville, who served throughout as a model of responsible speculation and scholarship, helped me solidify many otherwise transient insights. He may well wish that at least some of these notions had remained ephemeral. Kuang-ming Wu, with the peevish wisdom of a Taoist sage, looked askance at my work and told me what he saw. Finally, I am especially appreciative of the imagination and artistry of Beth Neville who has contributed that by which (unfortunately) this book cannot be told.

The University of Texas   DAVID L. HALL
  at El Paso

Contents

Thinking from the Desert

FOR THE GREATER PART OF MY LIFE I have made my home in the Southwestern desert, a region with a special character perhaps incomprehensible to those who have never come under its awesome influence. The magnificence of the desert is impossible to describe, but it resides at least in part in the fact that it is at once a place of vast extremes and a place indifferent to extremes. The withering stillness of an August day threatens anyone unprotected from the sun; but the winds of March and April can as easily make the sand itself into a near lethal weapon. At times the desert presents itself as a desiccated emptiness, offering not a drop of water to sustain life; without warning, however, torrential rains can create dangerous floods, after which the desert blossoms with an inconceivable variety of living things. There are no half-measures here. And yet the contrasting expressions of the desert are played against a background of brooding, almost alien, constancy that renders them rhythmic and harmonious in some vaguely reassuring fashion.

When I first came to this area nearly twenty-five years ago, our culture was living under the threat of a mushroom-shaped cloud born from out of these very desert spaces. What irony, once having secured ourselves somewhat from the threat of Atomic disaster, that we should have turned our paranoid fears toward the "other mushroom," itself a product of the same desert environment. Here in the desert the two antithetical symbols meet: the psychedelic plant and the nuclear flower of evil. I reached maturity during that brief period in which our culture dangled between these two extremes, awaiting the judgment of history.

But such extremes have a way of being rendered less severe, not through adjustment or compromise, but simply by virtue of the vastness of the alternative possibilities that provide their background. The desert can well symbolize that vastness which is the primary occasion for hope in the face of the restricting dystopias that have begun to pattern our intellectual landscape.

As a symbol of the situation within which we find ourselves, the desert can also serve as a *source* of renewal. This may be so because the desert is, above all else, a place of solitariness; and it is only from solitude that renewal can come. We wonder as we wander, and only as we wander. In the mountains one struggles for the peak; in the forest each tall tree can become a familiar landmark indicating the proper way. But the desert shifts and changes, defying attempts to explore it, to chart it, or to tame it. The desert is a place for wandering. And in the absence of firm values and clear goals we need less to follow stoically well-worn paths and more to practice the art of wandering, which can occur only if we retreat into deserted regions of life or mind. The desert is both symbol and source of our attempts to renew the activity of wondering, which can give birth to a new sensibility. Thus, it should not be at all surprising that the initial stimulus for a culture's activities is to be found in its religious experiences, since religions arise, metaphorically (and often quite literally), from out of the desert.

The wasteland imagery employed by so many of our recent cultural prophets has perhaps misled us. There is a vast difference between a wasteland and desert. Ours is not so much a land laid waste, which, once cleared of its rubble, can be rebuilt through human effort. Doubtless, when the rains come they will rust and rot the artifacts of our tired civilization, but it would be a mistake to believe that we ought to use

our energies to renovate the collapsing structures of our traditional culture. It is time to look beyond, to the promises of the
desert. For when the rains touch the desert, myriad blossoms
shall spring forth.

Perhaps the hardest lesson we must learn is that we are
not rainmakers. Neither the passing away of the old nor the
birth of the new is within our powers to determine. We are
desert dwellers, and thus depend upon the grace or the judgment of our ambience. Our cultural desert is rife with possibilities, and only when some from among these potentialities
begin to emerge in more articulate form can any of us feel
capable of efficacious action on behalf of a novel future.

In the attempt to write a philosophy of culture I have had
continual recourse to such reflections as these, for it is clear—
at least to me—that the endeavor to promote cultural self-
understanding cannot result in a coherent vision unless that
vision is derived from a sympathetic consideration of what
may appear to be contrasting, and at times conflicting, modalities of thought. And it is equally clear that we must avoid what
I shall later discuss under the rubric of the Pelagian Fallacy—
that is, the argument from freedom in principle to freedom in
fact. Our public world is at present a sphere of determination
upon which we depend until such time as articulate possibilities for future attainment are manifest. This assumption concerning the lack of freedom in public activity will receive
sufficient explication in the course of the essays that follow,
but I must say more here concerning the contrasting modes of
thought upon which I have drawn in my endeavor to describe
our cultural condition.

My greatest hesitation concerning the speculations on our
cultural situation that follow this brief *apologia* is with regard
to the unbalanced relationship between the *principles* and the
metaphors that constitute the foundation and superstructure
of this work. "Principles," the beginning points of thought
and action, are valid only to the extent that they permit themselves to be disciplined by "metaphors," the means of evoking sensibility beyond sense. And metaphors are efficacious
only to the extent that they have a "beginning"—i.e., are
principled. A principle is not a beginning in itself, but the

beginning of something in particular. The answer to the question "The beginning of what?" requires at some point along the line the resort to a metaphor. And a metaphor is not an end in itself, but the end of a beginning—the means to a beyond, but to a particular beyond.

The struggle between metaphors as symbols of thought and principles as sources of thought, the special character of which Plato articulated near the beginning of our present epoch, seems to be peculiarly intense today. Neither our poets nor our philosophers seem able to supply us with that kind of sustenance that would allow us to meet our situation with fortitude. Poets, shepherds of the metaphors that incite, evoke, and reprove us, and philosophers, caretakers of the principles that situate, articulate, and organize our sensibilities, have quarreled throughout history. That it is, after all, a family quarrel, one that advertises the essential interdependence of the conflicting parties, has not made the discord any easier to resolve.

The philosopher of culture—unlike his more analytic and systematic colleagues—is condemned to (and often condemned by) the tensions and conflicts of his ambience. Thus, in addition to the many failings attributable solely to its author, this work reflects the mixed metaphorical imagery required to elicit the confusion that, willy nilly, characterizes our present situation. This means that the metaphorical structure is at times splayed and unfocused. On the other hand, the account of contemporary culture I have given skirts on the edges of inconsistency since it is involved in assessing essentially incompatible, and sometimes contradictory, principles, not so much to highlight their contradictions (though at times that *will* be the purpose) as to articulate their distinctive explanatory powers.

In articulating cultural importances it is necessary to take an extremely abstract and general perspective since what is discernibly important is widespread, pervasive, and characteristically blunt. As a consequence of the abstractive level at which I have operated I have often resorted to typological devices of a very general sort as a means of describing these pervasive cultural determinants. It is not my purpose to claim validity for such devices at any but the level of cultural self-understanding. I do insist, however, that this resort to typology and blunt characterization is essential to the task at hand. The phenomenon of culture per se has about it a quality of massiveness, which means that it is distorted if over-refined. It is precisely the penchant of most contemporary philosophers for analytic refinement rather than speculative synthesis that has led to the pernicious neglect of philosophy of culture so evident in our period.

Part of the difficulty I am recounting is grounded, of course, in the very nature of speculative philosophy of culture, which must involve that kind of *reflection* that consists in holding a mirror, a *speculum*, before the object of one's investigation and noting the variety and sinuosities of the captured images. One cannot, in so doing, attempt to over-clarify the reflections. It is useless to try to clean one's dirty face by polishing the mirror; the cleaner the mirror, the more clearly we see the soiled countenance. It took the special genius of Charles Sanders Peirce to recognize the existence of "the objective vague," that which could be clarified and articulated only at the risk of falsification.

Our cultural situation is objectively vague. The speculations that follow share in that vagueness by presenting a reflection of the form, the substance, and the shadows of our contemporary cultural experience. In order to present such a reflection it is necessary to make use of both metaphors and principles in ways that promote a sense of the vagueness and uncertainty of our situation. Before one is tempted to attribute the apparent stylistic inelegancies merely to unvetted prose, I do hope he or she will consider the special character of the communicative task that the author has set for himself, and the way that task has shaped the style and substance of this work. A recent faddish slogan to the contrary notwithstanding, in the speculations that follow the medium is precisely *not* the message.

Closely associated with the tension between the principles and the metaphors discussed above, and partly responsible for it, is what can only be termed the "aesthetic incompatibility" of the arguments and the conclusions of this work. This incompatibility results from the fact that many of the conclusions that may be plausibly drawn concerning the direction of our technological future are bizarre in the extreme. And I have not hesitated to draw them. On the other hand, the arguments leading up to, or defending, these conclusions are gathered from the broadest possible of cultural resources and are couched for the most part in traditional philosophic language. This has led to a disquieting feeling on my part that, while the professional philosophers who read this book are apt to appreciate its arguments, they may find the conclusions drawn from these arguments to be unacceptable except as utopian fantasies; and while the wider public will be quite interested in some of the conclusions concerning our technological future, they may not feel disposed to wade through the philosophic arguments—especially when they can get even more sensational speculations written in a much less demanding style.

But surely any such suspicion underestimates both philosopher and non-philosopher alike. For most contemporary philosophers have been forced to learn the lesson best expressed by Miguel de Unamuno: "The fact that the consequences of a proposition are catastrophic says nothing against the truth of the proposition." Nor should we believe that the non-philosopher is unsympathetic with Cervantes' insight, "The road is better than the inn." The first lesson teaches us to accept the consequences of our arguments no matter how bizarre they might at first appear. The second lesson shows us that arguments are not for the sake of their conclusions, since it is in the arguments themselves that we discover the flow of experience and the rhythms of life that ground all philosophic inquiry. "Conclusions" are mere stopping-off places that punctuate a journey without ultimate destination. We argue, we speculate, we reflect, because the road is better than the inn; we conclude our arguments only as a means of pausing for refreshment along the way.

There is yet another tension present in this work. It is that between the traditions of the so-called Western, or Anglo-European philosophy, on the one hand, and the thinking indigenous to classical Oriental—particularly Chinese—culture, on the other. This work is a sequel to my *The Civilization of Experience*,[1] a speculative construction of a theory of culture employing the conceptualization of Alfred North Whitehead, our century's foremost philosopher of process. Those familiar with that work may believe that I have here traveled too far in the direction of exotic philosophic sensibilities in my effort to demonstrate the relevance of the traditions of process philosophy for an understanding of contemporary culture. Comparative philosophy is relatively new, and we have yet to develop criteria with which to assess the feasibility of importing alien sensibilities into contexts that are *prima facie* incompatible with them. In defense of my use of Oriental philosophies, I can only say that those who are willing to reflect with me on the issues considered in this work should come to appreciate both the relevance of process thought for the articulation of our cultural ambience, as well as the manner in which certain Oriental concepts and doctrines clarify and render more effective the process perspective.

Finally, I should say something of a tension that is not explicitly present in this work, but one that, doubtless, many will think ought to be: I refer to the tension between my expressed views and those over against which my vision stands. Speculative philosophy of culture, as I conceive it, must refuse the gambits offered by both absolutist and relativist understandings. I have not been blind to the scandalous relativism that emerges from a broad assessment of cultural evidences. But I have not sought to resolve the dilemma associated with philosophical relativity by recourse to the traditional method of dialectical refutation. In ages of uncertainty philosophic thinking progresses, haltingly, through the gradual enlargement of understanding; attempts to reduce the intellectual anxieties attendant upon the variety of conflicting truth-claims through an overly confident employment of dialectics can serve us no better than does the skeptical accession to the Protagorean Principle. My arguments are, for the most part, to be construed as seeking neither to establish truths nor to claim that no such establishment is possible. The burden of the speculative philosopher is to present a vision of sufficient coherence, complexity, and generality that it may serve as a context within which more specialized assertions of the skeptics and constructive dialecticians may find meaningful engagement.

Given the apologetic context within which most philosophic endeavors proceed, this book must be counted somewhat eccentric, and not a little strange. I confess I am worried less by the likelihood that the work will not be sympathetically received and more by the possibility that the book is not *sufficiently* strange to match the strangeness of the times. I find myself hoping that some among the readers of this work, less fastidious than I, will be stimulated to speculations far beyond those I have provided. For I cannot escape the belief that any vision of the future that leads us beyond mere stagnation, or the decline into infrahuman existence, must be radical in the extreme. Having said this, however, I must insist that I hold no illusions about the nature and efficacy of philosophic speculation. Mine is not a clarion call. It is, rather, a celebration of the uncertainty of the future as a means of stirring the ashes of the old world, and of endeavoring to anticipate the form of the Phoenix and the direction of her flight.

NOTE

1. (New York: Fordham University Press, 1973).

THE
UNCERTAIN
PHOENIX

PERSPECTIVE

1

Speculation and Foresight

History is a nightmare from which we are trying to awaken.
                                                JAMES JOYCE

When you awake you will remember everything; you will be hanging
on a string.

                                                The Band

WONDER AND WISDOM

ONE OF THE PRINCIPAL SPEAKERS at the Darwin Centennial
celebrations held on the University of Chicago campus in the
winter of 1959 was Sir Julian Huxley, grandson of Thomas
Huxley. Speaking from the pulpit of the magnificent
Rockefeller Chapel, this spokesman of humanistic, scientific
culture sounded the death-knell of religion. Sir Julian's dramatic antisermon, delivered in a measured, persuasive manner, is
to this day, perhaps, the single most famous address given in
the Chapel of the University of Chicago. And, perhaps, the
most prophetic. For though he was unaware of it at the time
Julian Huxley's indictment of Western religion was being
echoed in even more severe terms by Christian and Jewish
theologians across the country. What later came to be called
"The Death of God" movement was underway. The principal
issue in this theological movement of the Sixties was the

proclamation of the collapse of Judaeo-Christianity as a dynamic cultural force. "God is dead!" became the slogan for those who recognized that the cultural influence of orthodox religious beliefs had shrunk to almost zero.

The irony of this situation is, of course, that the litany of scientific orthodoxy strikes no more responsive chords today than that of Judaeo-Christian religion. Julian Huxley himself lived long enough to see evidence of the fact that the fate of our scientific culture was intrinsically tied to the fate of its religion. Not just orthodox religion, but the scientific culture nurtured by it, has entered upon a period of stagnation and decay. With the collapse of the belief in God came the failure of *all* absolutes. The grand constructions of science, our world-views, our conceptions of truth, goodness, and beauty have all been fragmented by the loss of "God" as the source of meaning and value. Infected by a sense of radical relativity, our culture becomes a "nightmare from which we are trying to awaken."

It was, after all, the belief in a God who created a rational order and disposed it according to natural laws that provided a principal foundation of modern scientific theory. We have only to reflect on the significance of Isaac Newton's claim that his greatest work was not the *Principia Mathematica* or the *Optics*, but his writings on the prophecies of Daniel and St. John, to be reminded how firmly the pioneers of modern science were committed to theological beliefs. Scientific reason, which we have long accepted as the only sure path to truth, turns out to be nothing more than a peculiar combination of the two fundamental human attitudes of *faith* and *doubt*. Reasoning begins from the foundations of belief and doubts all but its assumptions. The purpose of the doubt is the discovery of incorrigible truths; the purpose of belief is to provide a firm foundation from which to doubt.

Modern thought, born and nurtured in the doubt that corroded the Scholastic synthesis, provided a series of interesting philosophic adventures. In addition to the Cartesian rational doubt, which has as its principal aim the discovery of clear and distinct ideas from which systematic certainty could be achieved, there is the doubt of the empiricists, culminating in that of Hume, which had as its aim defense of the facts which could be gained from experience. Both of these types of doubt sought to father certainty and to establish truths, grand or humble, about God, Man, Nature, and Society that would be final and permanent. Rational doubt differs from skeptical doubt only in that the former maintains an element of faith. Faith in the Order of Nature, and faith in the ubiquity of causal relations were the essential beliefs that undergirded the claims of classical science. Doubt seeking certainty served as a methodological tool employed to discover the consequences of faith in rationality and order.

Critical doubt is a highly successful means of discovering truth as long as the beliefs undergirding scientific activity remain firm. But if they are threatened, so is the entire edifice of reason and science built upon them. Without the necessary faith underlying one's activity of doubt, there can be no discovery of truth. Absolute values, in any form, are no longer to be found. Doubt ceases to be the father of certainty and becomes, instead, the child of relativity. Pyrrhonian doubt brings the final collapse of faith, issuing in an age of skepticism.

Until quite recently we believed in the reality of Absolutes, even if we experienced them only in their absence. Then, gloomy prophets clothing their prophecies in mushroom-shaped metaphors, drew the attention of the public with messages of *anomie* and alienation, predictions of destructive violence, and the inevitable failure of civilization. But no more. The voices of cynicism and despair are no longer heeded. Indeed, the turn from existential despair to the kind of urbane detachment characterizing so many of the recently published works analyzing contemporary culture is one of the most significant events of recent years. It would be a mistake to consider this turning from despair on the part of our intellectuals to be a consequence of any amelioration of the problems that once evoked such anxious, pessimistic responses from our cultural prophets. On the contrary, our problems have increased in both number and intensity over the past generation. Surely our present times would seem to be ideal for the expression of the most cynical and pessimistic of proclamations. For in addition to the nuclear bomb, we must worry about the population bomb; the fall-out from our nuclear plants is as serious a problem today as the fallout from atomic testing ever was in the Fifties, and in addition to the traces of radioactivity appearing in our food we find we must worry over the even larger amounts of pesticides. The enemy without is still a very real threat; but to that threat has been added the enemy within—radicals and revolutionaries who wish to protect us from an oppressive society, and political and policing agencies, armed with "clear and present danger" mentalities, who wish to protect us from ourselves.

It is true that we have experienced many hopeful signs of change in the past few years (the liberation movements— black, Chicano, feminist; the new sexuality, the ecological movement, the synesthetic revolutions in art), but, without exception, we now seem to see the decline, if not the failure, of the promise of a new cultural sensibility. Strangely enough, in spite of these developments we do not appear to be cynical or disillusioned. Though we may certainly not be characterized as truly hopeful of the future, we cannot be said to be truly pessimistic either. The uncertainty of our situation is complete. The future is open. Not only have we lost the naïve belief in inevitable progress, we have lost the belief in the inevitability of any set of consequences. We have learned, at last, the lesson our relativistic culture is best adapted to teach us: there are no absolute values; nothing is absolutely certain; *anything is possible*. So infected by relativity is our situation, so complex and multi-valent are the events characterizing our cultural activity, that even dismay can hardly be clear-cut or well-focused. For in a culture such as we possess, omni-credulity seems essential for survival. It is no longer the case that we must believe in *something*; it becomes necessary to believe in *everything* in its turn. Ours is a hotch-potch culture where nothing ever really dies. Each thought, theory, principle or value is saved, like last year's wardrobe, in case it comes back in style. We have lost our sense of finality and irrevocability. We have lost our impulse to discover absolutes. We have even abandoned the search for an unimpeachable argument for the total absence of absolutes.

The cure for our present dis-ease cannot be found in increased knowledge. Indeed, it is knowledge, a kind of malignant self-consciousness, that has caused our problem. This world—"too much with us"—has been rapidly and well-nigh completely bereft of spontaneity and novelty. In accordance with a winding down in obedience to a cultural corollary of the law of entropy, we are experiencing a loss of vitality that can only result from boredom in the face of the staleness of alternatives open to intellectual endeavor. Our cultural psyche never really recovered from the Freudian articulation of the connections between raw libido and the sublimated products of intellectual culture, which has left each of our actions open to the reduction to simple motives of sexuality. Since Freud the influence of the psychoanalytic method has continued apace. The essence of that method consists of raising to the level of consciousness the structure of every item of individual and social experience. Jung has stolen our dreams; the social psychologists have catalogued "the games people play." Waking or sleeping, alone or with others, we are unable to escape our newly emergent Hamlet mentality. By rendering conscious formerly preconscious and unconscious areas of experience many of us have been forced, in simple self-defense, to cover our consciousness with a sophisticated veneer that resists, and will continue to resist, the most vigorous attempts to remove it. We have awakened from our nightmare. And we remember everything.

The simplest and most direct characterization of our present cultural condition is this: The scientific doubt that served so long as a tool for the establishment of truth has given way to doubt, which results from a frustrated search for truth. Doubt no longer serves as a means to truth; rather, doubting advertises the absence of truth. Cultural relativity, the relativity of theoretical perspectives, the existence of endlessly competing ideological claims, reflects a condition in which thought not only begins, but *ends* as well, in doubt.

If we were to seek a way out of our situation the simplest and most direct path would be to seek a new faith. Faith need not be reasonable. There are, after all, no *reasons* for belief. Tertullian, at the beginnings of the Christian epoch, spoke for all believers when he advertised the absurdity of belief. From Tertullian's *credo quia absurdum est* to the Augustinian *credo ut intelligam*, we can trace the development of a system of rational belief that, for a thousand years and more, held secure against skepticism while uniting the claims of reason to those of faith. Following Tertullian's example we need only choose, from among the myriad absurdities we daily encounter, a candidate for belief, and then hope for a latter-day Augustine to come along to provide the articulation of our faith.

Those who feel they have been "hanging on a string" too long may well find this the only solution. Belief brings relief. There is no path to reason that does not lead through faith. If we wish to return to reason, we must first believe. But if we are to avoid the consequences of narrow, harsh, and dogmatic beliefs we must avoid the temptation to accept uncritically whatever set of values offers most immediate relief from the anxiety of indecision. It is essential that we remain open to a wide variety of experiences. Otherwise we may easily fail to discover the most promising path toward a worthwhile future.

We would do well to remember that the origins of our individual and cultural understandings are found in neither faith nor rational doubt. There is an attitude more fundamental than either of these, one that characterizes our humanness better than reason or faith. It is the attitude of *wonder*. Philosophical understanding, the paradigm of cultural self-understanding, begins in wonder. What makes us human is not our capacity for unquestioning faith, nor our ability to establish truths concerning the nature of things. We are human because we experience wonder, awe, astonishment—because we are *open* to experience.

The age of early Greek philosophy, the principal source of our Western cultural experience, was a period in which certain questions were asked for the first time, a period in which the ideas and values that have dominated the entire subsequent history of tradition were first constructed through the curiosity and speculation of those Greeks whose eyes were wide open in wonder. The origins of faith and doubt as well are to be found in the experience of wonder. There could have been no great Ages of Faith or Reason if there had not first been a period of speculative Wonder. Faith, requiring an already existing proposition that serves as a candidate for belief; and reason, employing critical or constructive doubt concerning the consequences of thought or action—both presuppose the experience of wonder in its purest form.

Because of the recent collapse of orthodox religion and science as cultural forces, we have been inundated with new varieties of ideas, values, and techniques. In place of the effete religious sensibility we have spiritual disciplines, from transcendental meditation to tantric mysticism. On the outskirts of traditional science we see the growth of occult sciences, from astrology to the *I Ching*. One of the difficulties of living in these times is that we must accept the responsibility of relating to these novel happenings. It is too soon to establish the importance of the new phenomena arising in our cultural consciousness. We do ourselves, and the generations that will inherit from us, an injustice if we refuse to remain open to the novelties in experience and practice that are just beginning to emerge within our society. We serve ourselves, and our future, best if we begin to cultivate the question, "Why not?" For if sufficient numbers do not strive toward openness, the attitude of wonder, which promises so much for us, will be crushed between the skepticism of the professional doubters and the dogmatism of the true believers.

From faith comes belief; from doubt, the claim to knowledge. The promise of wonder is that it will bring wisdom. The philosopher, as a lover of wisdom, must first love wonder. One who loves wonder understands that societies and cultures in transition do not survive by the strength of their convictions, nor by the productiveness of their intellectual activities, but by their ability to remain open to experience. We can learn a lesson from the owl, the traditional symbol of wisdom. For, as philosophers have always known, what best distinguishes the "wise old owl" (look for yourself) is the eyes, eyes open wide; eyes that see what others fail to see; eyes open in wonder.

Of the many ironies that afflict contemporary culture none is more exasperating than that suggested by the fact that just at a time when openness and wonder are required from our intellectual elites, it is the philosophers who seem least likely to respond. One is tempted to believe that there is some iron-clad law of history that requires that revolutions in culture take place without serious philosophic reflection. The vested interest of professional philosophers seems clearly to be on the side of conserving the passing culture and its institutions since it is precisely these that validate philosophers' claims to serious intellectual endeavor. We easily find psychologists, sociologists, literary critics, biologists, and physicists offering their assistance as interpreters of our cultural crises since their individual competencies do not depend upon the principles that interrelate the cultural complex as a whole, but only on some specialized segment of it. But the willingness of such individuals to attempt interpretations of radical developments in contemporary culture is seldom accompanied by a desire to include their own specialized methodologies within the context of their critiques. And the same narrow competence that makes a specialist confident in what little knowledge he does possess blinds him to the limitations entailed by specialization of any kind.

It is the primary function of the practicing philosopher to articulate cultural self-understanding. And if the philosopher fails to provide such understanding, he fails in a task which is his very *raison d'être*. Thus the paradoxical nature of any attempt to achieve a philosophic understanding of culture: Only the philosopher is equipped to consider the complex interweaving of cultural aims, objects, and interests that define and organize human social activity and its products; and only the philosopher is sufficiently sensitive to the fact that in attempting to understand a society in transition one cannot lay claim to that objectivity under which guise the intellectual is normally wont to proceed. The loss of the claim to objectivity is sufficient to prevent many philosophic spirits (philosophers are anything but bold) from pursuing the task of cultural self-understanding during a period of transition. For the most part, contemporary philosophers have had recourse to their traditional strategies of retreat: the retreat into the analysis of isolated problems of language, logic, or science, or into the development of speculative systems of thought that arise not from the concrete problematics of contemporary culture, but from the defects of other philosophic systems, or from the murky depths of Being-Itself.

The philosophers' retreat might go unnoticed but for the fact that the philosophic discipline has for some time been under attack. For it is a fundamental datum of social development that, with the dissolution of any cultural synthesis, it is the relevance of philosophy that is challenged first. It has always been one of the tasks of philosophy to construct a *speculum mentis*, a mirror of intellectual culture providing a vision of the principal values or interests of a social order and their relationships; and since it is precisely the co-ordination of such interests that is brought into question in an age of cultural crisis, the philosopher of culture must find himself one of the first victims of cultural collapse.

We may, however, have reached a point where the consequences of the philosophic sin of omission are sufficiently serious that some philosophers are willing to come out of retirement in order to address themselves to the central issues of our time. We should hope so. For the philosopher possesses an indispensable quality little in evidence in our most current attempts at cultural self-understanding: a sense of irony born of an understanding of the limits of understanding. The patron saint of all seekers after wisdom was wise only in his ignorance, in his understanding of *limits*. Disciplined by this philosophic sense of limits, it should be possible to provide speculative considerations of the revolutions in contemporary culture, which not only transcend the backward-looking enterprise serving merely to tidy up received wisdom (the work that Hegel described as "the painting of gray on gray"), but which allow us creatively to shift our tense and perform the forward-looking endeavor of entertaining possible futures. The danger of this shift of tense, of course, is that it will leave us without a firm place to stand. The experience of the extreme tenuousness of our standpoint is one of the essential ingredients in our recognition of the limitations under which we must proceed.

The speculative effort involved in the attempt to attain foresight requires four fundamental strains of investigation.

Concerning the sphere of intellectual culture two distinct questions must be asked: the first involves the *dis*junctive relations of ideas that form the basis for the competing theoretical claims that constitute a significant aspect of contemporary intellectual activity. The second concerns the *conjunctive* relations of theoretical elements that ground our attempts to achieve a synoptic understanding of the aims, ideals, and interests that together define our cultural present. In addition it is necessary to ask after the primary means through which theories, grounded in specific cultural interests, give rise to actions in the realm of praxis, and, finally, to consider the manner in which novel practices within that realm call for theoretical interpretation. The remainder of this chapter will consider these four issues in turn. I should stress that our initial treatment of these issues will be somewhat general and abstract. It is the purpose of the remaining chapters of this work to support and to articulate in detail the major contentions to be introduced here.

CULTURAL INSOMNIA

Cultural history, in one of its many aspects, records the spectacle of *actions* giving rise to *ideas*, which are then employed to interpret, as well as to elicit, subsequent activity. Sometimes these activities are the informed practices of reasoning individuals; more often, they are blind practices in response to the compulsion of natural, social, or political circumstances. This sinusoidal movement from the concreteness and particularity of human action, to the realm of ideas and values, leading again to a return to the world of praxis, armed with tools of theoretical understanding, is one of the fundamental strains of human history.

After the initial emergence of ideas from out of the resources of feeling and action, the conflicts of alternative ideas and the conflicts of individuals and institutions committed to these alternative notions provide a principal dynamic for the historical adventures of the ideas in question. In addition, the funding of cultural experience ensures that ideas constituting yet other alternatives to the dominant ideas and practices can "stand and wait," as it were, emerging into consciousness at an auspicious moment. The understanding of this complex set of relations between thought and action is the task of the philosopher of culture.

The sphere of intellectual culture is defined by the various interrelations of concepts or ideas, which are born as the rationalizations of practice, and are capable of stimulating novel activities. These ideas, functioning as "cultural aims," serve as defining characteristics of cultural situations, and as lures for further articulation or instantiation of knowledge and practice. At the most general level these aims may be expressed in terms of the commitment to the realization of values such as *truth* or *beauty* or *holiness*. To the extent that a society is successful in promoting such aims, they serve to define its character. Cultural aims are normally discoverable within the context of some specific "cultural interest." A cultural interest provides a specific direction for the organizing of theoretical and practical energies. As disciplines, cultural interests are expressed in such forms as "science," "art," "religion," etc. The distinctive manner in which a society attempts to organize its cultural interests in order to achieve its cultural aims is one key to the understanding of its nature and viability. The realm of praxis is the principal source, and contains most of the consequences, of cultural aims. Praxis includes feelings and actions respondent to the compulsions of biological, psychological, and social needs; the customs, conventions, and habits that form the received common sense of a community, and those activities forming relatively novel practices.

Philosophy of culture may be construed, in terms of the above, as *the articulation of importances*. As such, it attempts to delineate the important elements of intellectual culture and their relations, in order to discover the dominant interests and aims qualifying a given cultural epoch, as well as to characterize those aspects of the realm of praxis that form either causes or consequences of significant cultural aims and interests. The philosophic interest attempts to serve vis-à-vis the other primary cultural interests, in a mediating, facilitating, or enabling capacity, by clarifying the actual and possible relations among cultural ideals and practices.

One aim of cultural philosophy is to assess those data

from which one may derive *insight* into the meanings of the cultural present. And since insight into the meanings of a culture is primarily a grasp of those important items of cultural experience that promise efficacy beyond the present, insight leading to *foresight* is a principal goal of the philosopher of culture.

But this goal is subservient to yet another. For the articulation of cultural importances has given rise to the concept of "civilization," which functions normatively to describe that form of social order within which the specific data of the theoretical and practical realms are interacting in such a way as to provide heightened and intensified public experience. The civilizing of cultural experience depends upon the articulation and stimulation of practice by intellectual activity as well as upon the contrast of ideas generated through human practice. The principal aim of culture philosophy is to provide a cultural consciousness that will promote the civilization of experience. This involves the balanced commitment to *insight* and to *foresight*, and requires the most rigorous kind of analysis of the theoretical and practical components of the cultural present.

One of the most significant aspects of twentieth-century philosophy has been its increasing methodological bias. We seem to have raised to the level of consciousness all of the salient principles and presuppositions that have characterized our cultural tradition. We have learned that we are possessed of only a small finite number of ways of thinking, which includes the manner in which we characterize the meaning of fact as well as the way we construct a theoretical schema. We have not only failed to discover "the Truth," we have lost our primary excuse for not finding it—viz., the belief in the infinite complexity of that which is real. Our reasons for failing in the search for truth have less to do with the complexity of nature and experience, and more to do with the fact that the story of our cultural traditions can be seen to consist in the juggling of a few theoretical presuppositions that have been used to organize and articulate the meanings of intellectual culture.

The meta-theoretical endeavors that have become ever more popular among philosophers are concerned with the raising to the level of consciousness those fundamental sets of presuppositions that have guided Western intellectual endeavors since the Hellenic period. This movement, christened the "flight from first intentions,"[1] and the "flight from certainty,"[2] consists in the attempt to confront, in a non-reductive fashion, the issues of conflicting theoretical claims. This issue, itself the victim of a confusing mass of mutually conflicting analyses, has been one of the primary motivating factors in the development of what may be termed our "metatheoretical consciousness."

The concern with explaining the nature of conflict among philosophical ideas is of course not a new one. It is only in intensity and degree that our current situation stands out as unusual in the history of our culture. Indeed, Plato attempted to understand conflicting philosophic claims as resulting from a lack of clarity in the attainment of knowledge. His analysis of the Four Levels of The Clarity of Knowledge in Book VI of *The Republic* accounts not only for the stages of mental development in its pursuit of perfect knowledge, but, by implication, for the co-existence of alternative philosophies at variance with Platonic formalism. Aristotle, likewise, attempted to account for the phenomenon of competing claims. Book A of *The Metaphysics* contains an analysis of historical and contemporary philosophies based upon their emphasis upon one or more of the Aristotelian Four Causes— material, formal, final, and efficient. Thus, the greatest of the Hellenic philosophers provided not only the major philosophic concepts that have given rise to philosophic systems in subsequent phases of Western culture; they provided, as well, the primary means whereby we are enabled to understand the conflicting claims of the various forms of philosophic enterprise.

Over against both the Platonic and Aristotelian accounts of the problem of conflicting claims stand the volitional accounts of competing philosophies originating from the Sophistic perspective, which characterized human beings in terms of the concept of *expression*. As bearer of "words," as *persuader*, "man is the measure of all things." The power of persuasion, developed in the early Sophistic tradition and car-

ried on in the school of Isocrates, a contemporary of the early
Platonic Academy, established the adequacy of philosophic
points of view in relation to the principle of success in argument. The spoils of philosophic supremacy belong to the
victor in a contest of debate.

The Platonic, Aristotelian, and Sophistic traditions were
soon complemented by the materialist reductionism developed from the theories of Leucippus and Democritus, in
which competing philosophic systems were found to be conventional, ideological, epiphenomenal expressions of fundamental material determinants, reducible to those determinants
without remainder. Whatever is not explained directly in
terms of the least units of atomic theory is to be discussed in
terms of convention. This is, of course, the source of the
classical view that all scientific knowledge can be reduced to
physical principles and explained in terms of physical laws.

With the culmination of Aristotle's philosophic activity in
323 B.C., the sources from which derive the principal competing traditions of the West were already established. Not
long after, these various philosophic perspectives had been
elaborated in sufficient degree to establish themselves as
explanatory models that not only could account for the principal aspects of nature and knowledge, but also could explain,
with some adequacy, the coexistence of mutually contradictory philosophic paradigms.

The subsequent history of philosophy has had to contend
with the coexistence of these primary philosophic visions.
Which philosophic viewpoints would dominate a given cultural epoch has been a function of the nature of the theoretical
and practical ferment energizing the selected ideas. Direct
conflict of theory with theory has led to the emergence of a
dominant philosophical paradigm, as in the case of some of the
Scholastic conflicts of the Medieval period; reactions against
institutionalized modes of social practice have stimulated the
emergence of an alternate explanatory mode articulating new
forms of praxis, as was true of the Marxian philosophy.

Whatever the motives behind philosophic development, it
can hardly be called progress in the most fundamental sense.
Philosophic progress has consisted, for the most part, of a

progressive articulation and refinement of separate philosophic paradigms, and the attempt to produce more adequate systematic philosophies by the inclusion of elements of more than one of the distinct paradigms. The first movement has meant that we have developed more subtle materialisms, idealisms, and the like, while the second has more often than not been the only partially successful attempt to reduce the competitive philosophic paradigms to one of the several fundamental systems.

In the latter days of the history of philosophy, however, a new type of progress is in evidence. This is the progressive realization of the existence of competing philosophic systems as irreducible schemas of interpretation that apparently will not yield to refutation, reduction, or assimilation by alternate philosophic schemas. This has brought about the development of meta-philosophic efforts that thrive upon the examination of alternative philosophic systems, often without comparative judgments of adequacy. This trend amounts to a progressive development in philosophy insofar as it does not repeat the same futile juggling of alternatives, the familiar substitution of the philosophy of Tweedledum for that of Tweedledee.

Representatives of this meta-theoretical tendency include, among American philosophers, Richard McKeon, Robert Brumbaugh, and Stephen Pepper.[3] McKeon is perhaps the most insistent of these meta-theorists. Employing the Aristotelian method of organizing philosophic viewpoints, McKeon demonstrates that philosophic activity in Western culture is, for the most part, a result of the competition among irreducible, autonomous, internally consistent and coherent theoretical paradigms. Brumbaugh, playing Plato to McKeon's Aristotle, employs, instead of McKeon's "causal" analysis, a schema modeled after Plato's four levels of the clarity of knowledge, which suggests a hierarchical pattern of relations among the various philosophic visions. Stephen Pepper, working in the Sophistic mode, devised the concept of "root-metaphor" to characterize the fundamental principle from which derived each of our philosophic traditions. These schemas have been employed to characterize the interrelations of the various schools of philosophy constituting contemporary philosophic endeavor, with the consequence that the presumed novelty of contemporary philosophies is claimed to be due to the failure to understand the close family resemblances among various historical examples of a given theoretical tradition.

Not only is the claim to novelty undermined by those persuaded of the meta-theoretical arguments, but the significance of the interaction among the various philosophic movements has been challenged, since theoretical conflict is, more often than not, grounded in *semantic ignorance*. The realization that contemporary philosophy is patterned by distinct and autonomous traditions, energized by a small number of irreducible theoretical paradigms, requires a radical change of attitude, which must affect the rhetorical and apologetic thrust of philosophy.

Modern philosophy, born of the heuristic employment of doubt as a means of obtaining certainty, has progressed to a point where philosophic doubt has become a consequence of the realization that certainty is unattainable, or the realization that too many mutually contradictory "certainties" are possible of attainment. The most significant consequence of this realization is that without the authority of truth undergirding a given theory, that theory can only lead to commitment through the use of rhetorical persuasion, intimidation, or coercion. Meta-mentality invites a kind of intellectual fascism which elicits commitment to values and ideals, not because they are true, but for the sake of law and order, the harmony of society, or "the destiny of a people." The extreme of intellectual subtlety that finally succeeds in suspending belief in favor of the exercise of reason ends by affirming the necessity of arbitrary commitment if there is to be any commitment at all!

We have awakened *from* history because we have awakened *to* the presuppositions that serve as the organizing principles of thought, action, and feeling in our tradition. We have raised to the level of consciousness the structures of our beliefs, attitudinal biases, and prejudices. The mysterious, non-rational underpinnings that have provided the wellsprings of our human progress are now exposed to our view. We know ourselves too well.

The irony of our situation is intense. Until recently, the co-presence of alternate theoretical paradigms within a cultural present has militated against the threat of intellectual stagnation. Now stagnation threatens our culture not because we lack alternatives, but because we have developed a full-scale consciousness of *all* the fundamental alternatives that have served as either theme or variations characterizing cultural experience and expression. We have raised to the level of consciousness all of the salient principles, rules, and aims that have qualified our cultural epochs. Stripped bare of its superficial displays of novelty, the history of theory is shown to be a chronicle of changes in styles of thought, which, like changes in the length of dresses, are hemmed in by rather narrow limits. Awakening to each of the fundamental presuppositions that serve as the variant principles of our thought, action, and feeling has produced a situation more disturbing than any of the nightmares that have intermittently patterned our twenty-five centuries of dogmatic slumber.

THE MALADY OF REDUCTION

In the Western tradition, the harmonious relations among cultural interests and aims have been largely determined by the analogy between psyche and polis drawn by Plato and Aristotle in the fourth century. When Plato constructed his ideal polis by "writing large" the human psyche, he provided the major analysis of the analogy between the soul and the state, which was to form the main heuristic principle illuminating the relations of private and public existence. The psyche, in its rational function, mirrors the sphere of intellectual culture, while its volitional and appetitive functions reflect the components of the realm of praxis. Persons are *thinking, acting*, and *feeling* creatures, and the relations between reason, will, and passion set the crucial problems for human existence at both the individual and the social levels.

For both Plato and Aristotle, the problems of harmonizing the private and public forms of existence are resolved by patterning the forms of social existence after the functional interpretation of the *psyche* as a tripartite unity of thought, action, and passion. Each sought to accomplish this end through the construction of an educational program meant to convey the nature and right relative status of the theoretical, practical, and productive interests. The sorting out of cultural interests into the scientific, philosophic, aesthetic, moral, and religious was a continuing consequence of the Platonic and Aristotelian ideas in conjunction with Augustine's hebraicizing of the neo-Platonic tradition in the fifth century.

Until recently, the harmonious interrelations of the various components of intellectual culture were functions of the underlying harmony of these cultural interests and the primary aims they expressed. The distinctive character of our present situation lies in the fact that the philosophic aim of constructing theories of the organization of cultural interests is no longer much pursued. With the abandonment of the aim at the construction of synoptic theories of culture, the sphere of intellectual culture is left without articulated principles grounding the conjunctive relations of its theoretical elements. The result is that specialist and popular attempts at philosophy of culture dominate the cultural present. Most of these cultural analyses are theories that, though grounded in one of the specialized sciences, are extended, through the facile use of analogical generalization, to apply to the entire breadth of cultural experience. Without philosophic visions upon which to rely, these theories have, in the main, borrowed their theoretical principles from the biological, psychological, and sociological contributions of the Darwinian, Freudian, and Marxian paradigms. But unlike Darwin, Freud, and Marx themselves, their contemporary disciples have little recognition of the limitations of these theoretical systems.

Freud proposed a theory directed to the understanding of neurotic personality. The extremes of normalcy and psychosis are, strictly speaking, beyond the purview of the theory. Darwin proposed an analysis of the origin of the species and method of species-survival. Neither the goal of human beings, nor the contributions of specific individuals in attaining such a goal were meant to be considered by the theory. Karl Marx looked to a de-alienated future in which the structures of economic determination would be lifted and individuals freed to pursue the proper goals of human existence. But he recognized that just as all theory is tainted by the socio-economic order of which it is the ideological expression, meaningful discussions of de-alienated man must await the realization of the utopian community constituting the social destiny of persons. In a surprising number of instances contemporary cultural analysts have drawn from these theories, singly or in combination, to construct what they consider an adequate theory of the cultural present.

The fallacy of this type of approach is to be found in the belief of these thinkers that they will be able to solve the cultural dilemmas we face as easily as they solve problems associated with their own specialties. But without a recognition of the limited sphere of applicability of their various theories, those cultural critics can provide only parodies of cultural theory.[4] Such theories have in common the elaboration of a fundamental "truth" derived from a specialized science, or sciences (as in the case of the Freudo-Marxians like Marcuse and Fromm), and the assertion that the problem implied by this "truth" about man and society is the *fundamental* problem of contemporary culture, as well as the naïve and dogmatic employment of the selected "truth" to explain or resolve *the* problem.

Though the mass production of theories of this type is less in evidence today than just a few years ago, the impact of these reductive generalizations is still an important determinant of our cultural present. The failure of these theories to achieve any but the briefest of successes signals the defeat of the only influential theories of the co-ordination of cultural interests that could serve as the basis for viable conjunctive relations of ideas in the sphere of intellectual culture.

The conditions of both the conjunctive and disjunctive relations of ideas in the cultural present suggest a crisis as regards our past. For the established paradigms that have been employed as explanatory of our cultural situations are acceptable neither singly, as overarching organizational structures, nor as a set of interacting alternatives. The purveyors of intellectual culture seem embarrassed by their own self-consciousness. Having raised to the level of consciousness the alternative structures of our reasonings and practice, it is increasingly difficult to pretend that one decision is more rational than a series of others, or that one form of practice is any more reasonable than its alternatives.[5]

The crisis with regard to our past exists, also, in the relations between theoretical and practical spheres of culture. The skeptical attitude toward theory affects not only the conjunctive and disjunctive relations of theoretical elements, but equally affects the relations of *theory* and *practice* within our cultural present. In a dynamic culture, at home with its past, theory derived from prior modes of practice is employed to maintain those practices and to stimulate novel activities. This relation has broken down in our cultural present. Practices found to be theory-dependent fall under the shadow of that same skepticism that is currently directed toward all theories.

This situation radically affects our belief in the possibility of attaining to significant knowledge. Whatever in the way of empirical knowledge we may be said to have must, in principle, be open to falsification. That which cannot be falsified cannot be said to be *known*. Tautologies excepted, knowledge is, apparently, always open to challenge. Dogmatic certainty, therefore, is at once a signal of an improper grasp of the meaning of what it means to know, and an obvious display of the importance of the attitude of belief in determining the character of ostensibly rational commitments. The present relations of knowledge and belief derive mainly from the meta-theoretical activities within intellectual culture. "Factual" knowledge turns out to be theory-dependent; and what is fact for one theory may be fiction for another. The inability to accept one theory as more adequate than another has opened a great deal of significant knowledge to falsification. This precludes the feeling of certainty with regard to all theory-dependent propositions. The effect of this development has been twofold: either one dogmatically affirms the adequacy of a single theory, reducing all other theoretical approaches to it (the theoretical reductionism discussed above), or one attempts to avoid commitment to theory altogether. This latter, anti-theoretical, tendency has affected every major cultural interest.

In religion, the death-of-God movement of some years ago set the problem for our religious present. The demise of the Judaeo-Christian God has largely undermined the rationality of our primary religious tradition. The principal religious dynamic in recent years has consisted in the development of sectarian and fundamentalist movements within the mainstream religious tradition, as well as the increasing acceptance of novel religious and quasi-religious resources. The interest in religion is quite high among the young, but there is no evidence that they were led to this interest through doctrinal stimulation. What the new religionists seek are techniques for achieving heightened religious experience, not doctrines that establish a theological world-view.

Contemporary artists seem quite impressed by their first cousins, the technicians. The sheer variety and complexity of mechanical and electronic gadgets turn the artists' attention away from their inner, order-creating resources and toward the posited order of technology. The suppression of consciousness in the aesthetic realm has led to the development of such phenomena as action painting, kinetic sculpture, chance music, and innumerable types of cybernetic art. These movements suggest a general capitulation of large segments of our artistic community to technique. No one would suggest that the artist must work with ideas in his head. To do so would be to make architects of all our artists. But the analogue of theoretical commitment in artistic activity is the belief that some order other than that immanently present in technique itself is discernible in the created art object. This belief is actively denied by many contemporary artists.

A radical contextualist and intuitionist temper that refuses to act "on principle" has for some time characterized the developing moral context of our cultural present. Here, as in every other cultural interest, the meta-theoretical bias and the suspicion of theoretical principles as bases of action combine to prevent significant engagement of *theory* and *practice* in the moral sphere, with the result that theory is simply abandoned. Theory must capitulate to practice for the simple reason that technological practice produces a situation that seems unamenable to theoretical interpretation. In the realm of human engineering, for example, techniques for the prolongation of life, for the prevention and termination of pregnancy, for the artificial replication of life, for the surgical and medical alteration of sexual identity, and so on, tempt one to avoid the task of constructing ethical theories in favor of developing some pragmatic stratagems for meeting currently unforeseeable situations. In the ethical realm we really haven't time to theorize; practice is outrunning theory.

The same phenomenon is to be seen within the philosophic sphere. Most of those philosophers not already engaged by meta-theoretical work attempt to view the philosophic activity, simply as that—*an activity*. Philosophers become therapists for those with specific, technical problems. However much the dispassionate observer might be interested in the construction of a fly-bottle, the entrapped fly has a specific and immediate problem—how to escape. Thus many philosophers have largely become *technicians*, concentrating on logic and language, the "tools of the trade," rather than upon more traditional and substantive issues.

The attempt to escape theory-dependence is best seen in the scientific interest. This is due not only to the fact that the movements from theory to practice have, in the modern period, been most significant in this interest, but equally because science, more than any other discipline, has hidden behind a façade that Theodore Roszak has felicitously described as "the myth of objective consciousness." However, knowing has increasingly shown itself to be a tentative and uncertain enterprise. The objectivity of science has fallen under the impact of the realization that scientists, like all other members of intellectual elites, are the servants, if not the outright slaves, of their unacknowledged beliefs. Historians and philosophers of science have raised to the level of consciousness those presuppositions that scientists have unknowingly employed to construe "the facts." Meta-theorists have shown that theoretical understandings tend to cluster about certain broad traditional concepts inherited from the ancient Greeks, and that after twenty-four hundred years, the process of the civilizing of experience has not led to the establishment of significant criteria for deciding the superiority of any given theoretical understanding.

The scientist loses much of his creative energy if he is forced to think that the facts he discovers are determined *to be* facts only by the schema he chooses to employ. As a result of this development we find scientists increasingly attempting to dissociate themselves from theory-dependence. This occurs in two principal ways. The first is illustrated by the efforts of the historian of science Thomas Kuhn, who, in his now-classic *The Structure of Scientific Revolutions*,[6] claims that the history of science is the story of successive revolutions in theory in which the acceptance of a novel explanatory paradigm necessarily involves the rejection of its predecessors.

The denial of the continuity of scientific development has profound and disturbing implications for current scientific practice. Since the scientist seems no longer able to discover truth, the theoretical explication of morphological schemes and their verification through extended application is increasingly abandoned and the *ad hoc* employment of operational concepts is stressed. The search for truth, always recognized as a progressive and long-term process, has largely given way to attempts to meet short-term needs of the society via technical rather than theoretical means. Rationality is replaced by ingenuity.

The second attempt to dissociate theory from practice leads in the same direction. Behaviorism, certainly a dominant methodology in the sciences, can lead to the suppression of theory altogether. Strict behaviorism attempts to avoid the use of explanatory and descriptive theory in favor of the employment of an economical set of unarticulated and unsystematized assumptions. Behavioral psychology, for example, employs assumptions involving the causal interaction of organism and environment. The assumptions are used to elaborate a technology that is claimed to be precisely co-extensive with the discipline of psychology. Theory, as an explanatory scheme that purports to explain that which is directly experienceable in terms of that which is not, is considered worthless and, indeed, pernicious. Psychology is "technology of behavior."

Within the scientific interest, heretofore the most dramatic illustration of the productive relations of theory and practice, the chaos in theoretical activity and the success of technologies operating independently of any theoretical disci-

pline have brought about attempts to escape altogether from
dependence upon theory. This has caused science to move in
the direction of technique, in order to *do* what it cannot *know*.
One implication of this movement is that our technological
society, presumed to be the offspring of the theoretical interest of science, has increasingly little to do with scientific
theory. Technological society, as the primary expression of
contemporary praxis, is fast becoming one gigantic illustration
of the denial of theory.

José Ortega y Gasset's *The Revolt of the Masses* predicted the rise of technological society as a result of the revolt
against theory. What he termed the "vertical invasion of the
barbarian," the rise to dominance of a class of technicians
possessed of specialized knowledge, but ignorant of *principles*, is very nearly complete in our cultural present. The
greatest of our recent scientific triumphs, the landing of men
on the moon, constituted an appalling fulfillment of Ortega's
prophecy. NASA technicians, each possessed of only specialized knowledge, accomplished that great feat without any
single individual having an understanding of the complexities
of the entire project.

The question of the suppression of scientific theory in
favor of technical skill raises the question of values. If not the
members of the intellectual elite functioning as theoreticians,
who *will* decide the directions of technological development?
There are, currently, several non-theoretical ways in which
technological society is being shaped. First, as Jacques Ellul
has forcefully argued in *The Technological Society*,[7] technology is a self-augmenting complex of operations. It can
determine its own direction. In accordance with what has been
termed the *technological imperative* ("What *can* be done,
must be done"), we can see that the mere existence of a
technical possibility often determines the course of technological progress. Second, specific challenges to the social
system suggest necessary advances in technology. Disease,
pollution, population pressure, war, and the need efficiently to
allocate energy reserves, have occasioned new developments
in the realm of praxis. Finally, political strategies often involve the employment of technique, quite apart from motives

of necessity or economic profit. The most dramatic example of this is perhaps the U.S. space program, which greatly profited from the fact that the goal of landing a man on the moon was chosen by the Kennedy Administration as a means of projecting a New Frontier, a project intended ideologically to unite the American people.

Theories drawn from the sphere of intellectual culture increasingly play little direct role in the development of advanced technological society. The questions of the values determining the direction of technological progress, as much as the techniques that make that progress possible, are not involved in the antecedent construction of theories, but in the application of values derived from the compulsion of natural and technological circumstances, as well as from social and political ideologies.

THE CASTING OF POSSIBLE FUTURES

Our examinations of both disjunctive and conjunctive relations of ideas dominating the cultural present, as well as the investigation of the failure of theory to direct practice, suggest that our culture is not functioning creatively with its established theoretical forms. Meta-mentality, one expression of the intellectual failure of nerve which characterizes our present social situation, has led many to abandon the search for truth in favor of the articulation of the inevitable conflict among theories that makes that search futile. Truth-seekers, where they are found, try to make good their search by recourse to reductionisms that reduce all cultural significances to a single explanatory scheme drawn from a single cultural interest. In addition there are those who try to abandon theory altogether and concentrate on practical consequences of activity divorced from theoretical control.

The final element of our cultural present relevant to the task of gaining that insight upon which foresight may be grounded is that of the sphere of praxis insofar as it is open to theoretical justification and articulation. We now must ask whether, in the cultural present, there are important modes of

cultural practice that are leading to the demand for novel
forms of theoretical interpretation.

It is perhaps important to note that the discovery of the
means whereby to interpret our cultural present will not
ensure that we shall be able to initiate changes. The conditions
of our culture strongly suggest that we may be unable to
employ theoretical principles to direct practice in the public
sphere. But the understanding of the ideas that are being
energized by current cultural practice and the use of these
ideas to articulate our concrete circumstances can stimulate
our individual responses to what may in fact turn out to be the
inevitabilities of the future. It could be that, as Martin
Heidegger has so poignantly expressed,[8] the proper response
to the end of our culture is a silent waiting for the future. If so,
the attempt to articulate our circumstances can at least add a
dimension to our experience that prevents our waiting from
being merely the expression of a quietistic stoicism. For the
relations between theory and practice are mutual. Practices
reach out for theoretical articulation, requiring the best interpretations available, and generating new linguistic conventions whenever possible. But the fit is never perfect. Theory
construes and disciplines practice, determining its structure
and, to some extent, its limits. But the determination is never
complete. And though theoretical and practical endeavors are,
in principle, separable, it remains true that, to revise the
Kantian dictum, theory without practice is empty, practice
without theory is blind. An act of understanding is an act of
construal, and, as such, is immediately relevant to the form of
present practice.

The search for new theoretical principles must look
beyond the intellectual sphere of the cultural present since it
has, apparently, exhausted its theoretical reservoir. The search
for new principles requires resort either to an alternative culture, or to the origins of experience in its personal and cultural
forms. And, indeed, it does appear that all three movements
are being made in contemporary culture: the turn inward to
the origins of individual experience; the turn to Eastern and
"Third-World" cultures as alternative sources of values and
techniques of self-understanding; and a return to the origins of

our Western cultural experience in order to come to grips with our present experiences in terms of our own cultural beginnings.

The most significant activities in the sphere of praxis that promise novelty are to be found among these visionaries whose primary characteristic is religious imagination. The search for original forms of religious experience and expression has initiated a turning away from mainstream culture and a steady, if somewhat tortured, march toward new beginnings. The political impulse of the Sixties has given way to what can only be described in terms of spiritual motivations. The spiritual critique of our culture is based in large measure upon the realization that contemporary Judaeo-Christianity in its recent turn toward relevance has relied too heavily upon the resources of secular culture. And, in point of fact, the social, political, and scientific views of secular culture are direct descendants of the theological expressions of the Judaeo-Christian tradition. The enthusiastic melding of the interests of religion and its scientific culture that came out of the apologetic era of the Fifties has led to a condition in which Western religion has all but lost its distinctiveness. We have come to realize that a turning to Western religion is just one more way of turning to bankrupt Western science. It is necessary that we turn to other spiritual resources. And all such turnings are turnings away from the received wisdom of contemporary culture.

One such turning involves the turning *within*. It was the genius of existentialism, a philosophy born of cultural crisis and collapse, that it dramatically advertised the subjective and personal character of philosophic thought, finding the principal meaning of philosophic activity "in the seductive way in which one moulds his attitudes as universals for others."[9] Perhaps all philosophic thinking is, and has been, of this type. Be that as it may, the *recognition* of that character comes in a period of cultural transition. The turn within, the introspective mood, which we find in the great religious inaugurators, as well as in the founders of philosophic schools determining subsequent cultural development, is essential to the period of beginnings. The Buddha, Jesus Christ, St. Paul, Augustine,

Descartes, the contemporary existentialists—all have in common the fact that they made a turning within to search for new beginnings.

Our own turn within began with the existential reappraisal of our cultural values, and rose to its height with the emergence of the generation of the "counter-culture" whose introspection was aided by psychotropic drugs. Evidences of this introspective move have begun to show up in the writings of our cultural critics. We find increasing demonstrations of the manner in which reflection upon one's own idiosyncratic experiences, bizarre as they may seem when made the subject of conscious analysis, are valuable in providing novel resources for the re-evaluation of our cultural self-understandings.[10]

Most thinkers are not in the least ill-disposed to discover the roots of their opponents' philosophies in psychological attitudes and biases, but are forced by the need to claim objectivity to except their own thinking from idiosyncratic experience. It is for this reason that almost every great thinker can be shown, at some crucial point, to have fallen victim to self-referential inconsistency. But the subjective character of thought is no sin in a time of cultural transition. Indeed, the reasonable, objective thinker is merely one who conservatively accepts the criteria of meaning and significance derived from the fading culture and because of that fact denies that there is any radical change at all. We cannot depend on the past to tell us a great deal about the character of the future, for prediction must be something more than extrapolation. We are forced, therefore, into a radical stance that requires a turning within for the personal authority from out of which to tell one's tale.

If the present were nothing more than a perspective from which to watch a parade of events in which stable past gives way to expected future, idiosyncrasy would be of little value, at least insofar as foresight were concerned. But such is not our case. The novelty that will best put us in touch with a future none can clearly see is one that derives, at least in part, from the idiosyncrasy of personal experiences transcending the determinations of the past. One way of being freed from the past is by turning to the depths of our individual personality, the chaos of our inner feelings, the extremes of our experiential spectrum.

Like Augustine, whose anguished internal struggle for conversion was a struggle both for himself and for his age, and like Descartes, whose introspective turn provided a grounding for the rationalism of an epoch, those who would build a pedestal from which to view the future must find the materials for the foundation in the self's innermost structures. And though Augustine's wondering was captive to faith and Descartes' obedient to doubt, each nonetheless grandly illustrates that introspective turning that is the first modality of wonder.

A second cultural turning has been the recent turn toward exoteric ideas and experiences. The celebrity of Carlos Casteneda's spiritual affair with a Yaqui shaman, as well as the innumerable converts to Eastern forms of spirituality, suggest that we are seeking answers to contemporary questions in alternative cultures. The sheer quantity of literature published in the last half-generation that provides access to Eastern religious and philosophical sources is truly impressive. And across the country we are rapidly being inundated by missionaries and prophets from the East. No doubt many of these self-professed holy men are impudent scoundrels, pimping for false gods. Some are truly saints, however, with precious insights from the East, which, in their quiet way, have already begun to alter our cultural consciousness.

The interest in Oriental thought and practice is difficult to assess. In one sense it may serve as a temporary antidote for boredom for those who have tired of the trite rehearsal of old answers to new questions: Many of our intellectual sophisticates possess a fickle nature born of an extremely brief attention span, and we can expect these to seek novelty for its own sake. But the true test of the efficacy of the turn toward the East will be found in those who have felt the necessity for such a move because of their own need for introspection, and who supplement both the turn to the East and the turn within by yet another turning: a re-turning to the origins of our cultural experience.[11]

The inward turning of our new visionaries led, under-
standably enough, to a turning toward the East, where introspective forms of spirituality dominate. The third fundamental
turning characterizing the spiritually motivated is, likewise, a
result of the second. For it is as Antoni Gaudi i Cornet
claimed: "Originality is a return to the origins." The turn
within, aided by psychedelic drugs and sophisticated spiritual
techniques, involves one in a return to the original sources of
individual, personal experience. This return must be supplemented by a re-search of the origins of our cultural experience
as well. The turning to fundamentals of our cultural heritage is
a necessary consequence of the turning to the East. For the
only way in which the insights of the East can be made relevant to Western culture as a whole is if we are able to translate
those insights into the language of our own cultural experience. The task of translation is more than merely a problem of
differing languages. We must employ Eastern thought and
practice as a means of guiding us toward insights within our
own tradition that answer to these in direction and import.

The principal effect of exoteric doctrines imported into
our culture is to call attention to esoteric doctrines within our
own tradition that match in theoretical and evocative significance the functions of those ideas in their own cultural milieu.
Unless the exoteric views can be translated into the language
of our culture, they cannot contribute significantly to the construction of our alternative paradigm. If they can be so translated, it can only be that the context for the understanding of
these doctrines already exists somewhere within our culture.
If this is so, we are directed to already existing elements within our culture that represent variations of the imported views.
Thus when Benjamin Whorf set out to discuss the Hopi language, and the world-view presupposed by it, he found himself drawing upon the philosophy of Henri Bergson to explain
the process orientation of the Hopi semantic context.[12] Such a
move not only facilitated an understanding of Hopi thought
and culture, it promoted an increased understanding of the
thought of Bergson as well. The meaning of esoteric thought
can become clearer through reflection upon the novelty of
exoteric doctrines.

The search for novel principles outside one's culture must eventually lead one to look for novel sources within one's culture. And, since the search for new principles (*principia*) is the search for new *beginnings*, this must ultimately lead us to a return to the origins of our cultural experience. This return is necessary since all of our cultural self-understandings are couched in terms of the various paradigms that dominate our cultural present. The return to the origins is an attempt to move toward relatively unarticulated experiences and to discover interpretations of thought, action, and feeling that have been largely neglected by the tradition.

This return to the origins involves two distinct moments: one is a search for philosophic beginnings in theoretical principles; the second, a discovery of religious beginnings, consisting in the origins of praxis as recounted in mythical form. The concern for beginnings shared by both religion and philosophy is as old as culture itself. The word *beginning*, in its most fundamental sense, refers to that mythical time "in the beginning," which religious myths recount. While the function of myths as etiological tales is *practical* in the sense that they are primarily concerned with the evocation of ritualistic practices that provide access to a time of origins, the function of philosophic *principles* is largely theoretical, referring primarily to the beginning points of *thought*. The search for originality, therefore, will have impact upon both our mythical and philosophic sensibilities.[13]

The re-examination of the fundamental mythical and philosophic resources available to us was begun by Friedrich Nietzsche in the nineteenth century, although the significance of his work is just now coming to be appreciated. Nietzsche's reinterpretation of the nature of Greek philosophic culture has dramatically influenced contemporary understandings of our intellectual heritage.[14]

Hellenic society, paradigmatically illustrated by the Athenian city–state during and just after the Periclean Age, has served as the basic model of intellectual culture in the Western tradition. But this culture has been consistently viewed through the eyes of scholars altogether too credulous concerning the relevance of, for example, the *Funeral Oration* of

Pericles and the dialogues of Plato as expressions of the actual conditions of Athenian society. The dominant picture of Athenian culture obtained from such sources is of a society of high-born gentlemen involved in subtle and sophisticated discussions of subjects ranging from art and poetry to the meaning of justice; gentlemen who exercised the right of every Athenian citizen to absolute freedom of speech within a model democratic society. This vision is, in no small measure, the result of translators on the order of Benjamin Jowett, who filtered much of the bawdiness of Athenian intellects through the see-no-evil conventions of the British gentry. That this picture fails to account for the fact that it was Anytus, a hero of democratic reform in Athens, who was principally responsible for the trial and death-sentence of Socrates, or that, as Alfred North Whitehead has somewhere remarked, the primary function of the poet in Athenian society was to write an ode celebrating the prowess of the boxer, only slightly disturbs our faith in Greek gentility.

Beginning with the writings of Nietzsche and Rhode in the late nineteenth century, when the irrational aspects of Greek culture began to receive their due, a thin fissure appeared in the monolithic structure of Greek scholarship. Only recently did this new interpretation of the Greeks become really influential among culture philosophers. The appreciation of the non-rational elements of Greek culture is hardly to be taken as the result of dispassionate scholarship interpreting new and significant data. It is, rather, an illustration of the search for conceptual alternatives existing at the penumbral limit of the ideas forming the general climate of opinion of our cultural epoch. The current stress upon non-rational factors in classical culture is, thus, due to the efforts of scholars who have a vested interest in discovering alternatives to concepts and theories that seem no longer relevant to the interpretation of present practice. We are engaged in plumbing the depths of our past to discover novel ideas that can serve to ground our interpretation of present practice. The ultimate goal of this movement is the construction of a philosophic vision that can serve as a viable alternative to the major paradigms whose principles have been tried and found wanting in the spheres of both theory and practice.

The principal motive behind the turn within, to the East, and to the origins in search of cultural self-understanding is the necessity to turn with wisdom toward a future that stands unknown before us. Certainly there have been many individuals who have not felt that such complex turnings are required for an accurate projection of the future status of our culture. Futurists and social planners often remain content with simplistic extrapolations that predict *more of the same*. Such predictions, however, depend more on a knowledge of the past than a concern for the future. Ages and societies primarily concerned with tradition have as their principal occupation the recounting of the ways in which the past has given rise to the present. A firm dependence upon what has been accomplished leads to the modeling of present actions and intentions upon the more or less completed past. Thought under such conditions has about it a settled character that leaves little room for speculation. In such cases, routine or fixed habit dominates social activity. Prognostications, when they are made, are but thinly disguised extrapolations that continue the line drawn from past to present to an arbitrary point in the future.

Societies oriented to the pragmatic present are no better equipped to articulate a novel future than are traditional societies. For an emphasis upon the present is, likewise, non-speculative. Those who emphasize the here and now are often impatient with the past. The purpose of social activity under these circumstances is the application of intelligence and ingenuity to the solution of present and pressing problems. A premium is placed upon that form of intelligence that seeks short-term solutions to immediate problems. No doubt such activity need not conflict with the traditionalist attitude in every case. But the pragmatic mentality has more often than not expressed an indifference to the past that leads to the belief that one's present is *sui generis*. One of the simplest ways to feel original is to forget one's origins. But this commits one to a rootless existence, without intensity and depth.

Concern for the future, to be meaningful at all, must not blind itself to the present and the past. But the future lacks the firmness of both past and present. The future is not-yet, and perhaps not-ever. One cannot face the future directly without *wisdom*; and wisdom is nothing more or less than the recognition of limits expressed in the reflection upon knowledge *from* the past and *of* the present, which determines the way of realizing a future. In social terms, a wise consideration of the future is one that modifies traditional and pragmatic knowledge so as to produce an aim for future realization that is rooted in the past, articulated in the present, but realizable only in some as yet unactualized future.

Our society is currently enamored of the future. Indeed, the concern for the future is faddish in the extreme. No doubt this will pass. But at a deeper and more profound level, it seems that even our intellectual elites are ill-equipped to handle the problem of the future. Though ours is hardly a society based upon tradition and a concern for the historical past, we are dependent, to an extreme degree, upon routine. It is of the very essence of a technological society that routines be established and, once set, followed. Our inheritance of technique has, in large measure, determined the present functioning of our society. There is no guarantee that such will continue to be the case. Nonetheless, most of the outside observers of the developments in technological society seem satisfied that our future may be defined in terms of simple linear progress from the present. Such extrapolations may be either hopeful or despairing depending upon one's attitude toward the present status of technological society.

The situation is different when viewed from within. The technological state of mind eschews conscious interest in tradition and the past. The technician seeks to articulate and resolve the problems emerging within the present societal matrix. But ignorance of the past, combined with an interest in specialized problems in the present, leads one to an excessively impoverished vision of the shape of things to come; for the future is seen to consist in jumping from one technological lily pad to another. We seem to look in vain for evidence of wisdom, the talent for weaving tradition and ingenuity into a firm basis from which to speculate upon the issue of the future. Wisdom, as a philosophic attitude, has long been held in low esteem in our society. The flurry of concern over the future includes very few serious attempts to approach the subject with wisdom. Ours are, for the most part, instinctive and pragmatic approaches. The love of wisdom must lead us toward the attempt to wed present insights into a pattern of tradition capable of sustaining their growth.

The search for wisdom requires that we take seriously all three turnings in pursuit of novelty. It is easy enough to recognize the value of research into alternative cultures; and it is more than sensible to seek novelty in our own cultural origins. It is the introspective turn that seems to require defense. In the pages that follow I shall be employing visions of the nature of things that stress intuition, speculation, and the immediacy of our fundamental experiences. This choice of philosophic perspective might well have been determined by a simple dialectical exercise that sought to complement the dominant rationalistic visions of our contemporary culture. There need be nothing especially arbitrary or subjective about such a procedure. It is precisely because of his apparent objectivity that the philosopher of culture must advertise the necessarily subjective character of his work in an age of cultural transition.

In a stable culture, the prediction of future developments involves no more than a saying in advance what must surely come to pass. Jules Verne and H. G. Wells were able to predict with remarkable accuracy radical developments in knowledge and social practice because they were relatively simple to foresee as extrapolations of scientific theory and practice. Lacking the stability of that cultural milieu, we are forced to abandon *prediction* in favor of *forecast*. Forecasting, as opposed to a mere saying in advance, involves three essential activities: First, the speculative entertainment of the outlines of possible futures; second, the selection of one among these viable possibilities; and, finally, the casting of the form of the future in such fashion as to invite sympathy.

The two aspects of forecast that transcend any form of objectivity are the selection of one possible future from among a number of possibilities, and the *invitation to belief* in the validity of that choice. Every vision of the future in this age must be personal because of the introspective activity involved in making a selection of one possible future from

among equally viable possibilities. And if the enterprise of
speculation upon the form of the future cannot be hortatory,
cannot be mere preachment, it must be more than description.
It must be *prophetic*.

Prophecy has very little to do with the description of
future events. A prophet (*prophetes*) is one who "speaks for."
Prophecy involves a claim to speak with authority. We tend to
forget that the famous prophets of history are famous mainly
because their predictions came true. For obvious reasons we
hear little about the failures. There have always been as many
prophets as there have been significant messages to deliver.
And every prophet lays claim to authority. For those contemporary with the prophecies it is the better part of wisdom to
keep in mind that the intrinsic appeal of the prophecy is perhaps the only criterion that may be employed when one
attempts to decide whose message to believe. Rationality,
consistency, coherence, elegance of construction, reputation
of the proclaimer, have little to do with the validity of a message since, as we have previously stressed, by the time an age
finds itself in need of cultural prophets, the accepted wisdom
of a society no longer commands authority.

It is not enough, therefore, simply to present speculative
possibilities concerning the nature of the future. It is necessary to choose. Utopian fantasies—casual products of glib and
facile wits—are fast becoming the opiate of the people. And a
people perishes as easily from too many visions as from none.
The prophet who seeks that insight which alone makes possible significant foresight must claim authority. And the fundamental source of that authority is that subjective form of
certitude that provides his place to stand while delivering the
prophecy. It is from this place that he exploits the wealth of
untapped resources from exoteric thought and culture, and
seeks to transplant rootless abstractions of the present in an
original past. In this manner, and only in this manner, is it
possible to achieve sufficient transcendence of the determinations of our cultural past in order to serve the process of the
casting of possible futures.

If cultural self-understanding were a luxury, we would
probably be justified in abandoning the task because of its

obvious difficulty. But some understanding of our cultural present and the possible future is an absolute necessity. For along with the civilizing of experience comes the increased tenuousness of the whole of our cultural enterprise. We come nearer barbarism as we move toward an increasingly complex and more finely articulated cultural existence. The same technological developments that have provided the increased potentiality for complex interrelationships among intense cultural experiences have produced a situation in which the destruction of society and its culture is a distinct possibility. The more godlike we become, the more we are burdened by our mortality.

NOTES

1. See Mortimer Adler, *The Conditions of Philosophy* (Chicago: The University of Chicago Press, 1964).

2. See Richard McKeon, "The Flight from Certainty and the Quest for Precision," *The Review of Metaphysics*, 18, No. 2 (1964), 234–53.

3. I shall discuss the meta-theoretical understandings of contemporary culture in greater detail in subsequent chapters. Here I shall simply cite the principal sources from which an understanding of this movement may be drawn. Richard McKeon's most useful published works on this subject are: *Freedom and History* (New York: Noonday, 1952), and *Thought, Action, and Passion* (Chicago: The University of Chicago Press, 1954). Robert Brumbaugh's principal meta-theoretical writings are contained in a series of articles in *The Review of Metaphysics*: "A Preface to Cosmography," 7, No. 1 (1953), 53–63; "Cosmography," 25, No. 2 (1971), 337–47; "Cosmography: The Problem of Modern Systems," 26, No. 3 (1973), 511–21; and in a book, co-authored with Newton Stallknecht, *The Compass of Philosophy* (New York: Longmans, Green, 1954). Stephen Pepper's works include *World Hypotheses* (Berkeley: The University of California Press, 1966) and *Concept and Quality* (LaSalle, Ill.: Open Court, 1967).

Perhaps the most influential recent work by a meta-theoretical philosopher is Richard Rorty's *Philosophy and the Mirror of Nature* (Princeton: Princeton University Press, 1979). Rorty, a student of both McKeon's and Brumbaugh's, has written a very subtle critique of contemporary philosophical activity that argues for the abandonment of the vision of philosophy as a foundational activity serving to ground cultural consensus in favor of an understanding of philosophy as a continuing conversation aiming at "edification." The reader might also wish to consult Nelson Goodman's finely wrought work, *Ways of Worldmaking* (Indianapolis: Hacket, 1978), for a meta-theoretical essay written from the distinctly pragmatic perspective characteristic of so many contemporary American philosophical analysts.

Meta-theory is by no means restricted to philosophy. For a meta-theoretical account of various psychological theories, see Joseph Rychlak's Introduction to his *Personality and Psychotherapy: A Theory Construction Approach* (Boston: Houghton Mifflin, 1973). Rychlak's analysis of theoretical alternatives in psychology follows the same general approach, and draws roughly the same conclusions, as do McKeon's, Brumbaugh's, and Pepper's.

4. In recent years, Konrad Lorenz' *On Aggression* (trans. Marjorie Wilson [New York: Harcourt, Brace, & World, 1966]), Philip Rieff's *The Triumph of the Therapeutic: Uses of Faith after Freud* (New York: Harper & Row, 1966), Norman O. Brown's *Life Against Death* (New York: Random House, 1959), and Erich Fromm's *The Revolution of Hope* (New York: Harper & Row, 1968), among (all too many) others, have parodied the contributions of the Darwinian, Marxian, and Freudian paradigms in various ways, producing wholly inadequate theories of contemporary cultural experience.

The most fascinating illustration of this tendentious misuse of a specialized insight is to be found in E. O. Wilson's *Sociobiology: The New Synthesis* (Cambridge: Harvard University Press, 1975), and in the movement it has helped to spawn. The appalling combination of arrogance and philosophical naïveté with which Wilson writes is evidence enough of the deleterious consequences of the over-application of a narrowly based methodology.

I do not wish to indict all disciples of these three cultural innovators. The neo-Marxians have developed sufficient methodological consciousness to be able to assess critically at least some of the limitations of their philosophy. Jürgen Habermas, perhaps the most sensitive and acute of the contemporary neo-Marxians, in such works as *Theory and Practice* (Boston: Beacon, 1973) and *Knowledge and Human Interests* (Boston: Beacon, 1971), provides the groundwork for an interpretation of culture that is as adequate as the Marxian perspective allows.

5. Again, it is the neo-Marxian who is best equipped to deal with this condition of contemporary intellectual culture. The distinction between ideology (forms of thought that serve as rationalizations of current practice in alienated societies) and "critical theory" (forms of thought that promote revolutionary praxis by articulating the limitations of ideologies) allows the neo-Marxian to provide programmatic ideas for contemporary society. From the perspective taken in this work, however, the neo-Marxian is as limited as any other theoretical perspective since it must ultimately degenerate to a reductionism when it explains, or attempts to account for, alternative philosophic paradigms.

6. (Chicago: The University of Chicago Press, 1962; rev. ed. 1970). Even more radical is the work of Paul Feyerabend whose criticisms of theory-bound investigations lead him to affirm an ad hoc, "anarchistic," epistemology for science. See his *Against Method* (Atlantic Highlands, N.J.: Humanities, 1975).

7. Trans. John Wilkinson (New York: Knopf, 1964). Ellul has recently produced a new work on essentially the same themes. Entitled *The Technological System* (trans. Joachim Neugroschel [New York: Continuum, 1980]), this work purports to deal with technology as a system in contradis-

tinction to *The Technological Society*, which treated technological society per se. I must say that, as far as I can tell, the novel contributions made by *The Technological System* are primarily at the level of examples and illustrations rather than in terms of any new principles of interpretation. *The Technological Society*, I believe, remains the much more important work.

8. See especially his *The End of Philosophy*, trans. Joan Stambaugh (New York: Harper & Row, 1973).

9. R. C. Solomon, *Existentialism* (New York: Random House, 1974), p. x.

10. The writings of the psychologist R. D. Laing, especially *The Politics of Experience* (New York: Ballantine, 1972), and of the polymath John Lilly (see *The Center of the Cyclone* [New York: Julian, 1972]), among many others, are illustrations of this type of work.

11. We have an excellent literary example of these three turnings in Robert Pirsig's *Zen and the Art of Motorcycle Maintenance: An Inquiry into Values* (New York: Morrow, 1974). The book is an autobiographical account of a man's search for ultimate meaning which leads him beyond the culturally defined limits of sanity into the innermost sources of personal experience; the doctrines of Buddhism and Taoism; and, finally to a revisioned past, a novel set of cultural origins from out of which the author and his contemporaries might fashion an existence rooted in the present. Because of its explicitly autobiographical intent, it is the introspective turn that is emphasized most. But the book is, nonetheless, an extremely suggestive methodological study for those who would come to grips with the problem of cultural self-understanding.

12. See Whorf's "Science and Linguistics," *Technology Review* (April 1940), 229–48.

13. Part of the return to the origins of our cultural experience involves the curious fact of the re-emergence of the Gnostic sensibility. We must speak of *re-emergence* since Gnosticism has tended to reassert itself during previous periods of cultural transition. In the interim between the collapse of Hellenism and the rise of the Judaeo-Christian tradition, Gnosticism, as a recognized historical movement, was born in the West. Likewise, in the medieval and early-Renaissance period, Gnosticism again raised its head. In the contemporary period, visionary works such as Roszak's *Where the Wasteland Ends* (Garden City, N.Y.: Doubleday, 1973), José Arguëlles' *The Transformative Vision* (Berkeley: Shambhala, 1975), Jacob Needleman's *A Sense of the Cosmos* (Garden City, N.Y.: Doubleday, 1975), and, in particular, William Irwin Thompson's *At the Edge of History* (New York: Harper & Row, 1971), *Passages About Earth* (New York: Harper & Row, 1975), and *The Time Falling Bodies Take to Light* (New York: St. Martin's, 1981), are examples of the recourse to perennial wisdom for the reinterpretation of the nature and direction of contemporary culture. Roszak's book seeks to plumb the depths of the anti-Christian, anti-scientific metaphysics of the Gnostic tradition, particularly as displayed by William Blake, to develop an alternative sensibility in terms of which to characterize a promising future for our society. The revisioning of history that goes on in the works of W. I. Thompson is intriguing in its reliance on the presumption of a lost wisdom of prehistory. Needleman attempts to engage scientific theory and practice with the Gnostic sensibility, while

Arguëlles draws from myth, art, and literature in order to project a vision of the future congruent with the Old Gnosis.

An important scholarly work supportive of the speculative adventures cited above is Elaine Pagels' *The Gnostic Gospels* (New York: Random House, 1979). The best source in English for a philosophical interpretation of Gnosticism is still Hans Jonas' *The Gnostic Religion*, (enl. ed. [Boston: Beacon, 1963]). And, of course, Gnosticism thrives in the ultra-pop realm of cultural analysis. For a catalogue of the pervasive social instantiations of the Gnostic Sensibility, see Marilyn Ferguson's *The Aquarian Conspiracy: Personal and Social Transformation in the 1980's* (Los Angeles: Tarcher, 1980).

It is not surprising that the social and cultural movements nourished by the Gnostic sensibility have met with a strong reaction in recent times. The worldwide emergence of a new fundamentalism has taken the form in America of conservative politics and fundamentalist Christianity. It is doubtful that technologically advanced societies such as ours can sustain the reaction against the Gnostic modes of thinking. At the very least, the arguments of this essay will demonstrate some of the consequences of the Gnostic impulse.

14. Landmarks of this new understanding of the Dionysian elements of Greek culture in recent philosophic literature include: various of Heidegger's discussions of Greek philosophy scattered throughout his writings; Bruno Snell's *The Discovery of the Mind*, trans. T. G. Rosenmeyer (New York: Harper & Row, 1960); the classic work of E. R. Dodds, *The Greeks and the Irrational* (Berkeley: The University of California Press, 1951), and A. W. H. Adkins's remarkable study of the development of Greek personality, *From the Many to the One* (Ithaca, N.Y.: Cornell University Press, 1970). I shall have occasion to draw upon these works in subsequent pages.

GENESIS

2

Disciplining Chaos

History is thus inescapably a tragedy in which man may choose
between forms of tyranny but may never escape the tyranny of
form.

WILLIAM IRWIN THOMPSON

Very deep is the well of the past; shall we not call it bottomless?

THOMAS MANN

THE WELL OF THE PAST

CONSIDERATIONS OF THE CHARACTER AND CONDITIONS of
our present cultural milieu have led us to the view that we
must attempt a return to the origins of our culture if we are to
understand the crisis of our time. But how do we find "the
beginning"? We cannot, as might initially seem plausible, ask
the historian to be our guide, for the discipline of history has
never concerned itself with beginnings in the most radical
sense. And to search for some prehistoric artifactual evidence
of beginnings is to give over the enterprise to the anthropol-
ogist who must, himself, always be in some measure dependent upon philosophical principles for interpretations of his
findings. We have no choice but to be blatantly philosophical
about the whole affair and recognize that what must surely be
meant by beginning is that moment "in the beginning" of

which myths speak and those *archai* or *principia* that constitute "principles," the beginning points of all thought and
action.

The primary function of myths has always been to serve
as etiological tales, as stories of the origins, whose cosmogonic motivations largely determine cosmological structures of explanation—structures that provide the context
within which philosophic principles were born. Thus, the
question of origins is properly not an historical question at all.
It is rather a religious and philosophical issue. It is the purpose
of religious myth to tell the story of beginnings. Latterly, it
became the function of philosophic principles to provide
objective and less occult guidelines for the understanding of
beginnings. That which myths tell in sensuous metaphor,
philosophy attempts to characterize in language that refers
symbolically to conscious public experience. Early on in our
own tradition cosmogonic myth provided the raw material for
cosmological principles. This transition from sensuous myth
to rational principles we may recognize as the move from one
form of intending the world to another. The attempt to construe this movement as progress in some normative sense is as
naïve as it is tendentious. The ferment in our contemporary
cultural experience is evidence enough that we are finding
dissatisfaction not only with the scientific view of the world,
but with the mythical and philosophical underpinnings of this
scientific view as well. Furthermore, as our analysis of the
relations of *theory* and *practice* in contemporary culture has
shown, there is simply no way out of our present dilemmas
through any of the paths philosophic reason has provided for
us. Our contemporary rehearsal of Sophistic skepticism and
relativism has merely recapitulated the main themes of the
song reason has sung since the period of Hellenic culture. A
much more radical alternative is necessary if we are to overcome the desiccation of experience at the hands of contemporary masters of the rational arts. Such an alternative can be
found only if we are willing to untell the story of the past.

This process of untelling the story that is our cultural
tradition will involve us in two journeys to the past. The first
journey will be one in which we retrace the adventures of

those ideas that have dominated our cultural experience and expression since our beginnings, and will involve us in an attempt to advertise the fundamental presuppositions of our intellectual culture. And since we are likely to recognize our fundamental assumptions only after they have begun to lose their authority as controlling principles of cultural creativity, the very fact that we are able to perform this meta-theoretical enterprise would seem to give strong support to the view of some critics of contemporary culture that we are currently in the process of abandoning the cultural paradigm that has, until recently, served to coordinate and articulate our knowledge and practice. A second journey will require that we move toward the past in search of the grounds for novel beliefs and intuitions, the principles of novel ideas and practices. This is a much more fitful and tentative procedure. Though we can point to neglected and, therefore, unarticulated sources of thought, action, and feeling, the articulation and clarification of these notions can only be sketchily achieved, of course, since it is no part of the task of philosophy of culture to detail their future.

These two journeys to the past require sensitivity to the dual abstractive procedures that undergird the structures of intellectual culture. The first is that of *formal* abstraction, which has led to the development of the general ideas in terms of which a culture directs its interests and activities. The ideas of our contemporary culture, for example, are products of articulation, ramification, and generalization of more concrete notions found in the primitive past. One task of the philosopher of culture in testing the viability of his cultural expressions requires a thinking backward, which involves a "letting the air out" of abstract notions in order to discover their perceptual content. Only then may we gauge the extent to which these ideas are still able to evoke and interpret the perceptual experiences that gave rise to them. The method of discovering the concrete basis of an abstract idea involves, then, symbolic reference from the idea to the perceptual experiences that underlie it. But, of equal importance, once we discover the concrete basis in terms of which the formal abstractive procedures have been performed, is the process of characterizing

the *selective* abstraction that took place at the beginnings of
our cultural traditions. Selective abstraction has determined
just which of those data constituting the welter of primordial
experience will be employed to ground the interpretative ideas
and practices that provide us with the formally abstract constructions forming intellectual culture. Thus, the two journeys
to the past are made in accordance with the rules of the two
abstractive procedures that have given rise to our cultural
experience.

If in its criticism of abstractions philosophy increasingly
leads us to conclude that present cultural aims or ideals do not
seem to evoke or interpret what we have come to feel are our
most significant experiences, we may find ourselves alienated
from the past. This alienation may either result from a sense of
uprootedness from the concrete bases of our abstract ideals,
or be occasioned by a "falling away of the past" caused by too
narrow a selection from the experiential sources that are the
only foundations of the abstract notions of intellectual culture.
In the first instance, we find that the aims, ideals, or values we
once experienced in vital connection with emotional underpinnings no longer serve to evoke commitment or belief. They
become ghostly abstractions, hovering over us, mocking our
attempts to gain access to the vital sources of cultural activity.
Uprootedness leads to an outrunning of the significant bases
of cultural experience, producing a "chronological barbarism," a dwelling outside the civilized world by living
beyond it in time.

Accompanying the sense of uprootedness is the phenomenon of the falling away of the past brought on by an over-
concern with the assemblage of those traditional significances
meant to serve as the primary pool of experiences from which
our concepts, theories, institutions, and the justifications of
our current practice emerge. The falling away of the past is a
condition of culture resulting from the assumption that the
present assemblage of cultural significances are all that obtain.
This condition becomes intolerable when a change in the
affective and intuitional character of a culture requires resort
to novel intuitions and their interpretation in order to satisfy
burgeoning demands for meaningful experiences and expres-

sions within a cultural milieu. The falling away of the past results from our no longer attending to those peripheral ideas that do not directly apply to current accepted practices. For example, our contemporary technological society, with its emphasis upon those aspects of our environment that lead to short-term solutions to our problems, and to the implemention of cautious programs aimed at efficiency and economic gain, has allowed many of the finer and more subtle components of our tradition to fall away.

The return to the origins is necessary if we are to find original experiences from which to begin anew, or in terms of which we may provide access to the understanding of the novelty emerging in the present. A futurist orientation and a return to the origins are requirements of contemporary culture philosophy because all the principal theoretical alternatives that may be employed in the analysis of culture and in the construction of theories of cultural experience have been raised to the level of consciousness.

We live in an age of intellectual anarchy—i.e., an age "without principles." It is simply no longer true that a dominant ethos exists, if by the term we mean a *Geist*, or general world-view, held by a majority within society or by significant elites within the social complex in such a way as to constitute an accepted matrix of value orientations. We currently are sustaining a number of distinct cultures, and it is surely the case that something like culture-shock is a transitive and mutual experience in each of the distinct orientations. We find ourselves existing in an epoch patterned by extremes.

Ours is an age of extremes simply because only at the extremes, only in sectarian thought-forms, do we find anything like untried alternatives. And at this juncture the concern is not so much that we discover a final truth as that we find a set of ideas or principles about which we may seriously ask the question of truth. It may be that there is no such thing as truth. But it seems, nonetheless, that truth is a necessary postulate of the courageous pursuit of cultural significances. We must postulate the truth of an idea in order to find out its real value. The trouble with this age of meta-consciousness is that we are no longer in a position to take that postulate seriously regarding any of the cultural values that for twenty-four-hundred years have served us as the foundation of our cultural existence.

In our cultural present, sectarian extremes stand on a par with the established ideas of our intellectual culture. And for perhaps the first time we are prepared to take these forms of thought seriously, and to return with them to the origins of our common experience to discover whether or not they constitute valid intellectual alternatives. Apparently, then, it is only in terms of what we formerly thought to be extremes that we may be provided access to the past that has fallen away. We really do not have much experience of thought at the extremes. Most of our so-called radical thinking exists as a dialectical alternative to some posited view. But it is not possible to articulate positions dialectically in an age in which the primary thought-systems have been shown to have equal viability. Every dialectical ploy has been tried before. Every conceivable position has won its victory only to be submerged in defeat at the hands of its dialectical opposite. The dialectic is based on a concept of reason that has served Western society well, but that we have seen come to an end, at least "in principle," in this century of rapidly disintegrating *principles*.

The response to the collapse of the principles of cultural unity has been an interesting one. It has consisted in a frantic search for novel principles, which has given rise to a large number of bold visions of new directions for our culture, many of which were cited in the preceding pages. The principal difficulty such works encounter is that they are not sustained by a tradition that provides a concrete support to the insights and conclusions of the thinkers, and that also provides some kind of pragmatic justification, and theoretical verification, of those insights. The isolated thinker is not enough. We need the sense of a *tradition*, some augumented pattern of thought and activity that shows itself viable as a means of organizing human energies and aspirations.[1]

That we do not have such an indigenous tradition, of course, is not at all surprising. The dominant forms of theory and practice could not allow of such a parallel tradition without undermining their own orthodoxy. We are forced to search out such a matrix of thought and action through a revision of our own cultural tradition and through an examination of alternative cultural systems. By doing so, we can perhaps marshal the resources necessary to provide the materials from which a cultural paradigm suitable to contemporary technological culture may be constructed. Only in this way will our search for self-understanding be realized.

The ad hoc quality of contemporary cultural experience is due both to the sense of uprootedness brought on by the experienced irrelevance of many of our formerly efficacious ideals and values, and to the falling away of the past resulting from a neglect of all but the most utilitarian aspects of our culture. And the alienation from the past experienced in our culture can be overcome only if we approach the past armed with a desire for novel experiences, and discover in the interplay of the past and the present the beginnings of ideas that, selected from the past, nonetheless give rise to interpretations of our present experiences. For this to be successful, we must balance our two aforementioned readings of the past: the first, which views it as a primitive form of the present; the second, which sees it as a bottomless well from which hardly dreamed-of novelties may be drawn.

We must not be naïve about the question of objectivity. The only way we can plumb the depths of the past is if we already possess some predispositions. If we ask why we should attempt to investigate the past if all we seek is the verification of a bias, we must answer that it is through such verification or, perhaps better, *vindication*, that we come to recognize what our perspective really is. There is no other way of discovering what we think! The assumption that intuitions can be discovered apart from concepts depends on the conviction that there exists an isolatable realm of uninterpreted facts. Within our rationalistic culture such a conviction is as naïve as the belief that it is possible to take a rabbit from an empty hat. We can separate the *definiendum* from the *definiens* in any particular case, but *some definiens* is always present. Value-free investigations are free of only those few values that may be successfully isolated. We must, therefore, not concern our-

selves with the past *als zwar gewesen ist.* What could that
possibly be but a *mélange* of untold vagueness and complexity?
We must be concerned with the past *as present circumstances
invite us to view it.*

IN THE BEGINNING . . .

Our English word "beginning" derives from the Old Norse
gína and the Old English *gínan*, which mean "to gape," "to
yawn." As such, the word is etymologically related to the
term "chaos," which also has as one of its basic meanings
"gaping void, or yawning gap." The beginning, according to
The Oxford English Dictionary, is "the action or process of
entering upon existence," "that out of which anything has its
rise." Likewise, chaos, according to the same source, is "element," "the first state of the universe," "the great deep or
abyss" out of which the cosmos, or order of the universe, was
evolved. Both the Greek *arche* and the Latin *principium*
answer to the meaning of beginning as source. "In the beginning" was chaos, and, consequently, the concept of "beginning" we have developed in our Western tradition shares
many of the same connotations as that of "chaos."

"Beginning" and "principle," as synonyms for "origin,"
are directly related to the conception of primordial chaos,
which in cosmogonic myths is a basic formlessness out of
which all order arises. The opposite of chaos is cosmos.
Cosmos means order, or harmony, or the world or universe as
an ordered and harmonious system. The idea of bringing
cosmos out of chaos is at the very root of our conception of
beginnings.

A "return to the origins" is a return, therefore, to chaos,
a return to that "time of beginnings" before there was order or
harmony. It is a return to a time of unreason, for reason construed as that power or capacity by which we grasp *first
principles* can take us only as far back as the moment after
which cosmos came into being out of chaos. Reason and
reasoning are—as we shall see in the following chapter—
intrinsically tied to the notion of primordial beginnings.

Cosmologies are the groundwork of rational order. Cosmogonies, by recalling a "time" characterized by a basic irrationality, or non-rationality, remind us that beyond the conception of an ordered and harmonious universe lies chaos, disorder, confusion.

Chaos is non-rational because it is unprincipled. It is, therefore, an-archic, without *archai*; without, that is to say, determining sources of order, without a beginning or origin. Chaos is the indefinite in search of definition, the unlimited requiring limitation. It is lawless, obeying no rules. The dread of anarchy that is so much a part of our cultural heritage is in large measure related to the primordial fear of chaos that is its presumed attendant. The political anarchy that Carlyle found "the hatefullest of things" is but an expression of "the waste Wide Anarchy of Chaos," which John Milton saw personified as the "Anarch old." Being without princes to rule is but an instance of being without principles to guide, and being without an ordered and harmonious cosmos within which to find one's place.

Our most primitive conceptions of chaos have taken three fundamental forms. The Semitic concept, perhaps developed from the Babylonian creation myth, *Enuma elish*, and expressed in the Book of Genesis, speaks of a primordial condition ("in the beginning") in which "the earth was without form, and void, and darkness was upon the face of the waters." The characterization of the beginning of things as a formless, dark void parallels the description of chaos in terms of the "primordial waters" in Egyptian and Mesopotamian creation myths. The story of creation is in this instance a tale of the victory over chaos, which establishes order. In *Enuma elish*,[2] Marduk slays the dragon Tiamat and establishes victory over the forces of chaos. In Genesis, God's command "Let it be" establishes order from chaos. In these instances it is an act of the will, a deed or a command, which assures victory over chaotic beginnings.

But the imposition of order need not take the form of an explicit act of the will. Indeed Plato's cosmogony in the *Timaeus* is based on the imposition of order through persuasion—i.e., through the process of *rationalization*.

Desiring, then, that all things should be good and, so far as might be, nothing imperfect, the god took over all that is visible—not at rest but in discordant and unordered motion—and brought it from disorder into order, since he judged that order was in every way the better. . . .

Reason overruled Necessity by persuading her to guide the greatest part of things that becomes towards what is best; in that way and on that principle this universe was fashioned in the beginning by the victory of reasonable persuasion over Necessity.[3]

There is no concern in Plato's myth for supporting a *pre-existent* chaos; the only important consideration is that the persuasive agency of the demiurge reduces the threat of chaotic disorder and achieves the permanent possibility of harmony through the exercise of rational persuasion. Chaos is the permanent possibility of disorder, which exists, abstractly, as the condition of the world without reason. Chaos is "in the beginning" in the sense that it is what accounts for the exercise of reason as an ordering agency.

In the Genesis myth the origin of light from darkness, and the consequent creation of an ordered universe, depend upon an act of the will. *Creatio ex nihilo* is accomplished by a command, an *order*. Plato's "likely story" of creation involves the rationalization of a disordered and discordant chaos achieving the victory of persuasion over necessity. Power creates something from nothing; reason brings order from discord. There is a third dynamic capable of construing order from chaos celebrated in the myths that have influenced our traditions. This is the factor of Eros. And it depends upon yet another variant of the conception of chaos. In addition to the conceptions of chaos as Non-Being and as Discord, there is the notion, prevalent in fifth- and sixth-century Orphic cosmogonies, of chaos as "that which separates." This conception is closely associated with the root meaning of chaos as "yawning gap." Among Orphic creation myths, a prevalent theme is the separation of earth and sky and the association of chaos with the space between. Eros then becomes the means by which the primordial unity of earth and heaven, the female and male principles, respectively, is to be achieved.

The most consistent rendering of Hesiod's *Theogony* is

one that understands the emergence of the world in terms of the coming-into-being of earth and sky and of the region in between. The union of earth and sky, of which Hesiod makes a great deal in the myth, then becomes the rewinning at the cosmological level of a primordial unity ever threatened by the existence of chaos as the separating gap and ever rewon through the agency of Eros as the drive toward the reunion of the separated elements.[4]

The interpretation of chaos as the region between earth and heaven has etymological support since, as I have noted above, the root meanings of *chaos* include "gape" and "yawning gap." This could suggest influence by *Enuma elish*, where there is a division of Tiamat into sky and earth, and Genesis, recalling God's division of the waters below and above the firmanent by his creation of earth and heaven. This interpretation of Hesiod would lead to the presumption of a primordial unity out of which chaos comes through the separation of the One into earth and sky. This would, of course, conflict with *Enuma elish* and Genesis insofar as they claim that chaos consisted of "the primordial waters," or "the dark, formless void," out of which the world emerged or was created. But in Hesiod as clearly as in *Enuma elish* and Genesis, chaos, a necessary by-product of that process that leads to the coming-into-being of all things, is something to be overcome. The sexual imagery in Hesiod leading to the identification of heaven with the male principle and earth with the female suggests both that without the opposition of earth and sky nothing could be generated, and that the first thing generated by such opposition is chaos, the gap separating the two.

There is at least an echo of this notion of separation giving rise to chaos in Aristophanes' myth of the circle men. The re-establishment of that original unity of persons, sundered by an act of Zeus, is the goal of eros. Love is the drive toward unity that can overcome the separation, or gap (the *chaos*), that emerged when the sexes came into being.

Aristophanes' variation of the traditional Orphic cosmogony is prominently expressed in *The Birds*. It is eros that is responsible for the order of things and their creation:

> Love hatched us, commingling in Tartarus wide,
>   with Chaos, the murky, the darkling;
>   . . . .
>
> Then all things commingling together in love,
>   there arose the fair Earth and the Sky,
>
> And the limitless Sea; and the race of the Gods,
>   the Blessed who never shall die.[5]

Here the origins of cosmos from chaos is construed after the model of a birthing process, with eros and chaos the parents from which proceed all things. In Aristophanes' version of the cosmogonic myth, love plays the role given to reason in Plato's myth.

The myth from Hesiod's *Theogony*, and Aristophanes' variation of it, contrast with the Semitic cosmogonies and with the Platonic myth of the *Timaeus* in that although the latter suggest that chaos is to be overcome through will and reason, respectively, the former describe the conquest of chaos by eros—a drive toward primordial unity.

The three types of cosmogony describe the manner of overcoming chaos conceived in three ways—as Non-Being, as Disorder, and as a separating gap. In all these senses, the beginning of things consisted in an act of construal. Though these three versions of the creation of cosmos from chaos suggest the three fundamental means through which persons, in our cultural tradition, have conceived the possibility of the conquest of chaos, there is perhaps another conception of chaos that needs to be clarified in this context: namely, that which affirms that *this world* is chaos.

According to some Gnostic cosmogonies of the early-Christian era, this world is the product of a demiurge identified with the Old Testament God. The created world is the realm of chaos. And though human beings participate in this world through their bodily existence, the human *spirit* has as its proper home a world of light and harmony beyond this chaotic earthly existence. In this view, the creator of the world is responsible for "an imperfect or an abortive undertaking."[6] Whereas most early Christian apologists utilized a concept of free will to account for the disorderly elements in existence, the Gnostics, usually affirming some form of determinism associated with a dualistic cosmology, had to blame the demiurge. The assumption that the creator was, to a greater or lesser extent, responsible for evil in the world by virtue of the imperfection of his creative activity led to antinomian ethics. Complete cooperation with the laws of the demiurge would spell damnation. The sensuous realm must be resisted, and redemption of the spirit—that human element that has affinity with a higher deity, ruler of the realm of spirit and light beyond this chaotic world—must be sought. As Hans Jonas has written of the Gnostic view:

> . . . Whoever has created the world, man does not owe him allegiance. . . . Since not the true God can be the creator of that to which selfhood feels so utterly a stranger, nature merely manifests its lowly demiurge: as a power deep beneath the Supreme God, upon which every man can look down from the height of his god-kindred spirit, this perversion of the Divine has retained of it only the power to act, but to act blindly, without knowledge and benevolence. Thus did the demiurge create the world out of *ignorance* and *passion*.[7]

In the dominant theories of chaos from which we derive our understanding of cultural beginnings, the ordering element can be characterized in terms of thought, action, or passion. Gnostic cosmogonies have accepted this fundamental structure and have merely inverted the dominant views. The power of the creator is blind and reckless power; the result of ignorance and passion, disordered emotion. Chaos is the result of an abortive attempt at creation. As we shall have occasion to see later on, the Gnostic mentality provides a clear and dramatic alternative to the major characterizations of cosmological and ethical concepts associated with our traditional culture, but in regard to the question of origins, the Gnostic myths are not fundamentally different from those that undergird received wisdom—at least as far as the attitude toward chaos is concerned.

There is, of course, no semantic necessity to view chaos only in a negative sense. Indeed, Werner Jaeger has insisted, in speaking of the Greek conception of chaos, that

> The common idea of chaos as something in which all things are wildly confused is quite mistaken; and the antithesis between Chaos and

Cosmos, which rests on this incorrect view, is a purely modern invention. Possibly the idea of *tohu wa bohu* has inadvertently been read
into the Greek conception from the biblical account of creation in
Genesis.[8]

It is true that, for Aristotle, chaos meant merely "empty
space."[9] But then Aristotle's use of the term was itself quite
"modern" compared to that of the Orphics and Hesiod. And
even if Jaeger overstates his case by claiming that the antithe-
sis between chaos and cosmos is a purely modern invention, it
is quite likely that the continual interpretation of chaos in
terms of the myth of Genesis was largely responsible for its
almost universally negative connotations. On the other hand,
the tonality of the Orphic cosmogonies and of Plato's myth in
the *Timaeus*, rehearsed above, itself provides no little stimulus toward the understanding of chaos as negative.

More importantly, we should note that even if we were
not to take our cosmogonic myths seriously, we are disposed
on wholly philosophic grounds to affirm an ordering activity
involved in beginnings. Aristotle, who provided no explicit
cosmogonic myth, and who saw no metaphysical need for
creation in any radical sense, has nonetheless provided the
locus classicus for our understanding of the function of
archai, or principles, as determining sources of order. A
beginning, or a principle, we still believe with Aristotle, is that
from which a thing can be known, that from which a thing first
comes to be, or that at whose will that which is moved *is*
moved and that which changes changes.[10] Principles account
for, and establish, the order of the world. As principles of
knowledge, beginnings are the origins of thought. As principles of being, they are the sources of origination per se. Beginnings in the political or social sphere are due to *archai* or
principes—those who command. In any of its forms according
to Aristotle, a first principle functions as a determining source
of order. And standing behind the notion of principles as
archai, there is the object of the ordering function of principles
that our cosmogonic myths celebrate as chaos.

The claim that the association of chaos with confusion
and disorder is "mistaken" is hardly defensible except on the
grounds of a strict and narrow linguistic archaeology. Even if

one should wish to maintain that the contrast of chaos and cosmos is not required by some archaic understandings of these terms, the opposition, whether understood in its mythical or its philosophic guise, is an extrapolation and intensification of a tendency firmly present in the primitive milieu from which our most fundamental cultural self-understandings emerged. And, what is more important, these self-understandings have come to be dominated by the contrast.

We have learned two important things concerning the concept of chaos. First, it has developed an extremely negative connotation in the dominant Western characterizations of the time of beginnings. And, second, what is most interesting about the discussions of the overcoming of chaos is the offering of three distinct dynamisms (will, eros, and rationality) as agents of that overcoming. For these three dynamisms—variously described as action, passion, and thought, or practical, productive, and theoretical activities—formed the foundation for the concept of personality in the classical period of the Greeks. Both the Platonic and the Aristotelian philosophic syntheses accepted these elements as the variables in terms of which a functional characterization of personality, society, and intellectual culture was to be made. What we shall find when we consider the concepts of the psyche in terms of the late-Hellenic philosophic synthesis is that the characterization of human nature as it developed in Hellenic culture—which was then transmitted to the culture of the Middle Ages and so became the Judaeo-Christian standard in terms of which we gauge human behavior—is a concept construed in terms of cosmogonic myths: i.e., in terms of the struggle to win cosmos from chaos.

Imago hominis

The attempt to discover the origin of our concept of human nature, or personality, insofar as it takes us beyond the phase of written records, is a highly problematic venture, and must remain so until such time as a method of cultural analysis is invented that does not depend, explicitly or implicitly, on linguistic analysis. The most direct manner of construing the

development of individual and cultural self-consciousness
may be as the evolution of personal and social structures that
provide a means of ordering chaos. According to such a view,
the concept of the psyche, and the social and cultural institutions that reflect and are reflected by it, resulted from a tension between the threat of chaos experienced as confusion,
disorder, and disharmony, and the demand for the imposition
of order and the maintenance of control that were the only
means by which our cultural ancestors felt themselves able to
survive individually and as a species.

Claude Lévi-Strauss, following the inspiration of
Rousseau, has characterized as the central problem of anthropology that of understanding, in human terms, "the passage
from nature to culture."[11] The problem is, as are all problems
of beginnings, insolvable since the "nature" from which creatures (which we must only latterly term "human beings")
passed can be construed only in terms of semantic contexts,
which themselves are cultural objects. Thus, in discussing the
passage from nature to culture, we are acknowledging our
entrapment within culture and affirming our status as beings
whose articulated existence may be viewed in relation to
"nature" only after we have constructed such a concept.

Without this recognition, we are apt to assume that the
phenomena of animism and totemism, which so-called primi-
tives variously employed as means of expressing a unity with
their natural surroundings, were means of subverting any tension that might have been experienced between "self" and
"not-self." Granted: self-consciousness may well have developed from a more primordial consciousness of totality, of an
undiscriminated "ocean of feeling" in which the distinction of
self and not-self was not an articulated experience; still, the
tension must have existed between order and disorder, between cosmos and chaos. Nature conceived, insofar as possible, apart from human culture still exists as a matrix of
order—a cosmos—explicable in our Western cultural inheritance only in terms of an antecedent and all-too-present threat
of chaos.

The primordial tension of conflict that ultimately gives
rise to self-consciousness as the supreme cultural object was

not the tension felt between nature and the new demands of culture, but the tension experienced as the ongoing conflict between threatened destruction by chaotic disorder and the promise of control through the schematization of chaos in terms of intuition, action, and rationality. Unless we posit—as the evidence of our mythical heritage urges us to do—this kind of primordial conflict, there is very little reason to believe that our cultural evolution should have taken the course it did take. Why should the felt unity of our proto-human ancestors with their natural environments not have constituted a satisfying solution to the problems of survival and well-being? The answer we must give to the question "Why did self-consciousness emerge in the first place?" (if we are to take cultural evolution seriously and not merely characterize the development of human psyche and its institutional ramifications in terms of the occult concept of "mutation") must be based on the realization of the basic conflict experienced by our ancestors between order—whether the order of "nature" or of "culture"—and confusion, between cosmos and chaos.

Alvin Gouldner, in his sociological analysis of ancient Greek culture, has stated: "Without some tension with others, the boundaries of self become more permeable, and the line between self and others grows indistinct."[12] The comparatively late emergence of something like self-consciousness and individuality is, perhaps, due mainly to the fact that under tribal conditions these tensions with others were reduced to a minimum. But the tension with "The Other," construed as a religious object, was quite real from the most primitive times. Before the individual emerged as the psychic and social unit of existence, the group experienced itself as real over against the threat of chaos, which it could not altogether escape.

Though the extant cosmogonic myths include rational persuasion and action as well as the drive toward emotional or aesthetic unity in the repertoire of dynamisms that may be employed to overcome chaos, there can be little doubt that it was through aesthetic impression that persons first became aware of the original threat and of its overcoming. This experience was initially felt through the medium of the collective, and only later came to be in its fullest sense an individual, experience. Individuality had to await the emergence of individualized acts of the will: decisions or purposes envisioned as personal and, in some sense, idiosyncratic. This can occur only "as the I passes from mere emotional reaction to the stage of action, as it comes to see its relation to nature no longer through the medium of mere impression but through the medium of its own action."[13] This transition paralleled the development of technology.

The first acts of individualization, hardly recognizable as such, concern the process of self-creation, which was a part of the function of the earliest human being. In the process of creating a culture, *persons* came into being. Thus, "man might even be defined as a creature never found in a 'state of nature,' for as soon as he becomes recognizable *as* man he is already in a state of culture."[14] Technology, in the original sense of *techne*, was the medium through which culture and, with it, human being emerged. According to Lewis Mumford, one of the many proponents of a technical monism, technology had its beginnings in the organization of psychic energies and only later developed into tool-making as we ordinarily conceive it. But both kinds of "tool" developed from the same source: "the primeval repetitive order of ritual, a mode of order man was forced to develop . . . to control the tremendous overcharge of psychal energy that his large brain placed at his disposal."[15] Mumford finds in the symbol-making activity of primitive human beings the beginnings of technological development. More important, he finds the reason for this development to be the need to control "a tremendous overcharge of psychal energy," the need to bring order out of chaos.

If we accept this thesis, it is easy enough to understand how, throughout the process of individualization, of self-creativity, the feeling of anxiety in the face of the threat to ordered existence continually confronted human beings. A contemporary philosopher claims, "[man] cannot deal with Chaos. Because his characteristic function and highest asset is conception, his greatest fear is to meet what he cannot construe."[16] Anxiety in the face of what cannot be construed indicates the importance of the feeling that something is known or at least knowable. Thus, it is the characteristic indeterminateness of chaos that leads to anxiety. Chaos understood could not be chaotic. Intelligibility, or determinateness, and chaos are contradictories. But from the beginning of our tradition, the conception of chaos has often been accompanied by the ideal of a final and complete victory over disorder. And though the belief that the universe is an ordered whole is often an ideal of philosophers, it is even more often a religious ideal. For, "religious man thirsts for *being*. His terror of the chaos that surrounds his inhabited world corresponds to his terror of nothingness." [17]

This statement by Mircea Eliade, the phenomenologist of religion, is supported by the following sociological conception of religion: religion is "the establishment, through human activity, of . . . a sacred cosmos that will be capable of maintaining itself in the ever-present face of chaos." [18] Such a characterization of religion clarifies the negative attitude toward chaos not only among the religious, but in secular society as well. For "every human society, however legitimated, must maintain its solidarity in the face of Chaos." [19] The risk of falling into disorder, the threat of anarchy, is run by anyone who would set himself against the laws and customs of a given society. For the disorder consequent upon the breaking of the laws of a society threatens to lead one to "that yawning abyss of chaos that is the oldest antagonist of the sacred." [20]

Contemporary persons are so hedged about by protective and securing structures that it is a wonder that we can even appreciate the threat of chaos that dwells beneath the surface of our psychic, social, and cultural edifices. Even our forms of irrationality are ordered and limited for us by the cosmicizing motive. The various revolts against reason that occasionally have patterned our historical development are revolts not against order, but against the rational means of attaining it. Existentialism, on the one hand, and romanticism, on the other, have been the primary modes of opposing reason and rational structures. But each of these irrational or non-rational philosophies is but an expression of an alternative form of cosmicizing chaos. The romantics seek to substitute feeling for reason; the existentialist opposes will to rationality.

Knowledge for the romantic is a *mélange* of poetic insight and quasi-mystical intuition. The existentialist hopes to produce knowledge through the willful determination of the structures of his world.

Yet whether it be the existentialist claiming precedence for existence over essence, decrying antecedent rational structures, and struggling for self-determination, or the romantic claiming that feeling or intuition can be the only access to reality, that "only an artist can define the meaning of life,"[21] there is no real revolt against the fundamental principles of order that provide protection against chaos. Reason is not the only (nor, as we shall have occasion to see, the most fundamental) means of construing chaos. Passion and volition themselves are agencies of construal.

At more concrete and personal levels, we learn to experience chaos from illness and accident, natural disasters, social conflict, and war. If we find ourselves too distant from such threats, we will nonetheless seek ways of experiencing that chaotic disorder that alone seems to make worthwhile all the sacrifices of novelty and spontaneity made in order to provide security for ourselves. Much of the jester imagery often associated with foundational myths—e.g., those concerning Peer Gynt, Pulcinella, Til Eulenspiegel—is to be construed in terms of the notion of chaos, "the principle of disorder, the force careless of Taboos."[22] From the self-induced fright associated with the late-night horror show on television to the participation in daring sports and the exposure to risk in the challenging of nature, in the struggle against "the elements," we can discern a tendency in human beings to experience the chaos of primordial beginnings. The need to test oneself against chaos, to win a victory over the chaotic threat to stability, is the desire to emulate the creator who first brought cosmos from chaos. Our voluntary experiencing of chaos has as its primary purpose the testing to see whether or not our cultural self-creativity, which has consisted in the disciplining of chaos, has been successful.

The evidence we have been reviewing supports the belief that both the *psychic* and the *social* development of human beings may best be construed, at least in our Western tradition, in terms of a struggle to win cosmos from chaos, and that employing this principle will allow us to clarify that development. If this is the case, it is important to discern the manner in which such a development, in fact, occurred and to investigate the consequences of the realization that human psychological and sociological experiences and expressions are primarily reactions to the threat of chaos.

When we arrive at Homeric conceptions of personality, we are not so much in the dark as we were in the discussion of tribal existence. There seems to be almost a consensus among those scholars who have approached the subject that "Homeric man has no unified concept of what we call a 'soul.' "[23] According to A. W. H. Adkins, "the Homeric poems . . . use language which suggests that Homeric man has a highly fragmented psychological, and also physiological experience. . . . In fact, it might be said that Homeric man experiences himself as a plurality, rather than a unity, with an indistinct boundary."[24] The Homeric period spanned the ninth to the sixth centuries B.C., and witnessed what Alvin Gouldner has termed "the greatest social revolution that Europe has yet experienced: the breakdown of tribalism and the emergence of the urban community organized on the basis of territorial propinquity—in short, the state."[25]

The passage from tribalism constituted the first crisis in the emergence of the Western conception of the self. Tribal organization as a complex system of remission and control mechanisms did not promote individualized expression except insofar as such expression was a specialized function defined by the needs of the social organism. The decline of tribalism was a decline in that form of social organization that, because it was organized around kinship ties, was considered as a family writ large. Emergence from this form of society and transition to a novel form led to the development of the conception of psyche, which has served to undergird much of our speculation concerning the meaning of persons up to and including our present period in the West.

But the development of the concept of psyche, and the peculiar self-image that accompanies it, was a slow process. The crucial stage of this process has been traced with great

care by Bruno Snell in *The Discovery of the Mind*. It is in the
literary creations of Homer that we can see the explicit outworking of the beginnings of articulate self-consciousness. For
Homer, psyche was not yet the fully developed notion it
would become in the writings of Plato and Aristotle. At this
stage psyche simply indicated "the force which keeps the
human being alive."[26] Besides the word psyche, Homer employed two other words—*thymos* and *noos*—to mean
"mind." "*Thymos* in Homer is the generator of motion or
agitation, while *noos* is the cause of ideas or images."[27] These
three terms—psyche, *noos*, and *thymos*—construed as organs
of "life, of perception and of (e)motion,"[28] are the prototypes
of what will later become, with the conceptualization of Plato,
the three functions of the soul: spirit, reason, and appetite. We
must be somewhat cautious, of course, about reading too
much of the later meanings into the Homeric terms. "Homeric
noos is not, though the word is the same, the pure intellect of
later philosophy: Homeric man does not engage in abstract
speculation, and is only concerned with practical reason."[29]
This statement by Adkins recalls Whitehead's distinction:
"There is Reason, asserting itself as above the world, and
there is Reason as one of the many factors within the
world."[30] The former is speculative reason; the latter, reason
in its practical mode. The broad contrast between reason in its
theoretical and practical modes forms a fundamental problem
for the philosophic attempts to integrate the human psyche, as
we shall have occasion to see.

   Prior to the speculations of Plato, there was little attempt
in the Greek tradition to present a systematic and authoritative
interpretation of the meaning of persons. Still, a series of inconsistent conceptions of the soul or self did exist in the classical age of Greece. The soul was seen as "the living corpse in
the grave, the shadowy image in Hades, the perishable breath
that is spilt in the air or absorbed in the aether, the daemon
that is reborn in other bodies."[31] Prior to Plato, too, there was
no orthodox vision of the soul. Plato's characterization of the
psyche, however, became the established pattern in terms of
which subsequent thinkers constructed the concept of both
human and divine persons that has served our tradition so well
until recently.

In the *Republic*, Plato assigns to Socrates the task of defining "justice," and Socrates proceeds to do so in a manner that has been largely determinative of most of the later attempts to provide an analysis of that concept; he defines the concept of justice as an *individual* virtue through an analysis of the same quality as it is found in a state. Socrates announces his intention to inquire into the meaning of justice in a state as a prerequisite to discovering justice in the individual citizen.

The problem of the psyche as Plato conceived it is construed in terms of a polar relation between the individual and society. The *locus classicus* for the consideration of the soul in these terms is Book IV of the *Republic* where Plato suggests an analogy between the state and the soul by demonstrating that those virtues in the state that are prerequisites for the attainment of political justice—wisdom, courage, and temperance—are the same as those we could find in a whole person possessed of reason, spirit or volition,[32] and appetite. In the whole person the rational element rules over both the volition and the appetites. Justice in the soul is the well-ordered harmony of its three functions. Similarly, in the state, right decisions based on understanding and rational self-control must be the primary motivating factor in social and political life. We tend to forget that the aim of the founder of political theory in this, his most famous dialogue, was, ostensibly, to discover the meaning of justice in the individual psyche, not, primarily, to construct a just social organization. Thus, Plato was attempting a psychological analysis just as surely as he was developing a political theory. For the most part subsequent generations have tended to be influenced by the political aspects of Plato's *Republic* without consciously embracing his psychological views. We have all but inverted the importance placed on the concept of justice as an individual virtue in our search for an adequate analysis of social and political meanings of justice. We may not, therefore, immediately recognize how much we have been influenced by Plato's vision of psyche and its analogy to the Hellenic polis, but it is, perhaps, one of the most important of cultural and psychological intuitions—if by "important" we mean that which has *import*, that which makes a difference in the public world. For the analogy did not lose its effect simply because Plato's ideal republic was never founded; nor did its influence diminish with the collapse of the polis as a viable political entity. It might well *have* been the case, however, that Plato's attempt to "write large" the human soul would have been lost as an effective element in our cultural tradition if Aristotle had not employed that insight *mutatis mutandis* as one of the principles in accordance with which his diverse philosophic writings were organized. It was also this organizational principle that was used to construct the curricular patterns of the medieval and modern universities, and that therefore forms one of the principal foundations of intellectual culture in the West, insofar as that culture is to be construed in terms of the pattern of university education.

"All thought," says Aristotle, "is practical or productive or theoretical."[33] These distinctions recall the Platonic division of the soul's functions into volition, appetite, and reason. Aristotle, in his organization of the *ways of knowing*, is concerned with the *principles* of those disciplines that have as their subject matters the various activities of the soul and the objects of these activities. Thus theoretical sciences consider "that sort of substance which has the principle of its movement and rest present in itself."[34] The theoretical, or natural, sciences treat of natural kinds of things, while the practical and productive sciences concern, respectively, ethical and political actions and the artistic products, which, as imitations of nature, must be understood on other than theoretical grounds. Thus, for Aristotle, metaphysics, physics, and biology are theoretical sciences; ethics and politics, practical; rhetoric and poetics, productive.

The analogy between psyche and polis first systematically articulated by Plato has been subsequently viewed in our tradition as expressive of a mirroring relation between the human mind and its cultural expressions. The university, intellectual culture in microcosm, mirrors the general cultural patterns of thinking, acting, and feeling, on the one hand, and those same functions seen as modes of being in the world intrinsic to each individual person, on the other. Philosophers concerned with either a general synthesis or a critique of human culture have sustained an interest in this characterization of the nature of psyche and of its cultural expressions.[35]

The forms of synthesis provided by Plato and Aristotle include more than just the psychosocial relation established by Plato's analogy between the soul and the state and the principle of the organization of the disciplines suggested by the Aristotelian system; in both thinkers there was the attempt to come to grips with the problem of the conflicting philosophic claims that threatened to confuse the intellectual order establishable through reason. Both Plato's discussion of the four levels of the clarity of knowledge and Aristotle's four causes are to be understood as providing a sense of a primary semantic context in which the diverse and often contradictory meanings of concepts and theories might be construed in relation to one another. One of the functions of a philosophical synthesis aimed at the coordination of the variety of significances of society is to account for contrast, conflict, and contradiction not only within the soul or among the various elements of society, but also among those who are attempting to characterize the data of intellectual culture from a variety of philosophic perspectives.

Plato's pedagogical theory contained in Book VI of the *Republic* considers the path from less to more adequate forms of knowledge, from the vaguest forms of sense perception to the most precise and most general reasonings. Furthermore, Plato's discussion in a hierarchical manner of the various approaches to knowledge has served, then and since, as the principal way of knowing a world. The first level of knowing is *eikasia*, the perception of shadows or images. At this stage knowledge is guess-work, or "gossip," and consists in the telling of myths or stories, in the perceptions of shadows or images, or in the reflections of things. It is the vaguest form of indirect, second hand, opinion.

The next higher level, the stage of *pistis*, of belief or conviction, provides a technical knowledge—what we would call "know-how"—but no understanding of rational principles. At this stage, we meet the ordinary visible things of our perceptual world and can, in accordance with past experience or opinion, manipulate these objects toward certain ends. But our knowing how to perform certain actions to achieve specific ends is not yet, on Plato's terms, knowledge. True knowledge begins with the stage of *dianoia*, understanding. To "understand" means to grasp a principle undergirding the particular object sensed or conceived. The particular is construed in terms of the universal idea or form it instances. But this knowledge is hypothetical, for the abstract understandings involved have not as yet found a place within any overarching structure such as a "science," in the sense of a system of true and certain propositions.

Dianoia is contrasted with *pistis* as "knowing that" something is the case contrasts with "knowing how" to perform certain practical operations in order to achieve a desired result. But above the *knowledge that*, which is *dianoia*, there is *noesis*, knowledge of the "why" of things. Understanding in the sense of *dianoia* is satisfied with deductions or applications derived from hypothetical principles; whereas *noesis* strives to evaluate the various partial descriptions or deductions of *dianoia* in order to construct a coherent explanatory schema encompassing the various specialized data found within the sphere of *dianoia*. This relationship may be understood in terms of the contrast between the knowledge of the scientist who seeks to confirm predictions made in accordance with certain hypothetical assumptions and that of the philosopher of science who seeks to criticize the assumptions and to place them harmoniously in relation to assumptions made by the other special sciences.

The objects of *noesis* are the forms of things themselves quite apart from their instantiations. The science of dialectic, that way of knowing that proceeds without the necessity of sense experience—i.e., reasoning in its purest and most abstract sense—is the method of *noesis*. One who reaches the level of *noetic* thought is prepared to make the final move toward the intuition of the single overarching principle that provides the ground of the cosmological order. Plato's Principle of the Good serves as the ideal of the unity of knowledge and being, aimed at demonstrating that there are, not various disjointed worlds approachable through *eikasia*, *pistis*, *dianoia*, and *noesis*, but a single world-system, a cosmos, united by a rational principle.

Plato's criticism of the philosophers who preceded him was based on his theory of the four levels of the clarity of

knowledge. His principal criticism of the history of philosophy, implicit in that theory, is this: because there had been
no successful approach to the principle of principles uniting all
theory and practice into a single cosmos, the history of intellectual culture from the Milesian materialists of the sixth
century B.C. up through his contemporary antagonists, the
Sophists, was a study in the conflicting and often contradictory explanations of the nature of things.

Platonic philosophy, therefore, not only provides the
basis for a synthesis of the various human dispositions considered in terms of a unified psyche functionally interpreted,
or of the relations between the thoughts, decisions, and
appetites of the individual and the phases and functions of his
social world, but seeks as well to provide a general theory that
accounts for the various ways of knowing extant in the Greece
of Plato's day. The Homeric world of mythology and poetic
metaphor may be construed in terms of *eikasia*. The Milesian
materialists and the Sophists with their emphasis on convention stress *pistis*—i.e., "know-how." The Pythagoreans who
investigated the mathematical principles of things, and clas-
sified them in terms of those principles, possessed *dianoia*.
The best example of a noetic philosopher is Plato's teacher,
Socrates, whose fundamental principle, "knowledge and virtue are one," served as the basis on which Plato was ultimately to ground his concept of The Good as the principle of the
unity of all things. If one accepts the Platonic insight concerning the existence of a single ordering principle that serves as
the ground and goal of philosophic wisdom, then all preceding
speculation becomes partial and in need of incorporation in
the final systematic explanatory schema of Platonic thought.

But is not necessary to accept these insights in order to be
able to see the cultural efficacy of Plato's organization of the
forms of knowledge. Just as many who are indebted to Plato's
theory of the psyche would have vehemently opposed being
labeled Platonists, so most of the subsequent thinkers who
have benefited from Plato's meta-philosophy have not felt
themselves heirs of the Platonic tradition.

Once more we see just how strong is the tendency to
order, the urge to construe chaos. The speculative tradition in

philosophy that provided us with our understandings of psyche, polis, and the organization of intellectual disciplines has likewise concerned itself with the development of a means of explaining the co-existence of mutually incompatible semantic contexts. And just as Plato's analysis of psyche and polis was reinterpreted along similar lines by Aristotle, so it was with Plato's meta-theory. In Aristotle we have an equally profound, and perhaps even more precise, rendering of the meta-theoretical problem.

Aristotle accounted for the conflicts among his philosophic predecessors by claiming that each had sought to explain the nature of things by recourse to a partial rather than to a complete causal schema. Aristotle's doctrine of the four "causes" or "reasons" was used not only as a device for adequate philosophic analysis but also as a means of demonstrating what he took to be the inadequate philosophic efforts of his predecessors. An adequate explanation of an item of experience or the world, says Aristotle, must have recourse to the material, formal, final, and efficient causes of that item. That is to say, we must have some knowledge of the stuff of which a thing is made, its formal structure or pattern, the end for which the thing exists or was made, and the process or maker through which or whom the item came into being. Providing a balanced characterization of the material, formal, final, and efficient explanations of things will mean that an adequate account has been given.

Plato discovered inadequacies in his philosophic colleagues based on their various emphases upon less viable forms of knowledge; Aristotle interprets inadequacy in terms of a failure to include a balanced emphasis upon each of the elements of the causal schema. Plato implicitly, and Aristotle explicitly, each argued for the adequacy of his own philosophic approach. This would no doubt be true of any thinker. But quite apart from this fact about the Platonic and Aristotelian systems, we can find in each the basis of a meta-theoretical system that provides a more or less neutral schema of interpretation in accordance with which we can understand the nature of varying philosophic perspectives and their relations, one to another. Part of the cultural impact of the philosophic syntheses of Plato and Aristotle has been due, therefore, not only to their construction of the outlines of the human psyche and its relations to society and to intellectual culture, but also to their systematic explanations of conflict among various theories of the nature of things.

Aristotle found, for example, that Thales, Anaximenes, and Anaximander, the first philosophers of Greece, stressed the material cause. Their search for *physis*, that of which the world is constructed, made of them the first materialists. The Pythagoreans, who construed the world in terms of number and harmony, employed the formal cause as the primary explanatory principle. Empedocles, with his stress upon Love and Strife as dynamic factors in bringing into being that which is, was considered by Aristotle to have emphasized the efficient cause. Anaxagoras, whose doctrine of *Noos* made of Mind, or Reason, the ground and goal of existence, explained the world in terms of final cause, or that for the sake of which things exist.

But what is important for our purposes is not the way in which Plato or Aristotle viewed their predecessors or their philosophical antagonists. Our purpose is, rather, to show that the development of self-consciousness, and now the development of meta-theoretical consciousness as well, was a result of the attempt to construe a world of confusion and disorder into a cosmos, a harmonious totality. And just as the concept of the psyche as a principle of organization of self, society, and intellectual culture forms one of the primary ways in which we bring order into our world, so has it been with the meta-mentality provided us by the classical Greek philosophies of Plato and Aristotle. The full potential of this fact was not realized until our own period in philosophy. One of the profoundest indications that we live at the end of an era is the attitude of many of our best minds toward the problem of conflicting intellectual claims. We are beginning to realize that we can do no more than classify, organize, and relate various schemas one to another. There is no way to decide among them. As I indicated previously, various contemporary philosophers have developed explanations of these conflicting theories by recourse to meta-theoretical speculations. The

most straightforward of these approaches employs the
Aristotelian perspective and demonstrates the development
of a primary philosophical type corresponding to each of four
explanatory principles. This schema, adumbrated in Chapter
1, can now be introduced in slightly more detail.

The materialist vision is grounded in a concept of material
or conceptual simples—basic building bricks—constituting the
nature of things. Classical atomism, with its assumption of
least material units from which the basic world-view of seven-
teenth- and eighteenth-century science derived, has given way
to slightly more subtle forms of psychological or linguistic
atoms as fundamental realities. The Freudian vision of man
and culture couched in terms of primal instincts or drives,
themselves fundamental and unanalyzable, is a perfect
example of the materialist paradigm. Logical atomism, similarly, is a materialist vision grounded on the supposition that
atomic facts, answering to Humean simples, form the basis of
our understanding of the nature of things. Proponents of this
view include such thinkers as Leucippus, Democritus, and
Lucretius among the ancients; Galileo, Newton, and Hume
among the moderns; and Marx and Freud among recent
thinkers.

The mechanical world-view of materialism involves an
affirmation of determinism. "Nature," conceived as atoms
and empty space, or physiological drives, or linguistic units, is
reductively explained. All relations are extrinsic; no room is
provided for human freedom, in any ordinary sense of the
word. Freedom is best understood in its psychoanalytic sense
as freedom from responsibility for that which one has become.
Materialism is backward-looking, in the sense that to understand is to account for the present. Causal analysis is the
primary philosophic method. The philosophy of culture that is
grounded by such a theoretical orientation is best exemplified
by Freud's *Civilization and Its Discontents*, a reductive
explanation of human culture as the sublimated products of
repressed libidinal impulses. On such a view, cultural objects
such as poetry, mathematical schemas, etc., are the result of
isolatable impulses within the physiological makeup of the cultural agent.

The formalist vision, based on the conception of *formal* cause, characterizes reality in terms of an unchanging set of forms, ideas, or essences, the intrinsic interrelations of which constitute the essential structure of things. The understanding of things is obtained by dialectical thought, which moves from particularity to universality in search of the primary principle, a principle of relatedness. Human agency is construed in terms of knowledge, its pursuit, and obedience to its dictates. Social and cultural experience is understood in terms of the fundamental ideas that guide the thought and action of individuals and the epoch. For such a vision, the primary analogate is the principle, or principles, that inform thought at its highest level—e.g., for Plato, the principle of The Good. In addition to Plato, idealists such as Spinoza, Hegel, Bradley, and Josiah Royce have employed this philosophic vision.

A third paradigm, stressing the notion of final cause, is what we may term "naturalism." "Naturalist," as I am using the term here, refers to a philosophic vision grounded in the concept of biological organism. According to this view, an organism is a whole, the parts of which functionally interrelate to achieve some purpose. The purpose defines the manner in which the various "parts" of the organism function. This biological metaphor is employed to understand not only living things, but social and political institutions as well. This vision is grounded in the Aristotelian form of naturalism and received its most significant modern expression in the nineteenth- and twentieth-century pragmatists—notably John Dewey—and in many of the philosophers who rationalized the Darwinian evolutionary theory.

The fourth paradigm is grounded in the notion of efficient cause. This vision, which we may term "volitional" philosophy, customarily affirms the arbitrary power of human decision and action as the fundamental reality. The slogan of Protagoras, "man is the measure of all things," describes this philosophy well. "Reality" is what "great men" decide. Those persons are great who are capable of persuading others of the validity of their convictions. In our century it is existentialism that best exemplifies this perspective. All relations are power relations. The paradigm for understanding social and political issues is the ruler–ruled relationship. On this view the primary analogate is *expression*, as *atoms* were for materialist, *ideas* for the formalist, and *organisms* for the naturalist. Man's being is self-made via expression. Language is the matrix through which the power relations of men are established. The importance of expression and the necessity of rhetorical persuasion are illustrated in existential philosophers such as Nietzsche, Sartre, Camus, and Heidegger, who draw heavily upon the use of evocative language to make many of their most significant and subtle philosophic points.

These four philosophic types have provided the fundamental semantic contexts in which the meanings of the terms and concepts employed in our intellectual culture have been determined. The traditions of thought derived from these general and abstract contexts have provided the semantic variations in terms of which we have considered various meanings of "knowledge," "power," "love," etc.—all those notions upon which we ground our cultural self-understandings. In addition, therefore, to the psyche and its analogues in society and intellectual culture, the process of cosmicizing has included the development of alternative semantic contexts to organize our cultural existence.

The most important conclusion to be drawn from this broad view of the passage from our cultural beginnings is this: for our Western speculative tradition persons are thinking, acting, and feeling creatures, and human culture may best be construed as a complex of aims, interests, and objects expressive of these three modalities of human existence. The principal dynamisms both of individual and of cultural experience, therefore, are the same as those uncovered in our considerations of the cosmogonic myths, which told of human victory over chaos. To say this is to say nothing less than that the making of persons and culture, which consisted in the coming-into-being out of the primordial beginnings of self-consciousness and the cultural expressions to which self-conscious beings give rise, is a making conditioned by the tension between chaos and cosmos, confusion and order.

Imago Dei

The adventures of the Greek concept of psyche did not end with the construction of the Platonic and Aristotelian systems. There was to be yet one other historical development of this fundamental cultural analogate, a development that, in large measure, provided one of the bases for the transmission of the later Greek philosophy into the so-called Judaeo-Christian culture.

In his arguments against the skeptics of the New Academy, Augustine of Hippo cited three truths that could be defended as unfailingly certain: self-existence, knowledge of existence, and love both of the existence and of the knowledge. "For as I know that I am, so I know this also, that I know. And when I love these two things, I add to them a certain third thing: namely, my love, which is of equal moment."[36] Augustine's analysis of these truths indicates that he holds them to be conditions for all forms of action, knowledge, and feeling. Knowledge of one's existence grounds the knowledge of all other existents, and love of one's existence and knowledge is the fundamental subjective form of feeling from which all pure passions derive. What is clear so far is that Augustine, heavily influenced by the dialectical side of the Neoplatonic tradition, is casting what he takes to be his incorrigible claims to existence, knowledge, and love in terms of an *a priori* dialectical structure answering to the Greek conception of psyche. But the crucial development takes place when Augustine offers a new explanation of the origin of that psychic structure, by claiming that "we indeed recognize in ourselves the image of God, that is, of the supreme Trinity, an image which . . . is yet nearer to him in nature than any of his works."[37] The pattern of our psychic structure is nothing less than the *imago Dei*, the image of God in man.

God, as "author of nature, the bestower of intelligence, and the kindler of love by which life becomes good and blessed,"[38] has determined that man's existence, knowledge, and love reflect the uncreated essence of the Holy Trinity.

God the Father as Will, God the Son as Logos or Wisdom, and God the Holy Spirit as Love thus become the primary analogates in terms of which the action, reason, and passion of human beings are to be understood.

Now, not only do we possess a matrix of analogical relationships between the self-conscious individual and his social and cultural milieu, but, after the Augustinian synthesis of Neoplatonism and Judaeo-Christianity, we also possess a schema in terms of which to provide transcendent explanations of the personal, social, and cultural functions and structures. In his magnificent tale of two cities, *The City of God*, Augustine drew upon each of these sets of analogical relations—psychic, social, and spiritual—to provide an analysis of the earthly and the heavenly cities and the relations of the individual to each. The parallels between the Trinitarian structure of the Divine Life and the triadic patterns of the psyche and society provide the background of Augustine's discussions of the psychological, political, and explicitly theological issues forming the substance of his work.[39] In many ways Augustine's *City of God* may be seen as a rewriting for Judaeo-Christian culture of Plato's *Republic*. Certainly the impact of Augustine's *magnum opus* has been, in many ways, as decisive as that of Plato's work. And the importance of both books is mainly due to the fact that each provides a paradigm that allows for cultural articulation and self-understanding.

The Augustinian synthesis, whatever its relations to the subsequent theological activity of the medieval and modern periods, constituted a fulfillment of the Platonic philosophic ideals insofar as they were to have cultural influence. Augustine, by writing the soul "even larger" and understanding God himself after the fashion of the Greek conception of the psyche, completed the cultural synthesis begun by Plato and Aristotle eight hundred years before.

This manner of handling the relations between the individual psyche and the transcendent "Persons" of the Christian Trinity has, of course, been of profound significance ever since the Augustinian synthesis was achieved. Concepts of reason, will, and passion as psychological "facts," and justice, power, and love as social relations, as well as the realms of praxis, nature, and the sphere of aesthetic feeling, may now all be expressed in terms of their divine counterparts. The final victory over chaos was achieved in and for our culture when both the human and the divine ordering agencies were characterized in terms of a tripartite structure that could serve as the basis for the understanding of the objective conditions of natural, moral, and aesthetic experience.

It would be a serious mistake to consider the conception of the Trinity from a purely theological perspective. The notion of the Trinity has functioned as a means of sociological, political, and philosophical organization and analysis at least since the Augustinian age. Though the history of the concept has been complicated by the distinction between faith and reason, which led some theologians to view the Trinity as a revealed doctrine, while others found it open to discovery through human reason, any review of the historical developments of the doctrine would indicate how it has been employed as a means for the understanding and organization of ideas and beliefs extending far beyond the strictly theological realm.

Thomas Aquinas, after Augustine the theologian who was to have the greatest impact upon general culture, did not believe that the concept of the Trinity was open to discovery by unaided reason. No doubt this was in part due to the fact that Aquinas followed the principle *nihil est in intellectu quod non prius fuerit in sensu* ("Nothing is in the intellect that was not first in the senses") borrowed from Aristotelian epistemology, and modeled his arguments on Aristotle's syllogistics, while Augustine, enamored of the Neoplatonic conception of a universe patterned by formal relations, employed the dialectical reasonings presupposed by that vision. Even though Aquinas considered the Trinity a revealed doctrine, this did not prevent him from using it as the means by which his theological system was to be organized. And the *Summa theologica* was a primary source of knowledge and action not only for believers, but for social and political philosophers as well. This great work, along with his many other writings, contains discussions of the concepts of power and authority,

law and sanctions, private and public existence, the nature of
the state and so on, which have profoundly influenced all
subsequent philosophic constructions. The analogies between
the persons of the Trinity and many of the central concepts of
social and political theory assured the perpetuation of the
doctrine into secular as well as theological traditions.

Perhaps the most influential theological synthesis developed outside the medieval context is John Calvin's. For
Calvinism has had as much impact upon social and economic
institutions as upon religious and theological speculations.
The structure of Calvin's *Institutes of the Christian Religion* is
based on the revealed doctrine of the Trinitarian structure of
God. The essential content of this revelation is that the Trinity
is an economy of three distinct aspects the distinguishing characters of which remain mutually untransferable and yet constitute an unassailable unity. Calvin affirms three separate functions within the economy of the one God: "To the Father is
attributed the beginning of activity, and the fountain and wellspring of all things; to the Son, wisdom, counsel, and the
ordered disposition of all things, but to the Spirit is assigned
the power and efficacy of that activity."[40] The functions of
creator and sustainer are assigned to the Father, and to the
Son is given the traditional Logos functions: he is "wisdom"
and "counsel," and he is responsible for the "ordered disposition of all things." That is, Christ is mediator between God
and man, and he is redeemer, the one who reorders and sets
things right again after the Fall. The Spirit is that element that
makes efficacious the will of the Father, functioning as a
dynamic mediator between Christ and persons, the ecclesias-
tical structures and persons, the Word of Scripture and
persons, etc., bringing about the will of God by communicating Christ to the elect.

God is in no positive sense an object of natural reason.
This means that unmediated knowledge of God is impossible.
Furthermore, since the Fall, nature no longer mediates the
knowledge of God. The principle structures through which the
knowledge of God comes to us are: Scripture, Jesus Christ,
faith, and the Church in which the word is preached and the
sacraments rightly administered. God, as the source of all

things and all activity, is formally revealed through certain Logos structures. But in Calvin's theology the Spirit functions as the mediator of God's *dynamic* character by making efficacious the will of the Father, in conjunction with the Logos structures of Scripture, Jesus Christ, the Church, and so on.

Again we must not be deceived by the explicitly theological language. The cultural importance of Calvinist thinking extends far beyond narrowly doctrinal concerns into the heart of the economic and social institutions of many of our European and American societies. The influence of Calvinism upon the rise of capitalist society has, of course, been examined in Weber's classic study, *The Protestant Ethic and the Spirit of Capitalism*. Less emphasized but equally important is the effect of Calvin's affirmation of the need for institutional structures as means of "rationalizing" the will of God. Not reason, but "institutes" and "institutions" are the proper mediators of God's will. The Logos structures necessitated by Calvin's treatment of the Trinitarian economy have led in Calvinist societies to the large-scale development of schools, hospitals, and other eleemosynary institutions, through which God's will may be done.

Also of great importance in understanding the impact of the Trinitarian doctrine on modern culture is the philosophy of Hegel. One has only to read Hegel's early writings in the philosophy of religion to understand how important he considered his speculative reflections upon the Christian doctrine of the Trinity.[41] And in his *Phenomenology of Mind* he provided a rationalized version of the Trinitarian elements, which he saw as "pictorial representations" (*Vorstellungen*) of the dialectical structure of the Absolute considered as Immediacy, Mediation, and Reflexive Unity. The bare notion of idea in its immediacy is seen as God the Father; the Self-Existence or mediating moment is identified with the Son as Logos; and the Holy Spirit is identified with the expression of the moment of reflexive return to self as subject, expressive of the unity of the dialectical process and its completion.

Although the content of revealed religion is the same as that of philosophic knowledge, we find that the form that houses that content is that of the various Christian doctrines of "Creation," "Fall," "Incarnation," "Reconciliation." All these are derivative from the central doctrine of the Trinity, which is the pictorialization of the life of the spirit constituting an inseparable unity with philosophic knowledge.

The secularization of the Trinitarian doctrine and its envelopment in philosophic concepts did not end with Hegel. Thinkers influenced by the Hegelian dialectic were willy-nilly affected by rationalized notions of the Trinity. Feuerbach found in the concept of the Trinity "the highest mystery and the focal point of absolute philosophy and religion."[42] "The secret of the Trinity is the secret of communal and social life; it is the secret of the necessity of the 'thou,' for an 'I'; it is the truth that no being—be it man, God, mind, or ego—is for itself alone a true, perfect, and absolute being, that truth and perfection are only the connection and unity of beings equal in their essence."[43] Feuerbach's conception of religion was that it constitutes a projection of idealized aspects of man's natural existence. Theology is ultimately anthropology. But this view does not prevent him from taking religious language and concepts quite seriously. And though he believed that religion in its transcendent guise was a reactionary force in human society, a proper understanding of the theological motive could contribute to the development of human potential. Feuerbach attempted to bring religion down from its other-worldly concerns and to interpret its doctrines in terms of material conditions. His consideration of the Trinity as a patterning of human relationships is an example of such an attempt.

Reflecting upon Hegel and Feuerbach, and each of the modern dialectical thinkers—both idealist and materialist (yes, even Marx himself)—we recall the beginnings of the concepts of thought, action, and passion as considered initally by Plato. The dialectical structure is again employed as a social, cultural, and historical principle of interpretation. The significant difference is that the theological form and content accrued over the centuries still cling to the concepts, in part determining their character and function.

Among contemporary thinkers, we find the theologian and philosopher of culture Paul Tillich expressing perhaps the

most balanced attainments of the mixture of the theological
and philosophical characteristics of the Trinitarian and dialectical concepts. His short book *Love, Power, Justice*[44] is a
critique of the theological, philosophical, ethical, and cultural
implications of the fundamental triad that has played out its
theme and variations since the Hellenic period. Justice and
power define the character and dynamics of public and social
relationships; love, as the drive toward a reunion of the
separated, largely determines the nature of personal, private
relationships. The unity of love, power, and justice provides a
dynamic model for the unity of persons in public and private
spheres of existence. The ultimate model of the triadic relation
is God, who is the source of love, power, and justice.

Whether the doctrine of the Trinity is seen as the gift of
divine revelation, the unexcelled object of rational discovery
and articulation, or merely as an adumbration of a more profound philosophic truth, it is clear that the doctrine has had an
extremely important effect upon our cultural self-understanding. For with the dialectical understanding of the concept of
God comes the possibility of providing an analysis of personal
and social structures from a transcendent perspective. The
addition of this perspective provides an increased richness of
resource for cultural self-articulation. When combined with
the various other conceptual resources we have considered,
there results a pattern of notions that, properly construed,
may be said to have served as the primary schema in terms of
which the cultural self-consciousness of the West has
emerged.

THE CULTURAL PARADIGM

With the addition of the concept of "God," we have provided
an articulation of the four principal elements of what we may
term the Judaeo-Christian cultural paradigm. God, nature,
passion, and praxis or social practice have served as the
fundamental notions through which the cosmicizing of chaos
has occurred; and the cultural interests that developed from
these fundamental concepts are the "disciplines," or disciplining agencies, that provided the matrix within which the

cosmicizing process has taken place. With the addition of the
Judaeo-Christian theological activity to the Hellenic organization of disciplines inherited from Aristotle, the dominant
forms of cultural interest became those of religion, science,
art, morality, and philosophy. Religion has as its object
"God"; science seeks the meaning of nature; art concerns
human appetitive, productive, and creative capacities; morality handles the judgments and activities of individuals *qua*
social and political creatures; and philosophy has as its
primary concern the articulation of the principles of each of
these disciplines and the consideration of the normative relations possible among them. These cultural interests answer to
the general qualities that define the human pursuit of value:
holiness, truth, beauty, goodness, and importance. These
qualities, at very abstract levels and in very general ways,
have constituted the cultural aims in terms of which we have
organized and directed our cultural interests.

The complex relationships existing among the functions
of psyche, the persons of the Trinity, the structures of society,
and the interests of intellectual culture have constituted the
primary paradigm that has, implicitly, served to organize and
direct our cultural activities until the present day. Thus when
Augustine asserted, not long after his conversion to Christianity, "I desire to have knowledge of God and the soul. Of
nothing else? No, of nothing else whatsoever";[45] and when he
added "O God, always one and the same, if I know myself, I
shall know Thee,"[46] he was hardly narrowing the scope of his
proposed inquiries. For, because of the specific development
of our cultural self-creativity, to know God and psyche is to
understand the principles in accordance with which our entire
cultural enterprise is to be understood.

This multi-valent interplay of psyche, society, intellectual
culture, and Divine Being, each interpretable in terms of the
other and all possessing a common structure—whether that
structure be determined functionally as a result of contingent
historical developments, or dialectically as a result of certain
innate, *a priori* "mental" structures, or whether it be *sui
generis* as Christians maintain—has in large measure served as
the fundamental matrix in terms of which we have been able to

raise to the level of consciousness the meanings of "God," "nature," "persons," "society," and so on.

Since the intersection of the Hellenic and Judaeo-Christian traditions, which resulted in the construction of the classical conception of the divine, the cultural paradigm has been mainly construed after the fashion provided by the theological interpretations of the myths of Genesis. These interpretations have, of course, borrowed heavily from the philosophical concepts of Hellenic culture. Nonetheless we can best recognize the organizing, cosmicizing force of the cultural paradigm if we see it displayed in the context of Genesis myths. There we find that God is primarily construed in terms of Power.

God as creator is the Supreme *Arche* construing chaos by virtue of the power of his will. Concepts of reason and love, which after the articulation of the Trinitarian structure came to be identified with "persons" of the Trinity, have variously functioned to qualify the volitional interpretation of God, but it is primarily in terms of the power of God who brought cosmos out of "the dark, formless void" that we understand our beginnings. The various elements of our cultural paradigm then can be interpreted as distinct ways of channeling power. Thus there are four vessels of power. There is, first, the power above nature, which we designate "God." This power is expressed in three modalities, directly through *command* and indirectly through the agencies of *rationality* and *love*. The other vessels of power are instantiations of the transcendent power of God. There is *physis*, *natura*, the power of nature itself; the power within persons, which we may term "passion"; and, finally, the power among persons, exercised through "social practice." God, nature, passion, and social practice are the four vessels of power that have been rationalized through our religious myth-structure.

In the Judaeo-Christian tradition, "God" is the *originator* who commands nature into existence. This command, expressed by the words "Let there be . . . ," provides the basis for the understanding of both the deity and his creation. God is he who speaks the words that command the world into being. Absolute *power*, the power to create *ex nihilo*; *rationality*, the quality possessed by the created products of nature by virtue of the fact that they were brought into being by words that *communicate* as well as *create*; and *love*, the dynamic that ensures communication, are the fundamental characteristics of God.

"Nature" is the object of God's creation. And since there was no antecedent matter from which God constructed nature, the world remains under his complete control. But this control is qualified by the fact that man was made God's "deputy." As such, nature is an *object* of *man's* control as well. He must establish power over it. But nature is also rational, having been created by a rational being. Therefore, man is enjoined to *understand* as well as to control nature. Science and technology, two key components of our culture, are here found to have strong support in the myths of Genesis, although, as we shall see, it is the technological motive of control that ultimately dominates the scientific motive of understanding.

Human passion, the power within persons, is also treated by the myths of Genesis. Sexual passion is correlated with the shame at the recognition of nakedness, with the pain entailed in the act of child-bearing, and with the obvious suggestions of male superiority deriving from the fact that Eve is, as are all the other animals in nature, named by Adam (who was of course named by God). And it is not simply sexual passion, but also the passion that leads to aesthetic expression, that are brought under the control of the myths. The story of the tower of Babel suggests that God confused the tongues of men because their desire for fame threatened the relationship between him and his creation. Only that creativity is divinely sanctioned that stands under the control of God.

God is he who speaks the words of creation and in so doing establishes the natural order as an object of control and rational explication. Man is deputy, lord over the created order, who is to subdue and control both nature without and the passions within. As sexual being and as artist, as procreator and as creator, man and his expressions are to be placed under the close scrutiny of God. Social practices, the bonds existing among persons by virtue of their public relationships, are established by God as those activities through which man carries out his task of the rational control of nature and human passion. Labor, which strives to win survival and well-being from nature, and the family, which nurtures and provides a stable context for children, are the two fundamental means of organizing social practice. But even here the rationality of human society is in no way complete. As the story of Abraham and Isaac so well illustrates, basic moral intuitions must at times give way to the arbitrary will of God. Human praxis, in the form of custom, tradition, or natural law, must, as clearly and as completely as human passion, be placed under the ultimate control of God. The power channeled through social and political institutions, as well as the dynamisms of nature and human passion, have as their ultimate source or *arche*, the power of God.

There were five moments in the development of our cultural paradigm: first, the construction of the psyche as a threefold functioning of reason, appetite, and spirit; second, the assertion of analogical relations existing between these functions of the soul and the classes or institutions in society or the state, in which the primary distinction was between the leisured intellectual class and the laboring class of slaves. Institutionally, however, this distinction between culture and utility[47] was sufficient to generate what Aristotle saw as a means of organizing the primary cultural activities into theoretical, practical, and productive spheres. The third moment in the development of the cultural paradigm was the identification of these activities with the ways of knowing: the natural sciences, ethics and politics, poetry and rhetoric, answering to the realms of thought, action, and passion, respectively. The meta-theoretical activities of Plato and Aristotle constituted the fourth step in the development of our paradigm. The construction of a means to organize and interpret alternative philosophic viewpoints provided implicitly and explicitly throughout the intervening period four principal semantic contexts, or, if you will, four main philosophic traditions, as perspectives from which to view and assess cultural interests and activities. The final development of our cultural paradigm was the emergence of the concept of God as a Trinity of Father,

Son, and Spirit, the persons of which were thought to be
analogates of the functions of the soul. With this development,
the capstone was placed on our quest for cultural self-consciousness. Henceforth, we were able to see ourselves not
only in terms of our internal psychic structure and its social
applications but also in terms of a transcendent realm parallel-
ing our own. The organization of our ways of knowing now
included religion and theology as interests and activities in
increasing separation from the sciences of nature, the ethical
and political interests, and the sphere of aesthetic activity.

In this manner, what we are terming the "cultural paradigm" emerged as a set of interrelations between God and the
soul. These relations may be identified primarily in terms of
the spheres of God, nature, passion, and social practice,
answering, in part, to the cultural interests of religion, science,
art, and morality, respectively. The main complication involved in analyzing this paradigm has stemmed from the recognition that each of the principal terms constituting the
paradigm may be variously defined in accordance with each of
the principal philosophic perspectives. Thus it matters, if you
wish to speak of the "natural" world, whether you construe it
as material and atomic structure, organic and possessed of
ends and goals, or, with the volitionist, as a mere construction
of human agency, or, as the formalist would see it, as pattern,
form, or ideal. Likewise if passion is understood, either as the
basis of art or as interpersonal dynamic, it makes a great difference to your argument whether you consider it primarily as
sensual pleasure, as one of the ends of organic activity, as the
motivation to, and reward of, conquest, or as knowledge of a
special kind.

The myth structure that has developed from Hellenic and
Judaeo-Christian sources has functioned as the basis of those
attitudes that, until recently, constituted the primary components of the realm of praxis in our cultural tradition. As
such it has been interpretable by each of the dominant philosophic paradigms forming our broad philosophic traditions.
God, whether as Great Mechanic, Divine Mind, Telos of
Nature, or Arbitrary Will, is recognizable as the principal element of the Judaeo-Christian paradigm. Likewise, with the

elements of nature, passion, and moral practice, the range of alternative interpretations extends to each of the major philosophic visions that, until the present, served as the dynamic elements of intellectual culture.

Much of the heavy-handed character of the foregoing presentation of the cultural paradigm will be qualified with successive applications of it that demonstrate the complex and multi-valent nature of the modes of interrelationship characterizing our cultural tradition. Yet at least some of this heavy-handedness is due to the fact that those who have applied the philosophic and theological conceptions forming our cultural paradigm have done so in such a manner as to perpetuate, in their actions and institutions, a rather blunt set of categories. Also, at least part of the reason for the apparently unrefined character of the paradigm is that it is in this form that the factors that have dominated our cultural development have been raised to the level of consciousness. We are impatient of refinements, in part because we feel that the concepts determining our cultural past have exhausted their usefulness—that they are inadequate to perform the tasks necessary to promote the civilization of individual, social, and cultural experience.

Much of what I have said about the character of contemporary culture in relation to its past can be read as an elaboration of the following words of Alfred North Whitehead:

> There is reason to believe that human genius reached its culmination in the twelve hundred years preceding and including the initiation of the Christian Epoch. Within that period the main concepts of aesthetic experience, of religion, of humane social relations, of political wisdom, of mathematical deduction, and of observational science, were developed and discussed. . . . Of course, since then, there has been progress in knowledge and technique. But it has been along the path laid down by the activities of that golden age.[48]

Contemplating this possibility is quite disturbing since it leads to the belief that from a purely intellectual and aesthetic point of view, there has been no fundamental novelty introduced into the human experience for perhaps fifteen hundred years and more. A number of serious questions are raised by

such contemplation, one of the most important being simply
this: if it is true that our cultural experience has consisted
mainly in the working out of the implications of intellectual
and aesthetic discoveries and inventions made in some Age of
Genius long ago, have we exhausted the variations of the main
themes provided for us by our creative ancestors? If so, can
we compose anew?

Questions such as these must be asked precisely because
we seem to have arrived at a point in our cultural situation
where the crisis of identity has at last reached to the very
depths of our soul. Many are no longer willing to interpret as
progress the mere substitution of more recent for less recent
assumptions. History, and its repetitions, have at least taught
us the lesson we could not have learned until now: it has all
been thought and experienced before. The fact that there are
new things to be done, new applications of old truths, does not
seem to suffice. We experience now the failure of nerve that
comes from recognizing that, in spite of all our novel postur-
ing, "there is nothing new under the sun."

We have, apparently, gone to great lengths to conclude that
our patterns of cultural development have consisted in the
disciplining of chaos. Certainly we have labored long to arrive
at what is for many a non-controversial, even truistic, conclusion. The significance of such a conclusion, however, will be
evident in a succeeding chapter when we consider that the
manner in which the primordial experience of chaos is construed in our tradition has not been the only means of characterizing chaos. That is to say, when we find that it is indeed
possible to envision chaos not as confusion and disorder but
as undifferentiated homogeneity, as harmony antecedent to
any given order, we shall be in a position to understand the
radical differences between our traditional heritage in
psychology, politics, and education and the heritage of
peoples conditioned by a dramatically different past. We shall
also be in a position to articulate, from the only truly revolutionary standpoint, the changes taking place in our own
present milieu as we reach the final crisis in our cultural experience, which, by calling all our cultural expressions into ques-

tion, requires a move in the direction of the only alternative for survival open to us. This alternative involves the affirmation of a new beginning, a return to origins from which we may progress only by re-experiencing chaos as positive homogeneity, as a wellspring from which we emerge as beings conducive to the overall harmony, rather than over against which we take our stand by imposing order and building a cosmos. But before articulating this novel vision of chaos, we must take a closer look at the consequences of our traditional view.

NOTES

1. Gnosticism, as a form of "perennial wisdom," has often served as such a tradition in the past. And, indeed, we shall find that the Gnostic sensibility is a valuable resource for many of the investigations we subsequently shall be making. But part of the burden of my argument in this work will be that we must transcend our culture in a radical manner if we are to discover the novel concepts that will articulate our burgeoning future. The "extremes" of our own cultural sensibility will, ultimately, lead us beyond Anglo-European culture to the matrix of Oriental, specifically Chinese, thought and culture.

2. For an interesting and informative commentary on *Enuma elish*, see H. and H. A. Frankfort et al., *Before Philosophy* (Baltimore: Penguin, 1949), pp. 184–98; repr. in *Theories of the Universe*, ed. Milton Munitz (New York: Free Press, 1957), pp. 8–20.

3. *Plato's Cosmology*, trans. F. M. Cornford (New York: Bobbs–Merrill, 1957), pp. 33, 160.

4. This interpretation is controversial, as are most interpretations of Greek mythical sources. A reasonably complete discussion of alternatives to this view is contained in G. S. Kirk and J. E. Raven, *The Pre-Socratic Philosophers* (Cambridge: Cambridge University Press, 1964), pp. 24–32. The disputes of scholars over this issue are of no consequence to my argument here, however, since any existing interpretation of Hesiod's concept of chaos suits my thesis well.

5. *The Birds* 701, 704–705, trans. Benjamin Bickley Rogers, in *Great Books of the Western World* V (Chicago: Encyclopaedia Britannica, 1952), p. 551.

6. Adolph Harnack, *History of Dogma* I (New York: Dover, 1961), p. 248.

7. See Hans Jonas' essay on "Gnosticism, Existentialism and Nihilism," in his *The Phenomenon of Life* (New York: Harper & Row, 1966), pp. 219 ff.

8. *The Theology of the Early Greek Thinkers* (New York: Oxford University Press, 1967), pp. 13–14.

9. See *Physics* IV, 1 (208B31–32).

10. See *Metaphysics* V, 1, for a discussion of the various meanings of *arche*.

11. *Totemism*, trans. Rodney Needham (Boston: Beacon, 1963), p. 99.

12. *The Hellenic World: A Sociological Analysis* (New York: Harper & Row, 1969), p. 106.

13. Ernst Cassirer, "Mythical Thought," *The Philosophy of Symbolic Forms* II (New Haven: Yale University Press, 1955), p. 201.

14. Lewis Mumford, *Myth of the Machine* (New York: Harcourt, Brace, & World, 1967), p. 46.

15. Ibid., p. 9.

16. Suzanne Langer, *Philosophy in a New Key* (New York: Mentor, 1958), p. 241.

17. Mircea Eliade, *The Sacred and the Profane* (New York: Harper Torchbooks, 1961), p. 64.

18. Peter Berger, *The Sacred Canopy* (Garden City, N.Y.: Doubleday, 1967), p. 51.

19. Ibid.

20. Ibid., p. 39.

21. Novalis, "Miscellaneous Fragments," in *Hymn to the Night and Other Selected Writings*, trans. Charles Passage (New York: Bobbs–Merrill, 1960), p. 71.

22. Joseph Campbell, *Primitive Mythology* (New York: Viking, 1959), p. 274.

23. Dodds, *Greeks and the Irrational*, p. 8.

24. *From the Many to the One*, p. 267.

25. *Hellenic World*, p. 79.

26. Snell, *Discovery of the Mind*, p. 8.

27. Ibid., p. 9.

28. Ibid., p. 15.

29. Adkins, *From the Many to the One*, p. 20.

30. *The Function of Reason* (Boston: Beacon, 1958), p. 10.

31. Dodds, *Greeks and the Irrational*, pp. 179–80.

32. I have chosen the term "volition" as a translation of the term *thymos* primarily to suggest congruence with the later history of the Platonic concept of psyche. It is obvious from reading the *Republic* 439A–440D that what Plato calls "the spirited part of the soul" is not in any simple sense to be identified with volition. But if we understand volition as the *power* of willing (see *The Oxford English Dictionary*), we can see that the drive (*thymos*) which allies itself with reason against the appetites (cf. *Republic* 440B) carries some of the connotations of volition. It is just such an interpretation which Paul Friedländer employs when discussing Plato's figure of the soul as a chariot and charioteer: "The two horses are of different kinds, the one being Desire (ἐπιθυμία), the other Will, Drive (θυμός). Either the mind bridles the two in balance, or they drag it with the charioteer into the abyss" (*Plato: An Introduction* [New York: Harper & Row, 1958], p. 193).

I am certainly sympathetic with A. E. Taylor's comment, "We must not make the blunder of trying to identify θυμοειδής with 'will'" (*Plato: The Man and His Work* [London: Methuen, 1960], p. 282), if one is trying to understand Plato's thinking strictly in its own terms. But the subsequent adventures of the distinctions of the "parts" of the soul in the thought of Aristotle, Augustine, and later thinkers were such as to stretch these terms beyond their original connotations.

In this chapter I am concerned, at a very general level, with the way in which we have come to employ certain notions in the attempt to arrive at cultural self-understanding. That in the process we have come to revise these notions is itself important to know. Thus I am precisely not sympathetic with Taylor's remark, in the same context as those quoted above, that "We must avoid every temptation to find a parallel between the 'parts' or 'figures' in the soul and the modern doctrine of the 'three aspects' of a complete 'mental process'" (ibid.). For, whether by misappropriation or by acceptable extension of meanings, such analogical parallels do in fact exist and have determined important aspects of our cultural history. Not only must such parallels be discovered, but their consequences in serving as general patterns of understanding must be investigated. Here I shall remind the reader that the philosopher of culture is concerned primarily, not with questions of the truth or falsity of this or that interpretation, but with the articulation of those important understandings that promote cultural self-consciousness.

33. *Metaphysics* 1025B25–26. See also *Politics* VIII for a discussion of the educational implications of Aristotle's organization of the disciplines.

34. *Metaphysics* 1025A20–21.

35. A principal example of this activity is the Kantian project, which sought a critique of reason in its theoretic, practical, and productive modes in *The Critique of Pure Reason*, *The Critique of Practical Reason*, and *The Critique of Judgment*. The work of R. G. Collingwood in this century, particularly his *Speculum mentis* (Oxford: Clarendon, 1963), evidences a concern for the construction of a "mirror of the mind" as a means of reflecting the various cultural interests and their mutual relations.

I have omitted, as not directly germane to the present discussion, consideration of the evidence for the thesis that many *cosmological* concepts were applied to the natural world by analogy from the social and political context. See Frankfort & Frankfort et al., *Before Philosophy*; F. M. Cornford, *From Religion to Philosophy: A Study in the Origins of Western Speculation* (New York: Harper, 1957); and G. E. R. Lloyd, *Polarity and Analogy: Two Types of Argumentation in Early Greek Philosophy* (Cambridge: Cambridge University Press, 1966), passim, for discussion of this view. I consider the arguments contained in these works to be generally supportive of the thesis of this chapter: namely, that there is an intrinsic analogical relationship among psychological, sociological, political, and cosmological concepts insofar as they may be relevant to cultural self-understanding.

36. *The City of God* 11.26, trans. Marcus Dods (New York: Modern Library, 1950), pp. 370–71.

37. Ibid., p. 370.

38. Ibid., p. 369.

39. See ibid., esp. Book 19.

40. *Institutes of the Christian Religion* 1.13.18, ed. John T. McNeill (Philadelphia: Westminster, 1960).

41. See G. W. F. Hegel, *On Christianity: Early Theological Writings*, ed. T. M. Knox (New York: Harper Torchbooks, 1961).

42. *Principles of the Philosophy of the Future*, trans. Manfred Vogel (New York: Bobbs–Merrill, 1966), p. 72.

43. Ibid.
44. (New York: Oxford University Press, 1954).
45. *Soliloquies* 1.2.7.
46. Ibid. 2.1.1.
47. See John Dewey, "Labor and Leisure," *Democracy and Education* (New York: Free Press, 1966), pp. 250–61.
48. *Modes of Thought* (New York: Free Press, 1968), pp. 65–66.

3

What "God" Hath Wrought

Reasonings are all in vain. We throw the sand against the wind which only throws it back again.

WILLIAM BLAKE

Monotheism contains the germ of every form of tyranny.

E. M. CIORAN

CHAOS AND REASON

THE CONCLUSION DRAWN FROM OUR INITIAL JOURNEY to the past in search of beginnings was that Western cultural experience has developed in accordance with a complex of notions that, after the emergence of our cultural self-consciousness in this present century, can be recognized as a paradigm organizing and interpreting the various ideas, actions, and feelings that constitute the data of our cultural present. Furthermore, that we are able to articulate the presuppositions of our cultural self-understanding suggests that we have reached a point in our development at which these concepts can no longer serve the same vital function they previously served. For, along with the development of methodological self-consciousness, we have experienced the relativity of various ways of characterizing the principal terms that intellectual culture comprises. As a consequence, the presumed certainties upon which our cultural significances have been grounded are increasingly open to question and to doubt. With this recognition we are made aware that the story of our cultural development, which we have characterized as the disciplining of chaos, has about it a disturbing air of arbitrariness and contingency. This is significant if for no other reason than that, since the means by which we have sought to order chaos are themselves arbitrary, there are no means by which we can maintain the authority of the *archai* or *principia* on which are grounded all our reasonings and practice.

This suggestion of arbitrariness is not especially remarkable in regard to the cosmogonic speculations involving volition and eros; it is the suspicion that reason itself is infected with the arbitrary and contingent characteristic attaching to the myths of creation and their subsequent cultural articulation that we must find disturbing. The interpretation of the concepts of reason and rationality as determined by a series of mutually contradictory attempts to discipline chaos would leave us unable to find rational solutions to our dilemmas satisfactory on any but dogmatic grounds. A close examination of the origins of reason would indicate that the charge of arbitrariness is indeed well-founded. The consequences for the principal elements of our cultural paradigm occasioned by the recognition of the suspect origins of reason will be examined as a means of understanding the crises in contemporary culture, which call for a second journey to the past.

Philosophical skepticism is generally a reaction against overly ambitious claims of reason. As a consequence, it is more often than not deemed anti-scientific since it is the scientist, and the logicians and mathematicians from whom he borrows his tools, who, by virtue of their methodological successes, are most likely to lay claim to certainty where no certainty exists. As David Hume recognized, one who attempts to employ doubt unqualifiedly as a means to truth would (the example of Descartes to the contrary notwithstanding) end in complete skepticism. Certainties are grounded in *belief*. Thus Descartes' appeal to "God" as a metaphysical principle guaranteeing the existence of a world external to the self derived its claim to certainty in part from

the subjective form of belief that had traditionally attached to
God as a spiritual being. Since, as Hume realized, "belief is
more properly an act of the sensitive, than of the cogitative
part of our natures,"[1] claims to certainty that are defended on
the grounds of reasonings ultimately do no more than advertise the inadequacies of reason to establish matters of fact.
Hume attacked the very bases of the scientific claims concerning the certainty of knowledge grounded in notions of space,
time, and causality. He avoided complete skepticism by
noting that claims to know are required by the necessity to act
and by reflections over the moral consequences of Pyrrhonian
doubt. But Hume's conclusion regarding reason was that it "is
and ought only to be the slave of the passions and can never
pretend to any other office than to serve and obey them."[2]
The fact that one of the passions to which reason is subject is
that of "belief" tends to prevent anyone from falling into a
complete skepticism.

But for those called upon to defend scientific rationality
criticism of the kind that Hume leveled against rationalism
cannot be left unanswered. The task of attempting to reclaim
for reason what Hume had given over to custom and belief
was left to the champion of scientific rationality, Immanuel
Kant.

In *The Critique of Pure Reason*, his magnificent attempt
to secure the authority of reason for subsequent generations of
philosophers, Kant argued that understanding "secures the
unity of appearances by means of rules," while reason
"secures the unity of the rules of understanding under principles."[3] The technical distinction between reason and understanding as means of knowing allowed him to distinguish the
faculty by which we grasp first principles (reason) from the
power by which we come to be possessed of them (understanding). The conditions allowing for understanding are *a
priori* forms of perception (space and time); the conditions of
reason are categories of the understanding (unity, multiplicity,
substance, causality, and so on). Reason's primary function in
its theoretical mode is to order the activities of the understanding in terms of principles that secure its unity.

The specific content of the Kantian doctrines is not relevant to our present discussion, but we do learn a great deal about the once and future fate of reason from the form of Kant's defense. Kant saw quite clearly that reason could be defended only if the means of grasping first principles could be separated from the means by which we come to be possessed of them. This he tried to accomplish through his distinction between reason and understanding and his claim that the categories of the understanding, as principles, are the necessary conditions of any knowledge that could properly be called scientific. The viability of Kant's arguments is hardly beyond question, as can be seen by a reflection upon the history of subsequent divergences from the Kantian philosophy on these very points. The continuing interest in Kant's attempt to secure the foundations of reason stems primarily from his assertion that the necessity to distinguish between the origin and the activity of rational thought is the fundamental, if ultimately futile, claim that must ground any defense of reason. We can see this most clearly by recourse to the first great crisis of rationalism in the period of the Greeks.

The skeptical aspects of the Sophistic movement in fifth-century Athens were largely derived from the reaction to the extravagant claims for reason made by the Parmenidean philosophy and involving a denial of the reality of change. The conflict between reason and sense experience this philosophy entailed led to an inevitable split between rationalistic "thinkers" and men of practical affairs. The spokesmen for these practical men were the Sophists, who took for granted the instrumental character of knowledge and claimed the proper sphere of "philosophic" thinking to be grounded in rhetoric as a persuasive art.

The Sophists were not alone in their attempt to call philosophy down from its Olympian heights of metaphysical speculation and to assert its fundamentally ethical character. No less a thinker than Socrates himself shared this vision. But the Sophists' understanding of the limits of reason prevented them from sharing with Socrates his hope of founding a rational science of philosophy. Many of the Sophists believed that one problem of reason lay in the origin of logos in *mythos*. Their enlightened attitude, so much celebrated by later champions of the Enlightenment, allowed them to understand that

myths could be rationalized; yet they did not believe themselves capable of disregarding myth altogether. It was given to
Socrates to understand that a firm ground for reason could be
established only if the power of *mythos* could be broken.

The Sophists had developed a method of rationalizing the
Greek myths in order to discover their "true meaning."
According to Ernst Cassirer, they became "the virtuosi of a
new art of allegorical interpretation. By this art every myth,
however strange and grotesque, could suddenly be turned into
a 'truth'—a physical or a moral truth."[4] Against this kind of
interpretation, Socrates' method was to ignore the myths and
to seek a new basis for philosophy in an examination of the
self, thus transcending the influence of *mythos* through an
introspective turn. As Plato has Socrates say in the *Phaedrus*:
"I must first know myself, as the Delphian inscription says; to
be curious about that which is not my concern, while I am still
in ignorance of my own self, would be ridiculous."[5]

Cassirer no doubt performs a real service in calling attention to the divergence of Socrates and the Sophists over the
attitude toward *mythos*, and to the consequences of this
divergence for the later development of Western philosophy.
But his characterization of the Sophists seems questionable.
He appears to recognize in the Sophistic interpretations of
myth a perspective that views the past as a primitive form of
the present, and mythmakers as primitive scientists. The end
of thinking as rational science is implicit, in a cloudy and
confused manner, in its beginnings.

But there is another, more relevant, possible assessment
of the Sophists. This assessment denies that they were
attempting to show that the myths of the Greeks were proto-
scientific in the manner in which such modern anthropologists
as Frazer and Tylor approached primitive myth, but sees the
Sophists defending the view that their scientific and philosophic colleagues were engaged in the same kind of activity as
were the mythmakers. The emphasis is not upon myth as
"primitive philosophy," but upon philosophy as sophisticated
and elaborated myth. And though the Sophists modernized
the Greek myths by providing "rational" explanations for
them, their aim in doing so was to use the interpretations as
other rational evidence was to be used: as the content of

rhetorical exercises that enhance an individual's power of persuasion. Thus the rationalization of myth did not have as its
aim the discovery of literal truths; it was meant to be a
continuing process to which every generation would return.
The acceptance of myth involved its use as an inexhaustible
reservoir of significances to which each generation would
have resort in order to continue the process of modernization.
One possesses truth in the Sophistic sense precisely when one
is able to define what is modern, fashionable, *au courant*.

The debate over the meaning and influence of the Sophistic movement is an interesting measure of the way our contemporary attitudes and beliefs lead us to revise the past. Until
the 1930s most of the interpretations of the Sophists were at
least mildly hostile. After that time, and increasingly into the
contemporary period, the Sophists have come to be praised
for their free-thinking and enlightened attitudes.[6]

This more positive assessment has paralleled the development of an increasingly hostile attitude toward the heritage of
classical science. Many of those who find in the Sophists the
forerunners of our modern, enlightened thinkers would be
hard pressed to explain the apparent relationship between the
contemporary reassessment of their movement and the collapse of scientific rationalism. I believe that John Burnet was
essentially correct when he claimed: "the 'age of the Sophists'
is, above all, an age of reaction against science."[7] That is to
say, it is a reaction against the belief that came to found the
classical scientific view that there were final truths to be discovered and that the methods of science provided a means of
discovering them. Burnet clearly saw the anti-scientific attitude of the Sophists because of his concept of the relations
between philosophy and rational science. According to
Burnet, "Philosophy is not mythology. . . . It cannot even
be said that [mythology is] the germ from which philosophy
developed. . . . There can be no philosophy where there is no
rational science."[8] Burnet has recognized, not surprisingly
given his Platonic vision of philosophy, that as long as we
view reason and rationality as continuous with mythical thinking, we shall remain subject to the power of myth.

The Socratic attempt to found logos on an examination of the self independent of *mythos* was based on the insight that every rationalist has been forced to rediscover in the face of the claim that truth is relative to time, place, and circumstance. Kant's attempt, in reply to Hume, to distinguish the functions of reason and understanding is but a reflection of the Socratic attempt to provide philosophical reasoning a place to stand other than on the mythical platform. If the Socratic turning within had led to a return to the origins of cultural experience, the history of philosophic thinking would have been significantly different. Instead, philosophic thinking proceeded along the lines required by the questionable assumption of the possibility of separating logos from *mythos*.

It would be the height of impudence to claim that Socrates, as interpreted by Plato, set philosophy off on the wrong foot. The greatness of the achievements resulting from the effort to separate logos and *mythos* places our cultural history beyond that kind of criticism. But, from the perspective of the cultural present, it does seem that the wisdom of our historical development is on the side of the Sophists against Socrates on this most crucial question. We are forced to take Socrates (as reported by Plato) at his word—he did *not* know himself, and as a consequence he did not know how intrinsically tied the concept of self or psyche is to the mythical accounts of the origin of all things out of chaos. The Sophists, possessed of a profounder self-knowledge, knew that logos detached entirely from *mythos* is an impossibility. For the self we know is knowable only by an acceptance of the myth that alone can account for it. The beginning (*arche*) of the self, like all other beginnings or principles in our cultural heritage, is a determining source of order that construes an antecedent chaos. Thinking from the beginning has depended on the continuity of the aims of *mythos* and logos.

Myths, as stories of the beginnings of things, when accompanied by their appropriate rituals, are meant to put us in touch with the time of origins, and to lead us into a direct experience of the chaos of beginnings. Cosmogonic myths allow us to experience afresh the time of origins, which includes the victory of cosmos over chaos. The experience of primordial threat and deliverance is the purpose of rituals that enact, and are interpreted by, myths. Here illustrated is the possibility of a grasping of chaos via participation in the myth and ritual associated with the ultimate origin. The logos of *mythos* is discovered when the principles of the myth are extracted and posited as the grounds for reasonings. These principles are defended on the basis of *other* principles and used to develop systematic understanding. The grasping function is rationalized. Henceforth what is grasped is not chaos in its primordial form but the principles of order abstracted from the story of origins. Participation is replaced by reflection, speculation, and rational construction. Thus the disciplining of chaos is achieved. The story of this disciplinary activity was traced in the last chapter.

The fundamental source of the relations of logos and *mythos* is to be found in the interplay of cosmogonic and cosmological speculation. The concern for origins and the concern for order are intrinsically tied since the nature of an ordered cosmos is to be found in the story of its origins. The proper sphere of reason has been, predominantly, that of cosmological speculation, which presupposes order and articulates the principles, the beginning points, of that order. The proper sphere of religious speculation has been that of *mythos*, the account of the origins of order itself. The attitude toward this separation of *mythos* and logos, which was a rather late development in Presocratic Greek philosophy, has qualified the character of metaphysical speculation at least since Plato and Aristotle.

Ontologia generalis names a general ontological pursuit that reaches to the very limits of rational investigation, asks the ontological question of the ground of existence, and thereby stirs the murky depths of primordial chaos and strains to see the bottom of the void. *Scientia universalis* constitutes a somewhat less radical investigation of the principles informing the cosmological structures of existence in terms of the ways in which they characterize the world. Philosophical speculation in neither of these senses has been able to remain content with reason alone, and has always found it necessary to employ myth as a means of evoking the sense of primordial chaos out of which cosmos arises. Whether this appeal is made at the very beginning of philosophic thinking, as in the case of the later Heidegger, or whether, as in the case of a philosopher such as Whitehead, following the Platonic tradition, the appeal to *mythos* in the form of a "likely story" is made as a last resort, the mythical element in speculative philosophy has never totally dropped from sight.

The various relations between logos and *mythos* gauge the peculiarly *religious* tonality of all philosophic speculation. In our Western tradition, it is as unlikely that one will find speculative philosophy apart from religion as it is that one will discover religious feeling maintained without the slightest recourse to reason. The search for philosophic beginnings, therefore, must involve us in a confrontation with the religious sensibility. For religion, more than any other enterprise, is concerned with the time of beginnings.

The relative detachment of logos from *mythos* was initiated in the attempt to separate myth and ritual in our culture. In the creative interplay of myth and ritual, we have one paradigmatic expression of the interaction of *theoria* and praxis in our cultural milieu. The rationalization of human experience that has led to an increasing detachment of *theoria* and praxis was initiated in large part by the dissociation of ritual and myth. For the element of rationality can dominate only when the mythical world-view and its associated dogmas can be entertained apart from the ritualistic activities that directly advertise the vested interests of theoretical understandings in the construal of chaos. The rationalists' disdain for religion is based, in part, on their instinctive recognition that in the beginnings of the religious sentiment are hidden the tainted origins of reason itself.

The presumption that logos and *mythos* have distinctive natures and functions, therefore, turns out to be highly suspect. For myths as etiological tales bear a strong family resemblance to philosophic principles, themselves concerned with the beginning points of thought, action, and feeling. The fact that rational and mythopoetic thinking share the desire to create cosmos from chaos is not surprising when we recognize that reason requires the existence of principles functioning as external sources of order. Philosophic differences that lead to different characterizations of the meaning of reason have revolved about the question of the methods of the discovery or the construction of principles, rather than about the question of the function of reason in relation to principles.

Properly understood, therefore, reason as the grasp of first principles always leads back again to myth, which functions to put us in touch with the roots of our existence. There are no objective *principia*. There is no way rationally to survey the origins. To reach beyond a principle is to be grasped by the primordial experience of chaos, to be offered up to the non-rational. Reason in its attempt to characterize reality reaches only as far as the arbitrary points of thought. To reach beyond, it would be necessary to remythologize reason. And reason remythologized ceases to be logos and becomes *mythos*.

Recent attempts to free reason from the power of *mythos* have perpetuated the distinction betwen types of rational activity that allow for at least a heuristic separation of logos and *mythos*. The theologian Paul Tillich has characterized reason in terms of its "ontological" and "technical" modes: ontological reason is "the structure of the mind which enables it to grasp and to shape reality";[9] technical reason concerns reasonings in relation to the employment of means, the kind of reasonings associated with applied science and technology.

The relations between the grasping and the shaping functions of ontological reason have been a serious concern in all philosophic treatments of the knowing process. Tillich notes that realisms stress the former, while idealisms opt for the latter. Our cosmogonic myths suggest that the act that established the possibility of reason was an act of shaping, which involved the organization of primordial chaos, or the establishment of order through the origination of principles. Subsequent acts of reason consist in the grasping of the principles of order established through the initial creative act, or, alternately, in a repetition of an act of construal. Since the advent of the Judaeo-Christian tradition, the predominant source of the principles of order has been God construed as omnipotent creator, who imposes upon chaos the order and meaning it is reason's task to discover. The notion of imposed order serves to ground the concept of reason in the volitional activity of God. Reason is the articulation of the commanding presence of God. It is the recognition of imposed order. The realists' claim that the mind is passive to the order of nature nonetheless involves an assertion of the existence of an order of a given type. And this claim has always been open to the charge of arbitrariness and contingency.

Tracing the development of cultural self-understanding in terms of the existence of antecedent principles is not sufficient for our purposes. We must try to understand how we came to be possessed of these first principles. Such an understanding undermines belief in their necessity, for we recognize that first principles originated with the construal of chaos, and the semantic contexts in which the act of construal has been articulated have taken several irreconcilable forms.

Whether the act of construal is characterized directly in terms of will as in the Hebraic cosmogony, or described in terms of the victory of persuasion over force as in Plato's *Timaeus*, or presented in terms of erotic motivation as in Orphic cosmogonies, the message is the same: the will that creates, the persuasive agency that organizes, and the love that unites—all are infected by arbitrariness since the end product in each case can be shown to lack necessity. Whether we construe the mythical story of origins directly in terms of a divine creator, or in terms of natural circumstances without transcendent reference, the result is the same: the coexistence of a set of conflicting and mutually irreconcilable world-views suggests that the original acts of construal that led us to the development of the conception of a coherent cosmos were *arbitrary* acts, which we later *rationalized* through a grasping and shaping of theories. It is thus impossible to escape from heteronomy through reason. The appeal to rational autonomy brings with it, *pari passu*, the appeal to the arbitrariness of the establishment of first principles.

Ontological reason consists in the grasping of principles that have their origin in the mythical and ritualistic participation in chaos and its organization. All our graspings at the

rational level serve the ends of the primordial shaping function, which itself is born in arbitrariness. This fact about
ontological reason is particularly significant because the fundamental distinction between ontological and technical reason
is supposed to lie in the relationship to *ends*. Ontological
reason is presumed to determine its own ends, while technical
reason "determines the means while accepting the ends from
'somewhere else.'"[10] This has prompted many of the criticisms of scientists and technicians, for example, whose ethical
standards seem to be suspended at times, leading them to
perform morally questionable tasks because they have been
enjoined to do so by industry or the state. Technical reason is
seen to be other-directed, obedient to extraneous ends.

The difficulty with the distinction between ontological
and technical reason is that, in the last analysis, it does not
seem to apply. For reason in its ontological mode also receives
its ends from somewhere else—namely, from the primordial,
non-rational grasping and shaping of chaos. In actuality there
is only one form of reason, and that is technical reasoning,
reason subservient to extraneous ends. What we have glori-
fied with the name "ontological reason" is reason in the
service of the shaping of chaos, reason as *control*.

The introduction of the subject of control brings us to the
very threshold of an understanding of our conception of
rationality. For behind the relations of reason and order,
which we recognize as incontrovertible, there lies the relation
of rationality and control. Our cultural self-understanding is
dominated by the conception of imposed order. And if this is
so, reason cannot be seen as a means of passively entertaining
an antecedent order; rather, it must be seen as *rationalization*,
the production of order, and as *control*, the maintenance of
order.

The examination of the principal elements of our cultural
paradigm is an examination of the broad structures of rationality, the patterns of our sense-making activities. Reason and
reasonings are as much a part of the operations of myth-
making and the articulation of myth as is every other human
function. If one asks the origins of our rationality, therefore,
the query must lead to the fundamental structure of our cul-

tural self-consciousness. And the peculiar character of rationality must be seen as a function of our particular manner of becoming culturally self-aware. The concept of chaos as it is understood in the myths of cosmogenesis leads to the interpretation of the epistemological function as primarily one of rationalization.

The suspicion of rationalization derives from our belief that it is an aberrant form of reasoning aimed at private advantage. Public forms of reasoning based on consensus are no more justified as viridical; they are simply more acceptable because they are likely to be of greater social benefit. The distinction between public, or objective, reasonings and private, or idiosyncratic, reasonings is of no intrinsic value. Whether reason is employed to solve problems relating to physical survival by increasing efficiency in obtaining food or shelter, or to resolve personal anxieties relating to the threat of chaotic disorder in the psychological sphere, the aim of reason is rationalized order.

The results of technical reason in achieving rationalized order so far outshine those of ontological reason as to lead one to doubt if the conception of ontological reason is a viable one. It was for years thought—such is the noble reputation of ontological reason in the Western tradition—that technique without ontological principles was useless. One of the most brilliant attacks on "merely technical reason," mounted by José Ortega y Gasset in *The Revolt of the Masses*, is most often read today as a conservative attack on the changes of social order deriving from the rise of technology, an aristocrat's demurrer in the face of "rising expectations," or an anti-democratic complaint against the future—but *not* as a philosophical argument whose inferences concerning the role of reason in a technological society are justified. We seem to be getting along just as well without the conception of ontological reason as with it. Technology is certainly no worse a solution to the world's problems than was the industrial period with all its rational apologists.

The recognition that reason is grounded in practical needs does not mean that the pure rationalists among us will have to abandon it. On the contrary, reason is abandoning us.

Advanced technological society is reason objectified. It stands
proof of the victory of technical reason. And the extent to
which we must resort to reason is markedly decreasing. Technological society is already informed; so we are not required
to inform ourselves. The forms and processes of rationality
exist increasingly outside the human psyche in the objective
structures of the technical order. The institutions, communications network, and industrial processes of a society become
nothing less than public habits, which in their status as custom
reduce the necessity of resort to independent thought.

As for the intrinsic enjoyments of the rational life, these
are fading fast in the light of the incurable relativity of thinking
per se. Concern for principles derives less from the desire to
understand and more from the wish to promote our reliance
upon objectified technical processes that organize our lives.
The attempt to maintain an interest in thinking for its own sake
is doomed in advance. Not only have we been unable to sustain the "quest for certainty" that seems to have lured so
many previous philosophers: we have been unable to attain a
significant unity of effort in our assault upon the infinite. What
has done reason in is not uncertainty but uncertainties. That
is, the plurality of the ways in which reason has chosen to
mount its attack upon the infinite has shown no obvious unity
of effort. An unanswered question is the romance of reason,
but the rank and acrimonious dispute over just what constitutes a legitimate question is debilitating to the aims of reason.
The pleasures of reason are fading fast in the light of the
relativity of rational approaches to existence. Having awakened to the full self-consciousness of its operational character,
ontological reason has suffered the fate of the unicorn, the
basilisk, and the tatzelwurm.

The most devastating critique of reason in its presumedly
ontological mode has come to us by way of the irreducibility of
certain primary theoretical characterizations of the world.
Which world is so shaped that reason can be said to grasp true
principles? The worlds of the mechanist, the formalist, the
naturalist, and the volitionalist are distinctly different. What
can reason tell us, finally, but the story of the mutually contradictory characterizations of the principles that are its objects?

The recognition of the internal consistency and mutual inconsistency of various cosmologies has produced such a crisis in our ways of understanding that it is doubtful that our intellectual culture can recover from it without a radical transformation of our sense of the character and function of rationality.

The principal effect of the recognition of theoretical relativity is the presentation of a profoundly ironical paradox reaching to the depths of our intellectual culture. The paradox is that our acceptance of a specific vision of the world entails the employment of a specific understanding of reason and rationality. Neither the understanding of the nature of the world in which we live nor the acceptance of a meaning of reason that allows us to defend that understanding, can itself be rational since the grounds for preferring one view of the world over a conflicting vision must be based on a conception of reason satisfactory to both points of view. More likely than not, the attempt to defend one's view of the world, or to convert another to one's view, must be grounded, not in reason, but in persuasion or coercion. Rhetorical persuasion appeals to the emotions in such a fashion as to alter the subjective form of feeling that attaches to propositions, aiming to produce conviction where before there was doubt or the suspension of belief. And although coercion cannot produce a change in subjective commitment (extreme forms of psychic coercion excepted), it can determine the behavior of individuals, leading them to act as if the world were organized a certain way.

Both persuasion and coercion as political tools are intimately connected with the volitional perspective. The fact that the relativity of philosophic visions seems to require resort to such techniques tends to verify the volitional view by suggesting that the kind of world in which we live is one that must ultimately find its rationale in the power of persuasion or coercion. This ironic fact was, in modern times, best recognized by Friedrich Nietzsche, whose insights into the *mythos* upon which our intellectual culture is grounded were so immediate and direct as finally to drive him beyond the slightest comfort of logos. It was Nietzsche's "profound aversion to reposing once and for all in any one total view of the world," his yielding to the "fascination of the opposing point of view," and his "refusal to be deprived of the stimulus of the enigmatic,"[11] which allowed him to see beyond the edges of disciplined chaos into the unordered abyss. He saw that in that chaos "there exists neither 'spirit,' nor reason, nor thinking, nor consciousness, nor soul, nor will, nor truth: all are fictions that are of no use."[12] Knowledge is but "a tool of power. . . . The measure of the desire for knowledge depends upon the measure to which the will to power grows in a species: a species grasps a certain amount of reality in order to become master of it, in order to press it into service."[13] Science, the most sophisticated of the cognitive activities, is "the transformation of nature into concepts for the purpose of mastering nature."[14] All knowledge—science above all—is instrumental, is but a *means*.

Many attempts have been made to mitigate the nihilistic consequences of this anti-epistemology. Max Scheler was to take over the Nietzschean argument in its essentials, but he applied it only to the objects of the experimental specialized sciences, which investigate "laws of fortuitous realities in the world and of their circumstance."[15] In addition to knowledge for the sake of control, Scheler believed *knowledge of essence* and *knowledge of metaphysical reality* to be open to human reason. The form of Scheler's attempted defense of reason was to become the paradigm for subsequent philosophers who took seriously Nietzsche's construal of knowledge in terms of will-to-power. It is Scheler who provided Tillich the grounds for his distinction between ontological and technical forms of reason, which we employed earlier to raise the question of the status of reason in contemporary culture.

Martin Heidegger, influenced by both Nietzsche and Scheler, attempts to distinguish between "calculative" and "meditative" forms of thinking, the former answering to Scheler's knowledge of control, the latter influenced by the poetic forms of intuitive thought. Heidegger, to a greater extent than Scheler, accepts the radical consequences of Nietzsche's theory of knowledge, but believes that although the tradition of Western philosophical thought culminated in Nietzsche's reduction of metaphysical knowledge to its volitional ground, a renewal of thinking is an open possibility.

With Nietzsche I would claim that *all* knowledge is open to critique in terms of its motivation toward *control*. With Scheler I would assert an internal connection between knowledge and the growth of the contemporary technological forms of domination. And with Heidegger I would claim that the end of our traditional forms of knowledge realized in terms of technology signals the beginning of a new cultural, or perhaps post-cultural, sensibility. And though I accept Nietzsche's view that all knowledge is grounded in will-to-power, I do not believe that this necessitates the acceptance of a volitional ontology. Our ways of knowing have developed contingently along lines that, because of the arbitrariness of their starting points, are easily characterizable in volitional terms.

I have argued that the volitional perspective is one among four dominant systems of construal that developed out of the cosmogonical theories that found Western forms of speculation. And though the volitional theory, because of its direct recognition of arbitrariness and contingency, has theoretical, or meta-theoretical, prominence in our tradition, this is not to say that it has any necessary standing. On the contrary, beginning with the next chapter I shall argue that there is indeed a significant alternative to each of the predominating strains of Anglo-European speculation. This vision, grounded in the concept of "creativity" understood in Taoist and Buddhist terms, I will claim, has a status qualitatively distinct from the four defunct philosophic visions and their many cross-fertilized forms. Thus, though my approach to the problem of the collapse of the conception of ontological reason will be to seek a means of transcending reason, I do not believe that such transcendence is possible without recourse to an alternative culture. And the appeal to elements of an alternative cultural tradition will involve a much more radical attempt at philosophic reconstruction than one that proceeds along the lines laid down by our own cultural tradition.

The radical nature of our attempted reconstruction will be due to the fact that we shall attempt to transcend reason and rationality, not by discovering a purer form of reason itself, but by discovering an alternative to reason as a primary means of characterizing the nature of things. And though this plan must seem profoundly tendentious at this point, it should become more acceptable as we proceed. For what we must do is to demonstrate that there is indeed a place to stand while critiquing reason that itself does not presuppose what it attempts to criticize—viz., the arbitrary activity involved in the disciplining of chaos. It is this demonstration that requires resort to an alternative culture.

The difficulty of trying to rehabilitate thinking without resort to cultural transcendence is illustrated by a number of specific movements within contemporary philosophy that have as their aim the renewal of thought. Perhaps the most uncompromising of these attempts was initiated by Edmund Husserl, who sought to pattern his defense of reason on that provided by Descartes in the seventeenth century. In his *Cartesian Meditations*, Husserl asks,

> Is not our situation similar to the one encountered by Descartes in his youth? If so, then is not this a fitting time . . . to subject to a Cartesian overthrow the immense philosophical literature with its medley of great traditions, of comparatively serious new beginnings, of stylish literary activity . . . and to begin with new *meditationes de prima philosophia*.[16]

The futility of attempting to echo the clarion call of Cartesian rationalism is evidenced by the subsequent history of Husserlian programmatic phenomenology. Far from initiating a revolution in our conception of reason, phenomenology has merely added to the plethora of philosophic techniques that may be applied to specific issues or problems in this or that cultural interest. If our current philosophic literature is not as immense as that encountered by Husserl, it is only because of the depressed state of the philosophical art rather than because of any realized consensus. The "medley of great traditions" is, of course, still to be heard; we are continually subjected to "comparatively serious new beginnings" (Husserl might claim this essay to be one such!), and contemporary philosophy is certainly not without the "stylish literary activity" that the art deco of any intellectual discipline comprises.

The Frankfurt school of neo-Marxians—pre-eminently Max Horkheimer, its founder, and Jürgen Habermas, its latest spokesman—have taken a somewhat less ambitious approach to the defense of reason. In *The Eclipse of Reason*, Horkheimer, echoing Scheler, claimed that "reason was born from man's urge to dominate nature."[17] In its objective mode reason is capable of seeking out the essences of things in a dispassionate manner. But in its subjective mode it is characterized in Nietzschean terms as that which seeks mastery over the things of the world by making them means to the realization of arbitrarily selected ends. Horkheimer holds that although objective reason is capable of transcending subjective reason, historical development has militated increasingly against such transcendence. The positivistic era of totally subjective reason constituted the end result of that development. The hope for the liberation of objective reason, which Horkheimer and other members of the Frankfurt school have discussed in various contexts, lies essentially in the employment of critical theory to promote changes in the social order that will decrease the political and social forms of domination and release public reasonings from the structures of domination that have been their context in modern times.

Jürgen Habermas has attempted to combine elements of materialist thought from Marx and Freud, idealist notions from Hegel, and naturalist concepts from the pragmatism of C. S. Peirce in order to critique the volitional indictment of reason deriving, ultimately, from Nietzsche! He has provided an extremely subtle analysis of the origin of knowledge in human interests and criticized the false consciousness resulting from the presumption that pure theory—theory unconditioned by practical concerns—is a currently realizable possibility. Habermas finds in the conjoined concepts of autonomy and responsibility "the only Idea we possess a priori in the sense of the philosophic tradition,"[18] and he indicates that "only in an emancipated society whose members' autonomy and responsibility had been realized"[19] would the life-impoverishing consequences of the implicit conjunction of knowledge and interest be circumvented.

Horkheimer and Habermas have accepted the eclecticism implicit in Marx's thought and attempted to revitalize reason through the cross-fertilization of various philosophic traditions. The problem with this or any other form of eclecticism is that its aim at achieving philosophic adequacy is continually threatened by the defect of logical inconsistency and incoherence resulting from the grafting together of traditionally incompatible principles. Moreover, since there are no accepted principles guiding the eclectic activity, the traditional divergences among the various philosophic paradigms are recapitulated within the family of philosophies springing from the inspiration of Marx.

The same phenomenon is seen with various of the other families of philosophers. Philosophers of logic and language who have narrowed the purview of philosophic investigation to logical and semantic analyses find themselves at variance with one another because of different preferences as to the system of semantics or logic that ought to be employed. There are no more acceptable rules allowing one to decide among such systems than there are among metaphysical systems. Ultimately, the sole appeal must be to intuition. Thus we have within the family of philosophical analysts a small-scale version of the conflict of theory with theory that has patterned the history of general philosophic activity.[20]

One of the more concerted contemporary efforts to avoid the effects of philosophic relativity involves substituting the notion of falsification for theoretical verification while, in principle, maintaining the objectivity of truth. The discovery of falsehoods and the uncovering of errors lead us closer to the truth. Progress in understanding comes through a series of "conjectures and refutations," to borrow a phrase from Karl Popper, the chief representative of this view. This theory derives, of course, from the epistemology of science, but it is not the majority view even within the scientific disciplines. Moreover, it grounds its methodological activity on a rather narrow selection of evidence, which precludes, for example, aesthetic and religious sensibilities from equal consideration with the scientific facts and ethical values of a privileged community of inquirers. The consequence of this rather ingenious response to theoretical relativity is the substitution of a *methodological* consensus (and a rather narrow one at that!) for an apparently impossible substantive one.

Perhaps the most constructive approach to the failure of philosophical reason is to be found in contemporary forms of process philosophy (about which we shall have much to say later on). Process metaphysics provides a *delimitation* of the function of reason, restricting its valid employment to the provision of approximations of the nature of things through a rendering of the abstract morphology of the processes that constitute reality. The incoherence of most attempts by contemporary process philosophers to employ reason in this limited mode is the result, as we shall have occasion to see, of the need for an adequate philosophic terminology with which to articulate the intuitions grounding a process view of the world. I shall be claiming that it is from the process orientation that we must begin to seek a way out of the dilemmas of our culture. But as long as we remain within our culture we shall not be able to exploit the genius of the process intuitions, since they are fundamentally at odds not only with each of the four semantic contexts that have existed in our intellectual culture, but with the *mythos* of our culture that determines that we shall characterize our beginnings in terms of a negative chaos.

The irony of reason's quest for order, which resulted in the disciplining of chaos, is that the result of the quest has been the production of a "chaos" of concepts and theories infinitely more resistant to organization than was the original chaos *in the beginning*. Chaos at least has the advantage of passivity to form. Theories that organize the dark, formless void are themselves impossible of harmonization, since only after reason has organized the chaos in this or that manner is it possible to recognize inconsistencies, incoherencies, and outright contradictions. It would not be flippant to claim that the adventures of the activity of reason, whether interpreted in its idealist, materialist, naturalist, or volitional guise, have ended, not with the conquest of chaotic disorder, but with the production of a chaos more threatening than that encountered in our time of beginnings. The consequences of the collapse of disciplined chaos and the victory of chaos over reason, once clarified, will serve as the initial stimulus toward re-searching a new beginning.

GOD OR THE WORLD

Our analysis of the origin and function of reason has emphasized the notion of control. God, nature, passion, and praxis or social practice, as constituents of the cultural paradigm, are, individually and in their systematic relationships with one another, means of recognizing order in things. They are rationalized components of an original mythical world-view. As such, they name power or control relationships the function of which is to ensure the recognition of a patterned set of relations forming the structures of rationality insofar as they are meant to give rise to cultural self-understanding. The elements of the cultural paradigm name relationships that characterize cultural experience. The examination of the meaning of "God" in cultural terms requires that we analyze the relation of God to the world. Likewise the understanding of "nature" requires us to focus on the meaning of the relations between persons and the natural world. "Passion" involves the relation of male to female; and "social practice" the relation of the individual to society.

These relations together constitute the principal rationalized structures that have supported our cultural self-understandings. The stress on the aspect of control in our characterization of the notions of reason and rationality should make us wary of interpreting these relationships as relations of parity. The rationalization of the mythical bases of our culture has given rise to distinctly dualistic rather than to polar relations.

In the Judaeo-Christian tradition the conflicts of light and darkness, good and evil, and so on, are placed in the context of an ontological continuum stretching from being to nonbeing. The so-called hierarchy of being, which establishes the natures of things by virtue of their place in the scale of being, renders seemingly polar relations of the type we wish to discuss no *real* relations at all, but conflicting opposites. Nonbeing is opposed to being; it is its negation. With this basic insight as model, each of the cultural relations we wish to consider must be seen in an implicitly negative and conflictual manner. God and the world relate as the fullness of being to relative non-being. The world is a created product and as such is an image of the divine. In its "fallen" character it is infected with evil and non-being. First as "image," then as "fallen," the world can be seen as inferior to God and therefore not possibly an equal partner in the relationship. Persons and nature have the same inequality. Though the agents of Original Sin, human beings nonetheless exist above the remainder of animate and inanimate nature. As ensouled creatures, human persons have a value not to be accorded to nature as a whole. Therefore, the relations of nature and persons cannot be one of equality or polarity. This same model is employed for the relations of male and female. It is for the male that the female was created, and *from* him, as well—at least, according to the most influential of the accounts in Genesis. The ruler–ruled status of the male–female relation destroys the appearance of polarity, turning it into a *political* relationship. The relation of society to the individual is in no greater sense a relation of parity. We are subject to "the powers that be." Individualism carried to its extreme is unacceptable because the claims of society must be seen as transcending the claims of any particular individual. No polar relation here. The individual requires a society, a language, a culture, to be human. Societies, as we have experienced on many occasions throughout history, can exist with only the barest minimum of individuality.

The seeds of our present cultural dilemmas are to be found in the conflict implicit in each of the relations that organize our cultural paradigm. After having the function of rationality as control raised to the level of consciousness, we recognize that these primary relationships reveal themselves to be ultimately unequal struggles in which one element must give way to the other. God stands opposed to his world, persons to nature, male to female, and society to the individual. The controlling power belongs to the initial component in each case. God's power subsists in his creative activity; the power of persons, in their status as deputies of God; the power of male over female is grounded in the presumedly derivative status of the latter from the former; and the power of society over the individual derives from claims that "the powers that be are ordained by God."

The greatness of our cultural development, we can now see, has been achieved at the cost of subordination and domination. And though we have for centuries accepted this pattern of domination and control—indeed graced it with the title of the civilizing process—the time has now passed when, in the name of progress, we shall be able to build a viable culture upon such relationships. For whatever causes (and we shall examine some of the principal causes in the sequel), a cultural paradigm based upon essentially disjunctive relations is no longer able to interpret what promises to be the novel emerging self-consciousness of advanced technological culture.

The most difficult of all subjects relating to our cultural self-understanding, the subject of "God," has become even more difficult of late because of the strange ferment in theological cricles that has led for the first time in our tradition to *religious* alternatives to the classical concept of God, which has served us culturally at least since the Augustinian theological synthesis of the fifth century.

The classical concept of God, which reached its culmination in the high Scholasticism of the Middle Ages, is an austere and finely articulated concept that serves very well the purposes of a reasonably well-integrated society dominated, at the level of intellectual culture, by the belief in the discovery of absolute truths, and characterized, in the sphere of praxis, by a stable and hierarchically patterned set of institutions and activities. For centuries the only viable alternative to belief in the classical Judaeo-Christian concept of God was an anxious agnosticism or a crusading atheism. We are prepared to accept the ministrations of a Voltaire or a Nietzsche or a Marx who at least affirmed the importance of Judaeo-Christianity, if only by making it the target of what they hoped would be fatal assaults. Indeed, we have turned such critics into prophets of a purified, trans-valued or humanized religion, which we find rather easily accommodated in the family of theological notions constituting our cultural orthodoxy. The apparent extreme of such critical assaults, the recent death-of-God "atheology," has constituted the medium through which many of the religious feelings customarily associated with theological orthodoxy have been channeled into intellectual culture. The plaint "God is dead" has, by virtue of the strange dialectical logic that has characterized our recent epoch, often evoked the same spiritual *tremendum* once associated with the proclamation "I know my Redeemer lives."

The theologians of the past two decades who tried to popularize the notion of God's demise were, in large measure, merely articulating an experience that constituted a brute fact of contemporary existence in an advanced technological society. Their service was not in identifying an experience or an event, but in providing an interpretation of the theological consequences of an experience widely recognized throughout contemporary society. The spectacle of theologians announcing the end of God to the lay public seemed at the time rather like a group of Santa's helpers proclaiming the death of Santa Claus to the children of the land. And the announcement had much the same psychological impact.

The result of the claim that "God is dead" was to create a new type of atheism, one that transcended the old forms of atheistic and agnostic denials of the conceivability or reality of God. This led to a widespread feeling of our having outgrown the need for dependence upon a Lord of heaven and earth, or, at the very least, to the conviction that we must accept a situation characterized by the absence of a being who formerly had constituted the principle *par excellence* in terms of which we had interpreted the meaning of our individual, social, and cultural existence.

Raising the subject of "God" raises a complex of semantic issues along with it. Few concepts have been employed by so many to mean such different things. Our Western, or Anglo-European, culture has employed the term in these principal ways: to mean either Divine Mind, Arbitrary Will, Telos of Nature, or Great Mechanic. These meanings have, of course, developed in the four main philosophic traditions that have characterized our culture. Which of these meanings of "God" we intend can have profound effects upon the patterns of our cultural development.

The theological notion of God as Arbitrary Will characterized a being who disposes according to secret criteria that only he can possibly know and who predestined each soul either to salvation or to damnation, without hope of appeal. The characterization of God as Divine Mind, possessor of all truth and wisdom, long provided philosophers with the notion of absolute truths and final answers discoverable by reason. Plato, at the beginnings of our culture, in seeking the Principle of the Good, and Einstein, toward the end, looking for a Unified Field Theory, were both imbued with this concept of God as Divine Mind. The deistic notions associated with the rise of modern science, in its Galilean and Newtonian phase, are based on the conception of God as the Great Mechanic who "invented" the world, and who is not disposed to interfere with the workings of his perfect machine. Finally, the assumption of some evolutionary theorists has been that God must function as the end, the goal, the lure toward perfection. In Tennyson's phrase he is "that far-off divine event towards which all creation moves."

These concepts of God, and the various permutations that have resulted from attempts to combine the specific visions into more adequate ones, have played about in our cultural traditions since the beginnings of Judaeo-Christianity. Sometimes one concept would be stressed, sometimes another, and the consequences of such differing stresses have been both obvious and profound. The novelty of our present circumstances is that, to a degree far greater than has been the case before, the concept of God in each of its various meanings has come under attack. We have run out of alternative characterizations of the religious object, the object of religious experience.

The volitional interpretation of God was the first to come under attack. The characterization of God as Arbitrary Will has fallen victim to the assaults upon authority of all kinds. We are, if not anarchists in our attitudes toward power and authority, at least cynics and skeptics, in the face of the empirically distasteful events of recent decades that have spelled the decline of the political process and of the nation–state. Also, the experience of the relativity of truth-claims and of the ephemerality of any philosophic or scientific explanation of the nature of things has militated against the acceptance of a concept of God as the principle of order or the source of truth, expressed in the notion of Divine Mind. The concept of God as the Great Mechanic is challenged by developments in scientific technology that have resulted in an increase in the possibilities of human control of the Great Machine. In addition, the complexity of advanced technological society is such that it becomes increasingly difficult to maintain a belief in the efficacy of mechanistic types of explanation. Electronic technology strains the bonds of the mechanical model beyond its useful limits. Finally, the view that God is the Telos of Nature has come under attack from those who sense the future as a radical openness, a set of contingencies in which real alternatives exist. The new science of futurism has persuaded many that the future is in the hands of human beings. There is no single possible future. The future is a set of real possibilities, which we are able to realize with proper initiative. Or, to quote the motto of the *Whole Earth Catalog*: "We are as gods, and we had better start acting like it."

The assaults upon the various conceptions of God have not been universal, but they have been strong enough to render acceptable to large segments of our cultural elites the pronouncement of the literary, philosophical, and theological *avant garde* that "God is dead." The cultural significance of the death of God movement of some few years ago lay in the fact that each of the possible, or principal, notions of God was brought under attack. The proclamation of the death of God was not just the claim that this or that notion of God was no longer viable. It was a full-scale attack on the conception of the Judaeo-Christian God in any form previously accepted. The curious result was that there was, implicitly at least, not one but *four* announcements of the death of God.

The most dramatic of these announcements was made by the existentialists, beginning with the statement of Ivan in Dostoevski's *The Brothers Karamazov*: "If God is dead then all things are possible to men." Nietzsche's proclamation, "God is dead," made about the same time,[21] and Sartre's somewhat belated conclusion that "all things are possible to man" completed the existentialist syllogism that provided the paradigm for all future announcements of God's demise. The

existentialists, specifically Nietzsche, described the death of
God as deicide. The will-to-power residing in persons could
not accept the concept of an Absolute Will that would make of
human beings only subjects or slaves. The recognition of God
as Will brought with it the revolt against an arbitrary power
standing over against the world and determining its nature and
destiny. God as Arbitrary Will must die.

It was no accident that this announcement of the death of
God came first. For, when the origin and character of the
elements of our cultural foundations are recognized, it is the
element of power that is first laid bare, and the sense of the
arbitrariness of our first principles that is realized. The concept "God" has always functioned as the interpretation of our
most profoundly religious experiences. Under these conditions, God as the Supreme *Arche* becomes the name for all the
blindly arbitrary power to which human experience has been
subjected throughout its history.

But, in addition to the generally pessimistic sounds of the
existentialists' funeral dirge, there has been a rather optimistic
strain of atheology that has persisted over the past decade and
more. The claim of this part of the movement was not that
God was murdered by his creatures, but that he committed
suicide. "God so loved the world that he gave his only begot-
ten son," and in the giving of his son, in the pouring of himself
into the world, he emptied himself. He gave "the last full
measure of devotion." God, as Transcendent Being, is no
more. The movement of the kenotic Christologists claimed
that in the realization or instantiation of the divine in and
through the person of Jesus Christ, the function of a transcendent being in bringing about the end of nature was realized.
Henceforth, the telos of nature must be immanent in the workings of the world. God, as Transcendent Telos of Nature, is
dead.

God's third demise resulted from the outworking of the
immanent goals of our technological society. The so-called
secularization motif in the death of God movement, which had
Harvey Cox's *Secular City* as its principal expression, accepted the fact of God's death as due to *natural causes*, to compli-
cations resulting from old age. According to this view, our
secular world come of age no longer needs the concept of God

in order to do its work. God, insofar as he can be spoken of at all, is *Deus absconditus*. The world has been left to its own devices and it is capable of resolving its problems without recourse to a Transcendent Being. The deistic motif, therefore, reached its culmination among the secular theologians. God as Great Mechanic is dead.

The final death of God, perhaps of all the most ironic, was announced by the so-called neo-classical wing of process philosophers and theologians. The classical Judaeo-Christian God, particularly as understood in terms of the notion of the perfection of being, has died—but quite by accident. He died, so we were told, from internal inconsistencies inflicted by overly zealous, incautious theologians who, in attempting to join the concept of God as Divine Mind from the Platonists with the concept of a loving being from Scripture, were unable to resolve the conflict between the notions of perfection and passion. God, as a "respectable chaos of unimaginable superlatives,"[22] came to strain the rationalizing talents of even the most subtle of theologians. In place of the God of St. Thomas and Christian orthodoxy, we find a God in process, a finite God, transcendent in potency and immanent in actuality. God as Divine Mind, as possessor of Eternal Forms, and thereby as distinct and separate from the world of flux and becoming, is dead. An unfortunate accident. Seen in this perspective, the death of God as a cultural fact can be summarized in this fashion: God, the God of Anglo-European culture, in each and every one of his guises, is no more. *Abiit, excessit, evasit, erupit.*

So much for the past. We have come to bury God, not to praise him. The announcement of the death of God, like the announcement of those of his earthly counterparts, the kings, should be an occasion of some joy as well as sorrow. "The king is dead; long live the king!" We must update a line from Oscar Wilde's threnody for the gods of the Greeks:

> Young Hylas seeks the water's springs no more
> Great Pan is dead and Mary's Son is king.

The pronouncement "God is dead!" should be accompanied by an announcement of the rebirth of the world. If we look around, therefore, for the current status of God or the gods in contemporary culture, we should discover something of the shape of our future insofar as it will be affected by belief in our commitment to the notion of deity. For this understanding we must look to those who, in addition to making the claim that God as we have known him is no more, have begun to renew or to advance theological activity along other lines.

We do not find much of a recognizable theology in the hardline literary atheist whose art once proclaimed God's death and whose representatives now maintain the anxiety felt at his absence. The literary atheist is one who, recognizing the fate of religion without God, proceeds to find in art the cultural surrogate of the religious sensibility. The function of the artist now becomes that of parodist or satirist, since in the absence of the real and living God we can do no more than caricature and satirize the theological models of the past. Satire, as Whitehead recognized, is "the last flicker of originality in a passing epoch as it faces the onroad of staleness and boredom."[23] The satires of Kurt Vonnegut, with his Bokononist Religion or his Church of God the Utterly Indifferent, placed within a context of extreme humane sensitivity, tell much of the story of the literary atheist who is without a primary religious object, but who in a very real sense cannot perform his art without it. "Lord, I believe; help thou my unbelief."

For the literary figure, it is, not the existence of God, but the *belief* in his existence, that is at issue. As the poet Wallace Stevens has claimed, whether or not he exists in actuality, "God . . . assuredly exists as a necessary postulate of the poetic imagination, embodying in concrete form, the perfected projection of life, which alone can satisfy the will."[24] The literary atheist is one who is, as every vocal atheist, preoccupied with the fact that God does not exist and who finds that his art must contain in some form the message of God's absence. Here we are unable to find, as yet, any positive source for the development of a new sensibility, unless it be in the hint that Wallace Stevens has left us that the absence of God leads the poets, as artists and literati, to a return to creations of their minds. If such is indeed to be the case, then we should expect the emergence of a new sensuous and concrete

literature and art, a recognition of transitoriness, an acceptance of impermanence, an emphasis upon functionality over
form, of becoming over being, of intuition over power and
rationality. These are the types of expression that could serve
as the sources from which a new sensibility could emerge. As
yet we look in vain for such expressions among our artists.

We might find a richer source in the process theologians'
revision of the concept of God. Alfred North Whitehead and
Charles Hartshorne are the principal representatives of a
school of thought that has tried to announce the end of the
classical concept of God while at the same time providing a
sophisticated and full-blown substitute for the old God.[25] This
neo-classical theology seeks to provide a concept of God infinite in possibility, but finite in actuality—a God in process. In
his transcendent nature God serves as the repository of all
possibility; in his immanent nature God functions as harmonized actuality. The relation of God to the world on these
terms is distinctly closer to a polar relationship than that suggested by classical theology, since the becoming of events in
the world contributes data to the experience of God. But
strait, indeed, is the gate, and narrow the way that leads to
such a subtle and finely articulated revisioning of the concept
of deity. It will be some time before we can see the impact of
this form of thinking in any but the most erudite of theological
circles.

I am inclined to think that it is neither among the literary
atheists nor among the theological revisionists that the new
concept of religion will be born. I believe that the principal
dynamic in the current cultural milieu, as far as theology is
concerned, is to be found in the tensions between the remaining two strains of atheological movement. The secularists,
with their faith in the inevitability of the loss of God with the
advance of technology, and the sacralists, who believe that
though the transcendent God has died, deity has entered the
world in immanent forms, promise most in the way of novel
theological speculation. For these two principles seem to
reflect the developments of our society very well. There is the
inevitable fact of technology, which leads to a secularized or
"worldly" mentality; but there is also a strong commitment to

spirituality in its immanental forms, as illustrated by the practical, technique-oriented mysticisms whose popularity among young and old continues to increase. The character of our future, as it will be determined spiritually, depends upon the manner in which these two phenomena interact. We shall address this subject directly later on.

Each of the arguments aimed at rejecting or re-interpreting the classical concepts of God are the direct consequence of theoretical, practical, and productive changes in the nature of the world in which we have come to live. The tensions resulting from the attempt to live in a set of circumstances to which the concept of God in any of the interpretations available to us seems irrelevant have become unbearable to many. And a simple atheism as a dialectical rejection of these concepts is also unsatisfactory. We are called upon to recognize that the form of the relation of God to the world and of the world to God is the real issue. It is not that one or the other element of the relationship may be rejected, for as long as we recognize the necessity of maintaining some concept of the cosmos as environs, milieu, or condition defining the basic "within which" human beings exist, it will be necessary to characterize that which has constituted the alternative pole of the relation. When, as seems to be the case in contemporary culture, that relation of conjunction threatens to become a disjunctive relation, our most significant alternative is not to accept the either/or situation, but to look to some new interpretation of experience.

The philosopher of culture is called upon to consider the richest and most vital of interpretations of our most profound experiences, and to proceed in as non-reductive a fashion as possible. He cannot serve the interests of a single type of experience but must answer to the breadth of civilized experience and seek in every profound experience the basis for the development of novel and productive concepts with which to express and to evoke the sense of significance that dwells within. "God," as concept, has always served to interpret religious experience, which experience has been conditioned and qualified by human existence in the world. We should seek not the concept of "a world come of age," which has no need of God, but an analogue of the concept of God as an interpretation of religious experiences that have now come to be conditioned and qualified in new ways in this new world.

The transitions in the cultural interests of art, morality, science, and religion that have begun to characterize this age lead us to speculate on the transitions to new cultural forms. It is the burden of the following pages to demonstrate that these transitions are indeed quite radical. But our argument will be that the truly radical nature of our emerging forms of experience and expression cannot really be understood if we yield to the impoverishment of our interpretative schema, as would be suggested by the simplistic capitulation to the atheist's proposal. The disjunctive relation of God to the world that has developed recently will be shown to be the signal of changes in cultural experience with far-reaching consequences. These consequences can be interpreted only if we are willing to remain open to experience in all its guises.

The revolt against the concept of God was brought about through a recognition of the fact of *control* as the defining characteristic of the relations of God to the world. With the deaths of God, the world is "out of control." The question raised by this condition is whether there is any alternative to the political character of the relations of the world and God. The affirmative answer we shall eventually be giving to this question must await articulation until after we have examined each of the remaining relationships that organize our cultural paradigm.

PERSONS OR NATURE

Unlike the concept of God as Supreme *Arche*, the idea of nature has a significant history prior to the wedding of the Hellenic and Hebraic conceptualizations. By the time of Aristotle's exile from Athens in 323 B.C., which marked the end of classical Greek philosophical activity, all the principal concepts of nature that were to play a part in the development of Western culture had already been examined with some subtlety. And though these concepts were to undergo some changes when introduced into an essentially theistic frame-

work at the beginnings of the Middle Ages, the changes were
not major; the concepts of God that were to be employed in
Anglo-European culture would be characterized in terms of
the same semantic contexts as were the various conceptions of
nature.

The investigation of *physis*, or "nature," had its beginnings in our culture with the Ionian Greeks, who asked after
the nature of *things*. The search for the meaning of *physis* was,
at the same time, a search for the *arche*, the origin, source, or
principle, of things. What is supposed to distinguish the philosophers of ancient Greece from the mythmakers is precisely
their differing attitudes toward the notion of beginnings.
Cassirer, as we have seen, tries to defend the uniqueness of
philosophy vis-à-vis cosmogony by virtue of the presumed
logos character of the former as distinguished from the mythical character of the latter. Claiming that mythical thinking
searches out a "commencement in time" while philosophy
seeks a "first principle," Cassirer finds in the Milesian
physicists the source of a rational consideration of beginnings.[26] In terms of the argument of this present work, however, such a claim is markedly beside the point. The function
of both mythical and philosophical *archai* as determining
sources of order ensures that the characterization of logos is
functionally identical with that of *mythos*.

Physis or *natura* is "that which is." It is the source of
motion, or activity, the ground of existence, variously described as water (Thales), *aer* (Anaximenes), material atoms
(Democritus), numbers (Pythagoras), Ideas or Forms (Plato).
Characterizations of the nature of things by the time of
Aristotle included notions grounded in materialist, formalist,
teleological, and rhetorical terms. The addition of the Judaeo-
Christian concept of God to the cultural paradigm provided a
supernatural context in which to place the various meanings of
the concept of nature developed in Greek philosophy. In addition to nature, there must be something above or beyond the
natural world. That is, besides *physical* being there must be
meta-physical being as well. The tendency to understand the
Greek term "metaphysical" in accordance with the Latin
"supernatural" was consistent with the need to subordinate

nature to God as creator. And though such an interpretation is based on a misunderstanding of the use of the Greek *ta meta ta physika* (which probably referred merely to the placement of Aristotle's work on first principles "after" his *Physics*), it signaled, early on, the tendency of the Western metaphysical tradition to view the fate of the concept of *physis* as physical nature in terms of the character and destiny of the transcendent being that our theological tradition has identified as God.

The principles employed to interpret the meanings of nature conform to the dominant theoretical systems already rehearsed. The Greek interpretation of nature as mind dependent or mind-like was advanced by Pythagoras and Plato, among others. The supposition that the structure of thinking and the structure of that which is real are one and the same forms the fundamental principle of formalist thought. The names of Leucippus and Democritus are associated with the materialistic or mechanistic interpretation of nature. For these thinkers "atoms and empty space" are the elements in accordance with which all things may be explained. The Aristotelian interpretation of nature in terms of aim-oriented, organic growth and change constituted perhaps the most rigorous and complex consideration of the nature of things in ancient philosophy. Finally, the Sophistic tradition claimed simply that "man is measure of all things; of things that are, that they are; and of things that are not, that they are not." This view of Protagoras and other Sophists introduced what in our age has come to be recognized as the notion of conceptual relativity.[27]

The principal answers our culture has given to the question "What is the nature of things?" have been four: nature is a field of patterned structures; a complex of organisms in interaction the activities of which are goal-directed; a blind swirl of atoms in empty space; or the rhetorical constructions of human beings for instrumental purposes. The history of our understanding of nature recounts the interplay of each of these four basic types of conceptualization. Because of the increasing importance of the cultural interest of science, the scientific conceptualizations of nature have usually dominated our understandings of that which is. And even though classical science did not emerge until quite late in our culture, the pre-scientific understandings of nature were such as to prepare the way for the scientific understanding of the natural world.

R. G. Collingwood, in his *The Idea of Nature*, articulates well the various changes in our understanding of nature from the Greek to the modern period. There have been three distinct periods in our understanding of nature: the Greek, the classical, and the modern. The Greek view was grounded in "the principle that the world of nature is saturated or permeated by mind."[28] Reason or mind was thought to constitute the source of order or regularity in nature. Greek science was thus rationalistic in the sense that it stressed the intelligibility of the natural world. Collingwood does not ignore the fact that the materialist, naturalist, and volitional interpretations of nature were present in Greek culture; he merely claims that what we have termed the formalist vision was the dominant image of nature in the Hellenic period. This understanding of nature in terms of ideas, forms, or patterns provided an important impetus toward the development of a rational science of nature.

The second major period Collingwood outlined is the Renaissance cosmology of the sixteenth and seventeenth centuries. For the Renaissance thinkers, beginning with Copernicus, the understanding of nature shifted away from one that saw nature permeated by mind toward one that was baldly mechanistic. Mind, in the form of a divine creator and ruler, was placed outside of nature. The Renaissance cosmologists saw nature modeled after the fashion of "a machine in the literal and proper sense of the word, an arrangement of bodily parts designed and put together and set going for a definite purpose by an intelligent mind outside itself."[29] Greek science, as Collingwood describes it, was based on the analogy between nature and human existence. The microcosm, represented by the individual psyche, serves as the basis for understanding the macrocosm of nature. The Renaissance view of nature, on the other hand, was grounded in the analogy between human and *mechanical* behavior. With the entrance of the idea of an omnipotent God, the construction of the mechanistic analogy was easily enough accomplished.

"As a clockmaker or millwright is to a clock or mill, so is God to Nature." [30]

The third cosmological moment characterized by Collingwood is that of modern cosmology, which had its beginnings in the second half of the eighteenth century with those historical writings (e.g., Turgot, Voltaire) that emphasized growth, change, and development. The stress on progress, translated to the sphere of natural science in the writings of Erasmus and Charles Darwin, Lamarck, and others, became the basis for the new conception of nature. The modern view of nature "is based on the analogy between the processes of the natural world as studied by natural scientists and the vicissitudes of human affairs as studied by historians." [31] The modern view stresses progressive, goal-oriented development and, therefore, affirms the organic vision of nature and natural processes. The focus is not so much on nature as a complex of substantial things as on the functions of the organisms in nature necessary to achieve their proper ends.

Each of these views of nature has its own special excellence. The Greek supports the presumption of a relation of persons and nature grounded upon the mind-like or mind-dependent status of the latter. When coupled with a vision of God as Supreme *Arche* functioning as the repository of the ideal or formal structures that provide the map of nature, this conceptualization nourished the strain of rationalism that has served as the primary *methodos* making possible the search for *a priori* truth and certainty. The classical view simplifies the meaning of nature by construing it in terms of external relations that can be described in materialistic or mechanistic terms. This construal allows for the construction of visible models of natural process that, so imitated, serve as the paradigms for mechanical invention and construction. When coupled with the concept of God as Great Mechanic, this view promotes the vision of the universe as a closed, mechanically determined, system completely understandable in causal terms. The modern concept of nature progressed from a concern with the mechanical to a concern with the organic aspects of nature, but maintained a causal, empirical emphasis expressed through the interpretation of nature in terms of quasi-historical principles and goals closely associated with the presumed "struggle for survival." Nonetheless, the naturalist view, when combined with a conception of God as the Telos of Nature, encouraged the interpretation of the relation of persons and nature in terms of long-range, transcendent goals that organized human existence and justified man's predominant place in the natural world.

Near the middle of the twentieth century, when Collingwood made his last additions to the manuscript that was to become *The Idea of Nature*, he thought that the future of cosmology ought to lie in the hands of those who were proceeding along the lines of some version of modern cosmology. But he also recognized that there was a significant challenge to that cosmology. Toward the end of his work, commenting on the possible direction of future cosmological speculation, he said "I have no guarantee that the spirit of natural science will survive the attack which now, from so many sides, is being made upon the life of human reason."[32] I believe that if Collingwood were alive today he might be extremely pessimistic about the possible survival of the "life of reason." For not only has the attack on reason he cited increased in vehemence; it has come to characterize the latest approach to the understanding of nature. Collingwood's modern cosmology has taken its place alongside the Greek and Renaissance views as a discarded alternative.

The new cosmology is variously expressed in terms of the operational, conventional, or behavioral orientations, which, as we have seen, are expressed most directly in terms of the instrumental characterization of nature. The volitional or instrumental approach to the understanding of the natural world has risen to dominance in our culture for reasons not unlike those that brought it briefly to the fore at the end of the Hellenic age. The breakdown of the intellect as a means of discovering truth, or of providing principles for the modeling of natural processes, or of defining proper ends or values, has caused that failure of nerve to which humans who are wont to see themselves as rational beings are always open.

If we should seek the dominant contemporary view of

nature, again characterizing what appears to be the principal approach of the natural sciences, I think we would find that it is distinctly instrumentalist. For contemporary theory of nature, like contemporary thought in general, is performed at the level of the meta-conscious we have previously described. Having raised to the level of consciousness each of the previously dominant paradigms for natural science—the idealist, the mechanistic, and evolutionary naturalism—and finding no logical, theoretical, or *empirical* reason for preferring one view to the others, theorists of nature have capitulated to the belief that science ought to seek only instrumental concepts. Accepting nature and its laws as *conventions* of the scientific community, natural scientists have reverted to a position first constructed by the Sophists of ancient Greece during a time of similar crisis and have ordained that, within broad limits, nature is as human beings determine it to be. The men who are "the measures of all things" are those who constitute the scientific and technological community. Now the meaning of "convention" is determined by the prevailing sense of "convenience." In our society that sense derives mainly from the technological state of mind that characterizes the aim of scientific understandings in terms of its instrumental power to organize and control the ecosystem.

The instrumentalist understanding of nature may not be satisfactory to those scientists who have prided themselves on being the guardians of and searchers after truth. The fact that we have tried and found wanting each of the various characterizations of nature leaves many of us in a dilemma much more severe than that posed by the deaths of God. For we would find it quite difficult to cease believing in nature! Unlike atheism, total skepticism has never claimed many adherents.

The instrumentalist understanding has captured each of the other cosmological orientations. When the instrumental motivation is raised to the level of consciousness within the formalist, mechanist, and naturalist perspectives, we find the emergence of conventionalist, behaviorist, and operationalist methodologies, respectively. These are the ways in which the traditions alternative to the volitional, each in accordance with its own distinctive genius, have recognized the element of

arbitrariness involved in rational claims and so have advertised the seriousness of the crisis in our understanding of the
relation of persons and nature.

These four contemporary philosophic methods, or movements, can best be understood as theoretical perspectives
within the epistemology of science aimed at acceding to the
collapse of the idealist conception of truth as the guiding principle of reasonings and action. The behaviorist, working within the mechanistic perspective, finds the end of reason in the
description of the behaviors, or motions, of the objects of
study. The conventionalist, in his formalist guise, claims that
theoretical concepts do not, and perhaps cannot, necessarily
reflect the order of things, but only the order of nature as
human minds are variously compelled to entertain it. Naturalist theories examine theoretical concepts as emergent from the
problematic situations that accompany the interactions of an
organism and its environment, emphasizing the operational
characteristics by defining all theoretical concepts in terms of
measuring operations involving the entities stipulated or described by the theory. Finally, instrumentalism envisions concepts and theories as instruments promoting the organization,
prediction, and control of events.

It is important to clarify the distinctive contribution of the
behavioral, conventionalist, operationalist, and directly
instrumentalist understandings of nature, especially since the
naïve presumption of the homogeneity of thought and practice
within the so-called scientific community is so much a part of
our cultural common sense. Often the confusions among these
various methodologies is unintentional. Almost as often, however, the attempt is made to combine them, in the hope that
the theoretical defects manifest in one orientation will be
rectified by an alternative view, and vice versa. But such
activity only postpones the recognition of the poverty of
theory per se.

It may well be impossible to attain semantic purity with
regard to these specific perspectives, particularly since the
terms to describe them are so often used interchangeably. But
we ought always to keep in mind the divergent orientations
regarding the critique of reason so as not to impoverish our

understanding of the complex arguments these critiques manifest. For while it is true, and for reasons I have tried to spell out in some detail, that the instrumentalist, power-oriented, volitional perspective is most in evidence among the various critiques of reason, it can hardly be otherwise than that once the volitional critique is made, each of the other perspectives must see its own rational foundations begin to crumble.

There is an instrumentalist bias implicit in each of the critiques of reason that emerges only if the presuppositions of the critiques and the consequences of accepting these presuppositions are raised to the level of consciousness. The idealist as reluctant conventionalist can stress the noetic function of theories only as long as he does not have to face the full consequences of the relativity of theoretical commitments. For then he must recognize the rhetorical character of the attempt consciously to persuade anyone of his theory. The naturalist as operationalist can remain satisfied with his approach to rationality only as long as there is the possibility of maintaining some organic relationship among beliefs in a given field of inquiry. Since beliefs are "habits of action,"[33] conflicts of practice announce differences of belief, and contradictory beliefs are expressed in serious conflicts in practice. The recognition of theoretical relativity both announces and is a consequence of conflict in the realm of praxis. In times of disciplinary, social, and cultural upheaval, it becomes necessary to impose standards capable of producing the minimal forms of organization among the members of a community of inquiry. Such imposition requires a resort to the means of power that cannot be justified in the context of naturalistic theory.

Materialists who employ the behaviorist orientation are better off than either the frustrated idealist seeking some scraps of knowledge, or the naturalist struggling to maintain some field of interaction that allows for the acceptance of common standards of measurement in the provision of operational concepts and theories; for all that is required from the behavioral standpoint is the simplest possible situation defined by stimulus–response or cause–effect paradigms. The difficulty is that behaviorism, as behavioral technology, must, as *all* technical reasonings must, obtain its ends or goals from somewhere else. The behaviorist must be subject to the value determinations of those outside himself. At times this means that he is asked to achieve ends grounded in principles that deny his economical vision of the nature of things. This is unavoidable since it is those who are persuaded most of the humanistic rhetoric, such as leaders in politics, business, and education, who most often fund the behavioral scientist. The ludicrousness of behavioral technologies employed as image-building devices in political elections, or to promote free enterprise and individual initiative in business, or to persuade students of their possibility to realize freedom and dignity— values unacceptable to the behaviorist theories that supply the means to realize these ends—does not escape even the partially benumbed wit of the behavioral technologist. And along with the embarrassed realization that the ends entailed by behaviorist means are partially subverted by the necessity to pursue rhetorically determined goals comes the recognition that the behaviorist perspective is simply one more instrument in the hands of the volitionalist who, consciously engaged in the quest for power, has achieved the level of methodological awareness ahead of the critics of rationality emerging within alternate points of view.

The instrumentalist interpretation of the relation of persons and nature is, in part, a consequence of the collapse of the relation of God as Supreme *Arche* to his created order. As C. F. von Weizsäcker has noted, "with the transition . . . to modern times, the emphasis in the thought and life of man is clearly moving away from God, toward the world. But now the world consists in the duality of man and nature."[34] The duality of persons and nature is patterned after the traditional conception of the relation of God and the world, which means that the function of nature in regard to persons is defined instrumentally as *control*. Evolutionary history construed as biological, social, or technical development is "no longer a drama enacted between God and the world, but a process that carries its power and justification within itself."[35] The power is the power of instrumentalized nature. The justification is

that of scientific theory, which itself is both cause and consequence of the instrumentalizing of our concepts of nature.
"Only that is still comprehensible to us which is of our
making. It has become clearer than ever before that knowledge and power belong together."[36] Werner Heisenberg
echoes these words when he claims that, with the rise of contemporary science, "every advancement of knowledge was
connected with the question as to what practical use could be
derived from it."[37] Natural science, in its theoretical mode,
now becomes meta-science since it deals with the character of
the relationship between persons and nature. Thus, "the science of nature does not deal with nature itself, but in fact with
the *science* of nature as man thinks and describes it."[38]

The instrumentalist understanding of the relations of
persons and nature reflected in recent epistemologies of science is but a consequence of the relationship of God to the
world as we have come to understand it. The deaths of God
result in our laying bare the instrumental character of our
relations with our natural ambience since the source of power
has shifted away from God as a legitimizing principle toward
human beings who themselves must now take responsibility
for the consequences of their actions in relation to nature.
These consequences are considerable, and largely negative.
The struggle to dominate nature has produced an ecological
crisis that challenges the viability of our instrumentalist
understanding of nature while stimulating us to struggle even
harder for the control of nature we are very nearly in danger of
losing. For we have not maintained the control of nature without experiencing the threat of the rebellion of nature against
us. Whether it be "the return of the irrational"[39] expressed by
primitivism in art or by the mass psychoses that from time to
time pattern our cultural development, or the revolt of our
ecosystem evidenced by the feedback effect of pollution and
waste upon our natural ambience, it is clear that the rationalization and instrumentalization of both psychic and physical
nature have not gone unavenged.

Even if it were possible to accept the complete relativity
of theoretical perspectives and to employ the operational or
instrumentalist view of nature, accepting whichever theoret-

ical paradigm happened to suit our present needs and suppressing the question of *truth* in favor of the criterion of *fruitfulness*, we should not be better off. For our views of nature cannot be detached from the Judaeo-Christian paradigm in which they have had to find their place. And the requisite interpretation of nature from within that perspective must always include the notion of a distinction between *human* nature and nature per se. It is just this distinction that has contributed so profoundly to the ecological crisis faced by every advanced technological society. The distinction of persons and nature, and the supposition that it is the duty, and destiny, of human beings to control nature, have led to a set of attitudes toward the natural environment that promise a total fouling of our nest if a dramatic change of our relationship to nature is not forthcoming.

It appears, then, that the concept of nature and of our relations to it that would best suit our present needs is one that leads us away from the exploitation of our environment and into a cooperative relation with it. But who really expects such a change? Far more likely than a redefinition of nature, and our relations to it, will be the last-minute attempt to solve our ecological problems through technological means. For, unlike industrial processes that have resulted in waste and pollution, technology seeks the most efficient use of energy and resources. It seems likely that our ecological crisis will be one of the prime determinants in the development of a vast, complex, and ubiquitous techno-system. We can expect no serious movement back to nature; rather, we shall see a movement forward to technology. The question of the proper attitude toward nature will be academic until such time as technology has completed its work. For the only viable solution to the problems resulting from our centuries-long assault on nature seems to be that we cannot survive partial control, but must proceed to a *complete* control of nature.

What the instrumentalist interpretation of nature has taught us is that what we had all along assumed to be the study of nature was, in fact, an investigation of the relationship between persons and nature, and in particular, of that relationship as characterized by the motivations of control and domination. The instrumentalist conception of theory showed us how to employ theory as an instrument of control and conquest. "Nature" has always been a culturally defined term. And, as such, the meaning of human personality has largely determined the status of nature as the object of human domination. As God's deputy, man has sought to subdue "fallen" nature construed as hostile and refractory.

The deaths of God that have left the deputy temporarily in charge of the created order exacerbate the crisis with regard to nature by raising to the level of consciousness the issue of the domination of nature and its ecological consequences. And whereas the concept of God has had relatively autonomous characterizations throughout our history, the concept of nature, in modern times at least, has been decided by the current view of the scientific interest. The formalist vision of nature prepared the way for the succeeding views by promoting the belief in the mathematical intelligibility of the natural world, while stressing the mind-dependent status of nature. The mechanistic concept of nature perpetuated an understanding of the external relatedness of events in nature and of persons to nature that supported the belief in the dependence of the natural world on the manipulative and constructive activities of human beings. The naturalist view stressed progress and future-oriented action disciplined by aims or goals, one of which was the progressive domination of nature. Finally, the volitional attitude toward nature promotes an instrumentalist understanding of the role of persons in relation to nature and succeeds in placing a capstone on the development of science from a cultural interest grounded in the disinterested approach to truth and knowledge to a complex technological activity seeking power over nature. We are forced now to attempt a re-evaluation of the relations of nature and persons upon which to build a viable future. This formidable task must be added to that of theological reconstruction called for by the collapse of the concept of God.

We saw that in order to save the conception of the world experienced in pluralistic and relativist terms, it was necessary to challenge the old conception of God. So, too, with regard to the conception of nature. We must redefine what it

means to be persons in relationship with nature if we are to
avoid the worst consequences of the ecological crisis that currently threatens us. This can be done because there is now the
possibility, for the first time in our tradition, of overcoming
the radical distinction presumed to exist between nature and
culture. For as we shall see in later chapters it is perfectly
possible to construe nature in terms of technological means
and activities, reducing, without pernicious consequences, the
conception of our natural ambience to the realm of culture,
and thereby transcending the traditional meanings of both
nature and culture as well. But, once more, we must postpone
the discussion of this novel development until after the consideration of the remaining elements of the cultural paradigm.

MALE OR FEMALE

Of the various relations that define the structure of our cultural paradigm, the most problematic is that expressed by the
interactions of male and female. This is the case since human
passion, which serves as the dynamism motivating these
interactions, has its origins in what should properly be the
private and intimate form of existence associated with human
sexuality. And the very intimacy of the context from which
the subject of passion emerges militates against its rationalization. We are most likely to encounter rationalized passion in
literary expressions that tell of the lover's frenzied excesses,
or of the artist's unremitting compulsion to create, or of the
driving need for greatness that leads some ambitious persons
to transcend themselves and their times. But literature tells
these tales in meter and metaphor that belie the erethic and
boundless character of passion.

The poet, however, is not half so futile as the scientist,
who in analyzing and cataloguing eros succeeds only in
advertising the dehumanizing consequences of passionless
activity. We may find a certain comfort in encountering passion through the purifying rhetoric of the poet or the sterilizing
statistics of the scientist. But passion celebrated by those
licensed to research our intimacies is but one more public fact.
And passion made public loses some of the intensity to be

found only in its original context. For this reason we must begin these comments with a reflection on the origin of passion in the private sphere associated with love as sexuality.

The understanding of passion may be sought through the institution of marriage or the concept of romantic love; it may be sublimated into a means of satisfying certain fundamental economic needs, or into the passionate striving for ideals; or it may be expressed as a dynamic ensuring the possibility of conquest. But each of these understandings blurs the distinction between the private and the public forms of passion. And though we cannot ignore the subject of passion as a public fact, we must view it initially in terms of the private and intimate context of its origins.

Our manner of discussing the concept of passion as an element in the cultural paradigm maintains a distinction between private and public forms of praxis that many post-Hegelian (pre-eminently Marxian) thinkers have not seen fit to emphasize. For Marx, praxis is sensuous productivity associated directly with economic activity. Art is reduced to *techne*, construable in terms of socially motivated productivity. Passion expressed in terms of the love relationship between two individuals cannot, for Marx, be isolated from the needs and demands of the economic sphere. Fine art, as truly as any other activity, is a function of the organization of the means of production, and of that alone.

It is certainly possible, however, to see praxis as a function of the demands of the private as well as of the public arenas. In such a vision, the arts, pure and applied, would result sometimes from motivations in one or the other spheres, and sometimes from tensions between the demands of public and private forms of existence. And though my final considerations about the form of the future will accede to the identification of art and *techne* in a way that bears superficial resemblance to Marxian theory, the consequences of my argument diverge greatly from the Marxian view.

The distinction between private and public forms of praxis implicit in the separate consideration of passion and social activity allows us to highlight an extremely important defect in many treatments of the concept of passion. That

defect is to be found in the handling of the notion of passion by
social philosophers. Marxian, existentialist, and pragmatic
philosophies have gone a long way toward revitalizing interest
in *action* and *production* as species of praxis, but the element
of feeling has suffered neglect all along. When contemporary
followers of Marx, or the pragmatists, complain about the
predominant stress on theory over practice in the history of
philosophy, they no doubt are justified. Nonetheless, they
share—for different reasons—a suspicion of intimate forms of
sensuousness. For all Marx's claims to have added sensuousness to the materialist conceptions of praxis, he added it only
as production, as making. The analysis of feeling per se,
whether the raw feeling that motivates activities of the most
primitive type or the acute intuitions and sensitivities of the
poet or mystic, is well-nigh omitted from consideration. The
complaint that theory has too often dominated practice is, of
course, justified. How much more justified are we, then, in
complaining of the champions of praxis that they succeeded
only in exchanging one form of tyranny for another? Action,
in the existentialist or pragmatic senses, or production, in the
Marxian, now bullies intuition and feeling in a manner not
unlike the way the demands of the intellect were once made to
dominate practical activity.

   In terms of its strictly cultural import, of course, passion
is not merely, or perhaps mainly, a private matter. It has
always extended beyond the sphere of intimacy and served as
one of the significant concepts characterizing the dynamics of
social existence. It was Freud, among contemporaries, who
employed the concept of eros as the *arche* determining the
character of human nature, social organization, and the
cosmos. Neo-Marxians sensitive to the deficiencies of Marx's
conception of praxis have recently begun to mine Freudian
theory for insights concerning the significance of eros as
arche. Since both Marx and Freud operated with materialistic
theoretical principles, the cross-fertilization of the Marxian
and Freudian conceptions of praxis has been particularly fruitful. But the concept of eros, as a reflection upon its various
historical adventures would indicate, may be characterized in
other than material terms. Indeed, the dominant form eros as

arche has taken in contemporary culture is to be understood in a broadly volitional manner.

The concept of passion as eros, as the drive toward the union of separated elements, is one of the three principal means of overcoming the chaos that is the presupposition of our beginnings. The primary elements of the cultural paradigm are directly tied to the cosmogonic myths that found our cultural self-understandings. God, as Trinitarian structure, is a reflection of the rational means of construing chaos that have come to be associated with the scientific and technological control of nature, with the power of rule that establishes the form of social relations between the individual and society, and with the element of love, which is the primary ingredient of the sphere of the private and the intimate relations among persons. "Love," "power," and "justice" are the names given to these forms of passion, action, and rationality at the level of social existence. The consideration of the concept of love on which we are about to embark will presuppose the concepts of God, nature, and social practice, which form the primary aspects of the complete cultural paradigm. And since, as we have repeatedly stressed, it is the element of power that dominates in these last days, the understanding of passion must begin by noting that the presumption of our culture that the elements of love, power, and justice are separate dynamics is increasingly open to doubt, since both love and justice are increasingly characterized in terms of the element of power.

One of the most provocative accounts of the concept of passion is found in Aristophanes' myth of the circle men in Plato's *Symposium*. The myth contains an account not only of the origins of love as eros, but of the beginnings of sexuality as well. In the beginning,

the sexes were not two as they are now, but originally three in number; there was man, woman, and the union of the two. . . . The primeval man was round, his back and sides forming a circle; and he had four hands and four feet, one head and two faces, looking opposite ways, set on a round neck and precisely alike; also four ears, two privy members, and the remainder to correspond. . . . Terrible was their might and strength, and the thoughts of their hearts were great, and they made an attack upon the gods.[40]

The councils of the gods deliberated as to how to deal with their insolence, and Zeus himself decided to punish them by dividing them in two. This he did, adding, "if they continue insolent and will not be quiet, I will split them again."[41] The splitting apart of the circle beings brought with it the beginnings of eros as a drive toward reunion of the separated halves. But the manner of Zeus's division threatened destruction of the human race, for when the two parts of a sundered being tried to unite, they merely became hopelessly entangled and prevented one another from autonomous activities. Thus they began to die of hunger and self-neglect.

> Zeus in pity of them invented a new plan: he turned the parts of generation round to the front . . . and they sowed the seed no longer as hitherto like grasshoppers in the ground, but in one another; and after the transposition the male generated in the female in order that by the mutual embraces of man and woman they might breed, and the race might continue; or if man came to man they might be satisfied, and rest, and go their ways to the business of life.[42]

Unfortunately for our general cultural understanding of passion, Aristophanes' account of the origins of eros and sexuality has not often been taken seriously. As one classicist remarks, "It would be vain to look for any very deep meaning in this very amusing piece of writing,"[43] and his words summarize a general attitude toward Aristophanes' mythical tale. Apparently the combination of Platonic irony and the low comedy of Aristophanes is simply too much for most of us. The deadly flaw in us, and in all satiric humor because of us, is that we tend to laugh only if the irony or satire points away. For this reason, though tragedy requires a noble protagonist, comedy demands something rarer still—a noble audience.

The ironic truth Aristophanes wished us to understand? Just this: eros, as the drive toward the reunion of the separated, has about it an irrefragable reference to the body. Eros is the drive to reunite separated bodies. But eros antedates specifically sexual desire, at least in the form of a physical tension. Such desire, which we have come to interpret in this post-Freudian age as *libido* (Greek: *epithymia*), has a strange relation to eros as Aristophanes describes it. For it is difficult to interpret *libido* as the desire for sexual *union* since it is precisely the orgasm, the end of sexual activity, that brings release from sexual desire, and from union as well.

Aristophanes distinguishes the procreative aim of sexual intercourse from its recreative function, implicitly finding in homosexual love a purer expression of sexuality unqualified by the procreative urge. The insight here is that whenever the procreative function of sex is replaced by the recreative, all contributions of eros as the drive toward the unity of separated halves are lost. The aim of exclusively sexual contact is to achieve release from that desire for union that prevents individuals from meeting their survival needs. After sexual climax, the partners may "go their ways to the business of life." Eros seeks union; sexual intercourse has as its fundamental aim *independence*.

The subtle insight into the psychology of sex contained in Aristophanes' account has often led to romanticizing about the *tristes d'amour*, but it has seldom led to the ironic conclusion that Aristophanes wished us to draw—viz., that the aims of desire and the aims of eros are fatally contradictory. It is not that this contradiction has gone unrecognized; it is that the irony has not been appreciated. Plato recognized the fact and sought to overcome the conflict by sublimating physical desire and defining love entirely in terms of a transcendent eros. Freud, at the end of our epoch, recognized it and sought to reduce eros to its material significance as a form of tension reduction associated with the pleasure–pain principle and, ultimately, with the tension between love and death. Perhaps closer than Plato to appreciating the irony of Aristophanes, he was as guilty as Plato of onesidedness. Whereas Plato saw in the soul's eros the guarantee of immortality with the achievement of ultimate union, Freud saw, as any materialist must, that the final victory would be awarded to death, the ultimate reduction of tension. In both cases there is a failure to recognize the ironic character of the relations of love and sex, and of the strange hybrid, which can only be named with a term that itself hints at contradiction, "sexual love."

According to Aristophanes, eros is originally a drive toward physical union without the blessings of sexual climax, which could make this drive manageable. The low-comedic ludicrousness of Aristophanes' imagery aside, how *does* one unite with the object of one's eros in other than a transitory, sexual manner? Lucretius describes the ultimate frustration of the drive toward physical union well when he says: "They greedily clasp each other's body and suck each other's lips and breathe in, pressing meanwhile teeth on each other's mouth; all in vain, since they can rub nothing off nor enter and pass, each with his whole body, into the other's body; for so sometimes do they seem to will and strive to do: so greedily are they held in the chains of Venus."[44] Without the blessing of sexual climax, such striving for unity would be disastrously consuming. Eros, as distinguished from desire, is not oriented sexually, but seeks the overcoming of separation. The love that at the human level can establish a lasting union cannot find its energy in sexual desire. Such a love seeks interpretation in terms of the sharing of common ideals, the forgoing of the bonds of friendship based on equality, or the establishment of a lasting union through conquest and interdependence.

We have already referred to Plato's resolution of the conflict of eros and sexual desire. In the *Symposium* Plato has Socrates characterize eros in this manner: It is the search for "true beauty—the divine beauty . . . pure and clear and unalloyed, not clogged with the pollutions of mortality and all the colors and vanities of human life."[45] Socratic eros loses its interpersonal reference and becomes a love that is expressed in a desire to unite with that which is fulfilling because it is more perfect than the lover.

Eros in this transcendent sense presupposes a concern for the process of self-perfection through the striving after determinate ideals. A contemporary interpreter of Socratic eros states simply that eros "strives for a union with that which is a bearer of values because of the values it embodies."[46] It seeks union with the sources of those values that sustain a cultural complex. The scientist's passion for truth, the artist's passion for beauty—each must be explained in terms of the quality of eros as a fundamental aspect of that love expressing itself in individual creativity. Socratic eros, at a personal level, is expressed as the desire for union with an individual as a bearer of some value.

Eros in its classical sense depends on an intuition of value existing in the object of erotic attachment. That intuition must be grounded in a sense of ultimate value. Plato used the concept of eros to name that dynamism of the human psyche that urged it toward transcendent understanding. In Christian mysticism God is the object of the soul's eros. Since the emergence of dogmatic theology within Judaeo-Christianity, the use of eros in the search for truth and holiness has been such an embarrassment to orthodox faith that theologians have sought to extirpate this concept of love from our religious tradition. The reason for this attempted rejection of eros lies in Christianity's introducing into the literature of our tradition the concept of *agape*. Unlike Socratic eros, which is a striving after an ideal, a love by an "inferior" for something "superior," agape is love expressed as an unselfish concern for the beloved. Agape is love by the fulfilled for the unfulfilled. As such, agape can be expressed only by God. Persons are recipients of agape, and only insofar as they may be a channel of God's love can they be said to approximate agape in their relationships. Agape is love freely given; it does not ask after the value of the love-object. Thus it is *spontaneous* and *unmotivated*. "When it is said that God loves man this is not a judgment on what man is like, but on what God is like." [47] According to this strict theological tradition, agape is "God-centered" love, and eros "man-centered." Love, as eros, cannot be accepted in this tradition because there is no viable route leading from man to God, unless it be initiated by God. Since the notion of striving for God comes perilously close to Pelagianism, heartily condemned by the Christian church, attempts within Christian theology to provide a place for eros alongside agape have been without significant influence. It is only within the mystical tradition that the concept of eros has had any influence at all. But the general dominance of dogmatic over mystical theology has mitigated any real effect it might have had upon the agape tradition.

Thus, in addition to the possibility that love would be confused with sexual desire, there was, after the advent of

Christianity, a strong tradition that identified love with agape—self-sacrificing, altruistic love. It was Christian theology that was largely responsible for the use of the concept of agape as a standard according to which all loves are to be judged. The first great theological synthesis, that of Augustine, did not altogether ignore the Greek concept of eros. Indeed, the natural striving of creatures after God was a presupposition of the Augustinian synthesis of love and will. But with the increased rationalization of religion in the Christian West, a process completed only in post-Reformation theologies, the eros character of love had increasingly to be suppressed in favor of the doctrine of the extreme transcendence of God.

The effect of the orthodox Christian interpretation of love was to deny validity to *libido* by identifying desire, or lust, with the sexual drive resulting from the Fall, and to understand erotic love in terms of the idealized concept of agape. Thus was eros secularized and denied any transcendent meaning. And eros without transcendence is expressed either as *epithymia*, simple desire, or else, as the love of conquest, *seduction*.

Moreover, the recent collapse of each of the conceptions of God as Supreme *Arche* has brought about a transvaluation and inversion of the concepts of eros and agape in which eros as love of conquest is complemented by agape as a form of adulation or "hero-worship." Thus libido serves to support a kind of narcissism, while eros and agape, in their degenerate forms, combine to promote sado-masochistic expressions of love.

The one remaining form of love that holds some promise for the promotion of humane forms of relationship has fared no better than the other three. *Philia*, or friendship, is meant to be the love among equals. According to Aristotle, who considered the topic of friendship in great detail in his *Nicomachean Ethics*,[48] true friends seek neither pleasure nor utility in their relationship but base their feelings upon the character of the other. *Libido*, based on simple desire, and eros and agape, each presupposing an inequality, are supplemented by *philia*, which is grounded on mutuality. Friendship is perhaps the only love that promotes the aims of mutuality. And *philia*, in contradistinction to each of the other loves, thrives on publicity. *Philia*, as the love of one's fellows, grounds the sense of community beyond the positivity of law and power, and is most obviously associated with the structure of society. The institution of friendship serves to bind the community of equals in the public sphere of a society. But, as we shall see when we consider the subject of "social practice," the general ill-health of society as a context in which public forms of togetherness may be found precludes the sense of individuality upon which the possibility of *philia* relationships is based.

Contemporary expressions of love can be articulated in terms of the traditional notions of eros, agape, philia, and epithymia, provided we recognize the transmutations of these concepts. The principal symptom of these transmutations is the contemporary discussion of the tensions between love and sexual desire. As Aristophanes' myth suggested, the origins of love and sexuality are of such a different nature as to determine an inevitable conflict between the two, since eros strives for permanent union and sexual desire has as its primary function the temporary overcoming of the necessity of union. Sexual encounter can be no more than a means of verifying Oscar Wilde's droll insight that "The only way to avoid temptation is to yield." Contemporary forms of sexuality advertise this aspect of sexual desire, since sex separated from love is more often a means of avoiding relationships than of promoting them. Libido translated into desire for transitory pleasure can lead away from relationship and toward anonymous forms of sexuality.

Love primarily motivated by the sexual drive is self-contradictory, for the aim of love as the overcoming of separation is in direct conflict with the principle of libido, which is grounded in the drive toward autonomy. Zeus invented sexual intercourse primarily in order that the drive toward union of the separated halves should not prevent individuals from pursuing their own activities. "Sexual release" is a release from the need for union and interdependence. As such, sexual intercourse is a disciplining agency ensuring that the reunion of lovers will be viable because it will be, in its most direct form—the form of the embrace—quite brief.

The separation of sexual intercourse from the various forms of the love relationship advertises the fact that the immanent principle to be realized in libidinal activity is the principle of autonomy and independence. Insofar as one may speak of the goal of libidinal sexuality as involving relationship, it is the relatedness to an anonymous partner as an object of narcissistic fantasy fulfillment that is sought. Traditionally it has been prostitution that has provided such an anonymous partner.

The anonymity is carried one step further through the institution of the massage parlor dedicated to so-called "erotic massage." The onesided character of the activity is nearly complete in this instance. But not quite. Sexual technology has provided access to libidinal satisfactions through the instrumentation of auto-eroticism. Mechanical and electrical masturbators provide, according to their advertising, the "ultimate in satisfaction" and "without the hassle of waiting for an available partner." Such auto-erotic techniques, in conjunction with the artificially enriched fantasies provided by the pornography industry, allow us to realize the goal of libidinal sexuality. Narcissistic sensuality and voyeuristic peep-show stimulation make a mockery of any concept of desire disciplined by the drive toward the reunion of the separated. Pornography, pornophony, and pornesthesia are the ways we parody the concept of desire and announce our sensual numbness.

But it is precisely at this point that we begin to recognize the really crucial issue determining the character of our sexual self-expressions. It is that we have begun to realize the true character of the alienation that it is the task of eros to overcome. We remember the threat of Zeus—"If they remain insolent . . . , I will split them again"—and recognize that we are the victims of that further division. The function of sexuality—whether as procreation, recreation, or the strictly creative activities of the artist—is to achieve self-unification. This is easily seen if we look at the artistic activities in contemporary society. Art as expression, as opposed to mere "allusion" or "mention,"[49] has taken as its aims the achieving of pleasure or power. Fantasy and ideology are its forms, narcissism and sado-masochism its motivating energies. Fantasy becomes important when the pleasure derived from mundane objects can no longer be direct. Ideology becomes important when power has lost its rationale. But fantasy and ideology exact a price. The creators of fantasy, and those too who consume it, are narcissistic to the extent that pleasure is achieved directly from fantasy. But fantasy employed as a means to the achievement of a goal inevitably becomes ideology promoting the sado-masochistic response to power.

Although the most prominent attempts to overcome self-alienation have depended on social and political ideologies of a broadly Marxian perspective, some few artists have begun to search within the self and to articulate their individuality in terms of introspective fantasies aimed at self-realization. The body as the means of experiencing pleasure may be celebrated by the artist quite apart from the political orientation that finds in the objective conditions of society the grounds for self-alienation. Granted that the politicization of passion has dominated and continues unabated, we must not overlook the efficacy of private forms of aesthetic expression which seek novel stratagems for self-actualization.

The crisis with regard to the conception of passion has led to the increased concern with love as an expression of power. The sexual liberation movements—feminism, gay liberation, and so on—are grounded in the need for autonomy and self-determination in terms of sexual relations. The recognition that the sexual relation has political characteristics has led to the declaration of freedom from traditional modes of relationship. The extreme of this declaration has come with regard to the issue of sexual freedom, of course, but it is not limited to the sexual aspects of human passion. Art itself seems to be slowly feeling its way toward a revolution in aesthetic sensibility that recognizes the radical nature of the changes in human relationship.[50]

It is a short step from the recognition of sexual activity as a means of achieving autonomy and independence to the understanding that auto-eroticism is the primary means of achieving such autonomy. Passion as sexual desire then becomes a private celebration, a masturbatory episode. The end of sexuality, implicit in its origins, is realized with the winning of sexual independence. Passion as the drive for union disciplined by the strictly sexual drive becomes a dynamic that aims at the overcoming of self-alienation and the unification of the divided self.

This may turn out to be a positive development if the alterations in the institution of heterosexuality promised by contemporary liberation movements continue apace. For if heterosexuality continues to be interpreted solely in terms of strictly libidinal satisfactions, the social inequality of females vis-à-vis males will prevent the self-actualization of women to the same degree possible to men. As is the case with the relations of God to the world and of persons to nature, it is necessary to redefine the male–female relationship if we are to save what has been considered its subordinate member. Unless this is done, the realization of the immanent principle of sexuality in terms of fantasy and ideology will simply mean that males will continue to realize their integrity at the expense of females, who will serve primarily as fantasy objects or as passive partners in sado-masochistic relationships. If the presumed complementarity of the sexes is to be realized, and thus is to serve as the model for the overcoming of individual self-alienation, the political character of the sexual and interpersonal forms of love must be subverted.

SOCIETY OR THE INDIVIDUAL

Our traditional attitudes toward social and political authority have been determined in part by theological beliefs developed within the Judaeo-Christian tradition. The covenental relations between God and man in the Old Testament entailed a set of social obligations to other members of one's community as well as political obligations to the sovereign powers of the social order. The erosion of respect for political authority is a result of the slow development of a secular and positivistic concept of society and the state. From the ancient alliance of priest and king, to the concept of the Divine Caesar, to the notion of the divine right of kings—which finally emerged in modern times as the rule of reason in accordance with natural law—to the contemporary notion of *Realpolitik* and the amorality of international relations, we have witnessed a trend toward the recognition of the artificiality of the institutions of state and society. But this recognition does little to provide viable alternatives to the social and political structures that have provided the context for individual existence and activity. We experience the arbitrariness of our public institutions and are alienated from them for that very reason. But since we believe public life must be maintained, we have no choice but to swallow our alienation and disillusionment and to accept our roles as citizens on grounds of self-interest alone. And since self-interest comes in all shapes and sizes in our pluralistic societies, we find that a social and political order cannot accommodate itself to the wants and wishes of all its members. The resulting loss of individual freedom is experienced as the loss of individuality itself.

Freedom within a social context has been variously described in terms of the possibility of significant choices or decisions limited by objective circumstances, as the intellectual freedom associated with the right to learn and to act in relation to one's knowledge, as the power to actualize one's individual and idiosyncratic personality, or, finally, as the result of determination in accordance with the contingencies of social, economic, and political conditioning. Though it is in this latter, materialistic, sense of freedom, best expressed by current forms of behavioral theory and practice, that the character of the objective environment takes on the greatest significance, it is obviously true that each concept of freedom as something more than mere abstract possibility depends upon the nature of the social structures within which an individual acts.

A society is composed of a number of interacting elements. First, there is a material substratum, a realm of *objects*, which as the result of or resource for human activity serves to provide the basic inventory of the social complex. In addition to the material order, there are *laws* that define the manner of relations within the material order and of the individuals of the society to that order and to one another. The *power* of a society is characterized principally in terms of the sanctions that undergird the laws. The final element is difficult to characterize; the closest one might get to defining it is in terms of the concepts of *ideal values* which serve as the defining characteristics of a society at the most abstract level, and which, in addition, qualify the significant actions of the influential persons and institutions in the social order. The relative achievements of a social order are the results of the realization of aims that either are consciously entertained or can be discovered *ex post facto* to have been the underlying motivations directing the energies of persons at the individual and institutional levels.

Each of these characteristic elements has served as the basis for theoretical interpretations of the nature of the social order. Idealist theories of society have stressed the element of ideals and have examined their intercommunication in terms of the forms of knowledge extant within the society. Naturalist theories have sought to articulate the organic character of the institutions of the society in terms of the rules or laws that guide their functioning. Materialist characterizations of society have examined the concepts of "material necessity" and the economic relationships that organize the means of producing the commodities that meet these basic needs. Volitional theories concentrate on the notion of political power, those who gain it and lose it, and the manner in which it is gained and lost. Theories of society that attempt to criticize the contemporary forms of social order must answer the question "What is wrong with our present societies?" in terms of the principal element isolated by the theoretical perspective. Together these various perspectives provide the basis for an indictment of the contemporary social order, which can be discussed in terms of the vulgarity of objects, the injustice of law, the oppressiveness of power, and the poverty of ideals.

The objective order of a society comprises those items that may be managed, consumed, or possessed. The principal elements of this order are the products of industry and the industrial processes that constitute the *thingliness* of the social world. In our contemporary societies, the objective order has undergone changes that (and this judgment is independent of the Marxian theory from which it usually arises) bode ill for the maintenance of ownership as a primary means of managing it. The increased complexity of industrial processes and the increased dependence of social stability on planned obsolescence require that goods and services be produced that have little durability. We can romanticize all we wish about the effect of this cheapening of our industrial products on the worker or on the potential purchaser of the goods, but Marxian apocalypticism to the contrary notwithstanding, little can be done to reverse the trend away from quality in the production of goods and services. The increased emphasis on use over ownership tends, of course, to dematerialize our social environment by identifying the quality of an object in terms of its function rather than its nature or character as an object. But until such time as we are able to transcend our need to possess things, the increasing vulgarity of objects will contribute to our sense of alienation from the purposes and direction of contemporary society.

The second element governing the structure of society, the element of *law*, has met with its own peculiar crisis in our technological milieu in large measure because of the near impossibility of attaining practical justice. Even in the commonest senses of justice as "the rendering each his due" or "the adjudication of rightful claims," it is almost impossible of attainment because of the increased variety and complexity of the ends of social action sought by members of society, and the conflict of right with right that must inevitably result. There are obvious wrongs in society that are capable of redress. But the real difficulty derives from the fact that the milieu of contemporary society has changed in so many ways, making unjust many attitudes, customs, and laws that formerly were above reproach. How, in any significant manner, can society alter the long history of injustices against blacks, Chicanos, Indians, women, and so on without completely transforming the status of contemporary social relations? Members of minority groups must choose whether to accept integration into the dominant society, with the consequent loss of cultural identity, in order to achieve some kind of equal rights, or to hold out for cultural autonomy at the risk of maintaining intolerable tensions with the dominant society.

The fact that laws applicable to *all* segments of society tend to be unjust to *some* segments is a function of the conflict of cultural ideals defining social activity and its products, and of the resulting rejection of dominant authority in the political sphere. If laws are experienced as unjust because of differential relevance or uneven application, the power providing the sanctions that stand behind the laws must be experienced as oppressive. Without the belief in the authority residing in those who exercise political power, nothing short of a profound sense of alienation can be the consequence of membership in a society.

As is the case with each of the other relations defining our cultural situation, it is the aspect of power that advertises the most crucial symptoms of cultural collapse. It is the sense of the illegitimacy of power exercised by social and political authorities over the individual that characterizes the weakened and rotting structures of our social order. Individuals are prone to deny the authority of those in power because of a sense of the vulgarity of objects, the injustice of law, and the poverty of ideals. This attitude toward authority will no doubt continue as long as these characteristic failings remain.

The laws of a society are rules that regulate the activities of the social organism in its pursuit of certain ideals. These cultural aims, as abstract values, are defining characteristics of a society. Cultural aims range from the most generic, such as "truth" and "goodness," to the slightly more specific values of "economic self-determination" or "technical efficiency." They are often entertained as contrasting pairs of values—freedom and equality, or beauty and utility—in such manner that one feels forced to choose the maximization of one value at the expense of its contrasting ideal. The "poverty of ideals" names a condition of contemporary society that has resulted from the awareness of a dearth of realizable values because of the generally impoverished condition of our cultural present.

The increasing emphasis on those values associated

almost exclusively with technological processes has caused a falling away of the past, which has resulted in a loss of significant alternative ideals. The abuse of those ideals we do profess stems from our failure to promote them for other than rhetorical ends, and has produced a sense of alienation and disillusionment. But beyond these symptomatic characteristics of our value crisis there lie other, more profound, issues. We find ourselves willing to accept the narrow and dull values of technological society and to brave the alienating hypocrisy of our contemporary leaders, principally because we no longer believe that the coordination of worthwhile ideals capable of promoting their harmonious realization is possible. We certainly do not claim to have any insight into the mind of God from which we could derive a sense of harmoniously realizable ideals. More specifically, we have lost a sense of generally applicable ideals because we find ourselves in a society with a rapidly disintegrating public arena, leaving us with a swollen sphere of the private and the personal.

The rise to dominance of the sphere of the private and the personal has threatened to alter completely the very basis of society as we have known it. Existence as an individual has been understood largely in terms of the ability to achieve something of value in the public sphere. And the desire for *greatness* has been the primary motivating factor in the lives and activities of those who would be understood as individuals. Not that everyone must strive for greatness; but there must be some models of the truly great if there is to be a dynamic and viable society. The striving for personal greatness has largely determined the romantic history of the race. Without that striving we should be hard put to realize values that are absolutely essential for existence in the public sphere—values such as *excellence, deference, risk,* and the irrational quality of *suffering,* which stands proof of risk.

When individuals achieve a certain excellence in some area of public life, be it politics or painting, deference on the part of others at once signals the recognition of that excellence and provides the most important reward for it. Both the achievement of excellence and the recognition of it are essentials for a worthwhile public life. In a pluralistic society in which innumerable excellences are recognized, almost everyone has the opportunity to achieve something excellent, and, conversely, no one is denied the opportunity to experience deference. A society that limits the possibility of attaining excellences to a specific class or caste, and in the course of so limiting does not allow the expression of deference among all classes and kinds of individuals in the public sphere, fails to exploit some real possibilities for the achievement of greatness.

The element of risk is necessary, of course, if there is to be any transcendence of the status quo. If the present degree of excellence is accepted as final and satisfactory, there would be no adventure, no search for new perfections. In open societies risk is the primary means by which one strives to increase one's status. But even in societies that have stressed the inheritance of excellence, risk has been at least symbolically important. Aristocratic societies have to provide those individuals who inherited their privileged positions with the proper training that not only would justify their position but would allow them to rewin their position if called upon to do so. Proving excellence by *improving* upon it is required because societies that are not to fall into a totally stale condition must provide not only models for realized excellence, but models for the manner in which new excellences might be achieved. Risk is the factor that produces the adventure of a society, and it is the single most important element in providing a warrant for the reasonably just distribution of power and privilege.

The contribution of suffering to the greatness of individuals and societies is hardest to understand. It is suffering that guarantees that risks have been taken. Perhaps there is no logic or reason in the requirement that individuals or societies manifest some degree of suffering before they are accorded proper deference, but it is nonetheless an easily recognized fact in any previous historical period. Without hardship, without sacrifice, without loss, there is no assurance that one's risk has been real. It is as if there were no maturity apart from suffering. As Whitehead has said, "Youth is life as yet untouched by tragedy." Tragedy, the loss of excellence by one who lays claim to greatness, is the fundamental form taken by suffering in the public sphere. No person of excellence can command authority unless he or she can demonstrate the proof of risk, which is suffering. If the hero does not combine daring with the demonstration that the risk is real—that he or she is risking death, or, what is worse, the loss of historic immortality—then he or she cannot hope to achieve any real greatness.

In a technological society, however, the values of excellence, deference, risk, and suffering are under attack. It is a truism that technology tends to level those distinctions that have served to define the primary relationships of social order. This is doubtless a virtue when those distinctions have been the more invidious ones associated with the relationships of privileged and oppressed classes. But the distinction between things of quality and excellence on the one hand, and mediocrity and cheapness, on the other, is one that cannot be sacrificed by a viable society. Excellence as a personal or publicly acclaimed value seems no longer desired, or even possible. No deference is to be shown where no excellences as idiosyncratic qualities are possible. Also no risk is desirable, or necessary. Risk becomes counter-productive, for what may redound to an individual's benefit in the short run is not likely to be of greatest long-term benefit for the entire society. The "back-up system" approach to technical advance is not only safest, but "best," in the long run. Where there is no risk, suffering becomes pointless and cruel. So we must be rid of it as well. Suffering, as proof of risk, is only proof of wasteful action in a society that must marshal its resources in the most efficient manner possible. Suffering must threaten the technical control of a recalcitrant nature that has not as yet yielded completely to the technological command. Suffering, that is to say, is inefficient; it is entropic; it is *immoral*.

Without excellence, deference, risk, and suffering, there can, of course, be no real greatness. And insofar as we think of life's meaning in terms of the search for, or appreciation of, personal greatness won in the public arena, we can in no way be happy with the developments of technological society. There can be no real greatness where uniformity is of high social value.

We shall continue to live under a cloud of Orwellian prophecy as long as we understand the character of our social organization in terms of the function of political power as sustaining public forms of togetherness. For as long as social practice is construed primarily in terms of the principle of political praxis, our experience of the oppressiveness of power will preclude the discovery or construction of viable objects, institutions, or ideals on which to ground our social commitments. Politics had its origin in, and has since been sustained by, a peculiar balance of public and private interests. The politician acts in public, but from private motives associated with the desire for personal greatness. To leave one's stamp on events in such manner as to find a place in history is the goal of the ambitious politician. But in a society that places little value on personal greatness, the politician is less inclined to ply his trade. Because politics depends upon a balance of private and public motivations, and because that balance no longer obtains in our contemporary society in its current state of transition, the quality of political life must be expected to suffer. Indeed the spectacle of a recent president of the United States risking his place in history through the incautious, unnecessary, and illegal manipulation of the powers of his office, while his vice president is involved in blatant graft, illustrates well the loss of efficacy of the desire for public greatness as a primary goal of political life. As the public rewards of political life decrease, the search for a compensating private gain will be undertaken.[51]

The loss of the public arena as a means for achieving one's sense of individuality has consequences beyond those that attach to our immediate social circumstances. The loss of the importance of the public sphere implies that history itself loses its import as a means of providing models for human action and attainment. Perhaps our present interest in anecdotal and psychoanalytic approaches to history is a measure of this changed attitude. In any case we must be sensitive to the possibility that the end of history may be realized in the near future, not by virtue of an apocalyptic event of spiritual or secular origins, or by virtue of the realization of a de-alienated society as the reward of revolution, but simply through the rendering irrelevant of the purpose and function of historical records. The more we find regular, institutional, and technical procedures for handling the significant events we encounter in what formerly was the public arena, the more we discover that we no longer need to search for the meaning of present events in terms of relevant antecedents. Consequently, we shall experience only *types* of occurrences that are easily interpreted in terms of policies and procedures already immanent in the order of technological society. Technology renders history irrelevant to the degree that the events constituting the repertory of human activities can be made amenable to pre-established procedures and techniques, or made to answer to the self-augmenting character of technological advances.

The decrease in the importance of the public sphere signals the end to the necessity of recourse to history as a repository of models of conflict resolution or as a means of understanding the derivation of the present from the past. Whether or not this will be interpreted as an unmixed evil will depend largely on the manner in which we respond to the challenge of the immediate future of advanced technological society.

The question "What is wrong with contemporary society?" can be answered as follows: we have reached a point at which the motivation toward the achievement of excellence on the part of individuals in the public sphere is no longer present to any important degree. This means that the values of deference, risk, and suffering are also absent. In large part this is due to the experience of the degradation of the elements that our social orders comprise. The sense of the vulgarity of the objects constituting the furniture of our world, the injustice of law, the oppressiveness of power, and the triviality of our ideals are sufficient to cause a failure of nerve that precludes our seeking to win recognition in the public sphere. The game seems hardly worth the candle.

The circumstances we describe here are the result of radical transformation in the public sphere. The very meaning of the relationship between the individual and the social order is in a state of transition. Heretofore, the individual has attained whatever value he might have as a citizen or a member of a social order by virtue of the possibilities of working for recognition within the public arena. Though the motives for such striving can always be traced back to the intimate and personal facts of an individual's private existence, the working out of these private motives and aspirations could be realized only in the public sphere. The sense of being a worthwhile individual has always been wrapped up in the relationship between the private and public spheres of social existence.

Artistic production, traditionally one of the most important means of achieving greatness, suffers the same fate as all other forms of public expression. The shrinking of the public sphere results in there no longer being an arena to house artistic expressions. Both the celebration of greatness through the medium of art objects and the achievement of personal greatness through one's art are precluded by the collapse of the public sphere. Social practice, reduced to its private and personal forms, leads increasingly to a stress upon experiencing over expressing, enjoying over producing. Praxis is understood not as action, creation, or production aiming at the attainment of greatness, but as *aisthesis*, as immediate experience, which has its origin and end in the private sphere. Though promising as a means of enriching one's private pleasures such a development has produced a crisis in our understandings of the structure and the purpose of social organization as a means of promoting the realization of individuality.

Technological society provides less and less of the kind of public space within which individuals may strive for excellence. Society dominated by material technologies usurps the power of individual self-expression and self-realization by promoting the aims of regularity and efficiency above those of novelty and spontaneity. We may be approaching a point at which the approximation to individuality can be achieved not in the public but in the private sphere. Precisely what this might mean for the future of the concept of citizen or member of a society we cannot tell for certain, but if we were to view the present crisis in the relations of the individual to society within the context of the three other shattered relationships—viz., those between God and the world, persons and nature, and male and female—we would experience a pressing need for speculations on the future that are sensitive to the global character of the transformations we currently are undergoing. The speculations that follow immediately should be judged in the light of the need for such sensitivity.

NOTES

1. *A Treatise on Human Nature*, ed. L. Selby-Bigge (Oxford: Clarendon, 1960), p. 183.
2. Ibid., p. 415.
3. Trans. Norman Kemp Smith (New York: St. Martin's, 1961), p. 303.
4. *The Myth of the State* (Garden City, N.Y.: Doubleday, 1955), p. 69.
5. In *The Dialogues of Plato* I, trans. B. Jowett (New York: Random House, 1920), pp. 235–36.
6. For examples of such an assessment of the Sophists, see W. K. C. Guthrie, *The Sophists* (Cambridge: Cambridge University Press, 1971), p. 48; and Peter Gay, *The Enlightenment: An Interpretation* (New York: Knopf, 1966), pp. 72–126.
7. *Greek Philosophy: Thales to Plato* (New York: St. Martin's, 1964), p. 88.
8. Ibid., p. 3.
9. *Systematic Theology* I (Chicago: The University of Chicago Press, 1951), p. 75.
10. Ibid., p. 73.
11. *Will to Power* 470, trans. Walter Kaufman and R. J. Hollingdale, ed. Walter Kaufman (New York: Vintage, 1968), p. 262.
12. Ibid. 480, p. 266.
13. Ibid., pp. 266–67.
14. Ibid. 610, p. 328.
15. *Philosophical Perspectives* (Boston: Beacon, 1958), p. 5.
16. (The Hague: Nijhoff, 1960), p. 5. See also his *Phenomenology and the Crisis of Philosophy*, trans. Quentin Lauer (New York: Harper & Row, 1965), passim; and *Die Krisis der europäischen Wissenschaften und die transzendentale Phänomenologie* (The Hague: Nijhoff, 1954), passim, for a discussion of the refounding of reason.
17. (New York: Oxford University Press, 1947), p. 176.
18. *Knowledge and Human Interests*, p. 314.
19. Ibid.
20. For example, the recent introduction of modal and deontic logics into philosophical methodology has meant that every traditional problem of ethics, metaphysics, and theology is now open to sophisticated logical analysis. Far from settling these issues, however, we find the logical tools employed to support and articulate the same divergent theoretical orientations as before. Not only can logics both "prove" and "disprove" the existence of God, depending on the interpretation of the logical status of

"necessary existence," "perfection," and so on, but for those inclined to accept the fact of the existence of God, logics can articulate dramatically different conceptions of the nature of the deity. One has but to peruse a work such as *The Ontological Argument* (ed. Alvin Plantinga [Garden City, N.Y.: Doubleday, 1965]) to see examples of this use of logic by orthodox and heterodox theologians and atheists alike. What is true in theology applies equally to every discipline touched by logic.

The loss of axiomatic certainty in logic has had consequences beyond philosophy per se. Morris Kline, in *Mathematics: The Loss of Certainty* (New York: Oxford University Press, 1980), pp. 31ff., has outlined the manner in which the failure of certainty in logical theory has contributed to the undermining of twentieth-century mathematical theory.

21. *The Brothers Karamazov* was published in 1880. Nietzsche's most famous pronouncement of the death of God came in *Joyful Wisdom*, first published in 1882.

22. Jorge Borges, *A Personal Anthology* (New York: Grove, 1967), p. 119.

23. *Adventures of Ideas* p. 358.

24. Quoted in Samuel French Morse, *Wallace Stevens: Life as Poetry* (New York: Pegasus, 1970), p. 55.

25. See Whitehead's *Process and Reality* (New York: Macmillan, 1929), passim; and Hartshorne's *The Divine Relativity* (New Haven: Yale University Press, 1964), passim, for discussions of the neo-classical conception of God. For an important critique of this concept, see Robert Neville's *Creativity and God: A Challenge to Process Theology* (New York: Seabury, 1980).

26. See "Myth," pp. 62–63.

27. There was at least one other conceptualization of nature that was articulated in ancient Greece but that never developed into a philosophic tradition. The view of Heraclitus that nature is a process, of the character of *events* rather than *substance*, was perhaps too far outside the family of concepts that later came to dominate our philosophic tradition to be acceptable. We shall have occasion, later, to consider such notions in some detail.

28. (New York: Oxford University Press, 1960), p. 3.

29. Ibid., p. 5.

30. Ibid., p. 9.

31. Ibid.

32. Ibid., p. 175.

33. See *The Philosophical Writings of Peirce*, ed. Justus Buchler (New York: Dover, 1955), pp. 28–31.

34. *The History of Nature*, trans. F. D. Wieck (Chicago: The University of Chicago Press, 1949), p. 68.

35. Ibid., p. 69.

36. Ibid., p. 71.

37. *Physics and Philosophy* (New York: Harper & Row, 1958), p. 197.

38. Werner Heisenberg et al., *On Modern Physics* (New York: Collier, 1962), p. 20.

39. See Dodds, "The Fear of Freedom," in *Greeks and the Irrational*, chap. 8. See also Whitehead's "The Romantic Reaction," in *Science and*

the Modern World (New York: Macmillan, 1925), and Horkheimer's discussion of "The Revolt of Reason" in *The Eclipse of Reason.*

40. In *Dialogues of Plato* I, trans. Jowett, p. 190.
41. Ibid.
42. Ibid.
43. G. M. A. Grube, *Plato's Thought* (Boston: Beacon, 1964), p. 99.
44. *On the Nature of Things* 4.1110–20, trans. H. A. J. Munro in *Great Books of the Western World* 12 (Chicago: Encyclopaedia Britannica, 1952).
45. In *Dialogues of Plato* I, p. 211.
46. Tillich, *Love, Power, Justice*, p. 30.
47. Anders Nygren, *Eros and Agape*, trans. Philip S. Watson (Philadelphia: Westminster, 1953), p. 75.
48. See especially Book VIII, chaps. 1–8.
49. See Borges, *Personal Anthology*, p. x.
50. Carolyn Heilbrun's *Toward a Recognition of Androgyny* (New York: Harper & Row, 1973) is an excellent example of the literary critic's burgeoning sensitivity to the erethic fervor among artists who seek expressions of passion transcending the power relationship. A good work on the general subject of androgyny is Joyce Singer, *Androgyny: Toward a New Theory of Sexuality* (Garden City, N.Y.: Doubleday, 1976).
51. I certainly do not wish to imply that this search for private over public satisfactions must be immoral per se. Whatever differences exist between Presidents Carter and Reagan at the level of political ideology, both are considered to be basically honest men. Each represents the sort of Christian fundamentalism that has occasioned a renewed concern for the presence of private virtues in politics, which is the more positive form of the de-emphasis of the public sphere.

CHAOS REVISITED

4

The Meeting of the Twain

East is East and West is West and never the twain shall meet.
R. KIPLING

For the first time the Male seeks the power of the Female.
I Ching

A RETURN TO THE ORIGINS

FOR THOSE WHOSE ROOTS ARE FIRMLY SET within Western
cultural experience, reason and rationality express themselves
most magnificently in terms of the act of theory construction.
Theoretical expressions are developed in accordance with
principles that, as *archai* or *principia*, serve as foundations
upon which intellectual systems are to be constructed. The
various sets of principles specify the differences among the
types of theoretical system that have come to dominate our
cultural self-understanding. In the discussion of the development of our cultural paradigm I outlined the contrasting kinds
of theory that, since the formative period of Hellenic culture,
have come to constitute the four basic philosophic paradigms
in Western culture.

The materialist paradigm resulted from the initial search
for *physis* or *natura*, the substratum of all things. The first

Western philosophers, the Milesians of ancient Greece, sought an answer to the question "Of what is the world constructed?" The search for a material "stuff" in terms of which to characterize the makeup of things was the principal task of the first materialists and has continued to be so for materialists ever since. Their principle is that of *physis*, physical nature.

Formalist or idealist philosophical systems have employed the principle of "knowledge." The characterization of the nature of things has proceeded in terms of mind-like, if not mind-dependent, "forms," "ideas," or "essences." One comes to understand the character of reality and of man's relation to it in terms of a noetic principle that provides the basis for an understanding of the coherent unity of all aspects of that which is.

The naturalistic philosophy, grounded upon the notion of organism, and constituting a whole with parts that functionally interrelate to achieve some purpose, stresses the principle of *law* and characterizes the nature of what is real, as well as the knowledge of that nature, in accordance with those rules organic entities must obey in order to achieve their individual purposes. Laws, construed as the laws of organic nature and human society, provide a distinctly different principle from either materialist or formalist philosophic systems, since the stress is on neither *matter* nor *form*, but on *purpose* and the means (i.e., the laws) by which the purpose is achieved.

Volitional theories characterize the nature of what is, the knowledge of that nature, and the laws or rules in accordance with which understanding of reality may be attained, in terms of the principle of *power* construed as the operation of individual will in conflict with others' wills. Power, as the power of persuasion, establishes the meanings given to "nature," "knowledge," and "law." If "man is the measure of all things," he can be so only by virtue of his exercise of the persuasive power of speech, which sets him, as logos-bearing creature, apart from all other creatures.

The history of Western philosophy is illustrated by a series of contrasting epochs in which now one philosophic perspective, now another, has dominated. Consciousness of the fact that philosophic history has often constituted no more than a cyclical series of Tweedledum's "no-how" and Tweedledee's "contrariwise" has led to a search for novelty and increased relevance through an attempt to encompass all traditions in a single system of thought. This has increased the adequacy of a philosophic theory but, alas, has also decreased its consistency. Those thinkers who are bound by the claims of consistency remain tied to a single tradition; others dissatisfied with the provinciality of a single perspective exercise the eclectic option and provide wider wisdom with decreased clarity and precision. Consistency and adequacy themselves, thus, have become meta-philosophical principles that dispose thinkers toward narrowness or width in the selection of principles on which to found a philosophic theory. That the history of philosophy cannot be construed in terms of a progressive realization of truth, but can only be seen as a kind of intellectual "war of each against all," strongly suggests that the claims of both consistency and adequacy cannot be met within the same philosophic theory.

The principal reason for the failure of philosophic theory is that the use of a single philosophic principle to found a system of thought disposes one to a self-defeating narrowness in the selection of philosophic evidences, while the attempt to include all principles on equal terms leads inevitably to incoherence and logical contradiction. In the first instance, an aesthetically satisfying consistency is maintained by construing all the conceptual elements constituting a theory in terms of a single principle. Thus, for the idealist or formalist, "nature" is a patterned structure of "ideas" or "forms"; "laws" are principles of understanding; "power" is the efficacy born of knowledge. To attempt, in the name of philosophic adequacy, to introduce correlative principles that are mutually non-reductive is to risk philosophic failure through fatal contradiction.

Cartesian philosophy is one paradigm of such inconsistency born of a striving for adequacy. The mind–body problem exists neither for the materialist for whom "mind" is reducible to material correlates of the basic building bricks of which all things are composed, nor for the idealist for whom "body" is an idea among other ideas. For Descartes, how-

ever, it was the essential disconnection of *res cogitans* from
res extensa that finally compromised the efficacy of his philosophy. The attitude of professional philosophers toward
Descartes' striving for adequacy depends on their degree of
insistence upon the criterion of either consistency or adequacy
in the evaluation of philosophic theory.

In our present age the hope that a philosophy may win
universal approval because of a blinding consistency that
prevents us from noting its partiality is all but dead. Equally
moribund is the view that if we are willing to overlook a major
inconsistency or two, or perhaps a failure of theoretical coherence, we may become satisfied with a speculative scheme that
interprets all areas of experience. In our Western cultural
tradition, the claims of reason and the claims of experience are
mutually necessary. Rational consistency and experiential
adequacy alike are essential characteristics of theory. The
only way out of our present philosophic dilemma is to refuse
the gambit offered by the division between the claims of
reason and the claims of experience.

Twentieth-century philosophers have recognized this
necessity. But, armed only with the tools of Western philosophic culture, they have been unable to make good their
Great Refusal. Analytic philosophy has claimed that no
dichotomy exists between reason and experience, for the
"logic of language" encompasses both. And if speculative
thinkers, poets, and artists seem to feel that something is missing in such philosophies, they are dismissed as muddled and
confused. Pragmatism, as radical empiricism, has suggested
that no real dichotomy exists between reason and experience
since life circumstances construed as a series of "problematic
situations" encompass both. And if individuals of a logical
turn of mind seek to hold principles apart from the flux of
circumstance in order to examine their systematic relationships as a means of predicting possible future relevance, they
are dismissed as compulsively simpleminded and overly rational. We cannot seem to gain satisfaction either from our
inherited dichotomy of reason and experience or from the
various attempts to overcome it.

Apparently we must reach beyond our Western cultural
experience for novel philosophic approaches if we are to avoid

the dilemma involved in trying to meet the mutually conflicting demands of reason and experience. This attempt must
involve the discovery of a novel principle or principles on
which to build a philosophic perspective distinguishable from
each of the four dominant traditions, yet which is not merely
an eclectic hodge-podge of the possible alternative principles.
This task cannot be accomplished, of course, unless the tools
allowing success of the endeavor already exist, at least in
embryonic form, in our culture. That is to say, the reach
beyond our cultural boundaries for new wisdom cannot be a
reach into the unknown. It must, rather, be a search for the
articulation of principles nascently present to our eyes.

In the final pages of *The Critique of Pure Reason*, Kant
called for a "History of Pure Reason," a chronicle of the
manners in which theoretical and practical reason have been
employed to understand the world and to provide persons a
place within it. Every major philosopher who has commented
on this story of reason, from Hegel to Heidegger, has called
attention to the importance of the crisis in the history of
reason occasioned by the thought of Parmenides and his disciple, Zeno.

Parmenides of Elea, born around 515–510 B.C., was the
author of a philosophical poem containing two parts, *The Way
of Truth* and *The Way of Opinion*. The principal argument of
the poem is that "only being is; not-being is not." The true
path of inquiry is claimed to be grounded on the proposition
"it is" or "being is." The false way, based on the belief in
non-existence, is unknowable, indeed unthinkable. *The Way
of Opinion* is based on an attempt to combine the two dis-
juncts "it is" and "it is not." The claim "it is and is not" is
that on which those who accept the common-sense world of
becoming, in which things come into being and pass away,
ground their belief. But this, too, is unthinkable, since to think
change is to entertain the notion of non-existence. The world
of becoming must itself reduce to non-being. Parmenides'
world was one and unchanging, a spherical plenum, without
additional qualities or distinctions.[1]

The influence of Parmenides' philosophy might have been
considerably smaller had his chief disciple, Zeno, not produced a charming and seductive set of puzzles and paradoxes

that challenged the common-sense acceptance of the reality of motion and change while at the same time refuting logical and mathematical defenses of these notions. Zeno sought to demonstrate by *reductio ad absurdum* that "change cannot be thought." Not only are his four paradoxes familiar to most schoolchildren even today, but they continue to exercise the wits of the more astute scientists, mathematicians, and logicians of each succeeding generation. The effect of Parmenides' doctrines, and of the paradoxes of Zeno, was to challenge the rationality of any thought involving change or plurality. And though no subsequent philosopher of major importance fully accepted the consequences of the Parmenidean proposition that "only being is; not-being is not," with its implications of a changeless, motionless plenum as constituting that which is, every major Greek philosopher after Zeno took the paradoxes extremely seriously. Democritus constructed a theory of atoms, mathematically divisible but physically indivisible, along with the definition of space as empty, in order to meet Zeno's challenge. Anaxagoras, following the example of Heraclitus, introduced the notion of continuity and indefinite divisibility, claiming that space, time, and matter are not discrete. This led to the vision of a world understandable in terms of process rather than substance. The Sophists introduced the notion of "convention" to avoid confrontation with the paradoxes. The proper sphere of the philosopher is the realm of praxis. Doing supplants knowing; "truth" is relative to culture and to the individual thinker.

Of the three main responses to Zeno's paradoxes, only the Democritean and Sophistic theories developed into major philosophic traditions in the West. When coupled with the general neglect of the views of Heraclitus, this fact helped to ensure that the metaphysical traditions of Western philosophy would be biased toward substance over process as the fundamental characterization of that which is. Confronted with paradoxes generated by the substance metaphysics of Parmenides, and resolvable on the assumptions of a process orientation, Greek intellectual culture expressed its selective bias clearly on the side of substance philosophies. Rather than entertain the possibility that the assertion "change cannot be thought'' might best be met by denying the necessity of a substance that undergoes changes, the dominant tradition ignored the insights that could, early on, have given rise to an understanding of *physis* as process. As a result, our cultural tradition has not had an opportunity to develop a process philosophy until this century with the appearance of Henri Bergson and Alfred North Whitehead.

The receptions of the philosophies of Bergson and Whitehead, ironically, recall the fates of Heraclitus and Anaxagoras, respectively. Like Heraclitus, Bergson is still remembered, if at all, as a poet and a mystic who, though eminently quotable, has had little real influence. Like Anaxagoras, Whitehead, honored both as scientist and as philosopher, made his major impact in the realm of theology. And, though celebrated as brilliant and original, Whitehead, like Anaxagoras, is generally considered by his contemporaries to have misspent his genius in vague and eccentric speculations of little philosophic import. Because of these attitudes, philosophies of process have hardly been given an adequate hearing in our cultural tradition. Things would no doubt have been significantly different if the cunning of history had produced a "Zeno" for Heraclitus. How different we can perhaps imagine if we proceed with a bit of ironic revisioning of the historical past. Imagine, if you will, the following paragraph to be an excerpt from a text in the history of philosophy.

One of the most significant archaeological finds of recent years is the set of philosophical fragments of Thelpis of Chimaera, a hitherto unknown philosopher who was a younger contemporary of Heraclitus. Thelpis defended the proposition "permanence cannot be felt" by arguing for the ephemerality of our subjective forms of feeling. Only by resort to concepts can permanences be found. Commenting on the statement of his master "You cannot step into the same river twice," Thelpis argued that the person, as well as the river, "flows on." Like a string of beads serially strung out in time, we come into being and pass away, each of our drops of experience characterized by spontaneity, novelty, and transience. The Thelpian fragments, though partial and incomplete, prove the basis of the construction of "Thelpian paradoxes" which, by taking serious raw feeling as the basic way of perceiving the world, would strongly defend the proposition contained in the final fragment [11c]: "only becoming is; not-becoming is not."

Thelpis is, of course, chimerical; and partly as a consequence of this fact, process philosophy is not a tradition, but only a perspective. But the presence of contemporary philosophies of process that recall neglected theoretical orientations within Hellenic culture is significant. It means that we have available an original set of philosophic *principia* in terms of which to interpret our contemporary cultural experience. It means that there is hope that we can provide again a fruitful marriage of *mythos* and logos, which will initiate a new paradigm in terms of which we may cast our future. For only by a return to the origins, which includes the search for both mythical and philosophic beginnings, can our attempt to cast a future be grounded on a firm insight into the tendencies of the cultural present.

Process philosophy requires a conception of positive, and relative, non-being. That is to say, the concept of the being–non-being dichotomy as its exists in Western philosophy cannot be affirmed in process thought. As long as non-being is considered after the fashion of Democritus' "empty space," which was invented, as we have seen, in order to circumvent the difficulties consequent upon the Parmenidean dictum "only being is; not-being is not," then process categories could never be developed. For the transition from one occasion of experience to another requires that there be, if not a continuity of becoming, at least a becoming of continuity. The characterless non-being of Parmenides and Plato was destined of course to be superseded by the negative non-being of Christian theology after Augustine. The Neoplatonic tradition, with its conception of a hierarchy ranging from the fullness of being possessed by the Uncreated Essence of the Holy Trinity to the merest wisp of empty space possessed of almost total non-being, established a pattern for our Western understandings that could in no wise allow for a true polar relation between being and non-being. The whole of creation was established as a vast continuum in which perfection was identified with the fullness of being, and decreased being involved decreased perfection.

The concept of process, or becoming, on the other hand, requires that non-being be placed on equal footing with being itself. For the coming-into-being of that which is not yet suggests a combination of being and non-being in which becoming is what is finally real. If this is to be true, then the concepts of being and non-being must be seen in polar relationship to one another; and each considered separately must be abstractions from becoming, which alone is truly real.

Parmenides' distinction between truth and opinion as constituting a contrast between being and becoming was to appear later in Plato's philosophy as the priority of the real world of eternal ideas over that of the world of appearance, the world of flux and change. This fundamental Platonic doctrine has found a firm place in the history of Western thought. With few exceptions, the doctrines of the priority of being over becoming and the assertion that non-being either is nonsense or possesses some mystical negating quality as opposed to being (a view theologians after Augustine often maintained), were affirmed throughout Western philosophy. Even those few exceptions emphasizing the importance of becoming can most often, on closer analysis, be found to affirm the orthodox view. Hegel, for example, whose great *Phenomenology of Spirit* traces the becoming of Spirit in history, holds that the process is defined by, and culminates in, Absolute Spirit, the permanent, unchanging Idea, which alone is fully real.

The principal adventures of this conception of being can be found by examining A. O. Lovejoy's *The Great Chain of Being*.[2] The conception of a hierarchy of being, graded from highest to lowest in terms of the principle of "fullness of being," well expresses the dominant attitudes of Western thought regarding the relations of being and non-being. What exists at higher levels of the hierarchy has more being, and is, therefore, more real, than what exists below it. Between God and empty space stretches a continuous, unbroken chain of graded existents.

The concept of a hierarchy of being serves to ground the identification of evil with non-being, which the Christian theological tradition accomplished. In Augustinian theology evil was discussed from two fundamental points of view, which established the twin foundations on which most subsequent theodicies have been based. Evil may be seen as a privation of being. Since nothing evil exists in itself but only as a privation of some existing thing, an existing thing is evil when the fullness of its being has been compromised. Moral evil, associated with the fall of the first creatures, originated because man turned away from the higher toward the lower good. "For when the will abandons what is above itself, and turns to what is lower, it becomes evil."[3] Lower beings in themselves are not evil; the degradation of the higher to the lower form constitutes the evil. The threat of evil, therefore, is the threat of displacement in the hierarchy of being. As long as each existent "keeps its place," there is no evil. "The Fall" is literally a fall from a higher to a lower state of being.

In addition to this concept of evil, Augustine discusses evil as disharmony. On this view, the created order, seen in its totality, is good. What appears evil from a finite, and limited, perspective would, on the larger view, be seen as contributing to the harmony of the total picture. Thus evil is disharmony; but all disharmonies contribute to the wider harmony of creation as a whole.[4] These two views of the origin of evil are, of course, intrinsically related, since the Fall is responsible for the apparent disharmonies in the existing order.

Subsequent discussions of the problem of evil have been dominated by Augustinian theology, and reflections of his views are found not only in St. Thomas, Luther, and Calvin but also in the theodicy of Leibniz. For the greater part of our tradition, including even the most recent discussions, the concept of evil has been associated with non-being and disharmony. Largely because of the influences of the Augustinian theodicy, most of our intellectual tradition still takes for granted the association of chaos and evil. For chaos has the meanings of "non-being" and of "dis-order." God created *ex nihilo* by bringing order into the formless void, by bringing "being" out of "non-being." It is quite understandable, therefore, that, despite a few voices to the contrary, the association of being with reality, of non-being with evil, and of evil with chaos, has dominated our intellectual traditions. Those few thinkers who have sought to express alternatives to the orthodox theology have had little impact.

Although the dominant philosophical perspectives accept the fact of chaos as a primordial condition or an undesirable by-product of the act of creation, there is what may be called a dualistic view that affirms chaos as one of two necessary originative elements, neither of which is ontologically prior, or axiologically preferable, to the other. The dualist position is graphically illustrated by the cosmogonical theory of Christian von Ehrenfels. According to Ehrenfels, "not 'out of Chaos' did God make the world, but 'out of himself,' against Chaotic resistances."[5] God is the "eternal venturer" and chaos is the "inciter to ventures," each deserving of love because of its indispensable role in the creation of things. No victory over chaos is to be sought. And as chaos and God have always existed side by side, there is no primordial unity to be rewon. God and chaos are truly dual, in the sense that they have polar relations one to the other. "All Unity and Universality come from God, all manifoldness from Chaos. Without Chaos God would be just as incapable of producing the world as Chaos without God."[6]

Whitehead comes close to this vision of chaos in the cosmological speculations of his *Process and Reality*:

> if there is to be progress beyond limited ideals, the course of history by way of escape must venture along the borders of chaos in its substitution of higher for lower types of order. . . . the immensity of the world negatives the belief that any state of order can be so established that beyond it there can be no progress.[7]

Though Whitehead does not quite affirm Ehrenfels' position, in his characterization of a universe evolving in its types of order, chaos takes on a positive character and "The right chaos, and the right vagueness, are jointly required for any effective harmony. . . . Thus chaos is not to be identified with evil. . . ."[8] Indeed, there is in even the most qualified of process views of existence the acceptance of chaos as a factor necessary to the ongoing process: "There is a moment of 'chaos' between the old and new form, a moment of no-longer-form and not-yet-form."[9]

The advent of the process tradition, therefore, brings with it a new perspective on the chaos of beginnings. But process philosophy has not received widespread attention until

recently, when, because of the transmission of similiar doctrines from the East, a sympathetic climate of opinion has
gradually emerged. It is not surprising that the recognition of
this type of thought has been slow in coming. For until the
dominant conceptions defining the substance philosophies
outlived their usefulness there could be little use for theories
so at variance with the major presuppositions upon which our
cultural self-understandings were grounded. Thanks to our
increased understanding of Eastern thought, we find ourselves
able to draw upon fully developed thought systems that derive
from the intuition of change and process. Some Eastern philosophies, particularly the system of philosophical Taoism,
provide subtle and sophisticated presentations of process
thinking.

One of the principal difficulties in the discussion of philosophers such as Whitehead and Bergson has been the
apparently ad hoc character of much of their thinking. Original
in the profoundest sense of that term, because they are
dependent upon origins not augmented by tradition, these
thought systems have been difficult to appropriate for use in
Western culture since the sustaining environments in which
they existed seem so hostile to their presuppositions. And the
attempt to provide some support for twentieth-century
process philosophies by reciting the *panta rhei* of Heraclitean
thought, along with some of the fragmentary comments of
Anaxagoras, has more often suggested guilt by association
than defended the cause of process thinkers. Of late, however,
with the emergence of interest in Oriental cultures, we are able
to discover the ramifications of the process intuition and to
suggest some of the consequences of the acceptance of
process theories. Taoist and Buddhist philosophers were, for
the most part, free of the apologetic burden of having to make
their philosophy understandable to fellow-philosophers
imbued with a bias toward substance modes of thought. And
this freedom suggests that only in the East are we able to find
the process philosophical turn of mind expressed in an un-
compromised form.

The difficulty involved in the attempt to employ exoteric
concepts to revivify esoteric patterns of thought is that some

form of translation into our cultural milieu is essential if we are to appropriate the novel insights. In the present instance, the problem of such a translation is the one to which we have already alluded: how can an adequate translation be given when the language of the culture receiving the novel insights is dominated by substance categories? We can maximize our success in this endeavor only if we are able to single out, at the level of both *theoria* and praxis, novel experiences and concepts drawn from our own cultural milieu, and to employ them as a means of plumbing the depths of our own cultural past and of alternative cultural traditions highlighting whatever novelty is encountered. This method, which I have been employing throughout this work, involves three aims: a consideration of the cultural condition of the contemporary West, which, as I have suggested, evidences a running-down of received wisdom and a felt desire for novelty, combined with an increased interest in forms of recently developed process thought; a return to the origins of our culture to discover similar insights that have been ignored and in effect have "fallen away" from us; and a resort to exoteric theories and practices to supplement and interpret the novel ideas and practices that have recently come to light among us. The pursuit of these three mutually interpretative aims will supply us with the material necessary to construct a viable alternative to the exhausted cultural perspectives we now find no longer serve our most vital needs.

ACROSS THE GREAT DIVIDE

Only now that we are called upon to take our process thinkers seriously do we begin to realize that we are not at all well equipped to understand them. The vision of the process philosopher is so radically at odds with our received wisdom that we have little choice but to construe philosophers of process in terms of our more familiar substance categories, radically distorting their most profound insights. The principal difficulty is that we do not have a recognized intellectual tradition that allows the proper interpretation of the process perspective. For this reason it is necessary to turn to the East, where a fully developed process tradition does indeed exist, in order to discover a context in which to interpret our process philosophies. Though this might seem paradoxical, there can be little doubt that Anglo-European process philosophers have much more in common with Taoist and Buddhist thinkers than with extant Western philosophic traditions. Accepting our present philosophic visions as the sources of criteria in terms of which to judge the adequacy of thinkers such as Whitehead or Bergson can lead only to the rejection of the thought of these philosophers or to an interpretation that construes them according to substantialist principles, thus trivializing them while rendering them "respectable." The alternative is to employ Eastern philosophic traditions as sources of interpretative categories allowing for the development of an authentic process perspective in the West. But to do this it is necessary first to bridge the great chasm that heretofore has separated Eastern and Western philosophic thought.

The enrichment of Anglo-European cultural resources through the pursuit of novel evidences found in Oriental culture is one of the more pressing of the responsibilities of our philosophical elite. But the urgency of the task ought not to blind us to its inherent difficulty. As essential as it is that we develop rigorous comparative methodologies that permit responsible access to the philosophic riches to be discovered beyond our cultural boundaries, we must allow our comparative generalizations to be disciplined by those analytic and exegetical endeavors that interpret alternative cultural evidences *in situ*. For it is through such endeavors that the variety and complexity of each culture are to be recognized and the specific similarities and differences in cultural expression are to be uncovered. We can never remain content with piecemeal interpretations of this or that aspect of an exoteric culture, however. Adequate comparative methodologies require recourse to more general understandings that render specialized insights meaningful in the broadest possible contexts.

Obviously, there is something of the problem of the chicken and the egg here. We cannot understand another culture until we have a language and a schema allowing translation into a cultural idiom appropriate to our understanding, but we cannot develop such a schema in a satisfactory form until we have sufficient understanding of the similarities and differences illustrated by the exoteric culture. We ought not, of course, to yield to the Kipling fallacy, the presumption that "East" and "West" represent two monolithic cultures facing one another across an unbridgeable chasm. Neither should we claim that any single comparative methodology, including the one I am about to suggest, is adequate to highlight the full range of similarities and differences patterning the relations of Oriental and Anglo-European cultures. The only reasonable response to the difficulties that intercultural translations represent is to recognize that the development of a comparative methodology is an extended process of tentative and pragmatic endeavors which only gradually may approach philosophic adequacy.

Though comparative philosophy is still in its infancy, we are beginning to make some progress in articulating the relationships of Oriental and Western thought and culture. And though we should not claim too much for our comparative endeavors, since they still have the crudeness of mere first attempts, we are apparently at least beginning to see where the real issues lie.

Undoubtedly the best-known comparative methodology relating Eastern and Western philosophic perspectives is that of F. S. C. Northrop.[10] The basic distinction, according to Northrop, between the two systems of thought is to be found in the "concepts by intuition" emphasized by Eastern philosophies and the "concepts by postulation" stressed by Western. A concept by intuition "is one which denotes, and the complete meaning of which is given by, something which is immediately apprehended."[11] A concept by postulation, on the other hand, "is one the meaning of which in whole or in part is designated by the postulates of the deductive theory in which it occurs."[12] Or as Northrop states elsewhere: "A concept by postulation is one . . . designating some factor in man or nature which, in whole or in part, is not directly observed, the meaning of which may be proposed for it postulationally in some specific deductively formulated theory."[13] Concepts by intuition are "names for particulars"; concepts by postulation are "universals." [14] As names for particulars, of course, concepts by intuition are also universals. But the referent of the concept in the two cases contrasts as particular to universal. It is in terms of their function that the concepts differ. In most of Western philosophy, concepts are employed ultimately to refer to postulated entities that find their place in, and derive their meaning from, a deductively formulated theory. In Eastern thought concepts most often function as means of suggesting or evoking the immediate apprehensions from which they are derived. Herbert Guenther, a scholar of Eastern philosophy, has recognized the importance of Northrop's distinction between Eastern and Western thought in indicating the difficulties involved in the translation of Eastern philosophical and religious writings into Western languages. Guenther uses Northrop's comparative methodology to warn the readers of his translations about the ease with which one might misconstrue the intended significances of Eastern writings. [15]

Though Northrop's comparative philosophy has met with broad approval, particularly among Western apologists for Eastern thought, it is by no means universally accepted. Joseph Needham, in his *Science and Civilization in China*, has claimed:

> There is no good reason for denying to the theories of the *Yin* and *Yang*, or the Five Elements, the same status of proto-scientific hypotheses as can be claimed by the systems of the pre-Socratic and other Greek schools. What went wrong with Chinese science was its ultimate failure to develop out of these theories forms more adequate to the growth of practical knowledge, and in particular its failure to apply mathematics to the formulation of regularities in natural phenomena. This is equivalent to saying that no Renaissance awoke it from its "empirical slumbers." [16]

In criticizing Northrop's characterization of the distinction between Oriental and Western thought, Needham proposes an alternative basis for comparative philosophy. As we have seen, Northrop claims a distinction between Eastern and Western modes of apprehension: the Western mode leading to postulation and scientific hypothesis, the Eastern mode expressed directly through aesthetic intuition. This leads to a contrast of Western "scientific" with Eastern "aesthetic" culture. Needham, on the other hand, tacitly presupposes that the scientific mode of the apprehension of nature is the only viable mode and then finds contingencies in the social and economic system in China responsible for its failure to develop fully the scientific mentality. It is, perhaps, apt to characterize Needham's comparison of Eastern and Western approaches to *philosophia naturalis* as cosmological in contrast to Northrop's epistemological concern. That is to say, while Northrop calls for an attempt at epistemic correlation between the Eastern aesthetic and Western theoretic perspectives on nature, Needham wishes East–West rapprochement to be based on the Eastern acceptance of scientific methodologies that allow for the development of their proto-scientific hypotheses, and on the Western acceptance of the organismic conception of Nature, which rectifies many of the limitations of the atomistic and mechanistic vision of Western science.

These programs may not be so different as they appear. After all, the Western theoretical attitude led to the development of atomistic and mechanistic theories in the first place. We have only to recall that the main reason Democritus postulated the existence of atoms as the basic building blocks of the universe was that he needed the concept of a physically indivisible, mathematically divisible, entity in order to avoid the strictures of Zeno's paradoxes. Mechanistic science is hardly grounded on an experiential or aesthetic foundation; it is, rather, based on a set of postulated entities. The Renaissance philosophic debates leading to the establishment of Newtonian concepts of space, time, and matter depend primarily not on empirical data but on ad hoc adjustments in conceptual frameworks.[17] Because the Greeks placed ultimate value on the claims of theoretical reason, the philosophy of Parmenides, which led to the conclusion that "change cannot be thought," occasioned the denial of change rather than the criticism of reason. Eastern philosophies of process and their contemporary Western counterparts accept change as the fundamental reality and provide a critique of the inadequacies of the exclusively rational approach to the knowledge of nature.

A dominant assumption in Western thought, based on a

rational demonstration first put forward in Parmenides' *The Way of Truth*, is that "only being is; not-being is not." The correlative claim in the East—at least among many of its Taoist and Buddhist thinkers—is "only becoming is; not becoming is not." The West most often affirms the reality of substance, or being; the East gives reality to process, or becoming. A primary theme in Western thought is the overcoming of chaos through rationalization. Thus the signal importance of reason, and of concepts by postulation. Eastern process thought takes its beginning from a presumed positive harmonious chaos with which one must cooperate rather than against which one must struggle. Thus the importance of immediate apprehension, and of concepts by intuition. This distinction may be highlighted by comparing the Western conceptions of chaos cited in Chapter Two with the Taoist attitude toward Chaos (*hun-tun*) expressed in the following parable from *Chuang Tzu*:

> The Ruler of the Southern Ocean was *Shû* (Heedless), the Ruler of the Northern Ocean was *Hû* (Sudden), and the Ruler of Center was Chaos. *Shû* and *Hû* were continually meeting in the land of Chaos, who treated them very well. They consulted together how they might repay his kindness, and said, "Men all have seven orifices for the purpose of seeing, hearing, eating, and breathing, while this (poor) Ruler alone has not one. Let us try and make them for him." Accordingly they dug one orifice in him every day; and at the end of seven days Chaos died.[18]

This allegory, which succinctly expresses Taoist sentiments concerning the role of discursive knowledge in human affairs, no doubt strikes the non-Chinese mind as somewhat odd because of the solicitude shown for chaos. Indeed, James Legge, the British Sinologist, whose lack of sympathy with much of Chinese culture often led him to misunderstand the texts he so admirably translated, comments on his allegory: "But surely it was better that Chaos should give place to another state. 'Heedless' and 'Sudden' did not do a bad work."[19] Surely it *is* better that disorder and confusion give way to order, but is it better that undifferentiated homogeneity give way to rationalized organization? The Taoists answer "No."

Here we can see how radically different the orientations of the contrasting elements of Western and Eastern thought truly are. Such a difference would indeed justify the belief that "never the twain shall meet," had recent developments in Western intellectual culture not given rise to such profound critiques of the orthodox scientific tradition as to require recourse to conceptual foundations at variance with the fundamental presuppositions of Western philosophy. As such they cannot but form a bridge to the East. Perhaps the best example of such a bridge is to be found, paradoxically enough, in the work of Whitehead, who had but scant knowledge of Eastern thought.

In *Science and the Modern World*, his 1925 Lowell lectures, Whitehead was performing no less than the task urged by Joseph Needham: namely, that of supplementing and restructuring the anatomy of ideal scientific practice by recourse to an alternative metaphysical or cosmological scheme that, though common enough in Eastern (particularly Chinese) philosophy, was as yet untried in Western thought. This effort of Whitehead's, by virtue of its now-classic status in the history of science and philosophy, can be seen as one of the pivotal works laying the foundation for future cross-cultural interactions between Eastern and Western cultures at the scientific and philosophic levels. The work is all the more important because it does not represent an artificial attempt to bridge the cultural chasm between East and West, but is the result of one seeking necessary alternatives suggested by the limitations of the contemporary conception of science as a cultural interest. Whitehead, himself ignorant of Chinese philosophy and science, could not have written, as Leibniz might have, with the Taoist and neo-Confucian forms of organismic cosmology in mind. His task was the tracing of the rise and fall of a scientific paradigm, "how it attains its triumphs, how its influence moulds the very springs of action of mankind, and finally how at its moment of supreme success its limitations disclose themselves and call for a renewed exercise of the creative imagination."[20]

That "exercise of the creative imagination" led Whitehead to formulate a new metaphysics for modern science, denying the ultimacy of the "independently existing substances, matter and mind" and beginning, instead, with "the analysis of process as the realization of events disposed in an interlocked community."[21] For Whitehead, it is not substances as subsisting entities that form the building blocks of the universe. "The event is the unit of things real."[22]

Whitehead terms his novel perspective "the philosophy of organism." For him the term "organism" refers to a process of creative becoming, which is at once intrinsically related to every other actuality in the universe and autonomous by virtue of its transience, freedom, and novel purpose. The organisms of Whitehead's universe are self-created. As such, process philosophy, insofar as it constitutes a philosophic paradigm, might best be termed the philosophy of creativity or, if one takes into account the explicitly organismic presuppositions, the philosophy of *creative synthesis*.[23] It is the notion of "creativity" that, in contradistinction to the concepts of nature, knowledge, power, and law underlying the major traditions of Western philosophy, provides the foundation of process thought.

The contrast we have been considering can hardly be said to be one that exists in any strict sense between Eastern and Western thought as a whole; the distinction exists, rather, between substance and process philosophies. Thus, though it is obviously a mistake to believe that the terms "East" and "West," as broad geographical designations, name monolithic cultures at variance with one another in every respect, it is nonetheless true that there is a significant cultural difference based upon the process orientation of much of the former and the substance orientation of almost all of the latter.

Neither Northrop nor Needham grasps what seems to be most essential in the strictly philosophical distinction between Eastern and Western world-views. Northrop finds the difference to be grounded in ways of apprehending nature, and seeks, through the use of scientific method, the development of epistemic correlations between the types of apprehension. Needham views the cosmologies of the East (in his case, those of Chinese civilization) as containing "proto-scientific hypotheses" that could properly have led to a science more adequate than that of the West if China had been awakened from its "empirical slumbers." Whitehead, innocent of the complexities of Eastern thought, but extremely sensitive to the shortcomings of Western philosophies as sources for the interpretation of the Anglo-European cultural tradition, provided a more suggestive set of reflections in terms of which one could develop a comparative philosophy. This is the case precisely because Whitehead provides a basis in his epistemology for the notion that all viewpoints (and he would have included *a fortiori* the divergent philosophical traditions of East and West) are abstractions from the concreteness and particularity of experience as ongoing process. Furthermore, he claims that abstractions are neither pernicious nor unreal, but a necessary means of getting into the depths of reality itself. Thus, in embryonic form, Whitehead's philosophic bridge between East and West is one that attempts to relate the particularity of concrete process with the efficacious generalizations of abstract speculation without disdaining either the particular or the universal aspects of experience.

This project initially seems to be exactly the one espoused by Northrop. But, unlike Northrop, Whitehead rejects the dualism implied in the acceptance of a radical distinction between intuition and postulation. For Whitehead, "thought" cannot be a source of knowledge strictly independent of "sensation." Mathematical space and time, for example, must derive from sensed space and time. Intuition is the basis of postulation. Northrop, criticizing Whitehead's identification of nature with the "terminus of sense perception,"[24] claimed that

> it is not permissible to reject the Galilean and Newtonian contention that there are two components in any scientific knowledge: the one empirical, *a posteriori*, and directly observed; the other theoretical, hypothetically *a priori*, and neither directly observed nor abstracted from the directly observed.[25]

Whitehead demonstrates the relation between what Northrop terms the "two components in scientific knowledge" by indicating how the latter could be derived from the former through a process of "extensive abstraction." In the case of a color perception, let us say, "red," Northrop would

claim that the immediately sensed red is the aesthetic component of the knowledge of red, which provides the concept
by intuition, while a number associated with a wave-length of
light in confirmed, deductively formulated, scientific theory
provides the meaning of red, given in a concept by postulation. The experimental verification of a relationship between
the two concepts establishes an epistemic correlation of the
type sought by Northrop between the two kinds of concept.
Whitehead's theory suggests that the color red is scientifically
explained when the connections between red as a factor in
nature and other factors in nature, such as light-waves as
electromagnetic disturbances, are discovered. An equally
valid explanation of red could be made by showing, in the case
of so-called illusory perceptions, that the sensed red must be
referred to a pathological bodily condition rather than directed
to light of a certain wave-length. In both instances a scientific
explanation of color would have been given.[26]

The actual procedure for demonstrating connections
between the two types of knowledge would be essentially the
same in the case of both Northrop and Whitehead. The difference, and it is an important one, lies in Whitehead's assumption that experimental verification involves the demonstration
of an *ontic* rather than merely an epistemic correlation
between the two types of knowledge. This assumption allows
Whitehead to treat an illusory perception of the color red on a
par with the veridical perception. The problem of illusory
perceptions is thus transformed into a problem of illusory
judgments. The judgment "I experience red" is, of course,
true in both the instances cited. But error would be introduced
if, in the latter instance, a further judgment referred the loca-
tion of the color red to a spatial region outside the body of the
perceiver. Yet in both cases the experience of red is a real,
veridical experience with ontic connections to other natural
occurrences.

Whitehead certainly did not wish to argue against
Northrop's claim (following Galileo, Newton, and much of
classical science) that one can distinguish concepts by intuition and concepts by postulation. Clearly, Democritus' ad hoc
assumption about the nature of atoms as mathematically

divisible but physically indivisible suggests the possibility of such a distinction. And it was this assumption, countering the threat of Zeno's paradoxes, that provided a latent basis for the development of classical Western science. What Whitehead does claim is that ad hoc assumptions can lead to errors in judgment that cannot easily be uncovered since we tend to discover what we anticipate in nature.[27]

Whitehead's concern for the direct relationship between universals and particulars sets him apart from Northrop's comparative philosophy. But it is this difference that places Whitehead in a more sympathetic relationship to Eastern thought than Northrop. It is somewhat paradoxical, therefore, that Whitehead has often been criticized by Northrop and the proponents of his comparative philosophy for his extremely Western or "postulational" orientation. Thus, Herbert Guenther states, " 'Eternal Object' is Whitehead's substitute for the traditional 'universal.' The very choice of words emphasizes the Western emphasis on the object."[28] But the misunderstanding evidenced in this comment could hardly be more severe. The genius of Whitehead's thought is found in one of his most fundamental comments concerning the function of philosophy: "Philosophy is the critic of abstractions."[29] This task requires the maintenance of a balance between form and function or substance and process. Thus Whiteheadian process philosophy, though at variance with the mainstream of Western thought, does not completely abandon the presuppositions of Western philosophy. For Whitehead has recognized that abstraction, which leads to incompleteness of thought if left uncorrected, occurs in two profoundly different ways. There is, first, abstraction from the actual world of experience. Thus a universal (or "eternal object" in Whitehead's terminology) can be employed to sum up or generalize upon many experiences of the same type.

The color "green" applies to all green things. If one believes that "greenness," as applicable to all green things, is somehow more real than the individuals to which it applies, then one affirms with the Platonic tradition that reality is to be identified with the permanent, unchanging realm of eternal ideas. But clearly this does not require the assumption that the real world is an abstract world if by that is meant a world derivative from the flux of circumstance. On the contrary, the Platonist would claim that what is abstract, in this sense, is the world of ordinary experience, not the realm of universals. On this view ships, sails, sealing wax, cabbages, and kings are all abstractions from the realm of eternal ideas. Process philosophies are closer to the common-sense view of abstraction. For Bergson a universal "is only a snapshot view of transition," [30] and reality is found in the process, not in the form.

In philosophies of form, universals point us toward a reality that is ever more generic and less specific; in philosophies of process, universals direct us to a reality that is ever more specific and concrete. In substance- or form-oriented philosophies, the function of universals is to lead us away from particulars toward increasing generality, which constitutes increasing reality. Process philosophies employ universals in order to drive more deeply into the welter of individual experiences. But just as Platonists must often begin with the world of concrete experience in seeking a path to the realm of eternal ideas, so the process thinker must often find his way through a world of formal abstractions in order to devise means of returning to the concreteness and particularity of experience. Thus, philosophy, as "critic of abstractions," must concern itself with both functions of universals. This involves two separate procedures, the "first of harmonizing them [i.e., universals] by assigning to them their right relative status as abstractions, and, secondly, of completing them by direct comparison with more concrete intuitions of the universe, and thereby promoting the formation of more complete schemes of thought." [31] Without the task of promoting deductive schemes of thought by assigning to abstractions "their right relative status," there could never be significant success in evoking the "concrete intuitions of the universe."

The process of articulating, or raising to the level of consciousness, the concrete particularities from which all abstraction begins Whitehead terms "rationalization." Rationalization, contrary to its common connotation, is a search for experienceable connections among isolated abstractions. As such, it is "the partial fulfilment of the ideal to recover concrete reality within the disjunction of abstraction.''[32]

Whiteheadian philosophy stresses, both in the formation of universals and in their employment as means of discovering (or uncovering) reality, what Northrop has termed concepts by postulation. But Whitehead insists that hypothetical–deductive schemes of thought can function to prevent the selective abstractions of the poets and artists from missing elements of concrete experience and thereby impoverishing the vision of concrete reality. The goal of philosophy is always to heighten the experience of what is real. And what is most real, for Whitehead, as well as for the Eastern process view, is the flow of experiencing. But, for Whitehead, concepts or universals employed as tools of ''rationalization'' are in no way pernicious, since they promote a deeper penetration into the concrete realities from which all experiencing has its origin.

This employment of concepts places Whitehead squarely on the side of those who claim that becoming has metaphysical priority over being. Whiteheadian thought achieves the aim Northrop assigns to the philosophical apologist who seeks a wedding of Eastern and Western methodologies: that of providing ''the epistemic correlation between the aesthetic and theoretic components of all things.''[33] That is to say, a philosophy capable of mining the distinctive insights of both East and West will be one in which concepts by intuition and concepts by postulation are employed in such manner that an intrinsic relation of symbolic reference exists between the two in which the former serves as the basis of ''philosophic generalization'' and the latter evokes the particular instances of intuitional experience.

We can find in Whitehead's philosophy not only the kind of epistemic correlation sought by Northrop but the satisfaction of Needham's desire for a perfected concept of nature as well. Needham himself has recognized in Whitehead's philosophy the perfection of a tradition of organismic thinking that, he claims, originated in Western thought with the philosophy of Leibniz. Needham speculates that Leibniz' originality may have owed much to his awareness of Neoconfucianist

modes of thought as transmitted to Europe by the Jesuit missionaries of the period. The claim that aspects of Leibniz'
philosophy, particularly his concepts of "monads" and of
"pre-established harmony," might derive in part from
Chinese sources would go a long way toward accounting for
the fact that, until recently, there have been few if any significant predecessors of the radically organismic conception in
Western thought.[34]

But Leibniz' form of organicism, though an advance over
Aristotelian naturalism in its acceptance of the comprehen-
sive nature of the harmonious relations establishing the
organic cosmos, is far from a process philosophy. The elements of self-creativity and novelty necessary to sustain a
vision of reality as change or becoming are rejected by Leibniz
in his attempt to maintain a consistent substance metaphysics.
The monads, or concrete actualities constituting that which is,
are completely without the capacity of self-origination or self-
creativity. The doctrine of pre-established harmony, which
maintains that in this best of possible worlds each monad will
act in maximal harmony with all other monads, requires that
each substance realize its aim or aims in absolute accordance
with its nature, which is brought into existence with God's
creation of the universe. The organicist aspect of the philosophy of creativity may well be traceable to Leibniz, but the
element of process had to await twentieth-century developments in the thought of philosophers such as William James,
Charles Sanders Peirce, Henri Bergson, and Alfred North
Whitehead.

It is not necessary to find a historical link in the seventeenth century between Chinese and Western philosophy in
order to justify the correlation between process and organismic philosophies in the East and the West. For as Needham
himself recognizes,

> there were (at least) two ways of advance from primitive participative
> thought, one (the way taken by the Greeks) to refine the concepts of
> causation in such a manner as to lead to the Democritean account of
> natural phenomena; the other, to systematize the universe of things
> and events into a pattern of structure, by which all the mutual influ-
> ences of its parts were conditioned. . . . Peering down the long
> avenues of time we can perhaps see the Newtonian Universe at the

end of the former view, and the Whiteheadian Universe at the end of the latter.[35]

In the "Whiteheadian Universe" we discover the grounds for both the cosmological and the epistemic correlations of Eastern and Western thought.

Both Northrop and Needham accept the aim of knowledge for both East and West as being scientific. Northrop hopes for a joining of present theoretic science with the aesthetic component of knowledge; Needham suggests that Chinese cosmology could offer to science the organicist conception that would challenge linear conceptions of causality and promote the concept of nature as a pattern of mutually interpenetrating elements. What each misses is that it is the specifically process-oriented characterization of the Eastern concept of nature that distinguishes it from that of the dominant Western philosophic traditions. Whiteheadian thought, which stands as the foremost illustration of the developing process tradition in Western philosophy, provides a bridge to the East, not primarily because it provides a method for epistemic correlation between theoretic and aesthetic components of knowledge as Northrop would wish, nor mainly because it suggests the outlines of a concept of nature illustrating the consequences of scientizing the proto-scientific conceptions of Eastern organicist cosmologies as Needham claims, but principally because it recurs to the theme of the process character of reality as patterned by aesthetic events, and insists on the necessity of continuity between nature so experienced and its construal in abstract terms. These two fundamental aspects of Whitehead's philosophy serve to provide the necessary bridge to the Eastern philosophic tradition, which, once reached, can be exploited as a means of elaborating the fundamental insights embryonically present in Whiteheadian thought. Each of these aspects must be considered in turn. We shall begin with the latter.

INTUITION AND PROCESS

The more we seek a common ground between Eastern and Western thought that will express what is most novel in our

Anglo-European tradition, the more we must stress the concept of *process*. Western thought has been dominated by the notion of *substance* and *being*, while in the East the concepts of *process* and *becoming* have more often been employed as the foundations of thought. The bankruptcy of reason in the West has led us to seek novel ways of interpreting our cultural experience and requires, therefore, that we abandon the received philosophic traditions, which have long since lost their usefulness in directing attention to nature, organizing actions in society, or evoking the sense of significance in relation to our immediate experiences of our world.

That we have in the philosophies of Bergson and Whitehead, among others, the expression of a novel process-oriented tradition has been of little cultural value to us because we have interpreted these novel philosophies in terms of our substance-oriented categories and in so doing have missed what is most radically novel in them. This could hardly have been otherwise since the theoretical perspectives from which to interpret philosophic thinking in the West have formed the semantic contexts from within which all cultural significances have been determined.

Each of our dominant philosophic contexts has developed in accordance with the notion of "reason." However great the differences among the various perspectives, each presupposes a general development out of a mythical, non-rational past. In the Western tradition, it has been the function of religious myth to tell the story of the time of the beginnings. Latterly, philosophical principles provided a more objective and less esoteric set of guidelines for the understanding of beginnings. What myths told in sensuous metaphor, philosophy attempted to describe in language that refers symbolically to conscious public experience. Early on in our own tradition cosmogonic myth provided the raw material for cosmological principles. The transition from sensuous myth to rational principles, which is variously described as "the discovery of mind"[36] or "the transition from religion to philosophy,"[37] we may now recognize as the move from one form of intending the world to another. The attempt to construe this movement as progress in some normative sense is as naïve as it is tendentious. The ferment in our contemporary cultural experience is evidence enough that we are finding dissatisfaction not only with the scientific view of the world, but with the mythical and philosophical underpinnings of this scientific view as well. Further, as the recent abortive attempt of the twentieth-century existentialists to achieve access to the non-rational side of man's nature has shown, there is simply no way out of our present dilemmas through any of the paths philosophic reason has provided for us. The existential rehearsal of the Sophistic skepticism has, more often than not, merely recapitulated the main themes of the song reason has sung since the period of Hellenic culture. A much more radical alternative is necessary if we are to overcome the desiccation of experience at the hands of the masters of the rational arts.

One of the principal difficulties, therefore, in establishing the viability of a process approach to contemporary philosophical dilemmas is that radically novel philosophic traditions have always, with no little justification, been suspected of yielding, in the last analysis, to a kind of irrational or mystical dynamic embedded in the metaphysical substratum. Bergson's mystical flights and Whitehead's metaphorical and analogical deliverances have at times embarrassed even the most liberal-minded of their disciples. This embarrassment has led to any number of misinterpretations of the nature of the process perspective.[38]

Precisely because of the radically novel elements in process philosophy, it is difficult for members of our culture to grasp its interpretative significance. The most characteristic response of all but a minority of Anglo-European philosophers is to find process philosophies vague, mystical, or irrational. Nothing could be more understandable than this reaction. From the perspective of philosophies that place a premium on clarity, unambiguous expression, and rational construction, process thinking must be unacceptable. Therefore, in order to obtain a hearing, process philosophers have had to demonstrate a concern for clarity, precision, and rational concepts, which has tended to militate against the fulfillment of the primary aim of process thought: the description of the world as composed of termini of acts of intuition. Process philosophy has had to wage an apologetic struggle against the received wisdom of the substance philosophies that form the mainstream of Western culture, and in so doing has hidden from view much of the original genius of the process perspective. The most dramatic illustrations of this unfortunate fact are found in the interactions between process thinking and the cultural interests of religion and of science.

One of the least celebrated scandals in our intellectual culture is that of the serious conflict between dogmatic and mystical interpretations of religious experience. One need but examine the phenomenon of Christian mysticism in order to understand the tension between intuition and postulation in the theological tradition. The clear testimony of the mystics is that the apex of religious experience is the experience of Unity, of Oneness. For the Christian mystic this is interpreted as the God–soul identity state. Yet the dogmatic theology of Christianity claims that "the beatific vision" is the highest form of religious experience. The beatific vision, the soul's envisagement of the uncreated essence of the Holy Trinity in the after-life, is distinct from the God–soul identity state, in the sense that the latter, if accepted literally, would entail a challenge to the concept of the impassibility (not to mention the infinity) of God, whereas the former conforms to the requirements of doctrinal theology. God, as the terminus of a mystic's intuition, is distinct from the God of doctrinal theology. Most of the tension between the empirical claims of the mystics and the doctrinal claims of the theologians within Christianity derives from the distinction. These conflicts are not evident in Eastern religions precisely because the relative importance of intuition vis-à-vis rationality is the reverse of that found in Anglo-European thought.[39]

One would expect process philosophies in the West to side with the mystical tradition, but this has hardly been the case. Whitehead labored to revise the traditional concept of God in order to conform it to a process view of reality, but the vision of a God whose "consequent" nature is qualified by the actualizations of the finite experiences of the temporal world, and whose "primordial" nature houses all possibility, is, in the last analysis, a rather half-hearted compromise with the rational theology of the West. This concept of God, in one aspect, is the terminus of an act of intuition, but in its primordial non-temporal aspect may only be inferred, as Whitehead himself recognized.[40] So-called process theologians, who constitute the greater number of Whitehead's disciples, have in their interpretations stressed the concept of God as a principle of *concretion*, or the ground of *order*, rather than emphasizing the function of God as a self-creative source of novelty. Attempts to de-emphasize the importance of the concept of God have come not from those interested in the direct deliverances of intuition, but rather from those intent upon naturalizing process metaphysics.[41] The aim of this effort is not merely to construct a Whiteheadian philosophy without recourse to the concept of God, but equally to secure Whitehead's metaphysics for the accepted canons of reason. The fate of process thought in its theological aspect has been that its rational and rationalizable components have been stressed at the expense of its intuitional foundations.

An even more important reason for the inability of process thought fully to realize its implicit dependence upon intuition as the primary access to the nature of reality is its relations with the enterprise of science. Process thought is a product of twentieth-century disenchantment with mechanistic science. William James, Henri Bergson, and Whitehead, each in his own peculiar manner, inaugurated his concept of process philosophy against the background of scientific materialism, and though, to a greater or lesser extent, each thinker made direct appeals to experience in the face of scientific claims of the importance of hypothetical–deductive schemes, the apologetic thrust of process thinking in the early twentieth century largely colored the development of that philosophical perspective. It could not suffice to show that process thought was supported by the aesthetic, moral, or religious intuitions of a given culture, or by the data of introspection. It was necessary to show that defects in classical scientific theory and practice required the perspective of process thinking for their rectification. For this reason Bergson, who otherwise made the strongest case for intuition, insisted upon working out his initial doctrines in terms of

contemporary scientific theory and practice. And it is instructive to note that Bergson's thinking has dropped into almost
complete obscurity except insofar as his thought has been
employed to criticize or supplement present scientific theory. [42]

Whitehead is certainly no exception to the generalization
that modern process thinking was born out of the critique of
scientific materialism. A mathematician and philosopher of
science before turning to speculative philosophy, Whitehead
revised the nature of the scientific enterprise in *Science and
the Modern World*, his first major philosophical work. And
Process and Reality, his attempt to construct a coherent metaphysical theory, had as its primary sources of philosophic
evidence many of the revolutionary concepts of twentieth-
century logic, mathematics, and physics. And though Whitehead certainly employed other sources of evidence,[43] the
broadly scientific foundation of his thinking most significantly influenced the nature of his systematic philosophy. As I
have just indicated, no relief from the hypothetical–deductive
burden of process thinking is to be found in the fact that so
much of the contemporary use of process categories is in the
interpretation of religious experience and expression. For
Whitehead's relation to philosophical theology is directly
analogous to his relation to science. In fact, it is quite possible
to consider Whitehead's revising of the classical concept of
God a result of the use of the relativistic concepts required by
contemporary revolutions in scientific theory.[44] The theological use of this revised conception by Whiteheadian thinkers
seldom involves a direct appeal to personal religious experience or private intuitions. In both theology and the philosophy
of science, process philosophers tend to operate mainly on the
conceptual and inferential level.[45]

It would be cranky in the extreme to criticize Whitehead
for his systematic, hypothetical–deductive efforts in relation
to process philosophy. One has but to reflect upon the fate of
the process perspective in the West, from its beginnings with
Heraclitus to the present, to understand the necessity for the
rationalization of intuitions of process. Heraclitus is viewed
within our tradition as more a poet than a philosopher largely

because process thinking unmediated by conceptualization and system does not fall within the purview of philosophy at all. Bergson, the modern counterpart of Heraclitus, has so little influence today primarily because, in addition to some of his novel cosmological suggestions, which were found relevant to the contemporary philosophy of science, he insisted upon intuition rather than reason as the primary mode of knowing. Whitehead, on the other hand, may be said to have survived as an influential philosopher precisely because he tied his emphasis on the necessity of immediate experience so closely to his systematic second-order constructions. By so doing, he, willy-nilly, forms a bridge to more radical forms of process thought. For now that it is no longer necessary for a theory to pay homage to the cultural interests of science or of classical theology in order to qualify as a respectable contribution to intellectual culture, we can begin to divest process philosophy of its apologetic accouterments and to develop this perspective from an experiential foundation. It is at this point, as we shall soon see, that the process philosophies developed within Eastern cultures become important.[46]

It is inevitable that process philosophers in our culture should be interpreted as vague, mystical, and irrational. Only insofar as their thinking contains elements deriving from the accepted *mythos* will they find acceptance within the philosophic community. But in the face of our cultural collapse, which, more than anything else, is constituted by a bankruptcy of reason, it seems necessary to stress precisely those elements in our process thinkers that challenge received wisdom. Thinking predicated on the intuition of positive chaos is the form of thought that promises to serve our future needs. Such an intuition would lead us directly into the flux of passing circumstances, into a relationship with our total ambience that is not characterized by subject–object distinctions or by mediation through symbolic filters, but that expresses the reciprocal interfusion of each with every other item.

The central claim of process thinking is that intuition, or feeling, provides a more ready access to the nature of things than do consciousness and reason. Concepts function, not as ends in themselves that directly name aspects of the real

world, but as tools for the evocation of intuitions. The claim of
Western process thought and of much of Eastern philosophy
as well amounts to this: since "change cannot be thought,"
and yet the very nature of reality is change, thought in the
form of reason and concepts cannot provide direct access to
the nature of things. However, since "permanence cannot be
felt," and feeling is the primary medium through which access
to reality is gained, permanence must not be a primary condition of that which is most real. Permanence, then, must be an
abstraction from process, and reason, which deals in concepts, must be the result of an abstraction from intuition. The
act of abstraction can be of positive benefit only if it provides
tools by which one may be reintroduced into the flux of passing circumstance. If reality is process, then the knowledge of
the real must illustrate the interpenetration of the knower and
the known. Conceptual knowledge, as an end in itself, separates the knower, as act of knowing, from the knowledge, the
content of the act.

Process philosophers often use metaphor and imagery to
evoke meanings that are literally inexpressible. Such language
serves two functions: first, a deeper penetration into the reality of experience is attained; and, secondly—and equally
important—a sense of the profound depths lying beyond the
reach of any words is gained. Non-literal, or metaphorical,
language is an essential tool of the process philosopher since
the subject of his thought and experience is capable of only
partial rationalization. Such language is meant to point beyond
itself to experiences transcending those characterizable in
words. In this way partial access to experiences beyond
reason is attained.

Language used in this fashion has often been criticized
since, at least in the Anglo-European philosophic tradition,
the most popular methods of philosophical investigation have
been those of analysis and dialectical reasoning. Analysis
presumes the subject matters of philosophy to be complexes
analyzable into simpler units that, when discovered, explain
the nature, behavior, or consequences of the whole that they
make up. Dialectical reasoning, in its normal form, consists in
the synthesis of elements or aspects of a given subject matter
through a demonstration of the incompleteness of "p" as long

as it exists outside of a systematic context encompassing both it and "not-p." Both analytic and synthetic reasonings tend to assume the univocality and unambiguous nature of the elements to be analyzed or synthesized. Metaphor and imagery tend to confuse, not to clarify, when such methods are employed. The method of the process thinker cannot be either straightforwardly analytic or synthetic. His subject matter is a process of becoming not yet complete. Only partial insight is ever possible. The process philosopher must stress, therefore, a kind of method that characterizes experiences capable of only partial realization. The method employed is a species of analogical reasoning that, following Dorothy Emmet in *The Nature of Metaphysical Thinking*,[47] we may call "existential analogy." An existential analogy is one in which language is used in order to suggest meanings not completely accessible to reason. Since the greater part of our experience is non-verbalizable in any literal sense, existential analogy is essential if we are to capture, or re-capture, the significance of the most profound undercurrents of our lives.

The fundamental problem in interpreting philosophies of process is that such interpretation, we must believe, involves *falsification* in a profound sense. "Substance" and "concept" share a fixed and static meaning, which easily leads us to the belief that the latter can interpret the former by virtue of an isomorphism. Indeed, the shared qualities of substance and concepts indicate that it was our emphasis upon conceptualization as a means of knowing the world that led us to believe, at least here in the West, that reality possesses a fixed, *substantial* character. But trapped as most of us are at the level of conceptual understandings, any attempt to characterize reality-as-process in conceptual terms seems to be futile in the extreme. A concept may abstract from a substance without losing the quality of permanence that characterizes it essentially. The concept of process, however, is a formal abstraction that tends to falsify the very meaning of process itself. Conceptual representations of process notions require, therefore, special care in their formation to ensure that they will always be capable of reference back to the intuitions from which they were derived.

In Whiteheadian philosophy, the correlation of an intuition and a concept is accomplished by *symbolic reference*. To return to the example discussed above: a certain wave-length of light symbolizes an immediately sensed color, and the immediate perception symbolizes that wave-length. In the case of an illusory perception, the referent for the sensed color has changed but the reciprocal symbolic relation remains. The *terminus a quo* is the bodily state occasioning the perception, the *terminus ad quem*, the perception as consciously entertained. The physical event in this illustration involves, in the case of the veridical perception, the stimulation of an optic nerve by light of a given wave-length. The consciously perceived color is presented to the senses as immediately perceived. In Whiteheadian terminology the "presentationally immediate" perception of color is an elaboration of the "causally efficacious" perception, which can be characterized in terms of the stimulation of the optic nerve of a perceiver by light of a certain wave-length. There is, therefore, a basis for claiming that the sensed color as presentationally immediate provides a concept by intuition with which to compare a postulated color conceived as light of a certain wave-length. For Whitehead the physical feelings, which are the most primitive factors in any perceptual situation, are feelings of the efficacy of a portion of the past actual world of the perceiver. These feelings are vague, massive, and relatively undifferentiated. As such, they conform to emotional tones. The basic perception of a color is, then, an *emotion*. Color perception provides an excellent illustration of Whitehead's interpretation of perception since we quite commonly recognize the emotional associations accompanying such perceptions. Though many theorists might interpret the emotional response to color as consequent upon conscious recognitions, Whitehead claims that the emotion is a subjective form of feeling that arises at the earliest stages of perception.

Implicit in this consideration of the perceptual situation is Whitehead's claim that there are more modes of perception than meet the eye. Perception in the mode of causal efficacy is the physical feeling of elements from one's past actual world. These feelings, in themselves, are unconscious, vague, and emotional. Conscious sensations of the variety we normally accept as the only valid forms of perceptions provide illustrations of perception in the mode of presentational immediacy in which, for example, a region of space is presented to the perceiver as qualified by a given color. A third mode of perception, "symbolic reference," provides a connection between causal efficacy and presentational immediacy by employing the content of one mode of perception as a symbol for the content of the other. A poet who expresses his feelings in words, and the reader of a poem who finds that the words evoke feelings, illustrate the reciprocal directions of symbolic reference. The conscious recognition of the meanings of words exists alongside relatively vague emotional feelings, which characterize either the occasion for the writing of the poem or the results of the evocative power of the poet's lines. That association of emotional tone and conscious recognition of meaning illustrates perception in the mode of symbolic reference.

The assumption that perception as presentationally immediate is the fundamental perceptive mode is both an illustration of, and a primary support for, the belief in the *substantial* character of reality. If sense data in the form of colored patches are presumed to provide access to the foundations of primitive knowledge of the external world, then it is little wonder that we have tended to accept without question the substance–quality characterization of what is real.

Symbolic reference can move in either of two directions: from the reality of intuited process to the world of consciousness and concepts, or the reverse. For example, "in the use of language there is a double symbolic reference:—from things to words on the part of the speaker and from words back to things on the part of the listener."[48] Expression, therefore, is a function of symbolic reference between the components of appearance and reality. As such, it necessarily involves symbols.

In the simplest cases, symbolic reference moves from reality to appearance. And the "sense of reality is of great importance for the effectiveness of symbolism. . . . [It] can never be adequately sustained amidst mere sensa, either of sound or sight."[49] For this reason "The abstraction, inherent in the development of language, has its dangers. *It leads away from the realities of the immediate world.*"[50]

The great advantage of language in human experience is that through symbolic mediation one can win freedom from the immediacy of one's environmental conditions. But this is also its greatest danger. For once words and concepts, as forms of mediation, are invented, it is all too likely that we come to accept the mediators, without their necessary function of mediation, as constituting fundamental realities. The primary aim of any philosophy of culture is to provide such a balanced critique of the symbolic activity that forms the basis of any cultural milieu that the symbolic contents of the culture can be construed as representations, mediations, of primary realities. We must see the words and concepts that form our discursive symbolism as tools for regaining the immediacy of concrete experience. The central problem in so construing our symbolic activity is that those expressions most closely associated with concrete intuitions are quite often the most idiosyncratic and difficult to communicate. By the time symbols have become universally interpretable they may have lost much of their evocative significance through overuse and abuse.

Primary expression is of relatively novel intuitions. If the expression is *too* novel, no interpretation in terms of the intuitions of the recipients may be possible. In that case, the expression is likely to constitute an unrationalized appearance that cannot be symbolically referred to the emotions of the recipients of that expression. Highly idiosyncratic works of art may be expressions of important aesthetic intuitions but still may not meet with an intelligent response on the part of critics and connoisseurs simply because of the novelty of the expression. In time, an idiosyncratic artist or his critics may educate the public, and eventually he may meet with wide, if posthumous, acclaim. Or his works may finally be dismissed as "meaningless." The success of an expression depends upon whether or not it is interpretable in terms of intuitions possessed by the potential recipients.

If an expression meets with proper interpretation, "the recipient extends his apprehension of the ordered universe by penetrating into the inward nature of the originator of the expression."[51] The bonds existing between the expressor and the recipients create a *community of intuition*. For this reason, Whitehead says that "Expression is the one fundamental sacrament. It is the outward and visible sign of an inward and spiritual grace."[52]

In conversation, the speaker's verbal expression requires symbolic reference from things to words, while the listener must refer from words to things. The same pattern is true for expression in general. The expressive sign, whatever it may be, may evoke the intuitions that interpret it. This is true, of course, only if the intuition is present in the recipient. If it is, "the sign works *ex opere operato*, but only within the limitation that the recipient be patient of the creative action."[53]

The major amount of expression is not of the primary sort. The most common type is that which expresses intuitions stimulated by the expression of others. Primary expression elicits intuitions in recipients that would not otherwise rise to the level of consciousness. The expression of these intuitions by the recipients is, then, "responsive." The predominance of responsive expression implies the importance of the linguistic, literary, and institutional traditions of a culture. Original expressions may be creative, banal, or evil. In any case, they are rare. Those primary expressions important to the founding of cultural traditions are most often products of the religious, aesthetic, or moral interests of individuals. It is *religious* expression, in its doctrinal form, that best illustrates how cultures handle their fundamental intuitions.

The most sophisticated type of religious expression is that of the dogma. The primary expression of a religious intuition is interpreted by the immediate recipients of the expression. The majority maintain the expression in the form of intermediate representations such as modes of worship, the popular forms of religious literature, and art. The criticism of these intermediate representations, and the rational construction of general concepts from the intuitions elicited by the relevant primary and responsive expressions, allow for the development of dogma. For once responsive expression has emerged there is the possibility of disengaging the expressed intuition from any particular experience through the formulation of a rational dogmatic construct capable of giving it abstract and general expression.

There are three factors, therefore, operative in the development of a dogma: the primary expression, the intermediate representation, and the rationalized dogmatic construct. Most so-called religious persons are responsive expressors, operating at the level of intermediate representation. Such representations are, of course, products of previous symbolic reference from the reality of the emotions and intuitions elicited by the primary expression. For such persons it is not the dogmas but the primary expressions that are of most importance. "Religions commit suicide when they find their inspirations in their dogmas. The inspiration of religion lies in . . . the primary expressions of the intuitions of the finest types of religious lives." [54]

Seeking inspiration in dogmas can lead only to a falling away from the reality of religious emotions and intuitions. Inspiration results from an act of symbolic reference from the appearance of imaginative representation to the reality of the relevant intuition. And it is not only religion that commits suicide if it places too much stress on doctrine or dogma. Each of the other cultural interests—art, morality, science, and philosophy—must exercise restraint in its handling of conceptual formulations.

The primary function of dogmatic expression is to satisfy the desire for rational coherence. The expression will be partial since it must stress generic rather than evocative and concrete linguistic forms; still the generalization of intuitions increases their relevance beyond the area of their origin. Furthermore, the use of exact statements in formulating intuitions ensures that identical intuitions can be singled out despite a wide diversity in the circumstances of their elicitation. For example, dogmatic formulations can aid in the examination of suspected commonalities between the various communities of intuition, and in this way facilitate the study of comparative religions.

In the light of the above discussion, the contrast made earlier between Eastern and Western cultures' varying emphases upon "process" and "substance" can be rehearsed once more in terms of the question of the relations between the experiences and the expressions that provide sources of significance for a given culture. Whitehead himself provides additional insight into this contrast in a brief comparison of Buddhism and Christianity as world religions: "The Buddha gave his doctrine to enlighten the world: Christ gave his life. It is for Christians to discern the doctrine. Perhaps in the end the most valuable part of the doctrine of the Buddha is its interpretation of his life." [55] The proper appeal of religion is to religious lives, and Christianity has in its founder a clear example of a religious life relatively free from initial theoretic emphases in his primary expressions. Even though we have not a detailed account of Christ's life, but only the initial responsive expressions (in incipiently rationalized form) of the disciples, still the reported sayings of Jesus tend to possess an evocative, pictorial, non-conceptual character. They "are actions and not adjustments of concepts. He speaks in the lowest abstractions that language is capable of, if it is to be language at all and not the fact itself." [56]

The primary expressions of Jesus Christ were interpreted by his disciples in terms of intuitions elicited into consciousness. These primary expressions and the response of the recipients created a community of intuition out of which grew the first attempts at rationalization, which are manifest in the responsive expression constituting the gospel accounts. The responsive expressions of the disciples and early apostolic fathers were responsible for eliciting in others similar religious intuitions and emotions. A derivative community of intuition was formed, and the tradition of Christianity entered upon its historical career.

The development of Christianity from the relatively concrete teachings of Jesus and his disciples to the ever more subtle characterization and elaboration of the primary intuitions into dogmatic form is one great theme of the history of Christianity. It is this theme that Adolph Harnack so stresses in his *History of Dogma*. The contrasting theme, of course, is the somewhat sporadic, yet recurrent, revolt against the finality of dogma in favor of a return to the concrete content of the

primitive faith. Tertullian in the second century; the
Protestant Reformation, particularly in its Spiritualist and
Anabaptist wing; the Spanish Mystics; and the modern day
Quaker sect—all bear witness to the desire to emphasize the
superior efficacy and spiritual significance of non-formular-
ized religious experience and expression. Those institutions
within the Christian tradition that possess a complex dogmatic
structure concern themselves with the delicate problem of
balancing the intermediate representations, the doctrinal
formulation, and the appeal to the fundamental realities underlying liturgical practice and dogmatic theory. The role of the
doctrine of the Holy Spirit has been to provide a defense for
the possibility of immediate access to spiritual realities without the mediation of dogmatic formulas.

We need only consider the long list of heretics in the
history of Christianity to realize that dogma rather than the
appeal to spiritual lives has formed the criterion of establishing
membership in the Christian community. On the surface, this
would seem to be an extremely ironic fact. For there is certainly *some* truth in Whitehead's claim that Christianity finds
its source and origin in the life of Jesus, and that Buddhism, in
many of its forms, stresses the Buddha's doctrines. And to the
extent that this is true one would expect the very reverse of
the actual relationship existing between the Christian and
Buddhist religions to obtain. For in Buddhism doctrinal affir-
mations are not nearly so important as the quality of the religious life evidenced by the mastery of spiritual techniques and
the employment of these techniques to attain wisdom, insight,
and a disciplined relation to the world. That is to say, doctrines are not meant merely to be candidates for belief; they
are to be used to gain access to experience. In Christianity we
discover an emphasis upon the necessity to *believe* correctly.
Practical forms of religious life have not received the same
stress. Christianity "has always been a religion seeking a
metaphysic, in contrast to Buddhism which is a metaphysic
generating a religion."[57]

Christ gave his life; his disciples and the later theological
tradition have tried to *express* the significance of that fact. In
the first instance, expression requires a movement from the

concrete to the abstract; in the latter instance, the reverse movement is required. Paradoxically enough, it is Buddhism that often finds its inspiration in the concreteness of spiritual life, while Christianity has, more than not, sought to rationalize the intuitions of its founder. The comparison between Buddhism and Christianity as broad traditions expresses well the fundamental contrast between symbolic reference from appearance to reality and the reverse operation. If we begin with the concrete world and end with abstractions, the danger is that we will remain content with those abstract expressions, refusing, or finding ourselves unable, to cash them in for concrete intuitional currency. From a religious point of view, it is far safer to begin with the world of appearance and, armed with a belief in its penultimate or illusory status, seek the reality that underlies it.

Words or concepts should serve as tools that refer symbolically to the source from which they derive. Otherwise, the tendency will be to confuse the tool with the fundamental reality.

> The fish-trap exists because of the fish; once you've gotten the fish, you can forget the trap. The rabbit-snare exists because of the rabbit; once you've gotten the rabbit, you can forget the snare. Words exist because of the meaning; once you've gotten the meaning, you can forget the words. Where can I find a man who has forgotten words so I can have a word with him?[58]

The difficulty with a point of view that is always directing one away from concepts and words back to the original "meaning" (which in this context refers to concrete intuitive knowledge) is that it must do so by employing words and concepts. If the reader or listener does not already know, concretely, the meaning that is meant to be conveyed, then how is he to avoid taking the words in their public significance as the aim of the communication? Wittgenstein's advice concerning that of which we cannot speak—that we should remain silent—would seem appropriate here. But those who seek to evoke some sense of reality as an ongoing process, as a creative advance into novelty, do not think they need to take this advice. Lao Tzu, the traditional author of the Taoist masterpiece the *Tao Te Ching*, was often chided by Confucian critics because, after beginning his work with the statement "The Way that can be spoken of is not the constant Way," he wrote an additional five thousand characters telling of the way. But the twelfth-century philosopher Wu Tzu offered an unobjectionable defense of Lao Tzu with these words: "I make an embroidery of drakes and let you examine and admire them. As for the golden needle, I cannot pass it on to you." [59] The needle is not in the embroidery but must be sought apart from it. Analogously, the intuitions are not in the words themselves but they can be discovered beyond the words.

PROCESS AND CREATIVITY

The construction of a philosophic paradigm that allows one to construe the world as composed of the termini of acts of intuition is guided by a metaphorical notion distinct from those employed in the mechanist, formalist, naturalist, or volitional philosophies that have dominated Anglo-European intellectual culture. That notion is "creativity." The philosophy of creativity, purged of the substantialist distortions Western philosophers have given it, provides a significant alternative to the primary versions of philosophy in the West. Such a philosophy, grounded in concepts of intuition, process, and self-creativity, already exists in Taoist, neo-Confucian, and Buddhist versions. We are attempting, by recourse to these Eastern sources, to construct a creationist paradigm [60] that may be employed to interpret the nature and direction of contemporary Western culture. In so doing we shall begin with the Whiteheadian concept of creativity and adjust it in the direction of Eastern process views. The resulting philosophic paradigm will, perhaps, be neither Eastern nor Western, but an amalgamation of the viable elements of each cultural perspective. I contend, however, that a fruitful amalgam is infinitely superior to the fruitless philosophic exercises that currently pattern Western intellectual activity.

Creativity, in Whiteheadian language, is the "pure notion of the activity conditioned by the objective immortality of the actual world." [61] It is "the universal of universals characterizing ultimate matter of fact."[62] Without character, it nonetheless *characterizes*, in the sense that it is responsible for the fundamental character of every existing thing. "The creative process is rhythmic: it swings from the publicity of many things to the individual privacy; and it swings back from the private individual to the publicity of the objectified individual."[63] The pulse of existence is a rhythmic process in which the many things of the immediate past serve as elements in the unification of an aesthetic process of experiencing in the present, which, upon actualization, itself serves as a datum for future experiencing. Nothing created is ever really lost. "The many become one, and are increased by one."[64]

This process of self-creativity that characterizes the nature of things suggests resolutions to the problems of relating unity and multiplicity and being and becoming. The process of self-creativity involves the coming together of all available things into the aesthetic unity of a drop of experience: the many become one. The act of creativity is an act of *concrescence*, an act of growing together. The many things find their unity in the act of self-creation. In creationist thought, being is defined in terms of becoming rather than, as is the case in substance views of reality, the reverse. The stress upon novelty requires that "becoming" constitute the primary term. For "to insinuate anything new into the permanent is to make it a new thing. The old with the least new factor is, as a whole, new. . . . Only abstractly, by disregarding the new, can we say that it is the very same whole."[65] Creationism characterizes being in terms of its potentiality for novel synthesis. The "many things" of the world, in accordance with which the growing together of experience (the aesthetic event) becomes, constitute *beings*. The aesthetic event itself is becoming. The creationist view of existence, therefore, sees two kinds of process: the process of self-creativity, which is concrescence, and the transition of beings into data for acts of concrescence. Creativity explains both concrescence and transition.

Creationist thinking is novel within the Anglo-European philosophical context because in its most complete form this type of thinking stands outside the *mythos* of our culture, which, as the source of all types of Western rationality, forms the root of each of our philosophic traditions. Seeking a novel philosophic paradigm leads us beyond the forms of logos that have derived from our Western *mythos*. For though it is perhaps impossible to discover an alternative logos to supplement the four primary philosophic traditions in the West as long as we remain within our present cultural milieu, it is possible to discover an alternative *mythos*, one that interprets chaos as undifferentiated homogeneity, as the positive contributing source of all order. This *mythos*, which we discover in Taoist metaphysics, stands in direct contradition to that which has given rise to meanings of reason and rationality in the West. Our inherited conception of chaos is one of "disorder" and "confusion," which requires organization via reason and rationalization.

"Creativity" and "process" as general concepts are the primary terms that interpret the reality of things as creative passage. Reality is composed of aesthetic events. These events are free, novel, and transitory. Creativity, as the spontaneous production of novelty, requires that there be freedom to produce the novel. Nature, as reality, must be incomplete, or no novelty would be possible. Creativity derives from a fundamental incompleteness both challenged and reaffirmed by the continued passage into novelty that is the essence of creative process. Since the meaning of creativity lies in the freedom that allows novelty, creativity must be seen basically as *self*-creativity. For the locus of freedom is the self. But, since nature is basically incomplete and since acts of creativity require some form of organic wholeness or completion to qualify as aesthetic, the actualization of self that is the paradigm of creation entails the consequence that the self is momentary, transitory, and in process. Aesthetic events are momentary acts of creativity that come into being and at the point of full actualization cease to be in the fullest sense. Process, therefore, is atomic in character. Otherwise there could be no full realization of novelty through aesthetic action. Aesthetic events, as free, novelty-seeking, and transitory, are the fundamental units of existence. Creativity is the self-creative action of finite events in process of becoming. Each such event, at full realization, loses its uniqueness. Reality, as an interweaving of freedom and novelty, therefore, must be seen as process.

Such a characterization of process philosophy, or "creationism," has its inspiration in Whitehead's thought. But it is in the writings of Eastern philosophers, principally Taoists and Ch'an Buddhists, that the creationist perspective finds its fullest expression. The indeterminism expressed by substituting the notion of creativity for the traditional concept of cause is well expressed by the Taoist Chuang Tzu: "All things create themselves from their own inward reflection and none can tell how they come to do so." [66] The fundamental element of self-creativity is freedom. No amount of analysis of experience will allow one to discover a cause of creativity. No component of experience—emotional or conceptual—can provide a reason for the self-creative act. For "beyond the determination of these components there always remains the final reaction of the self-creative unity of the universe." [67]

In Eastern thought this conception of the "self-creative unity of the universe" is expressed by the concept *Tao*. Tao, or "The Way" as it is normally translated, is without character, though it is the source of all characterization: "Tao is eternal and has no name." [68] Tao is said to be an "Uncarved Block," with a capacity for infinite characterization. It can be seen only in terms of its manifestations; otherwise it is without character. Tao is the ultimate intuition and doctrine about which all other aspects of Taoist metaphysics revolve. It is the source from which all things derive. As such it may seem to function analogously to the fundamental principles of other theoretical systems: Plato's principle of the Good, Aristotle's Prime Matter, and so on. But the analogy between the concept of Tao and the principles of Western philosophies is by no means exact. In the West ultimate principles serve most often as *archai*, or sources, distinct from the natural world for which they serve as source. The concept of *arche* in Greek metaphysics, at least since Plato, has been interpreted as a principle conceived as separate, in some sense, from physical nature. God as *arche* in the Western philosophical tradition serves to illustrate this point. As creator of all existing things,

God himself must not be construed in the same terms as actual existents. As uncreated essence, God is distinct from created existences.

Tao cannot be construed as an *arche* in this sense. True, Tao may be spoken of as the source out of which all things arise. But it cannot be said to be separate from the existing things of which it is the source. Taoist metaphysics is an-archic. The actual world presumed by Taoism is an anarchy in the sense that it is without *archai*, or *principia*, serving as determining sources of order and value distinct from the order they determine. The units of existence constituting the nature of things are thus self-determining. The becoming of the world is the coming-into-being of processes of creative synthesis. The process of becoming is a process of the self-actualization of the units of experience that make up the existing things of the actual world. This process involves the uniting of the many things of the actual world into a pattern of data forming the basis for subjective becoming for the individual experience, as well as the addition of the self-actualized units of existence to the totality of objective items of the actual world, which forms the available data for subsequent acts of self-actualization. For this process of epochal becoming to continue, some dynamism is required to account for the continuation of the process. Creativity is this dynamism. There is a sense in which creativity functions in relation to the process of becoming in quite the same way as Aristotle's Prime Matter functions in relation to individual substances. But there is also a significant difference: Prime Matter—like Plato's Forms or the classical conception of God—functions as an *arche* or principle distinct from the existing things of the world. Principles, in the tradition of Western philosophy, cannot be said to exist in the same way as the actual existing things they explain. There must be principles that function as the ground of potentiality and possibility in distinction from actualized existences. And since the process of actualization is only partially explained by the concept of pure potentiality and pure possibility, it is necessary to add a third *arche* to the explanatory scheme: *pure actuality*. Thus, three sources of the existing world are presupposed in most metaphysical accounts since Plato and Aristotle: potentiality, with its concomitant notions of possibility, and actuality.[69]

This conception of principles necessary for the characterization of the nature of existing things is a requirement of the *understanding*, for without such principles we cannot perform the rational act needed in order to characterize for our understanding the specific nature of things. In Northrop's terms, we form concepts by postulation in order to understand the intuited items of our experience. If we are concerned with increasing our access to the world through *intuition*, we must seek means other than the postulation of principles or *archai*, which provide the basis of a rational account of the world, and seek to penetrate to the experience of existing things themselves. The notions of Tao, or "creativity," function as termini of acts of intuition. Certainly, each of these intuitables could function as a postulated principle within a metaphysical scheme; indeed this is the manner in which these concepts are most often entertained within their respective contexts. But to interpret Tao as an *arche*, or principle, in the traditional Western sense is seriously to misconstrue it. Likewise, to conceive the notion of "creativity" as the source of potentiality in contrast to actualized existence is to see it in only its partial and ancillary role. *Archai* are objects of thought inferred from the existing things of the world, or from the description or interpretation of those things. As such they are not objects of intuition. Prime matter, the Receptacle, God (in his classical theological sense) are not intuited; they are inferred.

The basic difference between Western and Eastern ways of philosophizing is explained by the contrast, not between postulation and intuition, but between substance and process philosophies. A world of substances is discoverable through reason; a world of processes must be entertained through intuition. The primary notions underlying creationist philosophy must be referred symbolically to primitive intuitional experience rather than employed systematically as principles of coherence in the construction of hypothetical–deductive systems. If, subsequently, one wishes to systematize the intuitional basis into a conceptual scheme adequate to interpret scientific abstractions of the sort that for some time have dominated Western culture, this can certainly be done. But such a move is unnecessary unless one chooses to accept the continued dominance of such abstractions in determining the character and direction of the cultural milieu. And it is precisely this gambit that we in Anglo-European culture are increasingly prepared to refuse. Our refusal is not, we should stress, determined merely by the collapse of one set of abstractions requiring of us the development of an alternative theoretical system. On the contrary, it is the very act of theory construction in accordance with rational principles functioning as determining sources of order that is brought into question. Or, stated in terms of an argument developed earlier in this work: the roots of *philosophia naturalis*, out of which, and in accordance with which, *pari passu*, the scientific enterprise developed, are found in the conception of chaos as "yawning gap" or "gaping void," which can be overcome only through a rational act of organization. Science and scientific abstractions derive from cosmological systems, themselves determined by cosmogonical speculations and the myths that found them. And as we have already seen, those cosmogonies and cosmologies that have come to dominate the Anglo-European tradition are based on conceptions of negative chaos. But, again as we have previously noted, there are philosophical perspectives derived from conceptions of chaos as undifferentiated homogeneity. Indeed, we are now in a position to see precisely why it must be the case that Western or Anglo-European forms of process philosophy must pay tribute to the importance of reason and conceptualization if they are to meet with any but the most qualified acceptance. Our philosophic heritage has, as one its profoundest convictions, the mistrust of intuition. This mistrust is grounded in the belief that "in the beginning was chaos."

Tao, as the terminus of an intuition, must be process. For just as change cannot be directly thought, due to the static, form-endowing character of reasoning, so permanence cannot be directly felt due to the dynamic, form-excluding quality of intuition. "The Tao that can be told of is not the eternal Tao; the name that can be named is not the eternal name."[70] This statement does not entail a quietistic mysticism that refuses to express the ineffable. For in addition to the *nameless* qualities of things, the *nameable* characteristics participate in the Tao as well.

The understanding of tao-as-process requires the articulation of both the "nameless" and "nameable" aspects of the Tao. In the former sense, Tao is *non-being*; in the latter, *being*. "All things in the world come from being (Nameable Tao), and being comes from non-being (Nameless Tao)."[71] Traditional interpretations of Taoism stress the concept of *original* non-being, and as such lead to an interpretation of Taoism as a dialectical opposite of much of Western metaphysics, which accepts the priority of being expressed in the Parmenidean dictum, "only Being is. . . ." But that interpretation is one-sided in its own way, and leads to as many difficulties as the affirmation of being over non-being does.

A far better vision of Taoist "cosmogony," if the term is applicable, is the one expressed in the Second Chapter of the *Tao Te Ching*: "Being and non-being produce *each other*."[72] That is to say, Nameless and Nameable Tao are so related as to constitute two polar aspects of the same notion. In such an interpretation no final priority can be given to either being or non-being. Tao as nameable is manifested in the actual things of the world. As non-being, Tao should be interpreted in terms of the conception of creativity we have been elaborating.

As creativity is without character (though capable of characterizing) so with non-being: It is characterless, though it qualifies every existing thing. The *how* of this qualifying must be viewed in relation to the conception of becoming or process that names the polar relation of being and non-being. In contrast to Nameless Tao, or non-being, Nameable Tao might best be construed as The Order of Nature, provided the widest possible meaning is attached to that concept. Perhaps closest in meaning is the Whiteheadian concept of the Extensive Continuum—that initial matrix of order that pure extensiveness comprises. It is that "vast society [that] constitutes the whole environment within which our epoch is set, so far as systematic characteristics are discernible by us in our present stage of development."[73] Tao as being, then, is that matrix of real potentiality to which the pure potentiality of non-being is related to produce the actualities of our universe.[74]

It is impossible not to risk confusion at this point due to the unfamiliar use of the terms *being* and *non-being* required to explicate the creationist paradigm. Some confusion at least can be avoided if we indicate some of the more radical departures of this interpretation of Taoism from more traditional forms of Western metaphysics.

The relations of Tao as Nameless to the Nameable Tao are, as we have said, polar. Thus it is necessary to think of Tao as *that which is* as well as *that which is not*. Or better: Tao may be construed as *That Which*, and, thus, as characterizable in terms both of being and of non-being. That Which *is* and That Which *is not* form the polar relation that constitutes the dynamic of the Taoist, or creationist, universe. Tao is in the many things of the world in such a way as to constitute the acts of self-creation that are the only real things. This is to say that only becoming (coming into being, which illustrates some mixture of being and non-being) is; not-becoming (i.e., either being or non-being abstracted from its polar relation with its opposite) is not.

There are no *archai* external to the things themselves. No creator, no conditioner, exists. The Judaeo-Christian doctrine of creation assumes the existence of a Supreme Actuality, which created, out of non-being, Being-itself and the actualities of the world. Creationism has no need of a transcendent creator, because "everything creates itself without the direction of any Creator. Since things create themselves, they are unconditioned. This is the norm of the universe."[75]

This concept of self-creativity has far-reaching implications for the understanding of the radical process view we are elaborating. The denial of a creator or conditioner that is in some sense outside or beyond the self-creative events constituting process itself is tantamount to the claim that creationism is an-archic and thus without *archai* to produce or in-form existing things. Non-being is by definition uncharacterized. Being cannot be given any definite form by non-being. Thus the production of the things of the world cannot be explained by an *arche*, or principle, outside the things themselves. For the mutual production of being and non-being proceeds within the context of an indivisible unit, which means that neither is outside, beyond, or external to the other. And the things of the world themselves comprise nothing more than being and non-being. Tao as *That Which* both is and is-not is the dynamism of self-creativity. And to look beyond this dynamism for some dynamic *thing* is vain.[76]

The relations of being and non-being suggested by the interpretation of Tao as a dynamic, polar relation prevents us from interpreting the notion of becoming in terms of the conception of deficient being. The substantialist bias in Western metaphysics has prejudiced our understanding of becoming, or process, such that we are ready to believe that any mixture of being and non-being is somehow defective. It is the fact of novelty, which requires real instances of coming into being, that ensures the status of the element of non-being in the process view.

Finally, we should note how our conception of Tao precludes any necessity for giving priority to either one or many in creationist metaphysics. Tao as non-being is one; as being it is many. That is, non-being, as pure potentiality, is one and undivided; being, as real potentiality, is many in its potentiality for orderedness. Becoming, or process, as an indivisible relation of non-being and being, is both one and many.

The functioning of Tao as creativity is discovered only in and through things. This functioning reveals the power of Tao. And as the fundamentally polar characterization of Tao is necessary for more complete recognition of its status and functioning, the power of the Way is best understood in its basic being/non-being characterization. This polar relation is termed the *Yin / Yang* relation. *Yin*, associated with non-being, and *Yang*, with being, are intrinsically interwoven aspects of every instance of Tao.

In the creationist paradigm I am attempting to develop, the *Yin/Yang* conceptualization functions in relation to the atomic character of process to explain the rhythmic nature of the processes that constitute the natural world. The units of becoming, as self-actualizing, contain both passive (*Yin*) and active (*Yang*) moments. That is, the coming-into-being of the

event which process itself comprises requires a *passivity* to
the data of the past actualized world, and an *activity* of the
coordination and integration of these data into a novel organic
event. Viewed as passive, the event may be construed as an
effect of its past; viewed actively, it is a spontaneous act of
self-creation, *sui generis*.

At this point one is tempted to ask for a principle or
principles that provide some understanding of the manner in
which being and non-being are related in the becoming of an
event. The usual ploy in our Anglo-European tradition is to
suggest that the concept of *freedom*, characterized as the
novelty-producing capacity of a unit of becoming, provides
such a principle. Those units of becoming capable of introducing novelty into the integrations of their data are free; those
not capable are determined by their past. But this conception
of freedom associates the term almost exclusively with *action*,
and, in so doing, rips asunder the polar conception of becoming by placing a value judgment on the *yang* components of
events. This volitional interpretation of freedom and novelty
runs directly counter to the interpretation suggested by the
process view under consideration. Freedom is no more to be
identified with novelty-producing action than determination is
to be exclusively associated with passivity. We have here one
of the most subtle forms of anthropomorphism, a form that
has vitiated much of Anglo-European philosophy. For to
identify freedom with activity suggests that actions over
against nature are preferable to "actions" in accordance with
the flow of events.[77]

The unquestioned status of principles in Anglo-European
philosophy has blinded Western thinkers to the unique genius
of some forms of Eastern thought. Indeed, most of the modern
interpretations of Taoism and Neo-Confucianism by Eastern
as well as Western philosophers employ the conception of
principles as *sources* of the being and becoming of that which
is. The notion of Tao as non-being (the Nameless) and being
(the Nameable), coupled with the conception of process or
becoming as the reality of things, allows one to refuse the
gambit offered by almost all of Western and much of Eastern
thought. Becoming has no principle outside itself. And as

becoming is epochal or atomic, the processes of coming into being are their own reasons for becoming. Thus, there are as many "principles" explaining the nature and functioning of units of becoming as there are units themselves. The appeal to *archai* outside the process of nature is of no assistance in providing a grasp of the nature of becoming. The appeal to principles is thus shown to be a fundamental bias of substantialist metaphysics, which itself is either cause or consequence of the conception of reason as *ratio* or logos measuring or ordering an antecedent irrational surd, identified in our cosmogonic myths as chaos.

NOTES

1. Some recent philosophers have attempted to show that Parmenides' arguments—and presumably the metaphysical doctrines based on them—turn on a logical fallacy resulting from a confusion of "predicative" and "existential" propositions. The claim is, for example, that the negative predicative proposition "X is not P" is distinct from the negative existential judgment "X is not." But it is doubtful whether the claim that existence cannot be a predicate (a claim whose fortunes wax and wane depending on which philosophic dispositions are in vogue) touches the basic intuitions of Parmenides. His claim seems to involve a broader issue. To think is to think the intelligible; and to think the intelligible involves one in thinking *what is*. The subsequent, more sophisticated claim made of what is—namely, *that it is*—may lead to subtle difficulties, but that is hardly crucial to Parmenides' argument. The "mistake" that grounds Western metaphysics is not, I take it, to be found in a fallacy that all but the most naïve would instinctively avoid. I prefer to find the inadequacy of metaphysical speculation deriving from Parmenides' perfectly *rational* judgment that, since "change cannot be thought," one ought to deny the reality of change rather than challenge the validity of *reason*. I would only add that the time has come to examine the alternative path: that of accepting the fundamental reality of change and, by reconstructing our ways of knowing, to ask how change can be known.

2. *The Great Chain of Being: A Study in the History of an Idea* (New York: Harper Torchbooks, 1960).

3. *City of God* 12.6, p. 386.

4. See *The Confessions of Saint Augustine* 8, trans. Edward B. Pusey (New York: Modern Library, 1949), esp. pp. 134–38.

5. *Cosmogony*, trans. Mildred Focht (New York: Comet, 1948), pp. 218–19.

6. Ibid., p. 219.

7. *Process and Reality*, p. 169.

8. Ibid., p. 171.

9. Paul Tillich, *Systematic Theology* III (Chicago: The University of Chicago Press, 1963), p. 50.

10. See "The Possible Concepts by Intuition and Concepts by Postulation as a Basic Terminology for Comparative Philosophy," in *The Logic of the Sciences and the Humanities* (New York: World, 1959), pp. 77–101.

11. Ibid., p. 82.

12. Ibid., p. 83.

13. *The Meeting of East and West* (New York: Macmillan, 1949), p. 447.

14. Ibid., p. 448.

15. See Guenther's *The Life and Teachings of Naropa* (New York: Oxford University Press, 1963), pp. 124–30.

16. *Science and Civilization in China* II (Cambridge: Cambridge University Press, 1962), Section 18, p. 579.

17. For a succinct discussion of the philosophic debates preceding the establishment of Newtonian orthodoxy, see Ivor Leclerc, *The Nature of Physical Existence* (New York: Humanities, 1972), passim.

18. *The Texts of Taoism*, trans. James Legge, 2 vols. (New York: Dover, 1962), I 266–67.

19. Ibid., 267.

20. *Science and the Modern World* (New York: Free Press, 1967), p. 208.

21. Ibid., p. 152.

22. Ibid.

23. See the work of Charles Hartshorne, perhaps the foremost living representative of process philosophy, *Creative Synthesis and Philosophic Method* (LaSalle, Ill.: Open Court, 1970). My conception of the philosophy of creativity drawn from a comparison of Whiteheadian and Eastern philosophies will differ significantly from Hartshorne's.

24. See *The Concept of Nature* (Ann Arbor: The University of Michigan Press, 1957), pp. 3–4.

25. *Meeting of East and West*, pp. 441–42.

26. *Concept of Nature*, pp. 97–98.

27. The consequences of the assumption of the distinction between nature as sensed and nature as mathematically described that grounded modern science have been brilliantly outlined in Whitehead's *Science and the Modern World*.

28. *Life and Teachings of Naropa*, p. 127n.

29. *Science and the Modern World*, p. 87.

30. *Creative Evolution*, trans. Arthur Mitchell (New York: Random House, 1951), p. 328.

31. *Science and the Modern World*, p. 87.

32. *Modes of Thought*, p. 124.

33. See *Logic of the Sciences and the Humanities*, p. 384.

34. See *Science and Civilization in China* II, 291–92.

35. Ibid., pp. 284–85.

36. See Snell's *Discovery of the Mind*.

37. See Cornford's *From Religion to Philosophy*.

38. An interesting example of the inability correctly to interpret the novel process philosophies arising in the twentieth century is found in Stephen Pepper's meta-philosophical study, *World Hypotheses*. In this work Pepper uses Whitehead's metaphysical system as an example of

"eclecticism" in philosophy. His claim is that Whitehead has borrowed elements from various philosophic viewpoints and combined them in a basically incoherent and inconsistent fashion. Some years later, however, in his *Concept and Quality: A World Hypothesis*, Pepper revised his opinion somewhat, suggesting that Whitehead may, indeed, have developed the beginnings of a new "World Hypothesis" based on an original root-metaphor concept. The years between Pepper's first and second assessments of Whiteheadian thought were required for the novelty of the perspective to be grasped.

39. In many ways the mystical tradition can be said to form the sole ready source within Western culture for an understanding of the process view that requires one to envision the world as constituted by the termini of acts of intuition. The extreme difficulty Western thinkers have had in attempting to assimilate the insights of the mystics tells us a great deal about the implicit conflict between process and substance characterizations of the world. Unfortunately, by the time the insights of the mystics have been filtered down into the secondary literature of our culture, they have more often than not been masked by the rhetoric of substantialist metaphysics and are thereby lost to us. Indeed, any interpretation of mystical experience, even by the mystic himself, is of necessity rendered respectably Western, since the conceptualizations available which may be used to interpret one's experience are all to be drawn from substantialist thought.

40. And even that inference is a questionable one. See his *Religion in the Making* (New York: World, 1971), p. 69.

41. See Donald Sherburne, "Whitehead Without God," in *Process Philosophy and Christian Thought*, ed. Delwin Brown et al. (New York: Bobbs-Merrill, 1972), pp. 305–28.

42. It is likely that the second edition of Bergson's *Duration and Simultaneity* (1923) and the cosmological doctrines drawn from writings between *Time and Free Will* (1889) and *Creative Evolution* (1907) contain the most influential aspects of his thinking. The epistemological portions of his philosophy, grounded in the doctrine of the primacy of intuition, especially *Introduction to Metaphysics* (1903), seem to have had significantly less impact on contemporary philosophic thought.

43. See my *Civilization of Experience*, pp. 10–21, for a discussion of the sources of evidence in Whitehead's philosophy.

44. See, for example, the discussion of the process conception of "God" in Charles Hartshorne's *Divine Relativity* and *The Logic of Perfection* (LaSalle, Ill.: Open Court, 1962). See also John Cobb, *A Christian Natural Theology* (Philadelphia: Westminster, 1965). The discussions of God in these works borrow a great deal more from logic and second-order theological investigations than from the data of intuition.

45. This point is made well by James Wayne Dye in his "Heracleitus and the Future of Process Philosophy," Tulane Studies in Philosophy 23, Studies in Process Philosophy 1 (New Orleans: Tulane University, 1974), pp. 13–31. Dye's article contains a valuable set of comments on the importance of immediate experiences, rather than second-order theories, as foundations for process thinking.

46. There is an unquestionable irony in the contemporary interest among Western intellectuals in the philosophies of the East at a time when

Eastern countries have become so enamored of Western science and technology and the ideologies which sustain them. Of Communist China, capitalist Japan, and post-colonial India, none seems overly concerned with preserving its classical tradition. Indeed, the most fascinating and, perhaps for our present purposes, most relevant of the philosophic tradition—that of Chinese Taoism—can hardly be said to exist in either its religious or its philosophical forms within the boundaries of mainland China. Taoist ideas are to be found primarily within the *Ch'an* (Japanese: Zen) form of Buddhism which developed from the assimilation of Taoism and Madhyamika Buddhism after the second century. The practical form of Taoist mysticism, the yogic tradition, persists in some forms of Tantrism. Tantric Buddhism, associated until two decades ago with the secluded areas of Tibet, but now exiled by Chinese incursions into that country, has become increasingly familiar to Western thinkers and religious virtuosi because of the emigration to Europe, England, and the United States of displaced gurus and adepts.

47. (London: Macmillan, 1944), pp. 13–15.
48. Whitehead, *Symbolism: Its Meaning and Effect* (New York: Macmillan, 1959), p. 12.
49. Whitehead, *Modes of Thought*, p. 32.
50. Ibid., p. 39; emphasis added.
51. Whitehead, *Religion in the Making*, p. 128.
52. Ibid., p. 127.
53. Ibid., p. 128.
54. Ibid., p. 138.
55. Ibid., p. 55.
56. Ibid., p. 56.
57. Ibid., p. 50.
58. *The Complete Works of Chuang-Tzu*, trans. Burton Watson (New York: Columbia University Press, 1968), chap. 26, p. 302.
59. Quoted in Chang Chung-Yuan, *Creativity and Taoism: A Study of Chinese Philosophy, Art, and Poetry* (New York: Harper & Row, 1963), p. 30.
60. See my *Civilization of Experience*, pp. 23–29, for a detailed discussion of "creationism." I am no longer prepared to defend, as I did in that work, Whiteheadian thought as the most viable philosophy of creativity. The alterations which I shall make in the strictly Whiteheadian conception of creativity are due mainly to my reflections on Eastern philosophy. I should add that I have purposely maintained the term creation*ism* for the *theoretical* form of the vision which I am discussing in hopes that the "ism" will serve to advertise its tentative and penultimate status. I certainly do not wish to be guilty of the same sort of provincialism and dogmatism for which I have criticized other philosophers in our tradition.
61. *Process and Reality*, pp. 46–47.
62. Ibid., p. 31.
63. Ibid., p. 229.
64. Ibid., p. 32.
65. Charles Hartshorne, "The Development of Process Philosophy," in *Philosophers of Process*, ed. Douglas Browning (New York: Random House, 1965), pp. xix–xx.
66. Quoted in Chang Chung-Yuan, *Creativity and Taoism*, p. 66.

67. Whitehead, *Process and Reality*, p. 75.

68. *The Way of Lao Tzu (Tao Te Ching)* 32, trans. Wing-Tsit Chan (Indianapolis: Bobbs-Merrill, 1963), p. 157.

69. See the illuminating discussion of *archai* as metaphysical principles in Leclerc, *Nature of Physical Existence*, pp. 336–48. I should stress that my analysis of the importance of such principles in the process tradition is essentially opposed to his.

70. *Way of Lao Tzu* 1, p. 97.

71. Ibid. 40, p. 173.

72. Ibid., p. 101; emphasis added.

73. *Process and Reality*, p. 148.

74. My interpretation of the concept of Tao is a speculative attempt to reconcile several distinct doctrinal perspectives in Chinese philosophical thought, and my use of the concept may be orthodox in no classical school of philosophy. Nonetheless, I owe the reader some information concerning the sources from which my speculations are drawn. The fundamental source is the *Tao Te Ching* of Lao Tzu. Chief among the translations of that work which I have consulted are Wing-Tsit Chan's *The Way of Lao Tzu*, cited earlier; Arthur Waley, *The Way and Its Power* (New York: Grove, 1958); Gia-Fu Feng and Jane English, *Tao Te Ching* (New York: Random House, 1972); *The Tao Teh King*, the first volume of Legge's *Texts of Taoism*; D. C. Lau, *Tao Te Ching* (Baltimore: Penguin, 1963); and Chang Chung-Yuan, *Tao: A New Way of Thinking* (New York: Harper & Row, 1977).

In addition I have benefited from the writings of Chuang Tzu, principally as found in the second volume of Legge's edition of *The Texts of Taoism*, and in Watson's translation of the *Complete Works of Chuang-Tzu*; and from *The I Ching*, trans. Richard Wilhelm (Princeton: Bollingen, 1950, 1967). I have frequently consulted Helmut Wilhelm's *Eight Lectures on the I Ching*, trans. Cary Baynes (New York: Harper & Row, 1960), and his *Heaven, Earth, and Man in the Book of Changes* (Seattle: University of Washington Press, 1977).

I have also found Jung's commentary on *The Secret of the Golden Flower*, trans. Richard Wilhelm (New York: Causeway, 1975), pp. 77–137, quite helpful, as well as the selections from the *Commentaries* of Wang Pi and Kuo Hsiang on the writings of Lao Tzu and Chuang Tzu, respectively, contained in *Sources of Chinese Tradition*, ed. William de Bary (New York: Columbia University Press, 1960), along with the more recently published *Commentary on the Lao Tzu by Wang Pi*, trans. Arianne Rump with Wing-tsit Chan (Honolulu: The University Press of Hawaii, 1979).

Two excellent articles in *The Journal of Chinese Philosophy* deserve special mention: Sung-Peng Hsu's "Two Kinds of Changes in Lao Tzu's Thought," 4, No. 4 (December 1977), 329–55, and N. J. Girardot, " 'Returning to the Beginning' and the Arts of Mr. Hun-Tun in the *Chuang Tzu*," 5, No. 1 (March 1978), 21–69.

Finally, I must say that through conversations with my friend and colleague Kuang-ming Wu, a reincarnation of Chuang-Tzu himself, I have gained a sense of the "spirit" of the Taoist sensibility.

The position which I am taking lies somewhere between the neo-Taoist and neo-Confucian philosophies. With the neo-Taoist I stress the notion of self-creativity and the denial of *archai* external to individual things; with the neo-Confucianist I refuse to give priority to non-being over being, or to "one" over "many," in descriptions of the nature of process. In any case, because of my comparative methodology my views are not likely to be found in any complete form within either Eastern or Western contexts.

75. Kuo-Hsiang, *Commentary on Chuang Tzu* 2.2:46–47A, in *Sources of Chinese Tradition*, ed. de Bary, p. 243.

76. It is interesting to note the relation between the an-archic or "no-principles" character of Taoist metaphysics and the social and political anarchism of the early Taoist communities. Apparently, we have here the principal reason why the concepts of philosophical anarchism are so little represented in Western thought. As long as the conception of *arche* as determining source of order is affirmed, anarchy must be associated with *chaos* in the negative sense. Part of the significance of the importation of Taoist thought into Western culture should be found in the stimulus which it provides for the production of a metaphysics of anarchism. I am currently completing a book on philosophical anarchism, entitled *Eros and Irony*, which borrows heavily from the Taoist sensibility.

77. We shall soon have occasion to return to this point when, in the following chapter, we detail the concepts of *wu-wei* (non-assertive action), *wu-chih* (unprincipled knowing) and *wu-yü* (objectless desire).

5

The Way Beyond ''Ways''

''What is the spirit of the Ch'ing Liang monastery?''

''When you go to other places just say that you are on your way to Ch'ing Liang.''

A CH'AN KUNG-AN

The Way is forever nameless, and Uncarved Block.

LAO TZU

NEITHER THEORY NOR PRACTICE

ONE OF THE PRINCIPAL THEMES in the story of our developing cultural self-consciousness concerns the increasing skepticism directed toward the claims of reason and rationality. Anglo-European culture was decisively influenced by the theoretic attitude of the Greeks, which was grounded in the belief that one can know the nature of reality because of an isomorphic relation between reason and nature as that-which-is. If what one knows via reason conflicts with what one experiences in other ways, the claims of experience must give way to the authority of reason. In one form or another, this attitude has dominated our cultural tradition from the beginning, and has colored the manner in which ''practice'' has been conceived by those philosophers who have claimed priority for the practical attitude. Even the enterprise of science, which has stressed the importance of empirical methods since its modern origins, is grounded in the principle of sufficient reason and the belief in the ubiquity of causal relationships, which, in one form or another, have traditionally served to articulate the fundamental sense of the theoretic attitude. Recently, however, the skeptical attacks of the existentialists, Marxists, and meta-philosophers, directed against the sanctity of theory, have begun seriously to undermine the harmonious relations of theoretical and practical interests essential to any healthy society.

Though the interplay of the theoretical and practical attitudes has been extremely important in the creation of the institutions, understandings, and systems of value characterizing our culture, it was relatively late in the history of thought that the consciousness of this interplay was exploited to increase philosophic insight. One of the principal effects of our increased cultural self-consciousness in the modern period is that reason has begun to turn in upon itself and has mounted an exhaustive critique of its own foundations. Kant's programmatic critique of pure reason was further developed by Hegel, who, in his *Phenomenology of Mind* (1807) provided what is still the best example of a history of the theoretic attitude. A generation later, Marx, in a series of works in political economy, provided the most famous examples of the reading of history from the *practical* standpoint. Of course, David Hume, a century before, in his *History of England*, offered a paradigm of the consideration of history from the perspective of praxis as "custom." It was the naturalist Charles Darwin, a contemporary of Marx's, in *The Origin of the Species* and the *Descent of Man*, who illustrated biological evolution in terms of "natural practice." And John Dewey, in his *Quest for Certainty* (1929), wrote an exhaustive defense of the necessary pre-eminence of practice through an analysis of the negative consequences of the over-emphasis on theory in the history of thought. Unquestionably our primary concern in modern times has been the practical rather than the theoretical attitude. One of the principal grounds for this shift of interest is to be found in the importance of the evolutionary hypotheses of Darwin and Marx.

A consequence of this evolutionary perspective has been the recognition that practical reason has a much longer history than does the theoretical mode. The common presumption today is that thought has been one of the principal tools employed to ensure the survival of the species since the beginnings of humankind. As long as mere survival was the major problem besetting human beings, reason remained primarily a means for enduring and overcoming the challenges of the environment. According to this view, the beginning of recorded history coincides with the origin of speculative or theoretical reason. Reason divorced from the immediate necessities of survival celebrates itself through the self-articulation of cultural expressions. Such a use of reason, it is presumed, is a luxury that came to be afforded only rather late in human development.

In *The Function of Reason*, Whitehead illumines the notions of theoretical and practical reason by contrasting the figure of Ulysses with that of Plato. Whereas Ulysses employed reason in order to discover a method of resolving immediate dilemmas associated with the ends of survival and well-being, Plato used reason as a means of transcending any given circumstances in order to gain a general perspective on the world. There is nothing intrinsic to either the theoretical or practical reason that requires significant interaction. Indeed, it is Whitehead's view that these two modes of reason existed side by side without uniting for the greater part of the history of our culture. But "the enormous advance in the technology of the last [two hundred] years arises from the fact that the speculative and practical Reason have at last made contact." [1] This view entails the consequence that the desire to understand the products of human activity as well as the need to apply the principles of abstract knowledge have become efficacious only in modern times. There are cogent arguments in favor of Whitehead's claim. Even modern science in its beginnings was a speculative enterprise divorced from immediately practical concerns. In the development of modern scientific cosmology, the names of Copernicus, Kepler, Bruno, Galileo, Descartes, Gassendi, and Newton tell the story of a revolution in theoretical understanding. Even the telescope, a product of practical reason, provided nothing unanticipated by theory. The significant counter-influences that have led in contemporary society to the grounding of both theoretical and practical interests in technological needs began with the Industrial Revolution.

The motives for the use of theory in advancing practice are derived from the realm of praxis. The needs of survival, the increase in satisfaction through leisure, and self-revelatory actions leading to the attainment of greatness, are the primary motivations for the employment of theory. Weapons, gadgets, and techniques of self-aggrandizement characterize the sphere of praxis. The effect of this union of theory and practice has been the absorption of theory by practice (as discussed in Chapter 1). *Theoria* becomes *ideology*, the rationalization of, or apology for, a given practice.

We could have foreseen these circumstances. Francis Bacon's peculiar rendering of the claim "knowledge is power" (which, though echoing a fundamental Platonic doctrine, reversed the polarities and construed the former concept in terms of the latter) announced the strategy for the usurpation of *theoria* by the practical reason. Our present technological age stands proof of Bacon's doctrine. Action, which has as its primary goal the assertion of self through an act of the will, is now complemented by knowledge, which serves the same end. Knowledge of nature (science) and actions performed in accordance with that knowledge (technology) are both infected by a Faustian quest for power.

We have reached the point at which we can begin to understand the difficulty we have had in Western thought and culture in trying to maintain viable connections between knowledge and action. For in so doing we have often sought to unite two intrinsically conflicting modes of existing—*contemplation* and *the search for greatness*. The fundamental aim of knowing is the enjoyment of the immediate intuitive grasp occasioned by the theoretic attitude. Such enjoyment is intrinsic to the attitude itself. Action, on the other hand, is a *means* toward the achievement of greatness. It cannot constitute the dispassionate application of theoretic knowledge to experience. Nor can it serve as the source of principles of

understanding, which transcends the motive of achieving individual greatness. In our Western tradition, therefore, there
has been good reason for the separation of theory and
practice. And the union of the two, occasioned by the fusion
of science and technology, has perverted the aims of both
knowledge and action.

One of many ironies concerning our contemporary interest in the interplay of theory and practice is that our theoretical energies are expended developing *theories* of practice. The
presumed dichotomy of theory and practice is now recognized
to be the dichotomy of the "theory of theory" and the "theory
of practice." Even Marx, who saw this so clearly and made it
the main thrust of his complaint against classical materialisms,
has been victimized by his own disciples, who want nothing so
much as to develop an adequate theory of praxis. Perhaps the
only cultural movement that can claim to take praxis seriously
is behaviorism, which eschews theory whenever possible,
substituting instead the spare methodological dogma that
science as a means to knowledge can do no more than to
provide a description of behaviors as a means of promoting
their conscious control. The behaviorist promotes the development of technologies of behavior as self-augmenting systems of technique, immanently rational, and requiring, therefore, no transcendent theoretical principles for their guidance.
Whether this solution of the problem of relating theory and
practice will be any more successful than was the idealist
attempt to establish the conviction that *esse est percipi*
depends upon the fate of our technological society.

It is, perhaps, fortunate that the Marxians have not taken
their master too seriously. For if they had, we would not have
the quality of *theoretical* reflection upon the problem of praxis
that we do. Marxian discussions of the relations of theory and
practice derive, of course, from Marx's critique of Hegel. In
spite of Hegel's idealism, he did not conceive *theoria* primarily as a guide for practice or action, but as a means of articulating it. The development of Spirit was told in terms of the
self-articulation of the Idea, whose content was the substance
of intellectual culture. The aims of both *theoria* and praxis were
realized through the self-articulation of the Absolute Idea. The

unity of theory and practice was achieved by the self-reflective activity of the Spirit in somewhat the same manner as it
was achieved in Aristotle's conception of the activity of
"thinking on thinking." Marx sought to realize the unity of
theory and practice through the agency of "sensuous human
activity," and did so by reinterpreting classical materialist
conceptions in terms of the Hegelian dialectic, which meant
that the activity of Spirit was transformed into material forms
of production.

Existentialists, such as Hannah Arendt,[2] and neo-
Marxians, such as Jürgen Habermas, have begun a reassessment of the meaning of praxis that involves the resolution of
problems of alienation through reconstruction of the possibilities of action rather than a reconstitution of the forms of
production. One of the most fruitful attempts to interpret
praxis in terms of action is found in Habermas' discussion of
the grounding of knowledge in "human interest."

In his *Knowledge and Human Interests*, Habermas
accepts the notion that all theory is interest-laden, but
attempts to determine if there is in fact in *theoria* an interest
that can be united with self-conscious reason as critique and
revolutionary praxis in such a way as to realize the *telos*
immanent in both theoretical and practical endeavor. This
interest he discovers in the need for *emancipation.*

The aim of classical or traditional theory was to "provide
the subject with an ecstatic purification from the passions"[3]
by allowing him to locate himself consciously "in the unity of
a stable cosmos and the identity of immutable Being."[4] The
content of the idea of emancipation is the concept of
autonomy and responsibility, which defines the "good and
true life." The realization of this ethical essence of *theoria*
cannot be achieved by the presumption, via ontology and
cosmology, of a unified and stable cosmos since metaphysical
theories easily fall prey to the critical assaults of the Marxian
sociology of knowledge. The ethical intent of theory, however, can be realized to the extent that critical *theoria* and
praxis in the forms of self-reflection and revolutionary activity
can bring about an emancipated society. It is again to the
credit of Habermas that he has avoided the lock-step interpre-

tation of praxis as production in classical Marxian terms, and has introduced, via the pragmatists, especially C. S. Peirce, the interpretation of praxis as communication, and, thus, as a form of activity. The truth claims of theoretical knowledge are made in anticipation of the realization of the good life, which must await the development of a society as a context of communication in the form of "the non-authoritarian and universally practiced dialogue from which both our model of reciprocally constituted ego identity and our idea of true consensus are always implicitly derived."[5] Thus the pernicious— because alienating—objectivism entailed by the ontological claims of *theoria* are eliminated, "not through the power of renewed *theoria* but through demonstrating what it [i.e., objectivism] conceals: the connection of knowledge and interest."[6]

I do not wish to gainsay the brilliance of this attempted resolution of the problem of the relations of knowledge and human interest. My reservations with the theory are, however, potentially quite serious. The first is obvious from the nature of the argument in the initial chapters of this work. I do not believe that it will be possible to construct either a rigorously consistent *or* a reasonably adequate social theory that itself does not presuppose, and will not eventually advertise, ontological presuppositions of the kind spelled out in earlier chapters, which are, of course, objectivist in precisely the sense Habermas finds unacceptable. Such a theory translated or articulated in the form of institutions and organizations of a society will inevitably constitute potentially oppressive challenges to the pluralistic character of a democratic society. I have offered arguments in support of the irreconcilable nature of the self-contradictions inherent in the theoretical conflicts of theory with theory that pattern our contemporary culture. But even if these arguments are not found to be convincing, there is a second, much more serious, objection to the attempt to resolve the conflict of knowledge and human interest in contemporary society, one that directly concerns the understanding of praxis as *action*.

The difficulty with theories that maintain a distinction between praxis and *techne* in order to develop conceptions of practice grounded in the notion of "action" is that the concept of action is, because of its peculiar historical origins, open to suspicion. When it comes to the conception of action or practice, we have been mostly decisively influenced by the agonal spirit of the Greeks. Actions express *principles*, the defense of which is the purpose of the acts. This political concept of action has determined more than our understanding of politics. Actions aimed at the attainment of individual greatness are the subject matter of history, which, for all our intellectual posturings, we have always predominantly understood as a story of the deeds of great men, rather than a history of ideas, or institutions, or causal forces. Actions, whether as sources or consequences of principles, are activities of self-revelation; for this reason the act should, so we believe, be such as to reveal greatness, not triviality. "Because of its inherent tendency to disclose the agent together with the act, action needs for its full appearance the shining brightness we once called 'glory.' "[7] The desire for fame turns out to be not (*pace* Milton) "the last infirmity of noble mind," but rather the presupposition of nobility.

We find that the Hebraic roots of our concept of action are no less significant in determining our attitudes toward *practice*. The Western conception of "the domination of nature" is grounded in the belief in a creator God who deputized human beings as caretakers of his created order, but who then cursed his human creatures with the necessity of labor because of their prideful self-assertion, which resulted in the stolen awareness of good and evil, which in turn separated them from the rest of nature. Action turns out, ultimately, to be only a sublimation of labor, which advertises its origins in the enmity between persons and nature. In either the Greek or the Hebraic sources of the concept of action, we find a disposition to construe practice in relation to the agonal spirit that defines the quest for greatness.

Greatness is achieved only in the public sphere. The untold numbers who do not achieve fame we do not call great. This is truistic, of course, but it hides a less obvious truth: actions that are not aimed at glorification are seldom celebrated in culture and history, and are, thus, much less likely to have public import. The agonal spirit is the author of action in its truest sense. The function of practice is self-revelation of greatness. Such a revelation requires self-assertion. Action is aggressive, self-assertive, in its nature—at least this has been so in our cultural tradition.

The nature of social activity is such that it requires a place, a public sphere, that exists in sufficient dimensions to provide for significant actions. Public dialogue depends upon a consensual understanding that grounds and serves as the primary rationale for the public arena of a society. But the public arena is undermined in contemporary societies because consensus exists only in relation to ideologically manipulated issues. The instinctual recognition of this fact occasions the depressed sense of the importance of attaining to greatness and historical immortality discussed previously.

The search for greatness requires a public sphere in which there is a sense of importance deriving from the massive inheritance of traditional values, articulated through the medium of the various cultural interests that define intellectual culture. The desire for greatness derives from the existence of values and purposes that are by consensus deemed important and that form a cultural milieu serving as ground against which the figures of history are able to stand out. Theoretical thinking has increasingly and inexorably undermined the experience of the import of the cultural significances defining civilized existence due to the fact that we have lost even the hope for the re-instatement of a worthwhile consensus.

Theory, as interpreted from within our classical philosophic tradition, has about it an objectivist bias that can only be defended as disinterested if its truth can be established. The practical activities of persons in society are to be vindicated and justified by recourse to "true" principles. The pedagogical principles articulated in Plato's *Republic*, for example, had as their aim the stimulation and direction of the soul's eros in its quest for the Good. Actions in accordance with those principles are justifiable, we believe, only if they are in fact true. But the inability to appeal to truth that derives from the undeniable relativity of truth claims leads to the collapse of the public arena in which significant actions could take place. The claim that knowledge and human interest join in the desire for emancipation provides only a theoretical resolution of the conflict of theory and practice, for the possibility of emancipation is itself grounded in the existence of a public sphere that depends upon consensus as to the truth or falsity of the important beliefs of a society.

One way of recognizing the consequences of the collapse of the public sphere, and the limits of any attempt to revive it in our contemporary period, is to look at precisely why the resolution of the conflict of *theoria* and praxis has not been attained.

Theoria originally meant "contemplation," "looking at," "envisioning." It is similar in meaning to *thauma*, "wonder." Philosophy begins in wonder, in openness to the world, in a passiveness to experience. Theoretical endeavor was originally a contemplative envisioning of things as passively experienced. The development of the concept of theory from these beginnings to the present-day conception of theory as a conventional construal of nature is a history of the interplay between passive and active understandings of the theoretical attitude. It is clear that no real separation of reason and experience is possible on the original understanding of *theoria*. Only when extraneous criteria were applied to the construction of theoretical understandings did this development take place. Consistency and coherence as logical rules of theory construction tend to divorce reason and experience in some obvious ways. The tensions previously discussed between consistency and adequacy, for example, illustrate the possibility of separating experience and its theoretical understanding. A system of consistent propositions about the world is narrower than direct experience of the world since direct experience tends to be neither systematic (coherently organized) nor consistent. Ideally, a theory may lead us more deeply into experience than otherwise could be true. But this can be so only if the movement from *theoria* to theory is reversible in every case—that is, if it is possible to envision theory as a part of the experienced world and to understand it as guided by the claims of direct experience. This is the fundamental relevance of theory to practice.

Praxis has two original senses: The first meaning is "action," which involves the practice of an art as distinct from its theory. Praxis in this sense is the practice of theory, which may or may not involve the conscious recognition that one's actions accord with the theory, though this is normally presupposed. Aristotle defined art (*techne*) as "a capacity to make in accordance with a true course of reasoning." *Techne*, as opposed to mere experience, requires knowledge of the reasons underlying one's productive activity. Plato had already stressed this point in his distinction between "knowledge" and "right opinion." Without a knowledge of the principles of, or *reasons for*, one's actions, the successful completion of a task is merely accidental. The second sense of praxis, however, supports the conception of an artist as an unconscious practitioner of his art. Praxis as habitual action, accepted practice, or *custom* allows for the realization of a practical or productive end without conscious "know-how" intervening.

Of the two senses of praxis, the former is the more philosophically respectable in our tradition. Knowledge of technique is essential, we believe, to the proper exercise of a skill. For without the rationalization of techniques, the growth of technology as we have experienced it in the West would have been impossible. The facile identification of technology as "applied science" tells the whole story, for scientific technology purportedly stresses the conscious application or implementation of theory. Our tendency to understand technology only in terms of scientific application illustrates a rationalist bias that tends first to separate theory from practice and then to promote subsequent practice through the application of theory.

Aesthetic technique, perhaps the most difficult to see in rational terms, is viewed primarily as the application of consciously learned behaviors. We do not, of course, see the entire significance of art in terms of its technical perfection. In fact, there is no more common condemnation of an artist than through the faint praise of his technical skill. The perfection of art requires more than can be merely learned. Our disposition to believe in "talent" and "genius" illustrates our insight that the production of art requires more than the application of theoretical techniques. Indeed, *artis est celare artem*. But this passing recognition of the non-rationalizable aspects of artistic creation does little to counterbalance the general tendencies in our understanding that require the separation of theory and practice.

Not even pragmatic and Marxian philosophies have provided a significant alternative to our tendency to divide experience into theoretical and practical modes. A mere reversal of polarity does nothing to resolve the dilemma. The assumption of the rationalist that knowledge precedes practice tends to derogate sense experience and actions, and threatens to promote a narrowed and dulled sensitivity to one's life circumstances. The contrary assumption, that theory emerges only by reflection upon practice, tends to provide understandings with immediate, relevant consequences, but not the capacity for promoting long-range novelty.

Both theory and practice have come to be construed in terms of the concept of *principles*. "Theory" has come to mean "a systematic statement of the principles of." "Practice" is understood either as "action in accordance with principles" or "actions from which principles may be derived." In either case the presumed dichotomy of theory and practice stands.

It is not that conceptual solutions to the unity of *theoria* and praxis cannot be found. Indeed, Aristotle provided such a resolution in his claim that the highest form of *activity* is that of "thinking on thinking." The activity of self-reflective thought is both *theoria* and praxis. Likewise, the Platonic eros, which culminates in the vision of the unity of goodness, truth, and beauty, is given a practical function in Plato's social and political theories, serving as the foundation of the realization of justice in both the soul and the state. From Aristotle we learn that the highest form of activity is *contemplation*; from Plato, that the end of knowledge is the realization of justice. But from *history* we learn a different lesson: contemplation is all too often a luxury that can be realized only in isolation from the world, because "the world" is patterned primarily by actions that aim at power and greatness.

Searching for some means of harmonizing the claims of both knowledge and action has continued throughout our history. Contemporary attempts center in the concept of praxis. Dominant conceptions of praxis in the Anglo-European tradition have included the following: actions in accordance with principles of knowledge or understanding (Plato, the Idealists); actions in conformity to the will of the individual agent (Sophists, Existentialists); actions in response to problematic situations from which principles may be abstracted (Aristotle, the Pragmatists); activity leading to production aimed at meeting natural needs (Marx). In the first sense true knowledge provides the criterion for practice since "to know the truth is to do the truth." In the Sophistic and pragmatic senses practice is defined directly in terms of action. In Marxian philosophy, practice involves a making the character of which defines its relevance. These senses of practice are due to the dominance in our tradition of the notions of knowing, doing, and making as the primary means of being in the world.

None of these alternatives has served for any length of time as a satisfactory solution to the problem of harmonizing theory and practice. Consciousness of the inadequacy of all such attempts has led some contemporary philosophers to dig deeply into the philosophical tradition and to uncover a radical alternative that has as yet not been exploited in our tradition. Surprisingly enough the most radical critiques of reason and rationality that emerge from a re-interpretation of the relations of *theoria* and praxis come not from the neo-Marxian thinkers, but from the speculative philosophers.

Heidegger and Whitehead, though divergent in methodology and style, share a common concern of coming to grips with the questions of the function and grounding of reason. Heidegger provides an increased sense of what Milton Munitz has called "the mystery of existence" through his analysis of the Principle of Sufficient Reason,[8] and Whitehead promotes an expanded vision of the function of reason by virtue of his revisioning of the classical scientific sensibility.[9] Whitehead, in particular, is instructive on this issue since one of his principal tasks was the revisioning of the assumptions of science and scientific cosmology in such manner as to subvert the provincialisms expressed in our general cultural self-under-standings. That the effective outlook of our culture over the last three centuries has derived from the cultural interest of science has guaranteed that scientific rationality has dom-inated our discussions of the concepts of theory and practice. But Whitehead's philosophy is a joint production from his scientific and aesthetic sensibilities, a valuable bridge to an alternative conception of rationality, both theoretical and practical.

The beginnings of an aesthetic interpretation of reason are to be found in Whitehead's philosophy. Whitehead claims that "the function of Reason is to promote the art of life." [10] And he defines reason as "the self-discipline of the originative element in history." [11] Life, as "the clutch at vivid im-mediacy," [12] is an anarchy of aesthetic intensities. Reason promotes the art of life by promoting the self-discipline of vivid immediacy. Here we find the basis for a uniting of the aims of theoretical and practical reason in an aesthetic methodology. *Theoria* and praxis are united by *aisthesis*.

Aisthesis originally meant simply "perceiving the external world through the senses." *Aisthetikos* means "being preoccupied." It is the sense of being preoccupied with the external world as sensuously perceived that relates the con-cepts of *theoria* and *aisthesis*. John Ruskin, in his *Modern Painters*, made this connection specific when he characterized *theoria* as "the perception of beauty regarded as a moral faculty," in contrast with *aisthesis*, which is "the mere animal consciousness of pleasantness." [13] Each was construed as a form of preoccupation related to a manner of entertaining the external world of the senses. Aesthetics for Immanuel Kant was the science that treats of the conditions of sensuous per-ception, which has as its objects the characterization of the perception of *aestheta*, or "material things" as contrasted with *noeta*, "things immaterial." The commonly accepted meaning of aesthetics as "the science of the beautiful or of taste" derives from Baumgarten, a contemporary of Kant. This understanding of aesthetics has gone a long way toward producing a misappropriation of the meanings of *aisthesis*.

One way of reappropriating the term for use in philosophical understandings of the relations of *theoria* and praxis is by noting that modern characterizations of perception, particularly those of the twentieth-century process philosophers, have increasingly depended on the analysis of perception at levels more primitive than the conscious and the conceptual. The objects perceived are the facts of experience; the manner in which they are perceived defines the subjective sense of the world. The objective content of experience is received via a subjective form of feeling that characterizes the manner of the perceiver's preoccupation with the world. And it is precisely the manner of preoccupation that largely determines the nature and direction of one's interpretation of the world. The experience of "causal efficacy" as discussed by Whitehead,[14] the characterization of *Dasein* in terms of *Sorge*, or "care," considered by Heidegger,[15] Bergson's "intuition,"[16] and José Ortega y Gasset's "perspectivism,"[17] all depend upon some notion of "preoccupation" interpretable in terms of the subjective form of feeling the world.[18]

Aisthesis as praxis must be interpreted in terms of the creationist concepts of intuition, process, and creativity—concepts that allow for the interpretation of the world as composed of termini of acts of intuition—aesthetic acts. Praxis as *aisthesis* is fundamentally to be understood in terms of processes of self-creativity grounded in perceptual perspectives defining the form of preoccupation with the world.

In more traditional terms, the concept of praxis being developed here involves the distinction between *making* and *enjoying* common to the discussions of aesthetic experience and expression. Translating the conception of productivity from the sphere of economics into that of art, we find that the needs that give rise to the productions in the economic sphere may be translated into the enjoyments that inspire and reward creativity in the aesthetic sphere. A creationist theory of praxis would involve its interpretation in terms of *aisthesis* as self-creativity. The practicality of this notion is to be judged in terms of its success as a critique of principles as determining sources of order, and as a means of the evocation of sensibilities that conform to the realization of praxis as *aisthesis*. *Heretofore, philosophers have merely construed the world,*

*imitating the organization of an antecedent chaos; the point,
however, is to experience it in all its immediacy.*

The crucial question for this creationist vision of the
union of *theoria* and praxis in *aisthesis* is whether or not a
case can be made for the seasonal relevance of a conception of
being in the world that has as both its theoretical and its practical aim the aesthetic enjoyment of the world construed as the
sum of all termini of acts of intuition. Both *theoria* and praxis
are grounded in the self-creative enjoyments associated with
the aesthetic events that constitute the primary realities of
nature.

The creationist alternative to the interplay of theoretical
and practical activities is to deny the gambit that gave rise to
the dichotomy in the first place. Reason as the search for, and
obedience to, principles is eschewed. A principle is the origin
of knowledge or practice. Meaningful thought and action can
be traced to a principle that, as reason or cause, stands as *sine
qua non* for any instance of knowing or doing. Teaching and
learning involve the transmission of principles. Command and
obedience alike involve the articulation, in speech and action,
respectively, of principles, or so it has seemed. Creationist
thought, however, is *unprincipled* in the strictest sense. We
cannot speak literally of the philosophy of creativity as a
theory. It is the result of *theoria*—the product of intuition,
contemplation, wonder. *Theoria* is the source of all knowledge
and theory. In the West we have, largely because of our identification of our "source" with an act of creation that established the beginning of time, viewed our origin as a point from
which to progress. The movement from *theoria* to theory,
which has as its goal nothing less than the complete rationalization of experience, is one consequence of this identification. In the East, particularly in Taoist thought, we may view
the consequences of the conception of *source* as unprincipled.
The primary consequence of the conception of the relations of
knowledge and action is that thought never really progresses
beyond *theoria*.

It is customary to distinguish the original aims of theory
as *theoria* from the practical uses of theory in terms of the
speculative and contemplative character of the former as

opposed to the ideological tendencies of the latter. Theorial—as opposed to theoretical—thought seeks no systematization, delimitation, description, or application. Systematization provides no more than an arbitrary organization of the contents of the data references of a theory. The value of the systematic character of the theory is determined by the fruitfulness of the principle of organization. The delimiting function of theory promotes the use of stipulated definitions leading to a terminology that risks the hypostatization of "names" as surrogates for the things themselves. Description requires one to take an objective stand outside the events to be described. The need to apply a theory derives from a prior assumption of the separation of knowledge from action, which is overcome only if the theory can be employed as a tool determining or articulating activity.

Theoria, as contemplation, envisioning, is distinguished from theory in several ways, but none more important than by its approach to the issues of meaning and truth. Theoretical understanding requires that one establish the meaningfulness of a proposition prior to judging the proposition true or false. This is obviously necessary since truth claims can be justified only through a method of verification developed from some theoretical context. Theorial understanding, on the other hand, asserts the truth of a proposition prior to the discovery of its meaning. *Theoria* grasps the truth of its contemplation in an unmediated fashion. In *theoria* truth is *revealed*. It is the direct experience of truth that provides the motivation for the discovery of meaning.

All thought begins in the theorial attitude, and the thinking of Western culture is no exception. Philosophy begins in wonder. But in our tradition it did not remain there. The age of Speculative Wonder gave way to the ages of Faith and, finally, Doubt. The development of the four primary philosophic paradigms undergirding our intellectual endeavors was an exercise in wonder, in *theoria*. It was a meaning-disclosing activity. The subsequent theoretical enterprise of using each of these primary paradigms to determine meaning and truth intra-systematically has led to an extremely detailed, specialized, and almost completely rationalized complex of cultural understandings. Viewed from the most fundamental perspective, of course, the entire history of Western intellectual development has been continually sustained by the theorial attitude, by the immediate sense of revealed truth of the source of thought. But that "truth" may be entirely too subtle for the majority of Western intellectuals who believe that the judgment of truth or falsity may be made only after the proper exercise of a scientific method. But in a very real sense the healthy resolution of our present crisis in cultural self-understanding depends upon our eventual recognition that we have, fortunately, never progressed completely beyond *theoria*. The failure to realize that our intellectual endeavors, in their most fundamental dimensions, have involved us not in the search for truth among the meaningful elements of experience but in the discovery of but a small selection from the infinity of meanings found within the truth first revealed to us in *theoria* can only lead to a dogmatic closure that will preclude any further penetration of the truth encountered in the act of *theoria*.

The grounding of all thought in the theorial attitude, which itself is a mode of the aesthetic activity, provides us with a means of reinterpreting the aims of *theoria* and praxis. The separation of theory and practice, which has often been a separation of contemplation and the desire for greatness, can be overcome if the abstract character of the contemplative life is eschewed and the power motivations of the practical life are abandoned, each in favor of the aim at immediate enjoyment of those experiences associated with self-actualization.

The kind of knowledge that results from *theoria* the Taoist calls *wu-chih*. *Wu-chih* is, in fact, "no-knowledge." "It is called no-knowledge in that it is a state which is not that of knowledge; it is not a piece carved out of the total realm. It is a sharedness of the uncarved. totality."[19]

Such "knowledge" we in the West would call *mystical*. To see *sub specie aeternitatis* is to possess "cosmic consciousness." This insight into the Totality is often rather casually associated with ecstatic experiences. Taoism can be called "mystical," if the proper qualifications are given to the term. Traditionally, the mystical attitude has three fundamental termini: God, the soul, nature. Theistic mysticism, of the type exemplified by Christian mystics such as Teresa of Avila or John of the Cross, often involves an *ecstatic* experience. The soul leaves its proper domain and unites with God. Soul-mysticism, as practiced, for example, by certain members of the Hindu tradition, is not ecstatic but *en-static* since the focus of the experience is the soul itself, and the experience of unity involves an *in-dwelling*. Nature mysticism is distinguished from the other two forms since it focuses on neither ecstasy nor en-stasy, but on an experience of the togetherness of all things, which we may describe as "con-stasy"[20]—that is to say, a "standing with." It is a sense of the presence of all things standing together in a felt unity. It is not merely the sense of being one with nature, though that is part of it. It is the experience of the interfusion of each with each, the sense of *compresence*.

Constasy involves a mitigation of the intellectual tendency toward exclusive differentiation. It is *not* an experience of the "night wherein all cows are black." Things, events, phenomena still exist in themselves. But the sense of their self-existence promotes an experience of their relatedness rather than their distinction. A passage from *Chuang Tzu* illustrates this: "Everything can be a 'that,' everything can be a 'this.' . . . 'That' comes from 'this' and 'this' comes from 'that'—which means 'that' and 'this' give birth to one another. . . . When there is no more separation between 'this' and 'that,' it is called the still-point of Tao. At the still-point in the center of the circle one can see the infinite in all things."[21]

The experience of constasy is the experience of relativity. Such an experience, if partial and incomplete, can lead to skepticism and cynicism. But if one reaches the "still-point of Tao" there can be no such result, for therein lies the sense of the sacredness consequent upon the envisioning of all things *sub specie aeternitatis*. Poets and mystics know that the sense of the value of some finite detail of the universe—a wildflower or a grain of sand—derives from its context. Value is relative to situation. But they see beyond this or that finite context to the Totality, which is literally completed by the sand or the flower. A knower who discriminates in order to discover the nature of things misses that nature. It is no-knowledge, *theoria*, the experience of constasy, the sense of the reciprocal interfusion of all things, that tells us of nature.

Wu-chih is not at all impractical, as it may first appear. To grasp that fact we must consider the process of unprincipled knowing in conjunction with that of *wu-wei*, or non-assertive action. The notion of *wu-wei* suggests spontaneous actions in accordance with the natures of things. Because such non-assertive actions appear effortless, and, therefore, do not appear to be actions at all, the term *wu-wei* is used. Our tacit identification of action with acts of will brings the Western conception of activity into direct conflict with the Taoist concept of *wu-wei*. We stress "Where there is a will there is a way," indicating that through sheer determination one can devise a means to a given end. The Taoist would reply that where there is a will, it and "the Way" are surely not in harmony.

The Taoist, in order to know or to act, must grasp the intrinsic natures of those events his field of inquiry or activity comprises. All things participate in Tao and manifest the fundamental Yin–Yang polarity. But each item in the universe has its own *te*, that is to say, its own *excellence*. Sometimes translated as "power" or "virtue," *te* means "that by virtue of which a thing is just what it is and no other thing." I believe the best translation of *te* is "intrinsic excellence." This term evokes the sense of uniqueness characterizing that by virtue of which a thing is just itself.

Everything possesses its peculiar *te*. The *te* of *wu-wei* is the attainment of goals non-instrumentally; the realization of "ends without means." But to realize a goal without striving toward that goal it is necessary that one recognize the *te* of that in accordance with which one is acting. To construe elements in nature as outcomes of causal sequences is to view them only in their extrinsic character, not as they exist in themselves. Such a construal is in fact tantamount to selecting a single order of nature from the matrix of all possible orders and calling that *the* order of nature. But each item, within or without one's immediate experience, suggests a value orientation that lays claim to an order from the perspective of that valuation. Intuitive understanding requires that one understand from within that which is intuited in such a manner as to appreciate the world construed from its perspective. This is *wu-chih*. *Wu-wei* requires that one "act" in accordance with the intuition of the *te* of things. Such action is non-assertive in that it does not use these things as extrinsic means, but walks the ways of the things themselves. In this manner one promotes the harmony of Chaos (*hun-tun*) by acting with rather than against its elements.

In addition to *wu-wei* and *wu-chih*, there is a third mode of participation in the processes of nature—*wu-yü*. *Wu-yü* is the concept of objectless desire, which is the subjective form of feeling associated with instances of *wu-chih* and *wu-wei*. Together, the three notions of *wu-chih*, *wu-wei*, and *wu-yü* articulate the differences between the notion of creativity and the correlative concept of power with which it has often been confused in Western thinking.

Whereas "power" often suggests the correlative concepts of domination and control, "creativity" is a notion that can be characterized only in terms of self-actualization. Unlike power relationships that require that tensions among component elements be resolved in favor of one of the components, in relations defined by creativity there is no otherness, no separation or distancing, nothing to be overcome. *Creatio ex nihilo*, as it is normally understood, is in fact the paradigm of all *power* relationships since the "creative" element of the relation is completely in control of its "other," which is in itself literally *nothing*.

There can be no *creation* from nothing unless "nothing" is given equal status alongside "something," that is to say, unless being and non-being are seen as polar concepts defining an organic unity that is *becoming*. Thus there can be no temporalizing the notion of creativity in terms of a movement from non-being to being. A polar relationship has no beginning; to claim otherwise would be to provide some concept of initiation and, thus, to give priority to one of the elements in the creative relationship.

The distinction between power and creativity underlies the distinction between polarity and dualism. The greater the

emphasis upon power, the greater the importance of the
notion of duality as defining relationships. Creativity, on the
other hand, requires that each element of a relationship be
continually in the state of creating the other. The Taoist conception of the Yin–Yang relationship previously discussed in
terms of Western conceptions of passivity and activity illustrates the contrast very well. Yin and Yang are moments in a
creative process. The aesthetic interpretation of experience
and nature precludes the necessity of dividing events into
those that express and those that experience the efficacy of an
action.

The significant contrast between the notions of power and
creativity as means of articulating the natures of things is suggested by Nietzsche's claim that "every center of force . . .
construes all the rest of the world from its own viewpoint, i.e.,
measures, feels, forms, according to its own force."[22]
Nietzsche sees the activity of the events of nature in terms of
"power displacement";[23] the acts of construal are acts in the
agonal sense familiar to Anglo-European philosophy. But
creativity requires passive acts of construal characterizable in
terms of *ek-stasis*, the experience in and through another. It is
the possibility of *ek-stasis*, and its complement *en-stasis*, the
sense of being experienced from within, that allows for the
exercise of creativity as opposed to power. Underlying both
ecstasy and enstasy in the creative act is the con-static sense.
This is the experience at one and the same moment of both the
enstatic and ecstatic intuitions of the Totality as individualized
in terms of the internal and external references of *wu-chih*,
wu-wei, and *wu-yü*. From these notions we are able to develop
an understanding of the harmony of individual acts of self-
creativity with the inexhaustible source of creativity. And the
creativity of individuals as aesthetic events depends on the
potentiality for this harmony to promote something more than
empty knowledge, futile actions, or blind emotion. This potentiality may be actualized only if the aims of *theoria* and praxis
can be grounded upon the self-creative process whose
dynamic is *aisthesis*.

THE UNCARVED BLOCK

In trying to understand the meanings of knowledge and action in a creationist universe, we have been led to the Taoist notions of *wu-wei*, *wu-chih*, and *wu-yü*, and to the elaboration of these notions in terms of the concepts of enstasy, ecstasy, and constasy. Our discussion has required us to conclude that the creationist sense of knowing, doing, and feeling may be articulated only if it is assumed that there are no external principles determining the nature of knowledge or action. This rather bizarre claim means that the creationist universe is anarchic. How is it possible to defend the claim that the most fruitful understanding of our world is one that requires us to believe that the cosmos is "without principles"? We must now attempt to answer this question.

The simplest expression of the naïve assumption that has undergirded so much of our theological and scientific understanding of the universe in the classical period is that from chaos, construed as formless non-being, God fashioned the world we know through the ordering activity of *creation*. From such a belief came the conception of *the order of nature*. The order of nature is understood in terms of natural laws expressible in the language of cause and effect. This understanding of the universe requires that we grasp the nature of the first ordering principle, and the principles of the order or pattern imposed upon chaos through the act of creation.

Though theologians have, by and large, maintained the belief in *creatio ex nihilo*, scientists have, since the classical period, increasingly abandoned this cosmogonical model in favor of one that was most influentially expressed by Plato in the *Timaeus*. According to Plato the universe was created from an antecedently existent "matter," which God made "as like himself as possible." "Finding the whole visible sphere not at rest, but moving in an irregular and disorderly fashion, out of disorder he brought order."[24]

These two cosmogonical schemes, the one presuming *creatio ex nihilo* through an act of the will, the other grounded

upon the concept of the rational persuasion of antecedent matter, have existed side by side in our culture since their respective beginnings. The Hebraic cosmogony was, of course, most
influential in the Middle Ages and well into the classical period
of science. The nineteenth-century interest in *evolution* reintroduced the Platonic cosmogony into intellectual culture,
and it has dominated cosmological schemes up to the present.
The two schemes share an assumption that makes them much
more similar than might at first seem the case: the view that
the world is *one*. On the Hebraic conception God created *the*
world from nothing. This world with its laws is the *only* world
God made. On the Platonic scheme, likewise, the created
world is one: "In order then that the world might be solitary . . . the creator made not two worlds or an infinite
number of them; but there is and ever will be one only begot-
ten and created heaven." [25] Both the Platonic and the Hebraic
cosmogonies involve the presumption that the world is *one*
and *rational*. And this has led to the dominant belief that once
a rational cause, law, or principle is discovered it must be
accepted as a necessary element of the one existing world.

Leibniz, who attempted to incorporate the two cosmogonical schemes into a single vision, formally introduced the
notion of "possible worlds" into cosmological speculation to
demonstrate that the actual world is the best among possible
worlds. But the total impact of his logical speculations must be
said to include the raising of the question of "compossibility"
and "compossible worlds," which has led in our times to
speculations concerning the co-existence of multiple universes, each of which forms a coherent world but which, relative to the others, is chaotic or disordered.

Recent scientific and philosophic speculations have
begun to contribute to a serious revolt against the conception
of the unity of the cosmos. Some few years ago, a symposium
on "The Concept of Order" produced a series of fascinating
speculations that reflected our increased skepticism concerning the single-ordered rationality of the universe. In speaking
of the progress of cosmological speculations concerning the
nature of the cosmos, Cecil Schneer suggested that we could
not expect our progressive understandings of the cosmos to

lead us to a single adequate cosmology, but that in place of such a theory, perhaps "we shall find only chaos, the formless nonbeing out of which the gods fashioned existence by ordering. In the end we recognize that our laws are of our own devising; that our science has fashioned finally a map of the human mind."[26] These words recall the oft-quoted statement of Sir Arthur Eddington: "We have found a strange footprint on the shores of the unknown. We have devised profound theories, one after another, to account for its origin. At last, we have succeded in reconstructing the creature that made the footprint. And lo! It is our own."[27]

It would be a mistake to classify these statements as no more than idealist interpretations of nature. The point of these claims is precisely *not* that there is an isomorphic relation between the mind and the cosmos, but rather that what we have claimed about the nature of the cosmos is a result of our failing to recognize that our understandings have been grounded in acts of construal that have produced *an* order from among a possibly infinite number of orders.

The words of Eddington and Schneer are representative of a dominant movement in contemporary cosmological thought and physical theory, which had its modern beginnings with such figures as Pierre Duhem and Henri Poincaré. This movement, which may be loosely termed "conventionalist," is at one level related to the idealist tradition, particularly as it derives from the Kantian attempt to establish the doctrine of the dependence of the world's order upon minds. But this relationship is by no means exact. Idealists usually suggest that the isomorphism of mind and nature is guaranteed by the existence of an Absolute Mind or a Transcendental Ego. More recently, the source of the *a priori* element in experience has been shifted from an absolute to a relative status. Anticipations of nature are assumed to be functions of mental operations under the influence of previous understandings, but free of any absolute criteria of meaning and significance. The so-called "conceptual pragmatism" of C. I. Lewis, for example, allows for alterations in our categories of interpretation based on continuing experience. There are no immutable laws, not even the laws of logic.[28]

The conventionalist interpretation of nature, by accepting a dependence of order upon mind but rejecting, or omitting consideration of, transcendent principles defining the nature and structure of reason and rational activity, eschews the belief in the unity of the world. Our theories of nature do, indeed, tell us something about our minds as order-contributing agencies. But since, as the conventionalists claim, and as the condition of our theoretical understandings so dramatically illustrates, our minds can encompass a variety of explanations of the world, it is at least an open question whether it is possible to speak in specific terms of a single order of nature. And if there is no single *order*, then it becomes unlikely that any absolute *disorder* exists. Chaos as well as cosmos is relativized. We may, in fact, think of chaos as "the sum of all orders, the matrix from which particular orders are derived."[29] What becomes of the opposition between chaos and cosmos? There is none—at least not an absolute one, for "the distinction between order and disorder tends to disappear when the domain of both is the universe."[30]

Once this possibility is entertained, the plausibility of any rigid distinction between chaos and cosmos is challenged. Chaos, or "disorder," we realize, "is nothing less than the order of the universe."[31] If it is true that chaos is *the sum of all orders*, what determines our selection of a particular order as defining the nature of our world is what is *convenient*. Here is the crux of the conventionalist view.

"Order" is a relative concept. "An order is an arrangement with respect to which *it would matter if it were otherwise*. . . . To say that something is ordered is to say that it embodies a value; to say that it would matter if it were otherwise is to say that it ought to be as it is."[32] *Order* and *value* are intrinsically connected. The order of nature construed in its broadest sense is the sum of all orders, an infinite matrix of arrangements, and the repository of all value. We could, for example, conceive any possible arrangement of physical particles and from it abstract at least some of the laws and causal connections that would obtain within it. We then could conceive a being, or a state of affairs, sustained by that arrangement and with respect to which, therefore, it would matter if it were otherwise. Relative to that being or state of affairs the arrangement is ordered. We could not, perhaps, conceive of the sum of all orders as a total sustaining environment for any given being or state of affairs. That would be tantamount to claiming that in all possible worlds "p" obtains. Or, alternately, that in no possible world does "not-p" obtain. Whether, beyond the limits of our conceptions, it is possible to intuit "the sum of all orders" we shall leave for later discussion.

If cosmos is to have any real meaning it must mean much the same as chaos. For the adequacy of any particular interpretation of the order of the universe depends on one's ability correctly to assign the role of evaluator of a universal state of affairs. For whom or what was the universe ordered? Cosmologies become special pleadings—rationalizations of types of arrangement that, with respect to the being performing the construction, it would matter if it were otherwise. Cosmogonies supply the basic *principia* providing the rationale of the cosmological order. But if a cosmogony is, as Plato said, but a "likely story," it is perhaps but one among many possible accounts of the origins of the universe. The story of beginnings is meant to provide a foundation for an account of the nature of things. If no specific conceptualization of order defined in terms of "principles," "laws" and "causes" is provided, there is no necessity to believe in a first beginning of all things. It is for this reason that the Taoist, with his claim that nature is an infinite source of creativity, a matrix of all possible orders, requires no explicit cosmogonical myth.

In the creationist philosophy of the Taoist, Nature is an "uncarved block" (*p'u*). It is chaos (*hun-tun*), undifferentiated homogeneity. As the sum of all orders, nature is an inexhaustible field of creative potential. Each item, within one's experience or outside of it, suggests a value orientation that lays claim to an order from that particular valuation. Nature is no more anthropocentric than it is to be seen exclusively from the perspective of an amoeba, a super-nova, or a god. Knowledge of the world and actions within it require an appreciation of the ways of things as seen from within. Theological beliefs, aesthetic tastes and sentiments, ethical principles, scientific theories, cosmological speculations—all tend to narrow one's understanding of the way things are. They are carvings on the uncarved block.

The artist in the Taoist tradition appreciates the necessity of seeing all things from within. Thus the value placed upon intuition and empathy in the Chinese aesthetic tradition. The artist's relation to nature is through the medium of *wu-chih*, *wu-wei*, and *wu-yü*. The value of Taoist art as an illustration of the creationist relationship to nature will be completely lost if Taoism is interpreted, as is often the case, as a species of romanticism. The romantic stresses the *human* experience of nature; the Taoist strives to construe nature in its own terms and not from a human perspective. George Rowley is one of the few Western commentators upon Chinese art who recognizes this fact. "The four essentials of romanticism were an assertive ego, the active emotion of revolt, a longing for the unusual, and the psychology of escapism. On all four counts the Chinese Taoist held contrary views."[33] Taoism is often identified with romanticism because both stressed intuition over reason in their understandings of nature. But "romanticism was a personalizing alchemy which turned things into what you wanted them to be; Taoism sought the truth of things as they are in reality."[34]

The Taoist does not stress transforming activity. Action assumes the necessity of control, which interferes with the natural spontaneity of things in themselves. The Taoist does not feel himself to be in conflict with his ambience, because he does not feel obliged to re-establish a decaying theocentric order. Nor for that matter does he feel obliged to single out any specific order as the true one. His vision of nature is as if it were an uncarved block, a matrix of possible orders passive to infinite patterning. The sort of understanding of nature I am describing is perhaps best illustrated through the examination of Chinese art.

Classical Chinese art strikes the Anglo-European as unusual not merely because of the distinctiveness of the techniques and subject matters employed, but because of the placement of the enterprise of aesthetic activity within its cultural milieu. There seems to be no great distinction between the practices of philosophy and art. It is as if the "quarrel between the poets and the philosophers," which Plato described at the beginnings of our intellectual culture, had never erupted in China. Artists may be philosophers, and religious virtuosi for that matter, without disrupting the character of their enterprise. We too have our scholarly and mystical artists, of course, but what seems more the exception in our own cultural milieu is a prominent characteristic of classical Chinese culture.

If we direct our attention to the painting of the Sung dynasty (960–1279), when the Buddhist and Taoist sensibilities had so creatively merged with the Confucian, we encounter a style of painting that, by virtue of its allusive splendor, is perhaps the very epitome of the aesthetic sense. Whether we select the expansive landscapes of the Northern Sung painter Kuo Hsi or the more restricted portrayals of Southern Sung introspective art, which reached its finest expression in the Ch'an Buddhist style of Mu Ch'i, we cannot but see that something strange and wonderful indeed is to be found in the aesthetic sensibilities of Chinese artists.

Naturalistic and representational art in the West, at least since the Renaissance, has been dominated by the understanding of nature as the terminus of sense perception. Reliance upon visual perspective subordinates the aesthetic experience of the natural world to the demands of geometrical perspective and the organization of objects in three-dimensional space. Whenever Western artists revise the rules of perspective, they are likely to be praised or blamed for their employment of "distorted" (i.e., "unreal") spaces. The idealized landscapes of Chinese art employ a different conception of space altogether. The painter develops his subject matter in relation to three or more plane surfaces representing various distances— e.g., foreground, mid-ground, background. Each distance expresses a focal characteristic of the painting. The presentation of depth and distance in this manner confounds the sense of single focus or perspective and draws the spectator into the painting, influencing him to consider the work from a variety of points of view internal to the depicted scene itself. There is no distortion here; in shifting our focus from place to place within the painting we are moving about in aesthetic space.

Art such as we are describing attains a subtlety of nuance

impossible to achieve if one begins with the presumption of the natural world merely as the terminus of sense perception. The narrowing strictures entailed in the necessity to conform to the presentationally immediate perception of the objects of nature means that aesthetic values are inordinately disciplined by visual perceptions. The truth value of Sung dynasty art, however, is that emergent from an aesthetic rather than a rational order. The possible harmonies to be attained are therefore somewhat richer than those found in Western Renaissance and Modern forms of naturalism.[35]

A significant characteristic of the aesthetic attitude as it is represented by Sung dynasty painters is that it is no part of the painter's task to *objectify* the world. The subject of the painter is not external to him; it is internal to the artist at the moment of creation. But this internalized perspective is by no means the result of a personalizing egoism associated with the extremes of the romantics or expressionists. The world is in the painter in the same manner as the painter is in the world. And the painting must be "entered" to be enjoyed. If we view a landscape by Kuo Hsi, or an introspective work by Mu Ch'i, we immediately see that simply standing "before" the painting provides us with no privileged place. In the case of the landscape, we are asked to come inside in order to envision it from a variety of perspectives associated with the trees, mountains, waterfalls, and so on. Ultimately, however, it is not the painting that is to be our concern, but the *world* that emerges from the perspective of the painting. The painting is a platform from which to view the world. Standing there we begin to understand the purpose of the artist—and of art itself. If we approach Mu Ch'i's famous painting of the "Six Persimmons," or his idealized portrait of the poet Li Po, we are asked not to look, but to meditate. And if we do, we experience the almost unbearable vitality emergent from the relation of the painting with its world. Here, perhaps, Keats is vindicated, beauty *is* truth—not the blunt truth of conformation, but the truth of realization, or enlightenment.

The understanding of aesthetic creativity that emerges from such art is strange indeed. Who is the creator? What, or whom, is created? An eighth-century Chinese poet knew the solution to this puzzle:

The wild geese fly across the long sky above.
Their image is reflected upon the chilly water below.
The geese do not mean to cast their images on the water;
Nor does the water mean to hold the image of the geese.

The created is unconstrained, uncaused, spontaneous. Creativity is *self-creativity*.

In classical China, the arts included much more than the traditional painting, poetry, music, and so on. Perhaps the most provocative and best known art form deriving from classical China would likely not be termed an art form at all by those who first encounter it. I refer to *T'ai Chi Ch'üan*, which is at one and the same time a meditative exercise, a technique for the maintenance of health and long life, a dance, and a system of self-defense. Above all, it is the single most direct and authentic expression of creativity as I have been discussing it in these pages.[36]

As a meditative exercise, T'ai Chi may be practiced alone or in conjunction with a partner. The movements are continuous and flowing expressions of the Yin and Yang polarity. The "push-hands" movements performed with another person promote an immediate sense of the firm and yielding aspects of every activity in nature and provide instances of *wu-wei* as grounded in the harmony of the ecstatic and enstatic senses. To be centered one must be relaxed, yet intent, focused and congruent with each aspect of one's psychophysical being. Centering involves a passive construal of one's ambience from one's focused perspective. This is enstasy. Centering makes possible "blending," which involves the ecstatic sense of the center of the other. The senses of "where one is" and "where the other is coming from" allow instances of knowing, doing, and feeling to be creative processes that promote constatic unity, and which thus preclude the necessity of rational, ethical, or aesthetic principles as determining sources of order.

T'ai Chi exercises promote the kind of sensitivities that allow one to recognize the *te* of things. Knowing, acting, and feeling in accordance with the *te* of each thing, including, of course, one's own *te*, requires the capacity to defer. Deference is action (*wu-wei*) in accordance with the recognition (*wu-chih*) of excellence (*te*). Deference patterns result from the mutual recognition of the intrinsic excellences of events in nature. At the human level, creativity is primarily a function of *wu-chih*, *wu-wei*, and *wu-yü* realized in response to the differential excellences defined by a given context of communication.

Doubtless, there are significant practical limits to an individual's ability to relate to his ambience through the media of *wu-chih*, *wu-wei*, and *wu-yü*. To see some phenomena from within might well lead to extreme confusion and even insanity. And to walk the ways of some things would likely lead to destruction. This is but to realize that there are patternings among events that are closed to our appreciation and orders in our natural ambience in cooperation with which we could not survive. The alternative, however, is not clearly superior; for the way of self-assertive knowledge, action, and feeling increases the short-term survival capacities of but a segment (the powerful and their beneficiaries) of but one of the living species occupying the surface of a single planet in this galaxy—itself but one of an untold number of such galaxies— and that at no little cost to the total ecological system. The way of non-assertiveness seeks a harmony with nature as becoming, and thus eschews motivations toward control, progress, and the domination of nature. Taoist arts, from painting and poetry to T'ai Chi Ch'üan, allow us to expand the limitations placed upon us by the sense of the finitude, ignorance, and perversity of human beings, which has developed, *pari passu*, with the civilization of experience. The principal art is, of course, the art of life. And the art of life is self-creativity.

If we view life as the "clutch at vivid immediacy," we may believe that the art of life is promoted best either through the functioning of reason as a means of realizing the balanced complexity of the aesthetic intensities inherent in the selection of a single order from out of chaos, or through the functioning of creativity as the realization, in a single intuitive insight, of chaos as the sum of all orders. The Taoist chooses the latter path. The realization of chaos (*hun-tun*) involves the constatic sense of the *te* of each thing as defining a world from its individual perspective. Borrowing from the Hwa-Yen Buddhist terminology, we might say that the realization of chaos (*hun-tun*) is the experience of "emptiness" (*śunyata*), which is neither void nor annihilation but Becoming-Itself (*Tao*), understood as the Uncarved Block. In Becoming-Itself no specific order is discriminated from the complex of orders whose members continually supervene one upon the other in the rhythmic (*yin–yang*) flow of creative process. This experience promotes the articulation and celebration of the intuitions of creative becoming in such a way as to sustain the self-creativity of the termini of those intuitions one's ambience comprises. For the Taoist creativity is the aim of life. It is a teleological notion in the sense that it is the immediate aim of each event as an aesthetic process, a goal ultimately realized through the attainment of "the still-point of the Tao," the undifferentiated homogeneity of chaos, the end without beginning.

The Taoist, or creationist, understanding of nature precludes any stress upon foresight promoting actions in accordance with unchanging laws of nature, or with knowledge of causes as external agencies providing a rational account of natural sequences. Thus it is essential that the creationist be able to provide a reinterpretation of traditional Western conceptions of the notions of "law" and "cause" as applied to natural events.

For the creationist, natural laws define orders that originate from the self-realization of natural events and are dependent upon the freedom of these events. Thus law is, to use Whitehead's term, "immanent." This conception of the laws of nature is in direct conflict with the notion that laws are based upon the dictates of a Transcendent Creator, a notion that greatly influenced classical Western philosophy. The doctrine of immanent law is no more congenial to the positivist conception of laws as based on the description of observed successions of events, which provide the means of articulating patterns of events persisting over time. On this view laws derive from the observed and the observable. No metaphysical speculations or extrapolations are allowed.

Few are left who would defend the concept of imposed

law in its most doctrinaire form. And the positivist theory is less and less in evidence in scientific writing. There seems to be little pressing need, therefore, to contrast the creationist view with these alternative conceptions. There *is* strong reason, however, to provide an account of the doctrine of immanent law in the context of conventionalist theory, which, in its instrumentalist guise, dominates contemporary discussions of the law of nature.

Conventionalism in science suggests that scientific laws and theories are fruitful and convenient ways of characterizing aspects of nature. And as there are, perhaps, any number of such ways of construing a selection of facts, scientific concepts are, within limits, *freely chosen conventions*. Henri Poincaré is often credited with originating modern conventionalist theory. Reflecting on the development of alternative systems of geometry, Poincaré claimed that the existence of a number of coherent and consistent geometrical systems that could, nonetheless, be translated into one another raises the question of the status of Euclidean geometry as an adequate characterization of physical space. Geometrical axioms cannot be synthetic *a priori* intuitions as Kant claimed, or we should be unable to conceive consistent alternatives. But neither are geometric axioms experimental truths, for if that were so geometry could not be an exact science and would then require revision.

> The geometrical axioms are therefore neither synthetic à priori intuitions nor experimental facts. They are conventions. Our choice among all possible conventions is guided by experimental facts; but it remains *free*, and is only limited by the necessity of avoiding every contradiction. . . . In other words *the axioms of geometry . . . are only definitions in disguise.* . . . One geometry cannot be more true than another; it can only be more convenient.[37]

It is important to avoid too simple-minded an application of this concept of convention. In the first place, merely different systems of measurement do not alter the facts of nature. To be crucial, differences among conventional interpretations of nature must direct attention to alternative selections of facts and must, in the last analysis, suggest ways in which opting for one interpretation over another makes a significant practical difference. And we must be careful not to interpret the notion of "practical difference" along traditional lines as meaning simply that some different activity could be accomplished through the employment of one convention rather than another. This is no doubt the case if we remain content with classical Western conceptions of praxis; but we cannot forget that we have argued already at some length for a conception of praxis as *aisthesis*. Granted that when one chooses between competing scientific laws or theories one is involved in making a value judgment, the intrinsic connection between order and value must not be construed only in the sense of *rational* order. To do so is to limit too much the conception of value. In other words, the connection between order and value demands that a choice among values necessarily involves a choice among orders, and the orders are as many and varied, and as complex, as are the values. Aesthetic values are a great deal more complex than logical values; and aesthetic harmony much more variegated than logical harmony. If we construe praxis and *aisthesis*, then the question of "practical differ- ence" can be understood fundamentally as "aesthetic differ- ence." And as beauty is a broader concept than truth since it is free from the necessity of logically consistent explication, so *aisthesis* promotes a praxis free from the necessity to realize an end construed in terms of consistent or rational principles.

But even on a narrow interpretation of praxis, it is easy enough to illustrate important differences alternative conven- tional interpretations would make. For example, Poincaré argued convincingly for the separation of geometrical space from "representational space," the space in which we repre- sent external bodies to ourselves through visual, tactile, and muscular (he might have added auditory, as well) sensations. According to Poincaré, "none of our sensations, if isolated, could have brought us to the concept of space; we are brought to it solely by studying the laws by which those sensations succeed one another."[38] That is to say, some combination of visual, tactile, or motor sensations is necessary to gain a con- ception of space. But, as Poincaré was quick to point out, the fact that geometrical space is not imposed upon each of our modes of sensation individually means "there is nothing, therefore, to prevent us from imagining a series of representations, similar in every way to our ordinary representations, but succeeding one another according to laws which differ from those to which we are accustomed."[39]

Poincaré, in fact, constructed a hypothetical world subject to laws radically different from our own, a world enclosed in a large sphere with varying temperatures, greatest at the center and approaching absolute zero at the circumference. The linear expansion of bodies in this world is directly proportional to its absolute temperature, and these bodies are continually in thermal equilibrium with their environs. Since a moving object will decrease in size as it approaches the circumference of the sphere, this world, though finite, will appear infinite. Whereas we are educated to consider geometry as the study of the laws of displacement of invariable solids, to the inhabitants of this hypothetical world geometry "will be the study of the laws of motions of solids *deformed by the differences of temperature.*"[40] By this illustration Poincaré wished to show that beings educated in such a world would, of necessity, construct a different geometry. Embedded in his exposition, however, is the striking acknowledgment that, in our present world, "natural solids also experience variations of form and volume due to differences in temperature. But in laying the foundations of geometry we neglect these variations; for besides being small they are irregular, and *consequently appear to us to be accidental.*"[41] Here we have the basis for understanding the meaning of conventions selected according to the criterion of convenience. It is obviously more *convenient* to employ our Euclidean geometry than the geometrical system constructed in that hypothetical world. Not that the alien geometry would be totally inapplicable, mind you; it might at least suggest some interesting observations about our world. It would certainly not, however, as an alternative scheme, be very convenient!

In developing specialized sciences, we tend to omit detailed consideration of the total environment presupposed by the science. Our tendency is, therefore, to assume greater relevance for a special science than is its due. The geometry of three dimensions, which we employ mainly in the natural sciences, is, though apparently derived from no particular sense, more relevant to some of our senses than to others. The sense of sight, for example, seems quite at home with the notion of three-dimensional space. This is, perhaps, to say no more than that, as Poincaré himself claimed, "we do not *represent* to ourselves external bodies in geometrical space, but we *reason* about these bodies as if they were situated in geometrical space."[42] And since, as seems likely, our reasoning is more often closely associated (at least in sighted persons) with our vision, the eye benefits from our construction of three-dimensional space. But what of the other senses? Poincaré claimed *motor space* to have many more than three dimensions since "each muscle gives rise to a special sensation which may be increased or diminished [so] that the aggregate of our muscular sensations will depend upon as many variables as we have muscles."[43] And auditory space, as Whitehead has remarked, may require many dimensions, as well, since "sound, though voluminous, is very vague as to the dimensions of its volumes, as between three or fifteen, for instance."[44] Our notion of a geometrical space of three dimensions derives from the ways we have educated ourselves in relation to a sensory apparatus dominated by five main senses. Our historic dependence upon the concept of three-dimensional space is a function of the specialized sensory capacities we have in fact chosen to develop. We could, perhaps, develop others. "The dogmatic assumption of the trinity of nature as its sole important dimensional aspect has been useful in the past. It is becoming dangerous in the present. In the future it may be a fatal barrier to the advance of knowledge."[45]

Whitehead recognizes the conventional status of many of our conceptions of order. Refusal to recognize that nature is passive to a variety of interpretations is a sin against the expansion of human understanding. Our understanding, Whitehead claims, advances in two ways: (*a*) by elaborating the details of a particular theoretical pattern, and (*b*) by discovering novel patterns. The first method consists in the elaboration of systematic schemes and the exploitation of their descriptive, integrative, and generative potential. The second method introduces novelty into experience by emphasizing previously undiscriminated, irrelevant, or accidental details. The "dogmatic assumption of the trinity of nature" has allowed for a tremendous growth in human understanding. Alternative assumptions that introduce novelty into our conceptual experience will, perhaps, provide the grounds for new directions in thought. These new directions are possible because "there are an indefinite number of purely abstract sciences, with their laws, their regularities, and their complexities of theorems—all as yet undeveloped. . . . [And] nature in her procedures illustrates many such sciences." [46] This is to say that nature is a matrix of orders that serves as the source of scientific laws. "There is thus a certain amount of convention as to the emergence into human consciousness of sorts of Laws of Natures [sic]. The order of emergence depends upon the abstract sciences which civilized mankind have in fact chosen to develop." [47]

It is not necessary to confine our imaginations to the development of compatible sciences. We can well entertain the possibility of radically disparate sciences, based on radically different principles, emerging into consciousness contemporaneously. We shall have more to say about this possibility later when we discuss, briefly, the differences between "internal" technologies associated with the sciences of the East, and "external" technologies familiar to our Western tradition. Suffice it to say that the aesthetic possibilities of order are always broader than the logical possibilities, and it is precisely this that allows for the possibility of an evolutionary development from one type of order to another. Whitehead himself recognizes this fact when he says that, "while the harmony of logic lies upon the universe as an iron necessity, the aesthetic harmony stands before it as a living ideal moulding the general flux in its broken progress towards finer, subtler issues." [48]

It is difficult to distinguish Whitehead's position from the conventionalist view. His doctrine of the Immanence of Law, though it adds a cosmological dimension most conventionalists would eschew, does not seem to conflict with conventionalism in any important detail. Indeed, as we shall have occasion to understand later on, the fact that natural laws are

functions of the self-actualizing activities of events in nature
suggests the possibility that the processes of construal constituting the self-actualization of human experiences and culture
may themselves—if not now, then at some future time—reach
a point where they contribute significantly to the formation of
laws of nature. That is to say, if laws of nature are functions of
individual acts of construal, and if theories are conventional
construals of nature, and if we accept the fact that most of
human culture and experience involves theoretical processes,
then human beings, willy-nilly, may be profoundly influencing
the character of the laws of nature. We may, in fact, someday
be able to *dictate* to nature what its laws must be. This would
be the logical, if somewhat ironic, result of the Western conception of the struggle with nature. Victory at last; and a
return to imposed law.

There is a second, somewhat less speculative, manner in
which the doctrine of immanent law deepens the sense of
conventionalism: Whitehead introduces the notion of "cosmic
epochs," an ontologizing of Leibniz' conception of possible
worlds, as a means of explicating the significance of law as
immanent. In simplest terms a cosmic epoch is the "widest
society of actual entities whose immediate relevance to ourselves is traceable."[49] A cosmic epoch manifests the most
general types of order dominating the universe insofar as we
have important relations to it. But, as the term cosmic *epoch*
suggests, these types of order are not everlasting. There is an
arbitrariness about laws of nature. Laws are statistical and,
therefore, not always "obeyed." The order of a given society
of actual entities establishes the laws that dominate it. The
laws pass away if that social order decays. An evolving
universe may be changing in its fundamentals. The laws relevant to our present social order—the electromagnetic laws,
the character of space–time, the fact of measurability, and so
on—may have slowly risen to dominance amid the decay of a
previous order and may themselves be gradually losing their
dominance due to the decay of our present social order. For
example, "this planet . . . may be gradually advancing
towards a change in the general character of its spatial relations. Perhaps in the dim future mankind, if it then exists, will

look back to the queer contracted three-dimensional universe
from which the nobler, wider existence has emerged." [50]
Whitehead's imaginative claim is meant to be taken seriously.
And the phrase "mankind, if it then exists" is not a pessimistic nod to the possibility of self-destruction or to the necessarily catastrophic end of the human race, but a recognition of
the fact that the order evolving from this present one may not
be one that can accommodate the type of organic structures
that house living, rational beings of the kind recognizable as
human.

The doctrines of conventionalism and immanence as
regards laws of nature are not so different as they first
appeared. The immanent and changing character of natural
law strengthens the view that such laws are conventions since
these laws are but selections from among various possible sets
of laws in any given cosmic epoch. And the fact that cosmic
epochs themselves pass into one another indicates that even
those laws that are incompatible with our present dominant
order may be relevant to the character of a succeeding epoch.

The value of these speculations for the understanding of
creationist philosophy should be evident by now. In a universe composed of self-actualizing moments of existence,
order will be a function of the decisions of the primary units of
becoming. If there are no necessary laws to guide the self-
actualizing processes, then there is no reason to believe that
any single order should be absolute, final, or permanent.
Indeed, the universe becomes a vast matrix containing various
realized orders. This, however, seems more like *disorder* than
order. The cosmos becomes, like chaos, the sum of all orders.
And somewhere or somewhen every possible order is extant. [51]

Whitehead has clearly gone a long way toward establishing the creationist understanding of the natures of the universe. But he cannot make the case completely. For the
Whiteheadian universe is subject to principles as determining
sources of order. The creative becoming of the universe in its
march toward new types of order is "conditioned by the
objective immortality of the actual world." [52] And the primary
conditioning factor derives from the fact that the Universe

"exhibit[s] itself as including a stable actuality whose mutual implication with the remainder of things secures an inevitable trend toward order." [53] This must be so for Whitehead since "apart from some notion of imposed Law, the doctrine of immanence provides absolutely no reason why the universe should not be steadily relapsing into lawless chaos." [54]

Whitehead is referring here to the necessity to affirm the existence of God functioning as a general source of order and value. It is difficult to see how sufficient stability and harmony among the orders of the universe may be maintained if there is no source luring the processes of actualization toward mutually compatible self-realizations. On the other hand, introducing the concept of God (even Whitehead's concept, which is a far cry from that of the Celestial Tyrant of classical theology) threatens to give the doctrine of Immanent Law a mildly Pickwickian flavor. For, if, without God, disorder threatens the possibility of individual self-actualizations, then God's functioning must be sufficiently efficacious to overcome that threat. This simply means that, within limits, an order of nature results from the immanent and approximate realization of an imposed set of ideals, the source of which is God himself. In such a universe God may be required, by virtue of the only partial realizations of ideals on the part of the actualities of the world, to adjust his future ideals, so that no *absolute* imposition is possible. But, even on this view, the freedom of self-actualizing creatures comes perilously close to being reduced to triviality. Whitehead offers a conception of God that is a rather insipid compromise of the claims of spontaneity and order.

Whitehead's compromise is not one to be treated lightly, however, because it is necessitated by the context of Western metaphysics itself. Without some ground of order, there would be no reason for the existence of the world, only reasons for the character of succeeding states of the world. Leibniz raised the question of the rational basis of the world, as opposed to the basis for the existence of any given state of the world, in terms of the principle of sufficient reason. The reason for the existence of the world, or for the existence of *this* world rather than some other, cannot be satisfactorily

deduced from any given state of the world.[55] The question that
must now be faced is this: Do we in fact need an explanation
of the ontological status of the existence of the world? And if
we answer "No," then we must face the further question as to
whether or not we require an explanation of *any given* state of
affairs that occupies a privileged place among other possible
explanations by virtue of conformity with a principle or set of
principles functioning as a determining source of order. That is
to say, we must ask if there are any but conventional grounds
for the preference of one characterization of the world or any
state of affairs extant within it. If we find that there are not, we
shall be free to understand the fact that the cosmos, which
above all else we hold to be a rationally organized totality, is
but a compendium of accidents.

THE SCIENCE OF THE ACCIDENTAL

One of the primary determinants of the character of our
understandings of the nature of things is our prejudice in favor
of order and regularity. This prejudice received its classic
expression in Aristotle's discussions of the concept of "the
accidental." "We must first say regarding the accidental, that
there can be no scientific treatment of it. This is confirmed by
the fact that no science—practical, productive, or theoretical—troubles itself about it."[56] A science, as an organized
way of knowing, has as its proper subject matter that which
occurs *always or for the most part.*[57] Accidental occurrences
are neither always nor for the most part; therefore they cannot
constitute the objects of any science. As Aristotle maintained,
it is an accident that a man is pale, but not that he is a man.
That which causes his man-ness is a necessary cause, but that
which causes his paleness is accidental. It is not, of course,
that there is no cause of a man's paleness; it is that there is
no *strict and regular, isolatable cause.* There are too many
causes or reasons for paleness—emotional shock, diet, lack of
exposure to the sun, insufficient skin pigmentation, and so on.
Accidental events, on this reading, are accidental *relative to a
specific causal context.* Such events are, from within a specified context, *inconvenient to analyze.*

When in the sphere of knowledge or practice we establish a selection of objects or events as the subject matter of our inquiry or the field of our actions, we presuppose principles of knowledge or conduct. Meanings or activities within this context that cannot be conveniently understood or directed in accordance with our principles seem haphazard, accidental, and uninteresting. A simple change of context would permit us to reverse the figure and ground events in our conceptual or practical *Gestalt*. Whether such a shift would be valuable is, within broad limits, a wholly subjective question. To revert to Poincaré's illustration: we might not wish to alter our bases for geometrical reasoning from the consideration of displacement of solids to the concept of temperature change. But our decision not to do so is hardly grounded in any principle more, or less, noble than the need to survive with as little inconvenience as possible in the world *as we have come to construe it*. Thus accidental events are without a principle or cause in the proper sense. The consideration of unprincipled events with accidental causes is not presumed to be a valuable enterprise in our culture due to our reinforced disposition to seek regularities in nature and experience.

Accidents constitute a species of "contingency," which itself is a context-bound category. A law of nature operates within a given context characterized by the conditions defining the sphere of relevance of the law. This means that a law is in effect only to the degree that we are able to ignore the contingencies operating outside the context defined by the law. Also, it should be clear that contingencies are recognized by abstracting from the idea of necessary connection in precisely the same way that causes are recognized by abstracting from contingencies. Aristotle's claim that there can be no science of the accidental is grounded in the assumption that there is no productive means of investigating phenomena that are identified by abstracting from the idea of necessary connection.

There is a sense in which a science of the accidental is possible within the context of orthodox scientific views. Some laws of nature are, after all, laws of chance and probability, which consider the way random events (given sufficient number and duration) manifest statistical regularities allowing of approximate predictions. But even here it is the *regularity* of events that is measured. The events themselves may be in some sense contingent or accidental, but the laws defining the regularity of event complexes have the same status as other laws of nature.

There is, perhaps, a more literal sense in which we might characterize a science of the accidental, if we are allowed to revert to our Taoist interpretation of the status of events in nature. One way of introducing Taoist thinking into our present inquiry is through a critique of our dominant conceptions of *causality*. For it is our common sense and scientific belief in the ubiquity of causal relationships that prevent us from taking seriously the relevance of "the accidental" to our understandings of nature. And it is Taoist philosophy that provides the only sophisticated alternative to the notions of cause and law that are grounded by the principle of sufficient reason.

The most dogmatic and simple-minded of the interpretations of causality derives from the belief in causal chains or sequences. A cause is put forward as an explanation of an item that within the context of the explanation is termed the "effect." We do not look for the causes of events in nature that are in themselves and in their asserted context unremarkable. It is the dramatic and the useful events that draw our attention. But explanations can be manifold and multi-dimensional.

Criticisms of specific instances of causal specification (as opposed to criticisms of the theory of determinism per se) generally are based on the one-to-many and many-to-one aspects of causality. The fact that one causal factor may give rise to a wide range of effects precludes consistent certainty in the isolation of a given effect as due to a specific cause. Likewise, since many causes may be responsible for a specific effect, one cannot always (ever?) be certain that the proper cause has been isolated.

It is not just that there can be myriad perspectives taken with respect to a given event; it is also the case that we ask after the causes of events only if, for some reason, our attention is drawn to the event. As N. R. Hanson claims, "We ask

'What is its cause?' selectively: we ask it only when we are confronted with some breach of routine, an event that stands out and leads us to ask after its nature and genesis.''[58] We have individual and social criteria as to what constitutes an interesting question. Events that affect our survival, that give us pleasure or threaten to give us pain, are high on the list of interesting issues about which we ask the question "What is its cause?''

The disposition to ask for reasons or causes is part and parcel of the need to be able to predict and control events in order to achieve successful adjustments to one's ambience or to determine the character of one's environs through causally efficacious action. *Wu-wei, wu-chih, wu-yü* are dispositional states that do not necessitate raising the question of causal determination to the level of consciousness.

A theoretical perspective characterizes a world in a specific way that produces the context within which some issues are deemed interesting and others not. Among the events in nature whose relations are considered interesting or relevant there are causal connections, defined by the theory itself. A theory determining that the world comprises other kinds of entities or events would also determine what other kinds of causal connections obtain. Since "the causal laws that a thing satisfies constitute a fundamental and inseparable aspect of its *mode of being*,''[59] alterations in the answer to the question "What kinds of things are there?" will lead to the development of different characterizations of causal laws.

> Causes certainly are connected with effects; but this is because our theories connect them, not because the world is held together by cosmic glue. The world *may* be glued together by imponderables, but that is irrelevant for understanding causal explanation. The notions behind "the cause x" and "the effect y" are intelligible only against a pattern of theory, namely one which puts guarantees on inferences from x to y.[60]

That causal laws are theory-bound can only mean that the *principle of sufficient reason* is a heuristic principle at best, one that determines that causal explanations may always be profitably sought, but that makes no claim as to the adequacy of this or that theoretical context serving to guarantee the discovery of causes. That is to say, the principle of sufficient reason turns out to be an inference entailed by any theoretical context, simply because a theory is a systematic structure of propositions from which a specific complex of inferences may be generated. As "inferential nets," theories can always be seen to guarantee the discovery of sufficient reasons.

The principle of sufficient reason generalizes our sense of the ubiquity of causal relationships, but cannot, without additional support, guarantee that these relationships all obtain within the same theoretical context. Leibniz supplemented his discussions of sufficient reason with the arguments for the notion of a privileged order, "the best of all possible worlds." The interrelations of the principle of sufficient reason and the ontological claims about the nature of this actual world as rationally and morally preferable to its alternatives, establish an argument for the belief that the production of order from out of the chaos of possibilities required an *exclusive* selection.

Viewed ontologically, the principle of sufficient reason makes a claim that all entities or events are ordered in such a manner that any item may receive an explanation in terms of some other item or items. Viewed from the epistemological perspective, the principle claims that the act of knowing necessarily involves the construal of the objects of knowledge in such a way as to allow for the articulation of causal connections. It is possible to question the metaphysical assumptions of any proposition or theory on the grounds that the status of objects or events in nature is always inadequately characterized. If this is done it is easy enough to show that alternative conceptions of causality and of the types of causal connections obtaining within a given context are always possible. At least some of these causal sequences or orders may be shown to be inconsistent with the initial order. Thus the inability to resolve the issue of inconsistent causal explanations is shown to be a result of incompatible theoretical contexts, which is but to demonstrate that sufficient reasons are theoretical entities as surely as are the events or entities accounted for in rational terms. This places the burden on the concept of theory itself. It is the theoretical impulse that needs explanation.

The ontogenetic interpretation of the principle of sufficient reason has been expressed by the physicist David Bohm in this way: "Everything comes from other things and gives rise to other things."[61] But this apparently straightforward statement contains a nest of metaphysical ambiguities, and the concept of cause, and therefore the specific types of causal connections discoverable, depends upon the manner in which the ambiguities are clarified. "What is a 'thing'?" "What is meant by 'comes from' and 'gives rise to'?" "In what way may a thing be said to be 'other' in relation to the remainder of things?"

Depending upon how such questions are answered the status of causal connection will be variously determined. Opponents of strict causal determinism, for example, usually introduce the notion of "freedom," which involves the characterization of contingency in terms of the *causa sui* or *sui generis* nature of at least some events. Such an analysis is often aided by the introduction of process categories that require that the concept of a "thing" be an abstraction from a process of coming into being.

It is an open question as to the extent to which the concept of freedom and contingency can be made to dominate a metaphysical theory. According to the Taoist, freedom as self-creativity is an unlimited and unqualified notion. Introducing the idea of Tao as Becoming-Itself entails the recognition of an infinity of types of causal explanation. This simply means that any specific causal explanation is contingent with regard to a host of other, equally viable, explanations. This claim of the Taoist as creationist precludes the construction of a completely adequate cosmological theory, free from incoherence and contradiction. Such a theory is impossible in principle since no principle can establish a consistent and adequate conception of the nature of things. Or in the slightly paradoxical language of the creationist, "no-principle" determines a context that is itself the sum of all orders.

The relative indifference of the Taoist to the notion of causality is grounded in the view that aesthetic experiences, which are a significant part of everyone's existence, are not open to causal analysis. This is but to say that there are significant *meanings* associated with our experiences of the world that transcends causal determination. For the Taoist, or for anyone concerned with aesthetic experiences on their own terms, the disposition to construe the world in a meaningful way is more general than the need to construe it along strictly causal lines. Hume found the origin of our assumption of the ubiquity of causal connections in the passion of "belief." If such a passion is isolated it might be found to answer to the need, not simply for causal order, but for the experience of *meaning*. The function of *theoria* is not limited to realizations through praxis as action or production; it is equally germane, perhaps more germane, to realize *theoria* through *aisthesis*. And *aisthesis* is indifferent to causal analysis.

Recently, there has been an increasing interest in non-causal forms of meaning. Perhaps the most familiar is that discussed by Carl Jung under the rubric of "synchronicity."[62] What Jung terms "synchronicity" involves an interpretation of laws of nature against the background of "a-causal orderedness." The laws of nature are statistical. The exceptions to the laws are, in terms of the explanatory function of law, accidental. Some of these accidental happenings Jung construes as uncaused, contingent events. Synchronous events are instances of a-causal orderedness. Synchronicity refers to three separate types of events: first, the coincidence of a psychic content with a corresponding objective process perceived to occur simultaneously; second, the coincidence of a psychic state with a dream or vision corresponding to an objective occurrence at a distance that is discovered to have taken place more or less simultaneously; and, finally, an objective event occurring in the future but represented by a dream or vision in the present. In the latter two cases synchronicity is a function of the parallelism existing between a neutral psychic state and a dream or vision.

Jung developed his theory of synchronicity because of his interest in certain phenomena that might support his vision of psychic events as causally independent of physical or physiological causes. If it could be shown that there are formal principles of relationship among parallel events in nature, or between nature and the psyche, that do not reduce to causal explanations, this would provide the basis for a full-scale attack upon psycho-physical determinisms of all types. A model for a-causal explanations was constructed by Leibniz employing the concept of "pre-established harmony." But this theory quickly degenerated into the narrower conception of psycho-physical parallelism, which, in its turn, fell victim easily to the materialist reductions of modern science.

Jung traces the adumbrations of his concept of synchronicity to the alchemical and astrological practices in our ancient and medieval traditions, as well as to the Taoist stress upon the meaningfulness of non-causal connections. The most important assumption of Western astrology, for example, is no more or less than this: a meaningful relation exists between the microcosmic events characterizing the origination of a living organism's personal career and the macrocosmic events at the time of origination. Indeed, this assumption of "as above, so below" underlies all synchronistic interpretations.

One must be careful not to read astrological, alchemical, or other mantic procedures in terms of the scientific, causal, thinking that supervened upon them. For, examined closely, the scientist shows himself to be a magician who has experienced a failure of nerve. The reduction of the vast complexity of natural events, and all the possible forms of inter-action and correspondence that connect them, to principles of causal influence, constitutes a kind of simplification that one might well consider pernicious.

In Taoism, the *I Ching* and the tradition of divination that surrounded it required no causal explanations. We are asked only to believe that coincidental phenomena (the manipulation of coins or yarrow stalks, and the hexagrams selected thereby) provide meaningful correspondences. Nor does the Taoist shrink from the conclusion that accidental or coincidental happenings in nature are often sources of greater wisdom than the most precise causal knowledge.

The *I Ching*, which through a series of editions and translations is becoming increasingly familiar to Western audiences, is an attempt to chart the characteristics of change through the use of six-line symbols (Hexagrams, or *Kua*) formed by straight (——) and broken (— —) lines. The former represent the *Yang*, or firm aspect of change; the latter the *Yin*, or yielding aspect. *Yang* answers to such terms as Being, Light, Firm, Masculine; *Yin* to Non-Being, Darkness, Yielding, Feminine. The Hexagrams, sixty-four in all, represent the possible permutations of *Yin* and *Yang* aspects of change in nature. An understanding of these symbols of change and their transformations into one another provides one with some insight into the variety and complexity of natural processes. In Chinese metaphysics and popular philosophy, one finds a greater or lesser degree of faith in the efficacy of the *I Ching* as a book of oracles, but the status of the book as a symbol system the consultation of which can educate the intuitions to appreciate the importance of the element of change in characterizing the meaning of events in nature is hardly questioned. The *I Ching*, as Jung realized, is the profoundest illustration of the notion of synchronicity. And in terms of our present discussion it forms a veritable manual for the development of a science of the accidental.

The value of the *I Ching* for understanding notions of meaning that transcend causal determinations derives in large part from the notion of *Tao*. A possible translation of "Tao," one suggested by the Sinologist Richard Wilhelm, is simply "meaning." And, according to Wilhelm, "the relation between meaning (*Tao*) and reality cannot be conceived under the category of cause and effect."[63] According to Chuang-Tzu, "the sages of old took as their starting point a state when the existence of things had not yet begun. . . . When affirmation and negation came into being, the *Tao* faded."[64] The Taoist, who thinks holistically, must concern himself with aspects of existence that are related "by chance" and, therefore, simply in terms of meaning. This approach parallels the medieval Western doctrine of *correspondentia*, which is based, as is Taoist philosophy, on the organistic assumption of meaningful correspondence between the microcosm and the macrocosm. The doctrine of correspondence or meaningful coincidence, which the principle of synchronicity seeks to generalize, is implicit in the Platonic doctrine of Ideas, if we interpret it in terms of the existence of *a priori* meaning, which, existing from the beginning, *participates* in meaningful correspondences with events in the realm of becoming. Interpretations of Platonic philosophy that attempt to explain the participation of the Ideas in the events of the world of becoming solely by recourse to some causal model have not been able to make coherent sense of Plato's insights.

The principle of synchronicity establishes a connection without recourse to the concept of efficient cause. This is hardly as controversial as it may at first appear. Indeed the causal independence of contemporaries is by no means a controversial concept in Western philosophy, particularly in process philosophies wherein the completion of a quantum of experience can occur only if a given experiencing is protected from continual bombardment by contemporary occasions. This causal independence, however, does not at all suggest that meaningful coincidences are impossible or unlikely between contemporaneous events.

It is easy enough to misunderstand the notion of synchronicity, finding in it nothing more than the substitution of formal cause for efficient cause as the fundamental explanatory principle. Idealisms have, of course, always employed the formal cause as the primary explanatory principle, but they have had to affirm an *absolute* principle to account for the given order of things. If "God" or "Absolute Spirit" is invoked to explain the nature of things, it can only be that the order of nature is patterned by uniform logical characteristics. If such is the case, linear causality may be inferred from the patterning of events, ensuring a pre-established harmony between efficient and formal cause. In this instance, efficient cause is derivative from formal cause, but in no way in contradiction with it. There are passages in Jung suggesting that he means no more by the conception of synchronicity than this. But the weight of his writing on the subject, and, in particular, the phenomena he employs to illustrate his doctrine, suggests that he understood the primary fact about the creationist universe—that it is the sum of all possible orders resulting from the self-creativity of each event. That is: there are as many universes as there are events in the process of becom-

ing. The projected and accepted pre-eminence of one possible
order among others nonetheless leaves room in the interstices
for alternative universes the significances of which can be
understood if the character of events as efficacious along
strictly traceable linear routes is ignored and the understanding of co-incidental events and their relationships is sought
instead.

An especially interesting aspect of Jung's notion of synchronicity is that by it he has pointed the way toward the
development of a theorial attitude toward those interpretations of experience we have come to call "occult." For so-
called occult sciences are not sciences in the traditional sense
of the word. They are, in the language we have been using
here, sciences of the accidental—that is to say, sciences that
place their emphasis not upon the aspects of nature that have
been construed in linear, causal terms, but have instead
stressed the coincidental, meaningful correspondences that
obtain in nature by virtue of the ecstatic, enstatic, and constatic experiencing of each occasion of experience by every
other. It is the capacity of individuals for *wu-wei*, *wu-chih*, and
wu-yü that promotes the possibility of meaningfulness among
events in nature that are not construable in terms of efficient
cause.

The relevance of Jung's assertion of the principle of
synchronicity, and of the analysis of phenomena such as the *I
Ching* as sources of a science of the accidental is further
stressed when we realize that contemporary experiments in
the study of the human personality are beginning to articulate
a basis for the belief in the co-existence within the same
organic being, of both the disposition to think causally and the
disposition to entertain the world in an a-causal manner.

Among the more interesting of recent researches into the
nature of human personality has been that which has centered
in the investigations of the brain. Our modern descendants of
the phrenologists have gained some degree of respectability by
moving the locus of their concern inside the brain cage.
Charting the brain according to function is providing the basis
for a number of quite interesting speculations on the complexity of human experience. So-called "split brain" research has

developed in accordance with the discovery that the severing of the *corpus callosum*, which connects the right and left cerebral hemispheres, has sometimes led to the experience of two independently functioning brains.[65] This discovery is disturbing to say the least, since the indivisibility of conscious experience has long been asserted to be a primary reason for believing in the unitary nature of the self.

But the cerebral localizers have discovered not only the possibility that the two hemispheres of the brain are capable of functioning in separation from one another, but that they possess radically different types of function.[66] Joseph Bogen has characterized these different types of function in this way: the left hemisphere supports "propositional thinking," which means that it is concerned with abstract, analytic, and linear-causal types of thinking. The right hemisphere functions concretely, synthetically, and in a visuo-spatial manner. These latter functions Bogen terms "appositional," a term which indicates the capacity for comparing or correlating perceptions. The two types of functions have also received such designations as *digital* (that is, discursive and logical) and *analogic* (non-discursive and eidetic).

Speculations of this type have received an interesting organization at the hands of Arthur Deikman in terms of the supposition that the human being, as a biological and psychological being, is an organization of components that may be termed the "action" mode and the "receptive" mode. The action mode of organization functions to provide the primary means for the manipulation of the environment. "The action mode is a state of striving, oriented toward achieving personal goals that range from nutrition to defense to obtaining social rewards, plus a variety of symbolic and sensual pleasures, as well as the avoidance of a comparable variety of pain."[67] The receptive mode concerns the intake of the environment rather than its manipulation. Its attributes, in direct contrast to those of the active mode, are "diffuse attending, paralogical thought processes, decreased boundary perception, and the dominance of the sensory over the formal."[68]

In Western culture our orientation is primarily that of the action mode. This claim is supported by the fact that the concept of cause is often closely associated with the psychological sense of efficacy grounded in experiences of intention, decision, and action as expressions of power enabling one to produce intended effects, or alternately, from the sense of being acted upon associated with experiences of conflict, compulsion, and constraint. Elements of Eastern culture associated with meditational techniques seem to produce brain-states and behavioral states expressive of the receptive mode of consciousness. It is precisely because of the existence of a cultural context that expresses the receptive mode that we are prevented from dismissing that form of functioning as regressive, infantile, or psychotic.

If we take seriously the distinction between active and receptive functionings, we are able to provide some support for the view that the notion of causality is not a necessary principle determining our possible understandings of nature. It is rather a generalization of experiences in the action mode of consciousness.

Though the experience of causal efficacy seems to underlie our most fundamental meanings of cause and effect, that experience itself seems to depend upon the experience of temporality. In ordinary human experience *time passes*, and our most common experiences of time involve the experience of causal sequence, where the cause is the temporal antecedent and the effect the temporal consequent. One of the most persistent challenges to the belief in the ubiquity of causal relations has come from the tradition of religious mysticism, which lays claim to experiences transcending the temporal. Tantric mystics, trained in the art of visuo-spatial representations and interpretations of experience, assert with persistence that many of their meditative experiences are not at all bound by, or interpretable in terms of, linear, temporal, or causal categories. This is but to say that there is more than one important mode of experiencing in terms of which one is able to construe the world.

With the introduction of the speculations and researches of contemporary physiologists and psychologists concerning the nature of brain functioning, we have provided additional support for one of the principal theses of this work. For we have added reason to believe that the philosophic visions whose bankruptcy we have announced repeatedly in the course of this essay are themselves grounded in the volitional perspective, since that perspective can be seen as itself a function of the action-orientation, which in its more subtle guise appears as the causal interpretation of events.

What if we were to ask after the nature of things as construed from the receptive mode of consciousness? Would we not be required to envision the world in terms of non-assertiveness in thought, action, and feeling? And would not this lead us to picture the world as patterned by relations among events indifferent to causal explanations? And is not this just the Taoist, or creationist, universe we have been discussing all along?

For the creationist the world comprises a vast complex of mutually interfused events. The understanding of such a world is possible because of the sense of constasy, which allows one to experience the Totality as the sum of all termini of acts of intuition. F. S. C. Northrop termed nature, as experienced in what we are calling the constatic mode, the Undifferentiated Aesthetic Continuum.[69] The fact that the world is composed of mutually interfused events provides the grounds for a belief in order that is immanent, not imposed. There need be no reason for order extrinsic to the order itself. Every event in nature is *causa sui*. On this view the reason for the character of each event in nature must be found within, where "within" refers to an unchartable domain of spontaneity.

Herbert Guenther, explicating a Buddhist conception of causality, speaks for Taoism as well when he says: "Causality, if such a term is ever applicable, posits an interlocking system of hierarchically fluctuating cause-factors. That is to say, the cause-situation was already a 'network' of interdependent, co-existent and freely co-operating forces, and in this network at any given time any one factor may take the highest place in a hierarchy of causes and effect."[70] On this view there can be no isolatable cause that may be seen as an antecedent, of which an identifiable event may be said to be the consequent. And if it is true that any one factor may take the highest place in a hierarchy of cause and effect, then not only can there be no privileged agent defining a particular order, there can also be no privileged order! The Taoist denies what is most fundamental to the Western cosmogonical tradition, viz., that the actual Cosmos is *one world*.

The concept of efficient cause, which is the model for most of our Western notions of causation, entails the presumption of "strictly relevant antecedents." If no antecedent event can be isolated and determined to be strictly relevant to a second, subsequent, event, then the notion of efficient cause becomes questionable. Without a well-delimited doctrine of efficient causation, no concept of action can be made meaningful. And if action is not a meaningful concept, neither is the notion of order as the result of an *Orderer*.

I certainly do not mean to suggest that it is impossible to isolate causal antecedents; it certainly is possible. But the arbitrary and conventional nature of this procedure ought to be admitted. We feel compelled to discover *the* cause of a particular phenomenon in the physical realm for the same reason that we must feel capable of asserting ourselves with efficacy in the social and political spheres. An "action" requires an actor or agent who is its author. The concept of efficient cause requires that there be *strictly relevant antecedents* to account for events in nature.

A contemporary Taoist would emphasize the effect of the Judaeo-Christian myth of "the domination of nature" upon Anglo-European notions of freedom and determination. The myth has its origins in a Creator God who deputized human beings as caretakers of his created order, but who then cursed them with the necessity of labor because of the act of prideful self-assertion that separated them from the rest of nature. *Action* is, ultimately, only a sublimation of *labor*, which advertises its origins in the enmity between man and nature.

The primary fact about the Taoist universe is that it is the sum of all orders resulting from the self-creativity of each event. There are as many actualizable worlds as there are events in the process of becoming. Tao as Becoming-Itself is the sum of all orders, including any specific order realized from the perspective of a single event. Being is any specific order. Non-being is the potential for all other orders. Being and Non-Being are abstracted from the becoming of events. Becoming is the fundamental reality from which Being and Non-Being are abstractions. Taking the term "Cosmos" in its broadest sense, it is the sum of all orders, which is Becoming-Itself. According to the Taoist vision, Becoming, Cosmos, Chaos (*hun-tun*) and Tao as *That Which* are synonymous.

The organization of Chaos, a requirement of discursive knowledge, involves the carving of the Uncarved Block, which requires the establishment of a privileged order from among the sum of all orders. Such a privileged order insures a pre-eminent role for the organizer of Chaos—the rational or volitional being. Once that role is given, it is no longer possible to grasp the meaning of Tao, for reason cannot proceed except through delimitation and exclusive differentiations.

Obviously, if we insist upon a rational analysis, the notion that the Tao is Chaos as the sum of all orders will make little sense. For in place of the experience of "undifferentiated homogeneity" we shall think in terms of "incompossible orders," and the notion of *the sum of all orders* will translate as a confused mélange without coherent structure—in short, Chaos in the traditional Western sense. To grasp the Taoist sense of the equivalence of Tao, cosmos, chaos, and becoming or process, it is necessary to employ, not reason, but *intuition*.

Our faith in rationality has long been sustained by the myth of objectivity grounded in the belief in a single order of nature. Lately, however, we have begun to realize that the more we speculate concerning the nature of the cosmos the more we discover that it is but a *speculum*, a reflecting plane, which mirrors the human countenance. The conclusion we in the West have drawn is that "man is the measure." But this is to stop short of the full consequences of relativity. Eastern speculations likewise tend to arrive at the conception of nature as a mirror. But the difference between conventionalist theory and conceptions of the interfusion of each in all things lies in the increased complexity of the mirroring process recognized by Taoist and Buddhist thinkers.

Chinese Buddhist tradition provides a remarkably simple illustration of the mirroring process that is Nature-Itself. In

the T'ang dynasty, Fa Tsang was invited to the palace of
Empress Wu to expound the doctrine of Totality of Hwa Yen
Buddhism. This he did through a demonstration involving a
room whose floor, ceiling, and walls were lined with mirrors,
and in the center of which he had placed a statue of the
Buddha. In each mirror a Buddha image was produced, along
with the images in every other mirror. Holding a small crystal
ball in his hand, Fa Tsang illustrated how all the mirrors and
their images were reflected in it, and it in turn was reflected in
the mirrors, *ad infinitum*.[71] Not only was he attempting to
illustrate the reciprocal interfusion of all things, but he wished
to evoke a sense of the dependent co-origination of each item
in nature. This "dependent-arising," as the Buddhists term it,
suggests an indifference toward the isolation of causes viewed
as strictly relevant antecedents.

Nature, as the uncarved block, is not simply a convenient
construal from the human perspective, it is *the realm of all
possible construals*; not merely a reflection of the human
mind, but a mirroring of each in all and all in each that challenges the validity of the simply human perspective. To know
nature one must experience constasy, the sense of all things
standing together in a felt unity in which, nonetheless, each
item in nature maintains its autonomy and uniqueness. The
reciprocal interfusion of all things as illustrated by Fa Tsang's
Hall of Mirrors provides the basis for an understanding of
things that is not causally based. Though the Totality is the
ultimate object of knowledge in each occasion of an event of
knowing, it is the Totality as construed from the perspective
of the ecstatic sense of the other, the enstatic sense of oneself
as experienced by the other, and the constatic sense of each
member standing with all things. *Wu-chih*, *wu-wei* and *wu-yü*
discipline moments of construal in a creationist universe,
expressing the dominance of the receptive mode of consciousness over the active.

Conventionalism exposes the concept of action to the just
criticism that causal explanations are anthropomorphic and
are grounded in the conception of human convenience. This
relativizes cosmological speculation making it depend upon
current conventions. It should come as no great surprise that

the cosmologies grounded in the family of philosophic perspectives developed in our Judaeo-Christian tradition should
be no more at variance than they are. For the fact that our
Anglo-European culture can not only trace its roots to Hebraic
and Hellenic sources but can demonstrate a continuous development from out of these sources is evidence enough that our
cultural milieu forms a system of usages, customs, or conventions that has remained surprisingly constant over the centuries. Criteria of convenience change only if conventions
change. Conventions change with alterations in culture. There
have been no radical alterations in Western culture since its
beginnings. (This, we recall, was the burden of our discussion
of the development of our cultural paradigm in a previous
chapter.)

The family of conventions that have served us from our
beginnings are not the only possibilities for thought, however.
The a-causal, no-principles philosophic paradigm constructed
from out of Taoist and Buddhist sources is more than just an
ad hoc attempt to revitalize our intellectual tradition. It is
empirically grounded in the experience of constasy, which
derives from the felt sense that Chaos and Cosmos are one.
Relations to one's environment are not to be construed in
terms of self-assertive action but as sympathetic interfusion,
which calls upon each person to walk the ways of those things
he encounters.

The fact that these ideas, so at variance with the traditional philosophic notions in our culture, are found within
philosophical Taoism and in certain Buddhist sects (Hwa Yen,
Ch'an or Zen) certainly indicates that, even in the East, what
we are calling creationist thought has by no means necessarily
predominated. Our restructuring of a cultural paradigm for
decaying Western culture can certainly be nothing but an
exercise in futility if the philosophy of creativity has no more
to recommend it than novelty and the stamp of esoterica. A
philosophy of culture cannot depend upon elitist or esoteric
thinking for its explanatory and interpretative categories.
Such would be the most irrelevant of academic exercises.

Has the cultural context of Western thought altered
sufficiently not only to allow for the introduction of an an-

archist philosophy into the melting pot of ideas forming intellectual culture, but altered radically enough that one may
sensibly make the claim that this form of philosophical
anarchism provides the most viable interpretation of our
emerging sensibility? The "Yes" I here answer to this question will have a hollow ring until, in the discussions that
follow, I defend the view that the experiential context within
which the customs, usages, or conventions that form our cultural milieu are established is moving into a stage of qualitative
alteration that will call for a radically new interpretation, one
close to the creationist paradigm we have been developing in
these pages. The reason for this alteration, unlikely as it may
first appear, I shall find in the oft-celebrated phenomenon of
advancing technological society.

NOTES

1. *The Function of Reason*, pp. 42–43.
2. See Hannah Arendt, *The Human Condition* (Garden City, N.Y.: Doubleday, 1959), pp. 197–206.
3. *Knowledge and Human Interests*, p. 306.
4. Ibid., p. 307.
5. Ibid., p. 314.
6. Ibid., pp. 316–17.
7. *The Human Condition*, p. 160.
8. See *Der Satz vom Grund* (Pfullingen: Neske, 1957), passim.
9. See esp. *Science and the Modern World*, passim.
10. *The Function of Reason*, p. 4.
11. Ibid., "Introductory Summary."
12. *Process and Reality*, p. 160.
13. Vol. II, Part III, Sect. I, Ch. 2:1.
14. See *Process and Reality*, pp. 255–79 and passim.
15. See *Being and Time*, trans. John Macquarrie and Edward Robinson (New York: Harper and Row, 1962), pp. 255–73, and passim.
16. See *Introduction to Metaphysics*, trans. T. E. Hulme (Indianapolis: Bobbs-Merrill, 1955).
17. This concept plays a central role in Ortega's philosophy after 1916. For a concise statement of the doctrine and its consequences, see *The Modern Theme*, trans. James Cleugh (New York: Harper and Row, 1961), pp. 139–44.
18. Sophisticated Marxians may be quick to point out that the interpre-
tation of praxis as *aisthesis* seems to recall Feuerbach's reconstruction of
materialism, which demanded perception be substituted for abstract thinking as the materialist form of entertaining the world. And it was over against
this view that Marx introduced the conception of praxis as sensuous activ-

ity. The reply is obvious: I am not plumping for a materialist doctrine. If I were it would certainly be difficult to discuss "the subjective form of feeling," "intuition," or "preoccupation" in those terms. It is because of the poverty of materialism in this regard that Marx was forced to import an incoherent methodological tool (the Hegelian dialectic) into his theory in order to provide a dynamic interpretation of praxis.

19. R. G. H. Siu, *Ch'i: A Neo-Taoist Approach to Life* (Cambridge: MIT Press, 1974), p. 221.

20. I trust I shall be forgiven the use of this barbarism, which combines a Latin and a Greek root. The term more adequately expresses the concept I wish to describe than any of its more elegant alternatives.

21. *Chuang Tzu*, Chapter 2. Quoted from *Chuang Tzu: Inner Chapters*, trans. Gia-Fu Feng and Jane English (New York: Random House, 1974), p. 29.

22. *The Will to Power*, p. 339.

23. Ibid., see 340.

24. *Timaeus* 30, trans. Jowett. The Cornford translation of this passage is cited in Chapter 2 above.

25. Ibid., 31; my italics.

26. Cecil Schneer, "Science and History" in *The Concept of Order*, ed. Paul Kuntz (Seattle: The University of Washington Press, 1968), p. 135.

27. Quoted ibid., p. 135.

28. See *Mind and the World Order* (New York: Dover, 1956).

29. James K. Feibleman, "Disorder," in *The Concept of Order*, p. 10.

30. Ibid.

31. Ibid., p. 12.

32. Peter Caws, "Order and Value in the Sciences," in ibid., p. 106.

33. *Principles of Chinese Painting*, revised edition (Princeton: Princeton University Press, 1970), p. 22.

34. Ibid., p. 23.

35. If we were to seek a parallel for this kind of art in the West we could perhaps locate it in certain painters of the later Middle Ages, such as Giotto or Fra Filippo Lippi. See Jeanne L. Trabold, "The Influence of Chinese Painting on European Art of the Late Middle Ages and Early Renaissance: An Hypothesis," *Selected Papers in Asian Studies* (Albuquerque, N.M.: Western Conference of the Association for Asian Studies, 1976), pp. 53–59.

36. I am indebted to Audrey Joseph's unpublished paper, "Communication, Creativity, and T'ai Chi Ch'üan," and to conversations with Professor Joseph, of the University of New Mexico, for much of my understanding of the aesthetic character of T'ai Chi.

37. *Science and Hypothesis* (New York: Dover, 1952), p. 50.

38. Ibid., p. 58; emphasis deleted.

39. Ibid., p. 64.

40. Ibid., p. 66.

41. Ibid., my italics.

42. Ibid., p. 57.

43. Ibid., p. 55.

44. *Modes of Thought*, p. 56.

45. Ibid., pp. 56–57.

46. *Adventures of Ideas*, p. 177.

47. Ibid.

48. *Science and the Modern World*, p. 18.

49. *Process and Reality*, p. 139.

50. *Modes of Thought*, p. 57.

51. I should not suggest that Whitehead, on whose speculations I have depended in this account, would concur with the previous paragraph. For Whitehead stops far short of accepting the notion of the immanence of law in its strongest form.

52. *Process and Reality*, pp. 46–47.

53. *Adventures of Ideas*, p. 147.

54. Ibid., pp. 146–47.

55. See Leibniz' "On the Ultimate Origin of Things," in *The Monadology and Other Writings*, trans. R. Latta (London: Oxford University Press, 1898), for a discussion of The Principle of Sufficient Reason and the cosmological argument for the existence of God.

56. *Metaphysics*, VI, Ch. 2, 1026B4–6.

57. See ibid., 1027A19–21.

58. *Patterns of Discovery* (Cambridge: Cambridge University Press, 1958), pp. 68–69.

59. David Bohm, *Causality and Chance in Modern Physics* (Philadelphia: University of Pennsylvania Press, 1971), pp. 14–15.

60. *Patterns of Discovery*, p. 64.

61. *Causality and Chance in Modern Physics*, p. 1.

62. In *The Structure and Dynamics of the Psyche*, Vol. 8 of The Collected Works of C. G. Jung, trans. R. F. C. Hull (London: Routledge and Kegan Paul, 1969).

63. Quoted ibid., p. 487 (# 920), note.

64. Chuang Tzu, *Inner Chapters*.

65. See Michael Gazzaniga, in *Scientific American*, 217, No. 2 (August 1967), 24–29; reprinted in Robert Ornstein, ed., *The Nature of Human Consciousness* (San Francisco: Freeman, 1973), pp. 87–100.

66. See Joseph E. Bogen, "The Other Side of the Brain: An Appositional Mind," in *Bulletin of the Los Angeles Neurological Societies*, 34, No. 3 (July 1969), 135–62; reprinted ibid., pp. 101–25.

67. "Bi-Modal Consciousness," *Archives of General Psychiatry*, 25 (December 1971), reprinted ibid., p. 68.

68. Ibid., p. 69. I do not mean to suggest that the kind of brain research I have been discussing establishes anything definite in relation to the character and function of human personality and culture. To a large extent we are able to find what we seek in any type of research, especially when we discuss issues of such vagueness and complexity as the functioning of the brain. Certainly the neat classifications that suggest that there is a "right-brain" and a "left-brain" are excessively tendentious and bespeak a rather simple-minded wedding of dialectical methods and gross physiological observations. This aberrant form of "dialectical materialism" is hardly superior to any other.

If the reader wishes to consult a slightly less speculative treatment of the evidences from brain physiology I have been employing I would suggest Karl R. Popper and John C. Eccles, *The Self and Its Brain* (New York: Springer-Verlag, 1977).

69. See *The Logic of the Sciences and the Humanities*, pp. 95–96.

70. *Buddhist Philosophy in Theory and Practice* (Baltimore: Penguin, 1971), pp. 75–76.

71. This illustration is given in some detail in Garma C. C. Chang's *The Buddhist Teaching of Totality* (University Park: The Pennsylvania State University Press, 1974), pp. 22–24. The Hall of Mirrors is an alternative version of the doctrine of Indra's Net, which consists of an intricately interwoven network of crystal ornaments hung above the Heavens. The network reflects the entire universe and each crystal reflects all images, no detail being lost. See also Francis H. Cook, *Hua Yen Buddhism: The Jewel Net of Indra* (University Park: The Pennsylvania State University Press, 1977).

6

The Meaning of Making

O'er that art which, you say, adds to nature, is an art that nature
makes. . . . The art itself is nature.
WILLIAM SHAKESPEARE

. . . and all watched over by machines of loving grace.
RICHARD BRAUTIGAN

TECHNOLOGICAL FALLACIES

THE STRUGGLE OF HUMAN BEINGS against a violent and
implacable nature is one of the primary ingredients in the
romance of human history. The myth of creation in Genesis
tells the story of God's giving man lordship over nature and
charging him with the task of subduing the earth. Rule over
nature was, in the beginning, an effortless task as befits a
noble lord. But after the act of self-assertion that led the
primordial pair to eat from the tree of the knowledge of good
and evil, God condemned Adam and Eve with the curse of
labor. To Adam, God said, "with labor shall you win your
food" (Gen. 1:26). And to Eve, "In labor you shall bear children" (Gen. 1:29). Nowhere in the myth does God rescind his
initial command that Adam should subdue the earth. Because
of this the mythical foundations of so many of our cultural
attitudes toward the place of human beings in nature are
characterized by two incongruous themes: *lordship* and *labor*.

We do not have to question just how influential has been this understanding of human nature. Whether the Old Testament characterization of persons was determinative of our views, or merely codified attitudes already deeply ingrained in our cultural forebears, the themes of *lordship* and *labor* are easily discernible in our Western conceptions of the relation of persons and nature.[1] At least part of human motivation for struggling against nature might well derive from the sense of having once been rightful lord of creation. What was once the status of human beings by virtue of God's benevolence must be rewon through the hardships of labor. Nature is an obstacle preventing reunion with God. It is a constant reminder of self-induced separation, alienation from God. The human being is a lord laboring under a curse.

The dialectic with nature with which human beings have been engaged since the beginnings of cultural existence has led in recent history to a series of partial reconciliations between persons and their natural environs. But these reconciliations seem hardly to have led to the reinstitution of the lordly status of human beings. Freud claimed that just as Copernicus had destroyed man's vision of his privileged place in the universe as a physical system, and as Darwin had destroyed man's sense of having a special place as opposed to the animal kingdom, modern psychoanalysis had demonstrated that human beings are not even masters of their own ego. The effect of each of these revolutionary shifts in human perspective must be seen as ambiguous: It increased the sense of relatedness of human beings to nature, albeit in a fashion not at all acceptable to those who would be potential lords of creation. These "reconciliations," though, on the one hand, decreasing the alienation of man from his natural ambience expressed in the activity of labor, could but increase his alienation from his own self-image as lord and deputy. And as human activity shifted away from the oppressiveness of labor to the satisfactions of work and creativity sustained by man's increased control of nature, the motivations for domination increased. The shocks to our human self-image have been such as to alter finally and completely our attitude of *noblesse oblige* and our lordly condescension toward nature. The more we recognize our kinship with nature—which we can experience only as the result of a fall from grace—the more we seek to win a final and complete victory over it. Only through usurpation can the tyrant-to-be distinguish himself from his peers. This is a strange kind of reconciliation indeed! And it is not yet completed. We are currently engaged in reconciling ourselves with the technological milieu that comprises our most immediate ambience.

Bruce Mazlich has recently picked up this theme of reconciliation and given it an interesting twist. Accepting Freud's assessment of his and his predecessor's role in history, Mazlich points out that the "discontinuities" (he borrows the term from Jerome Bruner) between man and physical nature, the animal kingdom, and the irrational factors in his behavior, highlighted by Copernicus (Mazlich prefers Galileo), Darwin, and Freud respectively, have still left persons with a significant outstanding discontinuity—viz., that between human beings and machines. Mazlich claims the overcoming of this "fourth discontinuity" would overcome human distrust of machines and machine technology which "rests on man's refusal to accept his own nature—as being continuous with the tools and machines he constructs." [2]

This is certainly an interesting thesis. But surely the argument that the story of modern culture is the tale of the overcoming of discontinuities separating man from his true nature as physical, animal, irrational, and mechanical is altogether too tendentious to be generally applicable. The reconciliation of human being with the being of nature is itself, as we have stressed before, a cultural event. Our vision of nature has been dominated in modern times by the materialist world-view, which is but one of several possible cosmological schemes. And it is certainly no accident that the themes of reconciliation should be discussed in terms of Copernicus or Galileo, Darwin, Freud, and the proponents of machine technology, each of whom held, to some degree, the materialist or mechanist world-view. We must be cautious so as not to overapply theoretical insights that are so narrowly and provincially derived.

With this demurrer in mind, however, we can proceed to

consider the cultural effect of the contemporary attempts to overcome the presumed discontinuity between individual and machine. The revolution associated with Copernicus, Darwin, and Freud concerns the overcoming of a presumed dichotomy between "human" and "natural" existence. The attempt to relate persons and technology on a common ground seems a task of a different order. The effect of the three previous revolutions in human perspective was to destroy man's self-image as lord of creation. The only means left for human beings to regain favor is through the activity of labor. *Technology* is the means whereby humans may regain access to the garden of Eden. Or so they must believe.

Properly understood, the relationship of persons and technology would tend to provide a means of winning lordship over nature. Material technology, genetic engineering, and psychotherapeutic techniques are ways in which the privileged status of person vis-à-vis the physical universe, the animal kingdom, and the irrational forces of their own psyches might be rewon. Technology is the means by which humans can work their way back up through the ranks to reoccupy their lordly throne.

It would be a mistake to attempt yet another reduction of the human phenomenon to some aspect of the objective environment, be it physical or biological, or the irrationality of eros–thanatos drives. The technological phenomenon suggests a qualitatively different revolution in perspective from those encountered in previous developments associated with modern science. Technology underlies each of the subsequent developments, extends their consequences, and promises to resolve their dilemmas. The relation of persons and machines is one that promises to develop into a form of cultural symbiosis unhoped for in any of the other revolutions. Not, however, because humans accept their nature as being continuous with that of the machines they construct, but precisely because through construction of such machines they have the means to realize an aboriginal nature that could have existed only as potential as long as the curse of labor exhausted them in the quest for survival and goaded them toward a search for greatness. It appears that the understanding of technology is a prerequisite to the understanding of our future.

The conceptual confusions surrounding the terms "technology" and "technological society" have created a smokescreen behind which is developing the most significant single phenomenon on the cultural scene. The chief difficulty with the term "technology" is that it has no coherent set of semantic associations. One of the reasons this is the case is that technology has rarely been treated as a discipline within the sphere of intellectual culture. Whereas "biology" is seen to refer not only to the living things of a region, but to the logos of bios, the meaning of life, as well, "technology" is primarily understood in substantive terms and seldom designated the logos of *techne*, the meaning of making. It is the latter, disciplinary, context that provides the readiest means of establishing the meanings of terms and concepts, and of resolving problems that arise concerning a given discipline and its application. Though it is quite possible, in most cases, to ignore the theoretical dimensions of the technical phenomenon, there are often times when a general understanding of the cultural impact of technology is sought, only to be frustrated by the extreme difficulty of coming to grips with the meaning of technique and technology.[3]

The phenomenon that has come to be called "technological society" is the single given that affects every significant element of our cultural milieu. Technological society is the matrix that, for good or ill, is likely to serve as the repository of meaning and value for future generations. It is hardly possible any longer to ask whether or not we are willing to accept the development of technique and technology. Indeed, if we ever had a choice in the matter—and this is debatable—that choice has long since been removed from the ambit of possibilities forming our cultural existence. The principal question is not whether to accept technology, but "On what terms must we accept the technical phenomenon?" Before that question can be answered, however, it is necessary that we clear away what I shall take to be certain fundamentally confused and, indeed, fallacious understandings of the meaning and consequences of technology in contemporary culture.

The most serious, if only because the most common, confusion concerning technology is that it is quantitatively construable. This belief is based, of course, on a substantive definition of technology that perpetuates the notion that technology may be understood in terms of tools and machines. The traditional interpretation of technology has proceeded in terms of the conception of man as *homo faber*. The toolmaking capacity so readily identifiable in the anthropological approach to the study of human culture is said to define the uniquely human capacity. Hand-axes, bows and arrows, agricultural tools, and so on, are the prototypes of technological development from this point of view. The technologies of the industrial age are seen to be mere ramifications of the primitive tools of ancient societies. This view of technology is based in the fallacy of accepting as determinative for human development only those items of the cultural past that have *persisted* and are evident artifacts of the past. The substantive interpretation of technology as the sum total of material resources and their organization does not go very far in defining the nature of contemporary technological society wherein most of the technical phenomena are invisible—i.e., are identifiable only as the processes whereby a complex set of purposes are achieved. For example, the communications network, which more than any other single item characterizes the complexity of advanced technological society, is in no way reducible to the number of instruments of electronic communication. A vast system of usage is presupposed, a system that would in no tangible form survive the collapse of our cultural system.

Because, in modern times, the primary technological developments have been occasioned by events within the scientific realm, technology is often thought to be merely applied science. The theoretical understanding of technology, therefore, has been presumed to originate in the scientific theory that suggests the technical application. The resultant confusion has led to the claim that technology is merely a handmaiden of science, a claim that has radically truncated our understanding of the technical phenomenon.

The identification of technology with the tools and products of industry or with the instruments and equipment of science are two closely related instances of the tendency to view technology as a quantitative, linearly progressive, phenomenon. And such an interpretation leads to the belief that the future of technology can be divined by the use of simple extrapolation.

Theoretically understood, technology is often exclusively identified with "applied science"; concretely viewed, it is seen as a part of the history of industrial development. The former view tends to perform a double disservice to contemporary cultural understandings. In the first place, scientific progress is equated predominantly with the practical results of so-called scientific invention. The cumulative aspect of applied science viewed in this manner tends to suggest the same kind of linear progress on the theoretical side of science. But this hides the conceptual confusions, the theoretical conflicts, and the eminently *ad hoc* resolutions of problems encountered in research that characterize the history of science. The second disservice done by the too-ready identification of technology with applied science is that in this way we have remained all too ignorant of the technological significance of religious rituals, ethical mores, aesthetic techniques, and philosophic methods for our cultural development. Only by broadening the conception of technology can we begin to see that every cultural interest—art, morality, religion, philosophy, as well as science—has a technological aspect. Once this is seen we will be less likely to judge theoretical science as somehow more progressive than other intellectual disciplines and begin to understand what should have been obvious all along: quantitative progress is the only progress that we can clearly know, since only quantities are amenable to obvious accumulation and measurement.

Technology may be seen as applied science in precisely the same way that it may be considered applied art, or ethics, or religion. Each of our cultural interests has a technical side. There is none but a contingent, historical reason for claiming that technology is peculiarly related to science. Technology must be seen as the outworking in the sphere of praxis of principles of order and organization that derive from each of our intellectual interests. Cultural aims operating through the media of cultural interests are value-oriented. The values of *Truth*, as the conformation of Appearance and Reality, or

Beauty, as intense harmony in nature, artifacts, or institutions, or *Holiness*, as the sense of the transcendent importance of the finite detail among the Totality of things, all constitute aims toward which human societies have directed their energies. *Theorial* understanding does not require that such values be concretely defined or publicly realized. On the other hand, *theoretical* articulations of the meaning of Truth, Beauty, and Holiness are part and parcel of the development of the cultural paradigm, which is designed as a means of rationalizing chaos. Technology constitutes the regular means whereby cultural aims are realized in concrete form. Religious ritual is as much a part of the technical apparatus of contemporary society as are our manufacturing processes. That we pay less attention to the technical side of cultural interests other than science should not blind us to this fact.

The claim that technology and science are peculiarly related is given its most subtle support by technical rationalists such as Herbert Marcuse who, following Max Scheler, argue that there is an internal relation between science and technology since both are grounded in the motivation to control and to dominate.[4] This is but to argue that modern science is inherently instrumentalist in nature, and that the presumedly theoretical aspects of science are fundamentally practical in immediate intent. In this way the neutrality and objectivity of science are rejected and theoretical science is reduced to instrumentalism. Technology then becomes a slightly more obvious form of that basic instrumentalist orientation that has as its primary aims domination and control.

I certainly do not reject this claim of the technological rationalists. On the contrary I wish to extend it by arguing that culture itself has an inherently instrumentalist character and that not just science, but art, morality, religion, and philosophy, all are (or have been in the West) internally related to the technical phenomenon. Marcuse himself recognizes this more than do many others of his school, but he does seem to overstress the scientific interest as both cause and consequence of the instrumentalist, or "one-dimensional," character of other cultural interests.[5] To single out science as the primary cause of a creeping instrumentalism is to presume the possibility of a solution of whatever difficulties emerge because of this development by recourse to some other cultural interest. This, I believe, is naïve. The problem is not in our science alone, but in the motivation of reason itself. There is no recourse to be found within our culture. Recourse, if such there be, lies temporally and/or culturally beyond our present cultural milieu.

Martin Heidegger has poignantly expressed this claim in an essay entitled, *The End of Philosophy*. For Heidegger technology "includes all the areas of beings which equip the whole of beings: objectified nature, the business of culture, manufactured politics, and the gloss of ideals overlying everything."[6] As such, technology is "completed metaphysics," and "metaphysics is in all its forms and historical stages a unique, but perhaps necessary, fate of the West and the presupposition of its planetary dominance."[7] Technology is the peculiar end of the general articulation of Being, which is the activity of metaphysics. The human project, at its theoretical and practical levels, is realized in and through technology. Heidegger does not celebrate this fact, for like Nietzsche and Scheler, he finds technology functioning in obedience to the aim of domination. The technologization of culture is the result of a metaphysics immanently motivated by Will-to-Power. And its consequences are devastating.

> The decline [of truth] occurs through the collapse of the world characterized by metaphysics, and at the same time through the desolation of the earth stemming from metaphysics.
>
> Collapse and desolation find their adequate occurrence in the fact that metaphysical man, the *animale rationale*, gets fixed as the laboring animal.[8]

Here is technological rationalism in its severest form. Not only science, but every form of thinking defined by man's metaphysical interest, has its final realization in technology. Technology Heidegger deems "the highest form of rational consciousness," which sounds laudatory coming from a philosopher. But when he identifies technology and "experience," which he claims is "lack of reflection," "arranged powerlessness," we begin to understand the consequences of technological rationalization. The progressive development from unreflective experience to philosophic reflection and thence to technical competence has as its historical result the externalization of the concrete results of reflection, the creation of a technological ambience that serves as the environs of life and experience, and the identification of technical and experiential possibilities.

Heidegger's presentation of technological fulfillment does not include an analysis of the character of the novel world that lies beyond the current move toward technical rationalization. He is assured that "with the end of philosophy thinking is not also at its end, but in transition to another beginning."[9] But he refuses to extrapolate, and for that reason he seems to have grasped, as few theorists of technical rationality have, that the changes consequent upon fully developed technology will not be simply quantitative, but qualitative as well. You can't get there from here. Reason cannot see beyond the end of reason.

The extrapolator's mentality is best seen in the identification of technology and industry often made in popular presentations of the phenomenon of technology. The confusion here is especially pernicious in our period of ecological crisis since industrial and technological motivations tend, in many cases, in conflicting directions—one threatening disaster, the other providing perhaps the only viable resolution of crisis.

Though the industrial revolution provided an unequaled impetus for the advance of technology in the West, it hardly stands as proof that the principles of technology and those of industry are the same, or that they are even in harmony. Industrial development must be seen as the exploitation of natural resources primarily, though not exclusively, for profit. As such, industry is best interpreted along economic and, even more narrowly, *capitalist* lines. The primary goal of technology, however, is efficiency in activity. The aims of profit and efficiency can easily conflict. The making of personal fortunes by marshaling and organizing vast energies seldom can involve the efficient shepherding of resources. Industry has come to stand for waste, inefficiency, pollution, and planned obsolescence. Technology, however, has another aim:

absolute efficiency in the organization and control of experi-ence. In large part technology has been given support not by the positive aspirations of industry, but by its negative conse-quences. We can no longer afford smoke stacks belching tons of waste into our air, nor can we any longer pour wastes into our sewers and oceans, nor can we afford to use vast open spaces as homes for aged automobiles. The task of efficiency is forced upon us. But it is a burden joyfully accepted by those we have come to call "technicians." Where once the visionary *entre-preneur*, the ambitious industrial magnate reigned, we shall soon find the technician enthroned. Technological society has no room for the wasteful industrialist. Technology obeys but one rule—the rule of efficiency.

It is technology, not industry, that must resolve our ecological dilemmas. The management of business and industry is still in the hands of those trained to manage human beings. The personal exercise of power so enjoyed by the executive is more and more found to be in direct conflict with the efficient use of resources.[10]

Technology has, therefore, both positive and negative relations to industry. Technological efficiency can often serve the ends of industry by providing profitable tools and tech-niques to enhance industrial processes. It can also serve to clean up some of the sloppiness and waste promoted by the industrial aim at short-term profit. Neither of these aspects of technical development wholly accounts for the importance of technology in contemporary society, however. Beyond the incentives provided by industry there is an internal dynamic that must be clearly recognized. That dynamic Jacques Ellul had discussed in terms of the "self-augmentation" of tech-nology.[11] Self-augmentation is characterized by Ellul in terms of two "laws": the first claims that technical progress is ir-reversible; the second that such progress "tends to act, not according to an arithmetic, but according to a geometric pro-gression."[12] Technology grows internally through an increas-ingly large number of accretions, which are less the result of human insight than improvements upon present technologies suggested by the machines or techniques themselves.[13] The history of technological development shows itself to be the sort of accretive, self-augmenting process that aims ultimately at *perfection*, which must be construed as complete rationalization, complete order.

The character of technology as self-augmenting is not yet sufficient in itself to bring about the transition to a perfected technological order. There is no reason to believe that human beings are by nature efficient. The rapidity of our movement in the direction of efficiency and rationality must in part be attributed to the excesses of the industrial age. We are so in danger of fouling our nest that we have no choice but to turn to technical solutions to our problems. The combination of self-augmentation and vital need has brought about the situation that we find ourselves in today.

In his *Die Perfektion der Technik*, Friedrich Juenger quotes Rivarol's words, "Industry is the daughter of poverty." [14] No simpler manner can be found to characterize the difference between industry and technology than to claim that if industry is the daughter of poverty, contemporary technology can only be the step-child of excess.

The confusions of technology with science and with industry are grounded in the quantitative perspectives of the latter two. The claim that because technology is most dramatically visible in relation to the quantitative phenomena of our society we are able to understand the nature of technical development through extrapolation of the present into the future is made in the name of a species of determinism not unlike the old myth of inevitable progress. The fallacy that underlies this belief in determinism we may call the Jules Verne Fallacy. It consists in the belief that the future will be *more of the same*, only bigger, or better, or more powerful. This belief has sustained many technical enthusiasts since the beginning of the marriage of scientific theory with technological practice. The fallacy of this way of thinking derives from an insistence that all, or practically all, novelty must arise from current practice without the intervention of "unnecessary theorizing." Such an attitude creates a narrow and truncated view of future possibilities and leads us to what Marcuse has so well characterized as "one-dimensional thought."

Carried to its extreme, the Jules Verne Fallacy must inevitably lead to the belief in the self-augmenting nature of Technology. But the self-augmentation must not be interpreted mainly in quantitative terms. The future will not be "bigger and better." We have well-nigh reached the limits of our growth. The future will be more efficient. Or it just won't be. Comparisons with a bee-hive or ant heap would be too tendentious. We are neither ants nor bees. Political tyrannies have never been efficient. Doubtless, under Mussolini the trains ran on time, but little else worked properly. To know that our future society will be more technically efficient is to know very little. There are surprises awaiting us in the future.

Another serious oversimplification analysts of contemporary technological society are apt to make is the assumption that totalistic applications of technique in society are the result of, or unavoidably lend strength to, political machinations. Politics and social engineering are not that easily related to one another. Jacques Ellul is the most prominent example of one who has stressed the totalitarian nature of advanced technological society. Ubiquity of ordered, efficient techniques literally is to be equated in his mind with the realization of complete political control. This argument, as well as the completely pessimistic vision of technological society Ellul expresses, seems *prima facie* quite sound. But hasn't it been the tradition of politics precisely to shy away from the technical and efficient means of social control in favor of the personal, charismatic, visionary ambitions of power?

Max Weber was no doubt correct in his claim that bureaucracy yields power to the one at the top, but it is likewise true that the exercise of such power is in no wise nearly as satisfying as is the exercise of control over others based upon such intangibles as charisma, personal authority, command presence, and the like. In short, politics is a game of persuasion that cannot yield completely to control via technique. Behind the cool, efficient, bureaucratic Third Reich stood the personally inefficient, neurotic, wild-eyed visionary who would not play the bureaucratic game. The relations between technology and politics are much more complex than the gloomy prophets would have us believe. Our present technological system could as easily lead to a benign anarchy as to a totalitarian dictatorship. For it is technique applied to the leisure- and luxury-oriented existence of human beings, rather than directed toward the domination of nature and society, that best expresses the meaning and direction of contemporary technological society.[15]

The complex relationship of technology and politics is more easily seen if we take a look at the fate of the terms "politics" and "political" in contemporary intellectual culture. The significance of such terms, associated with both specialist and popular areas of society, is threatened in two important ways. The first is a death by qualification, which results from the narrow restriction of the extension of a term to only those phenomena highlighted by the methodological interests of a specialized elite. This results in a divorce of the specialist from popular culture, which leads to the second semantic threat. With no guidance from the specialist, the term is used without the recognition of any specific theoretical limits and suffers, thereby, from a too-generalized application. The term "politics" has suffered both fates. The behaviorist interpretations of contemporary political science have severely restricted the use of the term; at the same time its popular usage has become so bloated as almost to lose any specific meaning altogether.

At the level of popular culture, we speak of "Sexual Politics" (Kate Millet), "The Politics of the Family" and "The Politics of Experience" (Ronald Laing), and even "The Politics of God" (Schonfeld). The result of such usage seems to be that we call attention to the fact that power relations function as a primary aspect of every cultural phenomenon. Or put more directly, we have come to be aware of the artificiality of the way in which our cultural relations are decided. This in turn suggests that we have lost our sense of the inevitability or the naturalness of certain relations. The term "politics" classically was used to apply to the public relationships among men in society. The fact that we can discuss the politics of the family, or sexual relations, of our own private sphere of existence, and even of God himself, suggests that we no longer see these aspects of our cultural existence as being "natural" in the sense of having an *a priori* grounding in experience. As such these areas of our experience share in the arbitrariness that has characterized the contemporary political sphere.

As authors such as Thomas Szasz have so ably indicated, even the notions of what constitutes sanity are ideologically weighted questions. Thus not only have such respected minority groups as blacks, Chicanos, and women made out their case of political oppression, and in so doing defined, implicitly or explicitly, an alternative political scheme in terms of which their peculiar cultural and personal contributions could be made, but social deviants such as the criminal, the drug user, the homosexual, and the insane have been designated as sick in strict relation to the social norms that pattern the society of which they are members.

The problem is, of course, that if all relations are power relations, then the term "politics" as designating a particular sphere of cultural experience no longer has any worthwhile use. We are being forced to the conclusion that *culture is the packaging of power relations in a society*. Thus understood, culture provides the coating on the pill that we all must swallow. The fact that we are beginning to couch our understandings of our cultural experience in terms of power relations indicates that our traditional way of articulating these relations has lost its efficacy. The coating is off the pill; power is laid bare.

One of the more fascinating outworkings of this fact is the attitude toward political charismatics characteristic of our advanced technological society. One has but to pronounce the names of John and Robert Kennedy, Malcolm X, Martin Luther King, and George Wallace to make the point that those individuals from either end of the political spectrum who have had a charismatic appeal have suffered violent attack. Why this functional rejection of charisma? One is tempted to say here, perhaps too baldly, that the success of charismatic politics depends upon there being something mysterious, or at least something unarticulated, about the political art. The mere fact that we have raised to the level of consciousness the ubiquity of power relations in our society prevents any charismatic from functioning for very long. For one of the secrets of the charismatic is that he lays claim to the possession of power as a gift from beyond.

It was the concept of the "divine right of kings" that long provided the rationale for the claim to absolute political authority. The contemporary rejection of charisma is the last vestige of the revolt against divine right. This rejection must be traced at least in part to the fact that the nature and function of power-relations in society have become increasingly obvious. It is not the case that the politician has yielded his concern for the personal exercise of power to the rationalized technical apparatus. But clearly there is a conflict between technology and politics at many levels in contemporary society.

Though the technician is, by and large, satisfied with the self-augmenting nature of technological development, the politician, with a fundamental distrust of technology, is alarmed by the encroachments of technique upon the public sphere. Those who enjoy the exercise of political power could never be satisfied with the technician's dream of completely rationalized society in which order and efficiency reign supreme. Political behavior, though conditioned by the public arena, is ultimately personal insofar as it depends upon the desire to realize greatness through the exercise of the power of persuasion. Technology threatens to neutralize and frustrate the politician insofar as it rationalizes the decision-making process and renders obsolete the powers of personal suasion. No politician can be wholly comfortable with the realization that the decision to enter a nuclear war may have to be made (if it is to be made in time) by a computer at the Pentagon and not by the commander-in-chief. The complexity of political relationships and the rapidity with which many of our most important decisions must be made have almost necessitated that contemporary politicians hand over vast amounts of their power, and many of their prerogatives, to automatic, technical apparatus. Those politicians who maintain the illusion of power (and thereby remain in the truest sense politicians) are coming to constitute a very real threat to the societies they wish to govern by virtue of their unrealistic appraisal of the changes wrought by technological sophistication.

The politician makes one or the other of two mistakes regarding technology. He may claim that he can perform his function in separation from technical imperatives, in which case he may try to act contrary to the demands of technical routine. Or he may naïvely assume that he can manipulate technologies for his own ends.

Adolf Hitler, though a genius at the exercise of personal political power, had very little understanding of technology. The same technology and efficient bureaucracy that in the beginning gave him such vast power might well have served to make of him a world conquerer if he had but heeded those few scientists and generals who understood the technical machinery at his nation's disposal. Instead Hitler insisted upon making decisions without paying proper heed to the needs of the technical matrix. He wished to initiate policy, to exercise personal power, and as a result he came into terminal conflict with the efficient technology that had in part promoted his rise.

A more recent instance of the failure to cooperate with technological imperatives can be seen in the various troubles of the Nixon administration to which the name "Watergate" was attached. Though Nixon had shown himself capable of at least some cooperation with the technical apparatus when, in 1968, he employed Madison Avenue image-makers to "sell" him, in almost every other instance he showed himself unwilling to play according to the rules of technique. When members of the Nixon administration decided upon political espionage it was to the patriotic disciples of the cloak and dagger that they turned rather than to the technicians who could no doubt have accomplished the job without discovery. The resulting debacle in which Nixon found himself strangled by miles of recording tape has as one of its morals, "Don't send a political patriot to do a technician's work!"

We are still in the age of the politician, one who desires the exercise of power from a personal perspective. The bureaucrat is yet to enter fully into his own. We have employed bureaucracy in order to concentrate power at the top; we have used complexity as an excuse for inefficiency and corruption. Even though the majority of our recent Presidents have been task-oriented, they have not understood technology; nor have they, when the chips were down, taken the advice of the technical minds that could have advised them on efficient measures to be taken. The advice has come, more often than not, from special-interest groups, or the military leaders associated with the Pentagon, or others still addicted to power and glory.

It is less and less the case that the politician seeks to operate at odds with the technical apparatus; the more likely of his failings is that he assumes that he can use technology to his own ends. This is a frightening attitude at best. For the politician, who must have an instinctive antipathy toward technology, cannot be expected to understand it; his assumption that he can control it (an assumption the technician has long since happily abandoned), therefore, is insanely naïve. Underlying the new attitude toward technology on the part of the politician is the Fallacy of the Sorcerer's Apprentice. It is the assumption that the power of technology can be employed without an understanding of the "magic words" that brought that power into existence. This attitude is all the more frightening when we consider the fact that there is no longer a master sorcerer who can prevent the catastrophe that must result from the naïve and simplistic presumption that technology can be controlled by political decision-makers.

The technician with his Jules Verne Fallacy, and the politician with his Fallacy of the Sorcerer's Apprentice, are perhaps no less naïve than is that mass of individuals who are neither manipulators of technical apparatus nor wielders of political power, but mere consumers and passive participants. The naïveté of this largest of all the classes of our present social complex is wrapped up in what is perhaps the most vitiating of the fallacies harbored by the modern psyche: The Pelagian Fallacy. Pelagius, we recall, was immortalized by St. Augustine's attacks upon his belief that human beings could freely and responsibly cooperate in their own salvation. This belief, which argues from freedom *in principle* to freedom *in fact*, is one of the most pervasive characteristics of our present climate of opinion.

The question "Are we significantly free?" can, of course, receive two basic answers. We are either free or unfree because it is our nature as human beings to be so. Or our freedom or lack of it is a function of contingencies in the present. We might, in other words, be free in principle, but unfree in fact. An abstract understanding of freedom pervades Western, particularly democratic, societies and has led to the conviction that because we accept philosophical characterizations of what it means to be human that involve the belief in freedom, we must thereby be, *de facto*, free. This argument from principle to fact is particularly deleterious in its effect upon the morale of contemporary technological societies since it masks a two-fold consequence. In the first place, the Pelagian Fallacy creates a sense of freedom, which provides hope that, if we find our present circumstances unbearable, we can change the course of our future to suit our desires. This hope is, I believe, a false one. True as it may be that we are potentially free, it is fundamentally unsound to argue that human beings in advanced technological societies as currently constituted can freely determine the future. We seem to be unable to cooperate in our salvation (or damnation). Our technicians, who have given up the notion of freedom, who celebrate, and thrive upon, the concept of determination, are closer to the truth. To believe otherwise is to be dangerously and pathetically naïve. We *could* be free. Indeed, in the future we shall again be free. At present, however, we are compelled by forces that no one understands toward the realization of a future that can in no real sense be of our choosing.

The worst effect of the Pelagian Fallacy is not found in its support of a false sense of freedom for those who think they can choose alternative destinies, but in its creation of anxiety and guilt in those who, having the illusion of freedom, are also burdened by the concomitant sense of responsibility. If freedom is an illusion, so must responsibility be. Technicians, those who are busily engaged in creating our future, have no sense of personal responsibility for the developments of the future. Nor should they have. Time has long since passed when anyone could legitimately feel that he has a personal stake in creating The Future. The Pelagian Fallacy prevents the experience of guiltlessness, which could have provided some slight comfort for this age of unfreedom.

To call this an age of "unfreedom," after arguing in the preceding chapter for the Taoist conception of an a-causal universe patterned by self-creativity, might suggest a blatant contradiction. But the Pelagian Fallacy is not just a false sense of freedom where no freedom exists; it is a false sense of freedom as "free action," the belief in which precludes the development of the profounder sense of freedom as self-creativity. Ours is an age of unfreedom because our dominant senses of freedom, all of which are grounded in the agonal understanding of action, may be shown to be unrealizable. If the arguments developed in this essay are correct, however, we may expect that our technological future will be one that presents us with the possibility of realizing the kind of freedom expressed in the Taoist understandings of *wu-chih*, *wu-wei*, and *wu-yü*.

We must be careful to distinguish between the belief of the political elite in the possibility of determining the direction of technology and the lay belief in freedom of choice. The Sorcerer's Apprentice acknowledges the fact of technology but claims that its direction and control are viable political functions. The peculiar fallacy he commits presupposes the acceptance of technology as a given. The Pelagian Fallacy, as it is expressed in our democratic societies, is based upon a broad, if abstract, sense of freedom grounded in a faith in the efficacy of choosing or not choosing to implement technology. A significant portion of the lay public still holds to the Luddist conviction that, if and when we so desire, we can not only place limits on the growth of particular technologies, but even disassemble some of our more dangerous forms of technical apparatus.

We can see a poignant illustration of all three technological fallacies in the important debate over the industrial uses of nuclear power. The majority of our most influential politicians claim, with only a passing nod at the evidence pro and con, that nuclear power, if not currently safe, can assuredly be made so. A large portion of the lay public, ignoring the political and economic vested interests in the continuance of nuclear technology, naïvely wishes to abandon its use. The loudest spokesmen for the technical elite can be heard to say that, granted the significant risks involved, the technology is here and must be left to develop according to its own immanent rationale. Though these fallacious understandings are not universal, nor can they be so neatly assigned to distinctive segments of our society as I have perhaps too heavy-handedly suggested, there can be little doubt that these three modes of naïveté are conspicuously illustrated throughout contemporary technological society.

The three fallacies of contemporary thought discussed above are sufficiently ingrained in the intelligence of the various classes and peoples of technological society as to prescribe the dominant climate of opinion insofar as it concerns the casting of the future. The technician who has stolen the future from the other elements of society is close to the truth when he affirms that we are determined and are, therefore, beyond all claims to freedom and responsibility. He misses the mark to the extent that he remains timid and conservative, envisioning the future in terms of a linear development from the past. The politician has hold of a truth insofar as he claims one *ought* to be in control of technology, but makes a serious mistake if he moves from *ought* to *is* and claims the possibility of such control in the present. The layman's belief in freedom, though incorrect as a description of present possibilities, nonetheless states a truth about a future beyond our present determination, a future in which, perhaps, we shall be determined to be free.

TECHNOLOGY: INSIDE AND OUT

Because human pre-history is known to us primarily through the medium of persisting objects and artifacts, we have quite naturally come to construe the history of technology in substantive terms. Only recently have we begun to realize that such a reading of technological progress leaves out the initial and most important phase of the enterprise. Because we have too often understood the development of technology in terms of the increasing complexity of material objects, we have missed the fact that the most subtle and complex technologies were developed first. The pre-conscious tools associated with dream symbolism; the language of gesture and speech developed for interpersonal communication; religious and aesthetic rituals that served to unite the inner privacy of each individual to the public realm of communal existence—all were the technological *tours de force*. This thesis, defended by Lewis Mumford[16] among others, suggests that the earliest technical developments were ritualistic techniques invented in order to regularize and control the spontaneities and superordinal energies of the psyche. This view leads us far from the simple-minded understanding of technology as the "tools and machines of a culture." Technologies turn out to be techniques of organization and control.

Such a construal of the technological phenomenon requires that we accept the importance of technique in defining technology. Jacques Ellul is perhaps foremost in recognizing this importance. It is technique, claims Ellul, that characterizes technological society. The substantive aspects of technology are merely consequences of technique, which Ellul defines as *"the totality of methods rationally arrived at and having absolute efficiency* (for a given stage of development) in *every* field of human activity."[17] The phrase, "rationally arrived at," however, may seem to separate modern from primitive technique. Indeed, for Ellul, "technique certainly began with the machine,"[18] which means that "its characteristics are new."[19]

Ellul has understood the contemporary significance of techniques as means and methods rather than as tools and machines in defining the nature of technological society but utterly fails to place importance upon the ritualistic, magical techniques in non-literate societies. In fact, Ellul distinguishes between spiritual or magical techniques and the material techniques associated with the development of early technologies. And there is no evidence that Ellul sees any continuity of tradition within magical techniques nor any significant relationship between material and "magical" technologies.

The defect of Lewis Mumford's presentation of technological development is similar to Ellul's. Though he recognizes the importance of techniques of psychic organization in defining the origins of the technical phenomenon, he underplays their importance once machine technologies begin to develop. Ellul's ahistorical presentation allows him to dismiss the importance of primitive forms of psychic technologies due to their apparent insignificance in contemporary society. Mumford's decidedly historical approach, for different reasons, allows him to do the same. But each of these inter-preters of technology has made extremely significant contribu-tions to the interpretation of technology: Ellul by stressing the importance of technique as formal rather than substantive; Mumford by noting that man can be most properly seen, at least in the beginning of his development, not as tool-maker, but as *brain-maker*.

Drawing from the principal insights of each of these men, we may claim that a proper understanding of technology requires an acceptance of the following propositions: First, technology is a complex of means that organize and control human experience and expression. Second, these means may be both conscious and non-conscious in their invention and use. Third, technology is no more ubiquitous or totalitarian in its contemporary expression than in primitive societies. Fourth, though technical development can be discussed as an historical phenomenon, it is best to interpret the stages of technological growth as varying strands that have intertwined to form contemporary technological society.

The first characteristic of technology to be emphasized is its organizational quality. Technology first organizes and controls the primordial chaos encountered by the potentially human organism. The creation of consciousness and person-ality structure was both the presupposition of technical devel-opment and the initial consequence of human technology. This characteristic of technology as the disciplining of chaos has been rehearsed in detail already. It remains but to emphasize that advanced technological society promises no less than a complete and final victory over chaos for the human species.

Ellul's stress upon the rationality of technique needs to be qualified. Reason and rationality as modes of organizing con-sciousness are themselves technical constructs, as is consciousness itself. It is incorrect to presume that technology awaited the development of reason; instinct in animals grounds such technical skills as nest-building. As Mumford has claimed, "there was nothing uniquely human in tool-making until it was modified by linguistic symbols, esthetic designs, and socially transmitted knowledge."[20] Though *human* technology requires the employment of self-consciousness and symbols, there must have been a great deal of proto-human activity that could be termed technological. Technology is hardly a human invention; it is the human being that is an "invention" of technology.

A third misunderstanding of technological development is that the transition from primitive to modern times has led to an increasing technological organization in society. This assumption is based upon the interpretation of technology solely in material terms. The slightest reflection on the ritualistic organization of so-called primitive societies should make one pause before accepting the concept that a technological society is a contemporary phenomenon. Broadening the concept of technology to include ritualistic forms of organization should serve to provide greater perspective on the technical phenomenon.

We cannot expect to understand the nature and consequences of the technical phenomenon as long as we insist either upon the absolute uniqueness of contemporary technology or upon its strictly historical character. Both positions contain some truth. Indeed, I have argued that a simple extrapolation of the technological future from the present would lead to the grossest of misinterpretations. The continuity of technical growth is the continuity of developmental stages. Technology is an emergent phenomenon with an open future. It must therefore be understood *both* as unique and as historically conditioned. Just what this means should become clearer if we look at the various stages, or historical strands, constituting the story of technology.

Recognizing the arbitrariness of any strict division of the history of technology into epochs, we may nonetheless consider certain, admittedly artificial, stages of technological growth as a prelude to a more rigorous consideration of the technical phenomenon. The first such stage we could name that of *personalization*, or self-creation. In this stage, the primary technologies consisted of dream symbolisms that helped to order the preconscious experiences of early man;

religious rituals employed to put individuals in touch with the primary ontological realm; myths, functioning as the rationalization of ritualistic practice; and language, which created consciousness, signaling the final interaction of the environing occasions of experience that came to constitute the personality of the individual self. These techniques dominated the first stage in the development of technological society.

The stage of self-creation might have begun with the flourishing of *homo erectus*, perhaps more than 500,000 years ago. It was evidently during this period that the rapid development of the brain to its present size was achieved. *Homo sapiens* achieved continuous progress in material techniques without any associated increase in brain size. The increase in brain size must have led to stresses requiring increased internal organization and discipline. The size of the brain is, of course, less important than the complexity of its organization. But one primary stimulus to such organization might well have been the relatively dramatic quantitative increase in the size of the brain during the period just prior to the emergence of *homo sapiens*.

It is ritualistic activity that best enables one to co-ordinate and discipline superordinate amounts of energy. A ritual is a set of rhythmic, repetitive actions that function to save experiences on the one hand and to re-present or evoke experiences on the other. Rituals are symbolic activities that both co-ordinate and contain the original experience, and allow the experience to be re-collected. Ritual is associated with myth in the sense that just as myth is a rationalization of ritual, so ritual is an enactment of myth. A myth rationalizes paradigmatic events in the life of a people first coordinated by ritual, and then recollected in both ritual and myth. Myth plots the landscape of that ontological realm in terms of which life is lived. Ritual harmonizes the rhythms of social life with the character of one's experience of that realm. As we have seen, most myths, and the rituals associated with them, suggest primordial experience of the threat of negative Chaos. There can be little question that such was the experience of most peoples. But the existence of myths such as may be found in Taoism suggests that this experience was not universal.

It was religious ritual that dominated early societies. Such rituals have as their purpose communicating with what is eminently real and may be experienced as the source or origin accounting for one's existence. The communication may be for the purpose of placating, mollifying, ensuring future benefits, or merely for the sake of ecstatic enjoyment. But whatever the specific aim, ritual presupposes a distance between the actual and the ideal, which is to be overcome through prescribed forms of behavior. These behaviors are techniques, and the sum of these techniques constitutes the religious technologies of a society.

For Western man of recent vintage, ritual has had little significance. Habit has replaced ritual as the means whereby man comes into contact with his natural setting. Habits are simply the repetitive forms of behavior constituting social instinct. They consist in those things that can be done without taking thought. Rituals must be enjoyed to be efficacious; habits can function apart from enjoyment. A habit is as much a technique as is a ritual. Ritual has great efficacy in promoting personal richness of experience in relation to the ultimate source of meaning and value. Habits, on the other hand, provide the basis for the development of complex civilized cultures in a way that ritualistic societies never could.

The more that can be accomplished without thought the more time and intellectual energy can be saved to tackle the problems encountered in relating to one's immediate environment. So-called primitive societies could never "have done" with a problem; most aspects of existence were ritualized, and every ritual had to be participated in with conscious enthusiasm. The institutions of contemporary society such as banks, telecommunications systems, and superhighways are more or less regularized structures from which one may derive at least some benefit with a minimum of conscious thought. Social habits or institutions function as de-sacralized rituals for contemporary man. And that is to say no more than that technique has become *externalized*.

Early human beings, engaged in the process of self-creation, had a relatively small number of social instincts or habits. Living a ritualized existence required a great deal of effort because each individual was called upon to re-collect the

primal experiences that originated his people, to experience
the primordial threat of absolute Chaos, and to re-live the
security of salvation from Chaos. Such was the requirement of
one who was in process of creating a society from the communal form of sub-human existence and then of constructing a
single self from out of a given social context.

A second strand of technological development was that
characterized by *objectification*. This was the beginning of
homo faber in the traditional sense. The construction of tools
for molding the natural environment beyond the conscious
self became a principal occupation. This stratum had to await
the growing importance of the distinction between Self and
Non-Self. There is now a tendency away from the animism of
the earlier stage toward the establishment of an increasing
distance between human being and the being of all else. The
dichotomy of persons and nature is characteristic of this
period of development, which comprises almost the entire
recorded history of human culture, and is indeed a prerequisite for such history.

Technologies of two distinctive varieties now exist. There
is first the "internal" technology associated with aesthetic and
religious ritual. These are technologies of self-creation and
self-control. The phase of objectification produces the beginnings of "external" technology, associated with control of the
objective environment. The domination of nature takes place
in two phases: the control of Self and the control of Non-Self,
or the objective environment. The story of the human race, as
we in the West have chosen to tell it, is the tale of the progressive development of external technologies accompanied by a
decreasing recognition of the significance of internal techniques.

The co-existence of these two phases or layers—one
might say *dimensions*—of the technical phenomenon provided
the basis for the differentiation and specialization of various
cultural interests and activities. Religion provided the means
for re-collecting the mythical creation of cosmos from chaos;
rituals associated with art provided the means for construction
and manipulation of dream-images, imaginings, and the wealth
of perceptual data that, prior to the emergence of complex

linguistic forms, must have presented a private chaos for each individual. Art, concerned with the immediately sensed reality, and religion, with the communion of the self's immediate experience with the Totality, have served as the guardians of the internal development of mankind.[21] Morality, once detached from a religious context, and expressed in terms of law and sanctions defining the nature and limits of public activity, complemented science, construed as the interest in understanding and controlling the objective, natural world. Morality and science provided the guidelines for the objectification of technique and technology. The development of science in its modern form, as obedient to a mechanistic philosophy and a formal method, greatly accelerated the externalization of technology. The fallacious but commonplace presumption that technology is essentially related to science is dramatic testimony to the fact that scientific technology has obscured the other forms of technical culture.

Societies and cultures developing along lines of internal technique tend to shun external technology because of the potential damage it might do to the techniques of personal integration and self-creation. There is a popular Taoist tale that well illustrates a negative attitude toward material technologies. It concerns the attempt on the part of a disciple of Confucius to persuade a simple farmer accustomed to irrigating his garden plots painstakingly by hand of the value of a "well-sweep" as a means of increasing the efficiency and ease of the farmer's labors. The farmer, after listening patiently to the Confucionist, responded indignantly, "I used to be told by my teacher that where there are cunning contrivances there will be cunning performances, and where there are cunning performances there will be cunning hearts. He in whose breast a cunning heart lies has blurred the pristine purity of his nature; he who has blurred the pristine purity of his nature has troubled the quiet of his soul, and with one who has troubled the quiet of his soul Tao will not dwell. It is not that I do not know about this invention; but that I should be ashamed to use it."[22]

Expressions of this kind of attitude toward machine technology have begun to increase among contemporary cultural critics. These critics depend on a reinstatement of what we may term the "gnostic" sensibility, the re-emergence of which has been charted in both positive and negative terms by such thinkers as Eric Voegelin, Theodore Roszak, and Jacob Needleman, among many others. The essence of the gnostic sensibility is the appeal to traditional wisdom against the claims of science, and the stress upon "spiritual," or internal, as opposed to "material," or external, technologies. The emergence of the gnostic sensibility suggests the beginnings of a revolt against contemporary forms of technology.

The gnostic is quick to point out that the stress upon material techniques tends to blind us to the nature and value of traditional wisdom. The reliance on tools and machines has substituted external for internal techniques of remission and control. The extent to which societies opted for scientific and political technologies rather than ritualistic, spiritual techniques has largely determined the degree to which individuals in these societies are capable of internal self-actualization. So-called civilized cultures tend to rely on material techniques of obtaining food, shelter, and psychological welfare. And because of this stress upon external, civilized technique, we have tended to interpret the meaning and value of human existence in evolutionary terms, claiming that the transition from simple to more complex forms of external techniques defines a progressive realization of man's true nature. This leads to a continued de-emphasizing of spiritual techniques of self-realization associated with magical and occult activities. "Primitive" societies are so named because of their lack of material techniques. The superiority of "civilized" societies is recognized because of the dominance of external technology.

It is, of course, no longer the case that the external forms of technology are the only ones with efficacy in determining the character of our future, even though the most dramatic instances of technological growth concern external technique. Underdeveloped countries are absorbing material technologies as fast as they can be supplied. And though there is some talk among the aesthetic and spiritual elites within Asian and African countries about the need to implement Western technology in such a way as to maintain their principal cultural

values, there seems little recognition of the manner in which
this might be done. The case is less dramatic but equally en-
lightening in Anglo-European cultures, however. The increasing interest in Eastern forms of internal technology among
Western intellectuals is indicative of a growing sense of the
unsatisfactoriness of material techniques alone. Of course,
since spiritual hunger and dis-ease are no match for physical
starvation and illness, the rapid and well-nigh unqualified
acceptance of material technology seems to ensure a cultural
balance of payments favoring the West.

Whereas the Western, quantitative mentality seems to
chart a progressive evolution of societies and cultures in terms
of increase in material technologies, the gnostic mentality
views the development of civilized societies in terms of a
devolution, a winding down, a continuous loss of spirituality
in the face of increasing material progress. The gnostic recognizes our present period as that which the Hindus term Kali-
Yuga, the dark age, the final phase leading to the end of a
cycle of existence.

It is tempting for the irenic philosopher of culture to
believe that the two understandings of technology could be
complementary in nature. And such may prove to be the case.
It seems as of the present, however, that civilized culture will
be the setting for a rather uneven struggle between these two
forms of technique. And since each form is characterized by
excessive attempts dogmatically to reject one another—science seeing its opponent as psychotic emotionalism (what a
colleague of mine has termed "Zen Fascism"); the gnostic
decrying the barbaric materialism of externalized technique—
no rapprochement seems likely. Whether from the conflict of
these two sensibilities there will emerge a more balanced
assessment of the essential meanings of technology is a question about which we can only speculate.

The excesses of external technology have been rehearsed
many times. Critics of the dominance of material technology
define our contemporary age as one of *depersonalization* or
alienation. The industrial revolution has become the symbol
for the origin of the depersonalizing effects of technology. The
natural world, which had been controlled and objectified in

accordance with the aims of external technology, turned and found vengeance by requiring, as the cost of its submission, the remolding of human beings as mere extensions of the machine. The Marxist and existentialist critiques of the excesses of advanced technological society well express the point of view that technological advances can easily lead to the alienation and depersonalization of human beings. Identifying the emergence of this stage with the technological activities of the industrial revolution probably manifests a rather elitist view of history. As Mumford has indicated, the quasi-mechanical organization of labor for construction of the pyramids, waging of war, and other such efforts produced a human "mega-machine," which certainly served to dehumanize the laborers.[23] But the industrial revolution serves to name a period in which the mechanization of human beings was, in principle, generalized and began to affect princes and privy counsellors as well as the masses of the poor and disenfranchised. The externalization of mechanical techniques creates mechanical objects and institutions that require those who shall benefit from the machine to co-operate with its mechanisms.

A crucial question of the present is: Can we enjoy the benefits of externalized technologies without, in obedience to some inexorable dialectic, sublating or taking into ourselves again the results of our technical labor? Could it be that technological development, which began with the fashioning of organized structures within the brain-cage and then promoted the externalization of reason and order in the techno-structures of society, will find its culmination in a complex of cybernetic or symbionic interactions?

Two principal alternatives exist: we could proceed along the lines suggested by the tendency toward the internalization of the objective rational structures of technology. This mechanization or depersonalization would culminate in each of us becoming a technical object in the fullest sense. The other main alternative is that technology would free us from the necessity to express ourselves through the medium of labor. Perhaps what we term "evolution" has consisted in the increasing objectification and externalization of our mechanisms of defense in order that we might be freed from control by mechanisms of any kind. Perhaps. But many of the interpreters of technological society believe quite the contrary—that our future must be one of either absolute control or absolute chaos and disorder.

The alienation of individuals in our urban centers, and the increase in crime and violence, suggest the need for a transition toward a society in which anti-social behavior is not so much punished as *predicted* and *prevented*. The methods of behaviorism applied to human social existence would attempt to order the contingencies of reinforcement in such a way as to bring about harmonious and satisfactory modes of social behavior. The fact that it is possible, in principle, to determine within broad limits the public actions of every member of society through a program of behavioral conditioning seems to render academic the much debated question of free will. If the determinist is correct, why not a rational program of behavioral conditioning? But if he is incorrect, in principle he can nonetheless soon become *de facto* correct. Decisions made by social planners in this and subsequent generations could create a situation in which it would be unlikely that the question of freedom would ever again be raised for the simple reason that behaviorist programs of coercion would have determined that freedom no longer exists.

Behavioral technology is the attempt to internalize the techniques created through objectification. It is the *reductio ad absurdum* of the misconceived attempt to achieve self-creation by recourse to the wrong tools. Gnosticism with its emphasis upon magic and the occult sciences is the very reverse of the behavioral system. Whereas behaviorism strives to realize an internalization of external technology associated with mechanistic science,[24] the occult enterprises attempt to externalize the ritualistic technologies associated with spiritual and aesthetic activities. The conflict, only just beginning to emerge in contemporary society, between the internal technologies of gnosticism and the external technologies of science, characterizes the struggle that will decide the character of our technological future.

One of the more influential early works on the technical

phenomenon is Friedrich Juenger's *Die Perfektion der Technik* previously mentioned. Together with the German title, the English translation, *The Failure of Technology*, suggests the irony of Juenger's work. For it is precisely in the perfection of external technology that Juenger believes its failure may best be seen. The process of outworking in which technology finally realizes its potentialities is to be equated with a sustained and serious threat to human existence. This trend toward perfection, toward achieving a full realization of its potential, has as its parallel the process of the rationalization of social existence that has been a part of our Western cultural experience. Critics of material technologies seem to agree on the view that external technique tends to become internalized, with dehumanizing consequences. The arguments of such critics may be summarized as follows:

Persons are unique, but technology tends to destroy the uniqueness of individuals by demanding conformity as the price of efficiency, by requiring the kind of standardization and organization that precludes the need for individual contributions to the social order. *Persons are spontaneous, creative, original*, but technology is habituated, regularized, and predictible. *Persons are free*, and cannot, therefore, be explained in terms of an antecedently existing structure of causal contingencies constituting a complex of organized techniques, but technological society tends to reduce the areas of significant human choice by rationalizing the social process. *Persons are active agents, productive of vital changes within themselves and their environments*, but technology makes of persons the passive recipients of change who feel themselves done to, acted upon, serviced, programmed, controlled. *Persons thrive on mystery, paradox, the unattainable, the unfathomable*, but technology makes every area of social existence an accomplishable, solvable "problem." *Persons are masters of their environment*, but technology having collapsed the distinction between nature and technique, now challenges the distinction between persons and technique, between the vital and the nonvital, between *personae* and machines.

These consequences, coupled with the self-augmenting

character of technological processes, ensure that control is *immanent*—that is to say, the machines control themselves. It is with this last issue, that of control, that we come to the serious point upon which turns most of our current conceptions of technology. For it focuses on the crucial issue in deciding whether or not we may take up an optimistic stance toward the technical phenomenon.

Before the age of so-called Industrial Technology, the age of depersonalization, the primary aim of technology, at least as conceived by the best representatives of intellectual culture, was to increase our understanding of the world. With the advent of the industrial revolution and the Marxian critique of its excesses, the aim of technology began the change from that of understanding to that of control. Clearly, the aim of understanding *has* failed. We have found ourselves less and less moving toward a common or universal understanding of the nature of things and more and more accepting the fact that theory is, of necessity, absorbed into technology. In place of a general understanding, we have a set of possible understandings that may be conventionally employed in order that we may get on with the business of the day. The few disinterested speculators, concerned with the discovery of truth for its own sake, are not to be found waiting with anxious anticipation for the next most powerful telescope, or the next technical breakthrough in micro-physics. They realize that technologically aided advance provides nothing unexpected. The tools one constructs do not necessarily take one more deeply into the recesses of reality. We do have *different* understandings, and *more subtle* understandings; there is no question about that. But are we closer to The Truth?

It is a characteristic of contemporary scientific research that the techniques or apparatus employed in the investigations of nature can themselves interfere with the accurate observations of phenomena. But this truism is supplemented by an even more significant one, which is the fact that observations of nature are themselves determined in advance by the character of the apparatus employed. This same insight applies to theoretical paradigms that direct attention to only certain phenomena, lead one to expect the recurrence of these phenomena, and in the process make other phenomena in-explicable.[25] Instruments are extensions of our muscles or nervous system and serve our convenience. What we see with a telescope, microscope, or spectroscope is determined in advance by the nature and limits of the instruments employed and, more importantly, by the limits of the employer. Under-standing through the aid of instruments can be only instru-mental understanding. This is the major reason that the transition from attempting to understand the world to that of changing or controlling it has come to be accepted.

But we can no more succeed in controlling the world than we can in understanding it. If we mean by control, *rational* control, then it should be obvious why this cannot be. The self-augmenting character of technology places technical order outside the minds of individual persons and fragments the understanding of the whole into the understanding of a part. And to the extent that we do not understand the whole complex, we cannot remain in charge of it in the sense of deciding upon directions or determining priorities. Things are "out of our hands" and in the "hands" (prosthetically speaking) of the machines. If our ecological disasters are to be successfully weathered we cannot depend on haphazard solu-tions. Total commitment to technology seems the only answer. Control will not be our responsibility, but will be immanently "decided" by the necessities of efficiency and rational order.

The process of war-making has increasingly been given over to the technical apparatus. Each new weapon developed by our enemies requires that we respond in kind in our race to keep up with the Tvarskis and the Chans. A purely tech-nological imperative, at variance with all humane considera-tions, controls the situation. And we must not overlook the intrinsic technical satisfactions any technology provides to the technological personality. As any technician will tell you, it is often as satisfying to work on problems associated with, say, bacteriological warfare as with the search for a cure for cancer. The peculiar satisfactions inherent in each set of prob-lems are separable from the malign or beneficent conse-quences. It is more than just suspicion, or the aggressive impulse, or the immanent technological demands for efficient defense, that sends us always in search of new and ingenious weapons. It is equally the inherent satisfactions associated with doing one's job with consummate efficiency. Technique is, for the technician, an end in itself. Know-how is, after all, simply a kind of how-*knowing*, the pleasures of which are not defined by the practical result, but which are intrinsic. Technicians possessed of the technological state of mind work for the intrinsic rewards of the search for efficiency, order, and organization.

Even the pursuit of leisure presents our society with difficult technical problems. As Juenger long ago pointed out leisure is not the same as loafing. But as our contemporary leisure-oriented society has taught us there is little to be found in our leisure hours that is nearly so appealing as the kinds of labor we pursue to make a living. We are victims of what Marcuse has called "repressive de-sublimation" to the degree that even our ways of entertaining ourselves away from our jobs share all the repressive characteristics of our work. Leisure is itself a vast "industry" that creates a market place of technical gadgets, which guarantees more consumption leading to a greater dependence upon, and direct engagement with, the economic and technical enterprises of the non-leisured life. Bored and insecure apart from our jobs or professions, it appears that most of us enjoy making labor-saving devices more than we enjoy the consequences of saving labor.[26]

Sport as a form of leisure has itself become a profession. Professional athletes are doubly cursed; not only are their athletic performances a part of a high-paying job and the farthest thing from leisure, but they are extremely specialized in their function and increasingly alienated from their teammates and themselves by the necessity to develop their narrowly specialized skills. As a consequence, the *viewing* of sports, rather than participation in them, has become, literally, our national pastime.

We have failed in our attempts to employ external technology as a means of understanding or controlling the world, or of even enjoying it for that matter. And the crisis we face because of that fact is a serious one. As human beings we have no cultural needs left to satisfy beyond understanding, practical control, or enjoyment. We are thinking, acting, and feeling creatures, and if material technology finally satisfies the demands of neither thought, action, nor passion, then we are in bad straits. Here we touch the very roots of our present technological crisis; the basis of the contemporary conflict between the technologies of gnosticism and of science.

The cultural significance of behavioral engineering is that it provides, paradoxically enough, one possible solution to the current failure of technology. The reason for this is both simple and profound. As B. F. Skinner has claimed, it is the humanistic conceptions of freedom and dignity that account for much of the violence and misery patterning contemporary societies. If human beings only did not spend their energies seeking or defending "freedom," or demanding that others recognize their "dignity," activities motivated by "illusory beliefs," we should be able to achieve a more rational, more contented social order. How could this be done? By internalizing those external technologies that have been so successful in organizing the material system; by making the Inside over after the image of the Outside.

There is little reason to rant and rail against the behaviorist. He can certainly not be expected voluntarily to change his beliefs! If there truly is no freedom even in principle, then the behavioral program seems quite sound. We really have no grounds for impugning the motives of behavioral engineers since they are but attempting to carry to its conclusion a form of technological activity we have all depended upon in so many ways. Perhaps we have reached a point of no return where the only solution to too much material technology is more of the same. If we are unhappy at the thought of being mechanically determined, perhaps we can, by making a virtue of necessity, become happy by realizing that we are ourselves but physical systems like all else, and determination is the nature of things.

We can learn from behavioral technology that our need to understand the world is a false and frustrating need; what is really wanted is control of those contingencies of reinforcement that determine human experiences of pleasure and of pain. We can be programmed to enjoy the leisure material technology brings and reprogrammed to discipline the aggressive and violent impulses that so often erupt in us. Perhaps Juenger was wrong. The perfection of technology may not be its failure, after all. Behaviorism, as perfected technology, guarantees "success." And it would be naïve to ignore the real possibility of this direction for the future. The manipulation by science and the moral interest of the conditions of human existence as it is dramatically portrayed in Skinner's *Walden Two*,[27] and again ever so simply outlined in his *Beyond Freedom and Dignity*,[28] constitutes one method of resolving the present crises of technological society. Is this the *only* way?

THE FUTURE OF THE FOREBRAIN

One of the most popular fantasies of early science fiction writers was the vision of future human beings with weak and atrophied bodies but possessed of huge heads and massively enlarged forebrains. This vision, of course, was but an extrapolation of the presumed evolutionary development of the human species from out of its primordial origins. The story of evolution told in terms of the human brain is the story of a shift of dominance from midbrain to forebrain. This shift was coupled with an increase in brain size and complexity leading to the development of the cerebral hemispheres and the enlargement of the association areas of the neocortex concerned with high-level thought process. Why *not* assume that the evolutionary development associated with the increased size of the forebrain would continue? The only obvious argument against this conclusion is the apparent fact that there has been no significant development in brain size since the emergence of *homo sapiens*. This is hardly decisive, however, since even several hundred thousand years is a short period in evolutionary terms.

There is, of course, another less obvious reason for believing that the increase in brain size associated with the development of consciousness and reasoning will not continue. That is the presumption that, with the development of forms of intercommunication among human individuals, with the construction of material technologies, and the invention of complex social institutions, the functions of thought and consciousness are now discoverable more in the external, intersubjective areas of social existence and less inside the skulls of individual human beings. The sphere of intellectual culture, built upon material technology, is an evolutionary consequence that precludes the necessity for increased cerebral capacity. With the emergence of *homo sapiens* the brain might well have reached optimum limits for the successful realization of the functions necessary for the survival of the organism. A crisis was thereby reached in which beyond this point the organized structures of material technology and the intersubjective forms of communication began to ease the pressure upon the organism to amass more brain tissue. Culture rather than "nature" becomes the proper sphere of evolutionary change.

Beyond this scenario, which is rehearsed in various forms by thinkers such as Teilhard de Chardin, there seems to lie an unanswered—seldom even asked—question: With the advent of increased externalization of techniques and technologies, is it not possible that the rational capacities of the brain might, instead of increasing in size and complexity, begin to atrophy? Not, of course, shrink or diminish in size, but shift from one function to another? Humans, after all, still possess brain structures identical with those of less complex organisms, but with no identical function. It seems at least plausible that future changes in the human brain might be in terms of alternative functioning rather than alteration in structure or capacity.

The external and internal strands of technological development have reached a crisis wherein the conflict of Inside and Outside is visibly and palpably joined to form the most decisive battle in the history of the development of man's image of himself. Simply put, the alternatives are clear: objective technology can be successfully internalized, re-creating man in the image of but a fragment of his former self; or internal technologies, techniques associated with dreams and rituals and the spiritual relations of man's psyche with the

Totality of things, can be released into the world, continuing
the process of personal externalization that began with the
development of material techniques and the arts of communication. Or, finally, the two forms of technology may be
brought into some successful form of accommodation: maintaining the distinction between the Inside and the Outside first
established by the acts of self-creation that gave rise to the
development of consciousness and self-identity.

We can suppose that the reversal of the depersonalizing
trend that threatens to result in a behaviorally engineered
dystopia of a type only hinted at in *1984* or *Brave New World*
would be possible only if it were possible to reinstitute forms
of internal technique that regularized and rendered stable and
secure social existence. The less dependent the individual
becomes upon the forms of ritual and myth that allow direct
participation in the sources of meaning and value from which
human beings gain their sense of transcending the merely
natural world, the more will it become necessary that external
structures take over the regulatory function. The transition
from social forms of existence based upon ritual and myth to
those based upon rational organization (including legal and
institutional forms) and thence to the attempts to introject or
internalize forms of behavior through technical means is the
story of human social change told in terms of technological
development.

This story is, in large part, a story of the human brain. In
the previous chapter we noted the speculations of some contemporary brain physiologists concerning the divergent types
of functioning expressed by the brain. We have used the
notion of "left-brain" and "right-brain," somewhat loosely
and metaphorically, to suggest the differences between
"causal" and "acausal" forms of thinking, and between
"internal" and "external" technologies. We are now able to
articulate the consequences of these distinctions in greater
detail by noting that our Anglo-European culture is the result
of the pre-dominant emphasis upon those functions associated
with the left cerebral hemisphere, and the consequence of this
is that our culture has been formed in terms of the externaliz-
able functions of *reason* and *moral activity*.

I am not in the least claiming that this discussion of the evolution of brain in relation to culture is any more than a "likely story." After reviewing the various researches and speculations concerning the nature and function of the human brain I find myself in essential agreement with the expert R. W. Gerard who some years ago said, "It remains sadly true that most of our understandings would remain as valid and useful if, for all we knew, the cranium were stuffed with cotton wadding." [29] Fortunately our understandings of the world do not presuppose certain insight into the instrument we presume to be the source of those understandings. Having said this, however, it remains the case that the brain can serve as the symbolic and metaphorical focus for our discussions of the development of human culture in terms of external and internal technologies.

Western culture, in its dominant character, has resulted from successful applications and articulations of *reason* and the *moral sense*. Reasoning primarily concerns those problem-solving behaviors associated with the manner in which a mature human being attempts to cope with his environment in a conscious and purposive manner. The moral sense is grounded in the conviction that some activities are enjoined and others are forbidden. Characterized in this way, reason and the moral sense constitute qualities human beings have, more often than not, considered to be indicative of what is most noble in human experience and expression.

We can become clearer about the nature and status of these two types of activity if we see them in association with the directed interests of intellectual culture with which they are best associated. For several hundred years we in the West have been content to see in the scientific method the paradigm of rational activity. And we have referred questions of moral behavior to the claims of reason and natural law, specified in terms of positive laws of a state or nation. Moral injunctions, though most find their origins in a religious context, increasingly find their sanctions in the state and not in the religious sphere from which they came. The Ten Commandments of Judaeo-Christianity are hardly obeyed for religious reasons associated with the myths and rituals of Christianity and Judaism.[30] Those that still meet with general obedience are those protected by incorporation in positive law. Conscience, the name for the repository of profoundly felt injunctions associated with religious taboo, may still trouble us with regularity, but it is hardly capable of serving as a primary means of social stabilization.

Science and morality, though originating in individualized forms of activity, are capable of externalization. That is, these two forms of activity can be rendered *public* in a distinctly different way than can the other two principal cultural interests, aesthetic and religious activity. The organized institutions of a society rationalize social existence and decrease the necessity for active participation in the initiation of one's own actions. The existence of regulated traffic systems in an urban center radically decreases the need of an individual to choose a route to his destination. The more structured one's public behavior, the less one need think about what he is doing. Institutions are merely externalized habits that, along with their internalized counterparts, can provide the foundation for an untold number of significant activities. Laws preclude the necessity of wondering about the nature of one's moral obligations by defining those activities forbidden in a society.

The larger the area of one's life regulated by laws and institutional commitments, the less one is required to initiate rational and moral activity. No doubt the primary value of the rationalization of social existence would be that it would provide a substratum of habituated and regularized activities on which one could build yet more significant activities. But the lesson of the twentieth century, at least in developed Anglo-European countries, has been that regularized activity leading to social stability can become the means whereby societies are prevented from expressing the novelty and spontaneity that might threaten the establishment of external technologies.

Behavioral engineering is capable, either through common forms of operant conditioning, or by using direct intervention—e.g., drugs, electrical stimulation—into the brain, of directing the "moral" behavior of individuals. Computers, as information processing and retrieval systems, offer the possibility of providing predigested information for the use of whoever carries a portable terminal in his pocket. I don't wish to argue that this is the direction of contemporary society, at least not in this context; I merely wish to contend that reason and moral action are capable of being transformed into externalized public institutions without a dramatic sense of loss.

This is not the case with aesthetic and religious interests. We might romanticize about the need to maintain a subjective moral sense that would enable us to respond significantly to the needs of others. But most of us would acknowledge that the expert in the alleviation of suffering, be it the M.D., the psychiatrist, or the social worker, is more capable of aiding individuals than persons wholly without expertise. It is not even conceivable, however, that aesthetic activity could proceed without the private emotions of the individual; nor can religious experience be posited without the individual and personal sense of relatedness that characterizes religion.

Of course aesthetic experience, reduced to the most fundamental forms of pleasure, can certainly be excited by the introduction of drugs or other forms of stimulation. And psychotropic chemicals have often been employed as the agents of initiation into mystical experience. Nonetheless, most of us are bound to deplore such uses of technical means as a distortion of the meaning of these types of experience in a way that we would not in terms of the scientific and moral activities. The reason for this is that the externalization of the human capacities that led to the development of forms of public intersubjectivity and material technology was characterized by those forms of organization and regularization that could become self-sustaining and self-augmenting. Reason and morality can become so. Art and religion cannot. The mystical experiences that ground religions, and the novel and spontaneous emotions generated in the creative process, are more closely identified with the private worlds of individuals. Reason and moral action can be public almost *in toto*. They can be codified. Art and religion lie outside such codifications. This is only to say that in terms of aesthetic and religious activities, expression cannot exhaust experience.

Scientific method dwells upon those things that can be made public. "Private facts" are not facts. The assumption that everything of any importance can be subjected to scientific observation is simply the view that literal expression can indeed exhaust experience.

The reduction of human experience to those aspects capable of regularized expression is of the very essence of the contemporary distortion of the dialectical development of technology. Technology-in-itself subsisted in the acts of self-creation that originated the human experience. Technology-for-itself was constituted by the development of material technologies and the regularities of secular social life. Technology-in-and-for-itself would consist of the harmonious interrelationships of internal and external technologies rather than the domination of human subjectivity by external techniques turned inward for motives of regulation and control. The distortion of human experience and expression caused by the dominance of external technology is the result of a culture-wide failure to recognize the need to incorporate the expressions of internal techniques into the fulfillment stage of technology. The rationalization of social existence has increasingly secularized, and hence objectified, the expressions of those cultural interests that pattern Anglo-European cultures.

There has always been an alternative tradition existing alongside that established by the acceptance of reason and rationality as the basis of our cultural activity. And since the Hellenic period this tradition has periodically made itself known to the dominant culture of which it is a part. Usually this occurs with the collapse of an old pattern of thought and just prior to the emergence of a new one. The transition from Hellenic to Hellenistic culture was one such occurrence. The rise of the cults of irrationality, the mystery religions, testified to this alternative tradition. These religious sensibilities, which included the increased interest in *Tyche* (chance), and the pullulation of every form of magic and superstition, were released with the collapse of the social and ideological foundations of the Greek city–states. These sensibilities greatly influenced the Gnostic movement, which antedated and paralleled the beginnings of Christianity. And Christianity itself owes much to these gnostic antecedents. Between the collapse of the Scholastic Synthesis is the fourteenth and fifteenth centuries and the rise of the scientific mentality, the gnostic sensibility began to assert itself again. Alchemy, astrology, and a variety of the occult sciences were practiced by the most respectable men of the day. Ficino, Paracelsus, Bruno were all parties to this occult movement.

Gnosticism has a very ill-defined historical identity. This is due both to the esoteric and occult aspects of the movement, and also to the bad press to which it has been subjected with regularity by the purveyors of mainstream orthodoxy. Though it cannot be strictly identified as an historical movement, the sensibility can be outlined in terms of some prominent characteristics. By identifying this tradition we are better able to recognize the trend in contemporary culture that attempts to struggle against the depersonalizing effects of the behavioral engineers who wish to internalize the results of external technology. And we, also, come to recognize that the gnostic sensibility, on its practical side, is performing the opposite task; it is attempting to externalize the techniques of self-creation. The bizarre manifestations of "gnostic technologies"—e.g., astrology, alchemy, magic—are obvious. Would that we could as easily recognize the equally bizarre consequences of behavioral engineering.

The most basic contrast between Gnosticism and Science is that between the quantitative foundation of the latter and the qualitative nature of the former. The emphasis upon measurement in science is grounded in the quantitative assumption. The acceptance of discreteness rather than continuity in the characterizations of classical science distinguish it rather clearly from the speculations of gnostic cosmologies. One of the most striking implications of the contrast between science and gnosticism lies in the extent to which science in the sixteenth century constituted an extreme simplification of the gnostic trends emergent in the late Middle Ages and early Renaissance.

Because we are disposed to view science, including its history, in terms of its most recent manifestations, we are unable to appreciate how the beginnings of scientific methodology as we know it today constituted a massive simplification in the art of cosmological speculation. The qualitative assumptions underlying the Renaissance view of the elements, for example, according to which the four fundamental elements of Earth, Air, Fire, and Water were subject to alterations in terms of four basic qualities—Cold, Dry, Hot, and Wet—presumed a continuum of constantly changing forms of existence. The measurement of the qualities was not possible. "*How* hot?" "*How* dry?" were not questions that could be given an exact answer. Quantitative, atomistic science, on the other hand, provides the basis for exact measurement and, therefore, for the testing of theory.

One of the most oft-embraced fallacies in the recording of the history of science is that involving the presumption that the occult sciences, such as alchemy or astrology, are simple-minded attempts to understand aspects of the cosmos that materialistic science has more completely characterized. Anyone who has read the basic alchemical sources, for example, would never claim that they were simple-minded. The gnostic sciences are *qualitative*, as opposed to the quantitative character of the dominant modes of scientific endeavor in the West. The theories and procedures of the alchemist involve highly complex concepts and operations. And since they are qualitative rather than quantitative in their presuppositions, there can be no exactness. Whether the aim of the alchemist is the transformation of metals, or the transformation of psyche, there are no empirical guarantees. Gnostic sciences deal, not with what is "always or for the most part," but with the *exceptional*.

The most pernicious of the consequences of the quantitative view of classical science is found in its reduction of all relations among items in the universe to external relationships. If we maintain that no item is intrinsically related to any other, in the sense that its existence, significance, or value in no way depends on any other item, then we effectively reduce everything to The Outside. Such a reduction is accomplished in principle in behavioral technology, and its dramatic successes in therapeutic instances amenable to mechanistic techniques is a result of that reduction. The severest critics of behaviorism will grudgingly acknowledge its success in some areas. But its pragmatic success is not sufficient to gain it acceptance by those who are theoretically disposed to see the world of experience as composed of internally inter-related substances or events.

The truth of the matter seems to be that the more we construe the world along simple, clear lines the greater is our success in controlling it. Perhaps it was necessary in the beginning to see our world in extremely simple terms if we were to progress along the proper lines. Modern science cannot be accused, in its contemporary stages at least, of having an excessively simplistic vision of the cosmos, but there is every reason to think that if it had not had such a simple view as that provided by the Newtonian form of theologically-infused mechanism, science may never have gotten off the ground. If one reviews the debates concerning the meaning of "nature" in the late Renaissance it seems clear that the principal pragmatic gains of science were in terms of clarity and simplicity.[31]

Another major contrast between gnosticism and science was considered in some detail in the preceding chapter in terms of "theorial" and "theoretical" approaches to the notions of meaning and truth. Gnosticism reverses the stress of modern science upon theory and system, seeking to move away from the theoretical attitude that establishes truth or falsity in terms of concepts that derive their meaning from within some theoretical framework. Instead it clings to the revelations of traditional wisdom as antecedently true, and plumbs their depths to discover the profound meanings they contain. The truths of science are literal truths—*facts*; the truths of the gnostic are spiritual truths—*convictions*. A fact lies "out there" for all to see; a conviction lies "in here" and must be individual, personal, and private.

The contrast between spiritual and literal conceptions of meaning and truth is related to a third contrast between the gnostic and scientific sensibilities: that entailed by the esoteric character of the former and the exoteric character of the latter. The public character claimed for scientific evidence and conclusions suggests that it is the purpose of modern science to lay claim only to that knowledge that can be promulgated and made a part of the general store of human wisdom, accessible to anyone who would take it upon himself to draw from it. The extreme difficulty of contemporary scientific concepts and procedures compromises somewhat the public accessibility of scientific knowledge. But the practical results of science, its technological consequences, are there for anyone to use. Gnosticism, on the other hand, is esoteric in the extreme. One must be prepared for wisdom—either by being singled out as the recipient of a revelation, or by being initiated through some secret rite, or brought to the level of spiritual awareness by a *guru*. This applies as well to the practical side of the discipline. Technical applications, be they magical or mystical, are not for public consumption. The alchemist—the true alchemist, not the medieval charlatan—was concerned to keep his techniques secret because alchemy is an ancient form of *gnosis* aimed primarily at spiritual transformation. The transmutation of metals was but a symbol of the higher transformation aimed at salvation.[32]

A final contrast between gnosticism and science is most relevant to contemporary understandings of the changes in intellectual culture. Whereas science, at least since the nineteenth century, has tended to view things in *evolutionary* terms, gnosticism envisions the story of human history as a *devolution*. The gnostic assumption can be expressed something like this: human beings as they are currently constituted have de-volved from spiritual beings with capacities far beyond any we currently realize. The "progress" of mankind as secular history is apt to view it as nothing more than the increased and accelerating materialization of the spirit. This age of *Kali Yuga*, the age of "the reign of quantity,"[33] stands at the end of a downward spiral. The concept of an Ancient Wisdom compared with which our present wisdom is as ignorance; the myth of Atlantis, a civilization that far surpassed any present civilization—such beliefs as these give substance to the presumption of a downward process of devolution. The recent speculations concerning "gods from outer space," which have appeared in the popular press, constitute just one more variation on this gnostic theme, which claims that the source of all true wisdom lies in the primordial past.

All of the traditional occult sciences are in full swing in contemporary society: Astrology, the Tarot, the *I Ching*, even Crystal-Ball gazing (skrying). There are healers and telepaths, psycho-kinesists, and prognosticators; most of them are frauds and opportunists, but many belong to the Hermetic tradition, the tradition of Hermes Trismegistus, the mythical figure of ancient Egypt. Many jaundiced eyes see no more than odd-ball, superstitious eccentrics belonging to this tradition. More serious cultural observers may see the interest in the occult as a symptom of a pathological condition of our present culture. Few would see the gnostic sensibility as contributing to the curative process that promises to save contemporary society from its one-sided technological excesses. But unless we are willing to take a serious look at the alternative tradition it is doubtful that we will be in a position to understand, much less appreciate, many of the positive developments in our present situation.

One of the ways *not* to appreciate the gnostic contribution, although it would be somewhat cranky to complain over-much about this tendency, is the way in which many popularizing psychologists, biologists, and physicists are attempting to exploit the occult sciences, seeking to validate some of the peripheral manifestations of the movement, and to demythologize and render palatable as much of the doctrine and practice as possible. The commonest form of this activity is the attempt scientifically to demonstrate extra-sensory perception. Only slightly less grotesque has been the recent co-operative effort between scientists, yogis, and Zen masters, which has led to the measurement of the effects of spiritual, usually meditative, disciplines.[34]

Transcendental Meditation is perhaps the best example of a secularized, westernized, scientized form of gnostic discipline. There is no question but that it "works." The issue is that it is not being employed in the manner that befits an internal technique. We in the West seem to employ it to ease anxieties, to concentrate better, to relax, to sleep more deeply. In other words we use this discipline for all the wrong reasons, having mistaken its by-products for its ends. This can contribute to the continued dominance of means-oriented, power-saturated technique. Also, "westernizing" esoteric techniques tends to reinforce the idea of literal truth, and to make public a spiritual discipline meant only for initiates.

There are examples of gnostic technologies that—though they may be employed for all the wrong reasons—nonetheless serve as profound challenges to the scientific orthodoxy of the West. Acupuncture is an ancient healing art in China. It became known to the West primarily because Mao Tse-tung ordered the training of thousands of bare-foot physicians (i.e., folk doctors) as a stop-gap measure until medical doctors trained along Western lines could be supplied. Because of the recent propaganda value of the acupuncture techniques being imported to the West, it is likely that acupuncture is here to stay. The "theory" behind acupuncture's success involves the ancient conceptions of a mystical *ch'i* force, which flows through the body along meridia invisible to the eye and not discoverable by any dissecting tool. Neither Chinese nor Western medicine in their contemporary forms has an adequate explanation as to why acupuncture works. *That* it works is a continual challenge to the theoretical foundations (both, of course, materialistic) of Chinese Marxism and Western allotropic medicine.

For centuries Anglo-European culture has enriched its consciousness and increased its control over its environment primarily through the kind of concern with regularity and order that is pre-eminently expressed through the interests of science and technology. Classical science has employed a rigorous and impeccable method aimed at pursuing answers to the question "Why?"—questions that could be answered only in terms of rules or laws that defined regular relationships among two or more variables. Currently technology seeks to perpetuate this tradition by a vigorous application of scientific knowledge to answer the question, "How?" Pursuit of both the "Why" and the "How" has been characterized above all by the concern for order and regularity.

There has begun to be a change, however. Increasingly, the most advanced thinkers are attempting to break out of the rational order ordained by scientific and technical culture by pursuing thoughts that take them beyond the strictures of scientific orthodoxy. Eschewing questions such as "Why?" and "How?", our most provocative thinkers are likely to begin with the query "Why not?" Granted, this can lead into a situation wherein it becomes increasingly difficult to distinguish what is merely *non-science* from what is *non-sense*.

Asking "Why not?" has led in recent years to speculations on visitors from other worlds; radical reassessments of the history and age of our planet; investigations into the possibility of communication with other forms of animal life; the discovery of the creativity and authenticity of many of the persons we have been taught to believe are functionally insane, not to mention the canonization of Don Juan, a Yaqui Indian, as the patron saint and shaman for all those who wish to travel to "other places, other times," beyond logic-bound, rule-regulated existence.

Our minds are being stretched for us. We are being taught that the world is not just "out there," as profit-seekers think, for the *taking*; it is, also, open, amorphous, inchoate, "in here," for the *making*. So-called laws of nature are not, unless we wish them to be, final decrees of *Ananke*; they are ordinances, open to repeal. The more we impose order upon nature, the less imposing we find it to be. We have gained security from the belief that the control of our environment is based upon the demands of reason. But that security depends upon our believing that the order of nature and the laws we employ to characterize that order are in some sense final. The emerging suspicion many of our thinkers are entertaining is this: there is no final, necessary order. We are now asked to believe that much as rulers (*principes*) order societies of men, principles (*principia*) order our knowledge. But both the rulers of society and the rulers of thought may be deposed. The history of thought, like the history of government, is a story of oscillations between bloody tyrannies and bloodless, banal democracies. Consensus, imposed from above or sustained by public opinion, has dominated our consciousness of, and obedience to, both the laws of nature and the laws of men.

Thoughts such as these are becoming increasingly important because of the necessity to interpret the relativity of knowledge and the consequent challenge to the rationality of scientific orthodoxy. Because of the chaos of world-views, the hotch-potch of theories characterizing intellectual culture, we are coming to the realization that we have perhaps wasted too much of our time pimping for Truth, or whoring after it.

No doubt these thoughts seem altogether too radical. For without a cosmos of restricted possibilities there can be no assurance of the persistence of a public world within which laws, rules, habits, and institutions could function, as they currently do, as so many guard-rails against the threat of chaos. Without a common world of restricted possibilities there can be no easily discernible order in our thoughts, actions, or feelings. But it is increasingly the case that if we are to be adequate in our treatment of the width of human experience, it will be necessary to speculate upon conceptions of the character of the world that lead one rapidly into conflict with the aim of logical consistency. Of what real value is the principle of logical consistency if it requires that we omit significant items of experience?

One of the foundations of classical, "left-brain" science was the belief that a uniform causality operates throughout nature. The increased exposure to gnostic technologies has led to the challenge of that belief. One of the most dramatic of such challenges has come from the phenomenon of the Hindu fire-walking ceremonies. Imagine a pit of burning coals with a surface temperature, as measured by a pyrometer, of over 1300 degrees Fahrenheit. Envision a band of ecstatic Hindus dancing across the pit, barefooted, their only protection faith in the god Kataragama. They dance over the embers; reaching down they scoop up handfuls of coals and toss them over their bodies. Finally, they emerge on the other side of the pit, unscathed. Not even their clothing, which under ordinary conditions would have ignited immediately, shows any signs of damage. Such ceremonies, observed hundreds of times, investigated by research teams and reported to the public in such journals as *Scientific American* and *National Geographic*, constitute one vast exception to the generalization: fire burns. The Hindu belief in the god Kataragama is by all accounts an efficacious one—efficacious enough to suspend the operation of a significant law of nature within a local environment. By attending to an "accidental" characteristic of fire, that sometimes it does not burn, and by exploiting these accidental characteristics, the Hindu has demonstrated the importance of contingencies in nature.

Defenders of the orthodoxy of science will scoff at the above account, ignoring the facticity of the event. Others who accept the factual character of fire-walking will reach for a causal explanation that suits the orthodox paradigm. The first reaction is an obscurantist ploy that seeks to maintain an orthodox methodology. The second involves one in often ludicrous and fantastic explanations that rival the implausibility of the phenomenon one seeks to interpret.

Fire-Walking is most often "explained" by self-hypnosis. This is, of course, no explanation at all, since hypnosis itself has yet to receive a scientific explanation. Why shouldn't 1300-degree heat consume anyone, hypnotized or not? And does the devotee hypnotize his robe as well? The scientist cannot, no matter how much semantical obfuscation he employs, deny the exceptional status of the fire-walking ceremony. The presumed statistical character of laws, which derives from the recognition of accidental characteristics of nature, opens the door to the consideration of the relations among events in nature that are relevant to alterations in the statistics that define the dominant laws to which we conventionally attend.

Every exception to a law of nature is itself an instance of another law. All things are real possibilities. Chaos is an infinite matrix of orders. *Creation*, as the selection of a possible order from among the sum of all orders, is an event that can conceivably alter the character of the laws of nature as they are recognized by a given set of individuals within a given environment.

We can no longer define the nature of real possibility in terms of the conceptions of science and external technologies. The realm of possibility is vastly expanded by the recognition of the efficacy of internal techniques. The principal question, of course, is whether or not the two technologies can be brought into viable relationship. That depends upon whether or not the divergent cultural expressions of internal and external technology can be understood as important aspects of an organic whole that would emerge from a wedding of the two. One way of energizing interest in the achievement of such a union would be to recognize that the future of the forebrain—the future of that which distinguishes *human* being from the rest of being—depends upon the establishment of a working relationship between these divergent human functions.

THE EDUCATION OF NATURE

If we are to discuss the creative possibilities of life in our emerging technological societies, it is essential that we avoid the temptation to commit the Pelagian Fallacy. To claim freedom out of season is a futile boast. Such a claim can only produce a false sense of hope, which would then lead to an equally artificial feeling of efficacy. The aim of speculative philosophy, and *a fortiori* of speculative philosophy of culture, is not merely to understand the world in systematic terms; nor is it (*pace* Marx) to change the world. Its purpose is to heighten one's experience of the world. Speculative philosophy is a wondering meant to increase one's sense of wonder. What I primarily wish to do, therefore, is but to wonder how we might be open to the resolution of the dilemma facing each of us in contemporary technological society.

We know more about the Outside than we do about the Inside. Such is the character of knowledge, of course, that *we* know only things that can be made public. Private knowledge is knowledge "I" possess. But even at that, we have greater access to the Outside than each of us, as "I," has to his own Inside. We feel more at home *out there* than we do *in here*. This is not at all due to the different natures of the Inside and the Outside. It is due to the historical choices that we have made in the development of human culture. It could have been different. Whether it could have been a *great deal* different we shall never know. Certainly the threat of pain and death, which was a part of the environmental conditions of every human being from the beginnings of our animal existence, and which continues to plague most of us with undiminished force, could explain the cultural activity that led to the development of external technology and the primary concern with the Outside-as-threat. But whatever led to the present emphasis upon techniques of control and domination, we are increasingly aware that they are insufficient as fundamental human motivations. We recognize that external technology is an expression of our character and needs as human beings; but it is not a complete expression. We seek the luxury of completeness. And that can only come if we can relate the benefits of external and internal technique.

What is it that internal and external technique have in common? This question is hard to answer principally because most definitions of technology, as we have seen, presuppose the fully developed human being as the agent operating in accordance with the technique. Aristotle's conception of *techne* as "a capacity to make involving a true course of reasoning"[35] presupposes the existence of reasoning as a precondition for any making. This, of course, precludes the existence of what we are calling internal technology in its most primitive senses associated with the evolutionary self-creation of the human being. But there is one sense in which even Aristotle's definition of *techne*, which has been of overwhelming importance in the Western understanding of the meaning of technology, takes into account the principal activity involved in self-creation—the aesthetic process of creation associated with *feeling*. For the aims of *techne* as what we would call "fine art" include the evocation of pleasurable feelings. Art as imitation provided, for Aristotle, an occasion for learning. In addition, the tragic art provided for the catharsis or purgation of emotion, which clarified and sensitized the spectators' aesthetic sensibilities. As expressed, as externalized, *techne* is a making in accordance with *reason*; as experienced, as internalized, it is a feeling process, a process capable of rationalization. We can, of course, see right away the difficulty that was to befall later developments in the arts, pure and applied. Defining *techne* in terms of rationality, and considering its internal value only insofar as it rationalized, organized, and led to the controlled expression of emotion, heavily burdened future understandings of technology with the element of reason. The seeds of behavioral technology were contained in the first articulations of the technical phenomenon in Greek philosophy.

For both Plato and Aristotle, art was to be conceived as imitation of nature, though the senses of the term "imitation" are quite different. For Plato, the cosmos is itself produced by a process of imitation in which a Divine Artificer creates the world from a pre-existent matter, using perfect Ideas as models. The world, itself an imitation, is then the source from which the human artist draws his models for imitation. Human art imitates imitations, and is, therefore, twice removed from the reality constituted by the Eternal Ideas, which alone are truly real. For Plato, art imitates the *structure* of things, which answers to its true reality. For Aristotle, imitation is along *functional* lines. What is imitated for Aristotle are antecedently existing processes in nature. Nature itself is not an object of art. Nor are the products of Nature the objects of art. The objects of imitation are the *actions* of nature, including human actions as well. Moreover, the sense of imitation includes a kind of completion. Nature makes a tree; man makes a house from the wood of trees. The process employed to make the house is the same that nature would use if it were to make a house. In fact there is a sense in which man is the agent of nature for the making of the house, though Aristotle does not wish, by admitting this, to collapse the distinction between art and nature.[36]

The difficulties of this conception of art as imitation, in both its Platonic and Aristotelian senses, is that it presupposes the conception of reason and rationality as the guiding principle of what constitutes acceptable art. In Aristotle's case, no distinction is made between pure and applied arts—the shoemaker makes shoes and the painter makes a painting. Both are artists. For Plato, fine art and "craftsmanship" are distinguished by method: the craftsman or artisan has some knowledge (what Plato would call "right opinion") of the artistic process leading to the aesthetic object. The poet or fine artist may create from out of "inspiration," or "divine madness."

Though the two types of artist differ in the methods of, and resources for, their imitation, neither is able to give an adequate account of his creative activity. It is the latter type of artist we encounter in Plato's *Republic* as an enemy of the state; one who must be courteously, but hastily, escorted from the perfect society. The artist who remains is the artisan, the craftsman, what we would call the "mere technician." But he remains only insofar as he subjects himself to the guidance of the philosophic rulers, they who truly *know*.

Even as brief a survey of the two principal interpretations of the relation of art and nature as has been given ought to be sufficient to provide some interesting, and indeed, ironic speculations on the relation of our contemporary interpretations of technology to these philosophic beginnings. In the first place, only Plato allows art a definition and character other than that controlled by reason. And Plato, once admitting that the poet or artist is capable of divine inspiration, excludes him from his ideal society. Social existence is promoted and sustained by those who are capable of pure and applied rationality. Art which cannot be guided by reason is to be excluded from civilized life. Obviously, we have not taken the advice implicit in either the Platonic or Aristotelian accounts literally. With Plato, against Aristotle, we have more often than not promoted the distinction between pure and applied art; but with Aristotle, we have given the artist a status far above what Plato would have accorded him. It is true that we have continued the ghettoization of art begun with Plato; but the artist's ghetto has always had a particularly strong appeal. We allow our artists their idiosyncrasies on the condition that they do not attempt to disrupt society with undue claims of the relevance of their art. The "mere technician," meanwhile, we have allowed to remain free to re-make the society in which he resided, in the beginning, in the lowest echelon. At present, in fact, the technician seems to be a member of a generally acknowledged elite. It could have been predicted. Plato's ideal society, projected in the *Republic*, could only be made to work if techniques of behavioral engineering that we only now are beginning to develop could be employed. Plato's Utopia was the society reason demanded. But until such time as psychologists could become princes, philosophers could never be kings.

The most serious fault of the characterization of technology solely in terms of the claims of reason is that, when coupled with the Aristotelian distinction between art and nature, and the consequent notion of "the artificial," it leads to the very difficulties we now experience with the bold attempts to internalize external forms of technology. A natural object, such as a tree, has its "reasons" for being, what Aristotle termed its "causes" (*aitia*), inside itself. Its matter, form, end, and the dynamic process that enabled it to achieve that end, are implicit in the seed and realized through the growth process of the tree. A chair made from the tree is an artificial object; and though one could argue that the matter is that of the tree, the form of the chair, the purpose for which the chair was made, as well as the activity that eventuated in its construction, are all external. Art, or *techne*, as a making, may imitate nature, but the products of artistic creativity are *artificial*; that is to say, they no longer have their reasons for being inside themselves. The increased importance of external technology in contemporary society, a perfectly rational outworking of the characterizations of art and its place in society found in Greek thought, may lead to a society in which not only the tables and chairs and industrial products, but *the citizens as well*, are *artificial objects*, with their reasons for being no longer in themselves but within the technical directives according to which the society operates.

Plato and Aristotle, though they provided the most important characterizations of art and technique, did not exhaust the early discussions of the topic. Two other significant conceptions of art play throughout the history of Western philosophy. These consider the ends of art in terms either of *power*, or of *pleasure*.

Materialist conceptions tend to recognize the pleasure-giving capacities of both the production and enjoyment of art. Of course, this type of characterization could equally well be considered in terms of the concept of imitation since, for the materialist, the principles of pleasure and pain are fundamental to human nature, and the artist but imitates those natural processes that are pleasure-giving when he does art. But that seems to stretch the term overmuch. We have in the latter days of the materialist tradition received a characterization of the relation of art and nature from the materialist persuasion that is direct and unambiguous.

Freudian psychology, at its metaphysical extremes, allows us to understand art as the *sublimation* of nature. For the materialist, nature is nothing more than atoms and the void. The fundamental principles of nature as we have come to know it are those that lead to the integration and disintegration of basic particles. These principles, though they cannot ultimately be explained in terms other than those of chance, provide the primary reasons for everything that is. The conceptualization of Freud required an Eros–Thanatos dichotomy in order to cap his speculations about the nature of human life and its cultural context. Eros is a drive toward integration, which is the foundation of all pleasure and pleasure-seeking. Thanatos, the threat of ultimate dissolution, is the foundation of pain. But pleasure, as tension-reduction, though it presupposes Eros in the most fundamental sense, is ultimately identical with Thanatos, the final reduction of tension. It is within this context that art and technology are to be understood. Cultural objects, artificial objects, are the products of activities aimed at pleasure; but as these activities are themselves indirect, they are ultimately unsatisfactory. Sexual gratification, as the most direct and unmediated form of pleasure, is the primary goal of human nature. Art, in its production of human culture, is a *sublimation* of nature.

Various interpreters of contemporary culture have been enamored of the Freudian conception of the relation of art and nature, particularly as it applies to the interpretation of technological society. Herbert Marcuse and Norman O. Brown,[37] among others, resolve the dilemmas presented by their Freudian analyses by, naturally enough, suggesting that technological society could provide the means whereby human beings might begin to "de-sublimate"—that is, to experience more directly the sensuous side of their human natures. Marcuse and his disciples add a novel dimension to the Freudian theory by applying some neo-Marxian notions to their analyses. What they do, essentially, is to claim that some revolutionary dynamic is necessary since the repression of sensuality and fuller human capacities is maintained by a political elite for its own neurotic purposes. Variations of these Freudian prescriptions aside, the conception of art as the sublimation of nature provides the dialectical alternative to the characterization of *techne* in terms of rationality. Art is not guided by reason, nor is the principal aim of art intellectual penetration; art aims at the promotion of pleasure, the satisfaction of desire.

This hedonistic or epicurean vision of art as an aid in the increase of pleasure and the decrease of pain has itself played no little role in the development of our present technological society. Gadgets and weapons define the extremes of the pleasure–pain spectrum. And between these extremes lie all the technological products that promote the ends of an organized society through the promise of pleasure and the threat of pain. Behaviorism is again the natural result of this alternate vision of the relation of art to nature.

One traditional view of *techne* remains. It is the view that characterizes art in terms of "convention," a term that includes all human productions, not excepting the expressions of the theoretical and practical sciences. If, as the Sophistic cliché has it, "Man is the measure of all things," then the field of *techne* is inclusive of all human activity. Mere art is the *transformation* of nature according to human capacities and desires. The end of art is *power*. This must be so since, if there is to be a common world at all, some consensus must be gained. If there is no final, real and objective world to be known, but only the world as construed by human action, then it is human activity that must establish not only "the world," but must win acceptance of the world as well. The historian who tells the story of the "great men" who have made history must himself vie with others so that his interpretation of greatness will be accepted. In such a world, the primary purpose of art is *persuasion*. One must not only achieve: it is necessary that one persuade others of the greatness of one's achievements. *Rhetoric* is the fundamental art. Conventions are not to be established by accident, but in accordance with the motives of men seeking greatness. The concern that one receive proper credit for the invention or discovery that one claims as original, the desire to have "a place in history," the overriding concern for public life, and the fear of anonymity, are ultimately grounded in the view that there is no objective reality against which we may measure our success; it is up to us to make what will be.

No great subtlety is required to see how significant for the modern-day Sophist is the behavioral orientation of contemporary technology. The Sophist (we speak here mainly of the politician) certainly does not care what metaphysical worldview underlies our understandings of technique; each such understanding, after all, is simply a rhetorical ploy that has as its ultimate aim the attainment of power over others. Behavioral engineering is certainly a more efficient method than rational debate for the achievement of the aim of persuasion. We have learned at least this much from the current use of psychotechnology as a means of conditioning and controlling behavior.[38] There is every reason to believe that such uses of behavioral technology bode ill for the future of technological society. But as I have argued above, an overweening pessimism might just lead us to miss the one ray of hope that seems to remain for those not satisfied with the current program of the internalization of external technique. That hope lies in the fact that the contemporary coalescence of each of the forms of interpretation of the purpose of technology, though seeming to suggest the complete absence of any critical perspective from which to view the technical phenomenon, also gives evidence of creating a great amount of frustration and giving rise to a series of significant (dare a non-Marxist use this term?) *contradictions*.

In the first place, as I have already suggested, the alliance between the technician and the politician cannot be a very comfortable one. This marriage of convenience is based on the technician's need for funding, and the politician's need for the best possible solutions to a series of pressing problems. Politics knows nothing of efficiency and organization. The personal exercise of power is one of the sloppiest activities known to us.

There is at least the possibility that we shall evolve beyond the present tensions associated with the possibilities of international conflict and, following a course of internal development aimed at solving our ecological problems, we shall find ourselves turning into a technocracy in which the aims of domination and control will no longer define the production and employment of techniques for the simple reason that the ubiquity of technical organization has so rationalized the public arena that the quest for greatness in any of its forms will be looked upon as an idiosyncrasy of but a few. There is certainly nothing in this argument to convince anyone who still believes that man is "by nature" a power-seeker. But there is just enough evidence that we are no longer enamored of heroes and great men; no longer tuned into, or turned on by, charismatic leaders, to believe that the public sphere has lost its appeal. We seem more inclined to pursue private satisfactions. Perhaps we shall avoid *1984*.

Whether we shall also avoid a *Brave New World* is, of course, another question. If the concern for private satisfactions remains at the present level, it is certainly possible that we shall turn to the behavioral engineer for the production of techniques of gratification. But there is another tension or contradiction in our present situation that may offer additional hope that even this will be avoided. For without the political context from which to derive the goals and ends of behavioral control, the technician is at a loss. He does not wish to be the one who decides which values will be used as criteria for the development of techniques. Over and over again we recognize the fact that the technician is willing to perform his function for anyone. Like the soldier of fortune of a bygone age, he performs his task for the intrinsic satisfactions of his job. But if not the motives of political power, what *will* the motives be? There are many possible directions that efficiency can take in contemporary society. Who will decide?

If the politician retires from his traditional role as the guardian of social stability and of his own place in history, the job may be filled not by another single elite, but by a conglomerate of elite groups. The most interesting of developments currently, as far as the emergence of novel sources of value in society is concerned, is in the accelerating interest in the values of Eastern culture. Not merely, or mainly, in the fine arts and literature, or even in medicine, but also, and perhaps primarily, in psychology. Here, in the birthplace of the modern form of behavioral engineering, we are beginning to see our Western intellectuals drawing upon Eastern theories and techniques in order to re-assess the nature of the human experience and the means of meeting primary human needs. This "turning toward the East," which I have discussed heretofore primarily as a philosophical possibility, receives more practical expression in the several branches of humanistic science concerned with the understanding of human personality and values.

The emerging psychological elite includes not only classical psychoanalytic and behaviorist orientations, but humanistic psychologies, as well. The most recent movement among psychologists, strongly influenced by the spiritualist psychologies of the Eastern and Gnostic traditions, is that of "transpersonal" psychology, which includes a concern for the development of what we have been calling internal technologies.[39] As yet this movement has had little influence within the more academic and professional of cultural settings. It is, however, a stimulating source of responsible inquiry into, and speculation upon, topics such as altered states of consciousness, yoga, zen meditation, magic, the philosophies of Gurdjieff, Sufi mysticism, and so on.

The primary influences upon psychological attitudes come, of course, from out of the psychoanalytic and behaviorist orientations. It is from members of these orientations that we have obtained the notion of *techne* as *therapy*. In *The Triumph of the Therapeutic*,[40] Philip Rieff promotes the idea of a therapeutic society in which the principal mediators of social energies would be psychotherapists with techniques of remission and control capable of neutralizing pathological emotions and activities and of enhancing the expression of other aesthetic and moral actions. On the supposition that religions have long ago surrendered their function of the construction of a moral demand system and the integration of individuals within it, Rieff wishes to see the responsibility for this function passed to the therapist. If, as Rieff believes, it is no longer necessary that societies require a single, overarching system of values, it is possible to perform the task of properly channeling emotions and activities in a relatively piece-meal fashion without disrupting society. "Rituals of release" such as human sacrifice, which once functioned as a means of promoting social cohesion and the release of emotions that might otherwise become pathological, have no real counterpart in contemporary society (except, perhaps, in the diluted form of violent sports). In a therapeutic society, the individual therapist would take charge of the rituals of release.

The principal difference between contemporary therapeutic conceptions of society and societies in which religion served as the primary integrating force is found in the shift in the function of myth. Whatever his other advantages, the essential disadvantage of the psychotherapist compared with the shamans of primitive societies is that the shaman could assume a broad background of mythical presuppositions held in common by all of his "clients." The modern psychoanalyst faces a more difficult task. He is forced to create in the minds of each of his patients, from materials more or less present at hand, not only whatever mythical landscape is required by the theoretical structure of the therapy, but, in accordance with the dominant scientific attitude, must also dispose his clients to believe that his particular myths are *true*. He then must rehearse the myths for his clients, after which he guides them through the mythical landscape wherein they confront the obstacles predicted for them, and, with the aid of the therapist, overcome these obstacles. This constitutes a winning through to victory and serves as the crisis that promises a cure.

Psychotherapies, using that term in the broadest possible sense, require varying degrees of belief. Freudian psychotherapy requires many beliefs. The client must accept the importance of the past as a determinant of the present status of one's personality, the basic outlines of the dynamics of family relationships, the notion that the organism is fundamentally sensual and sexual, and so on. Without belief there can be no cure. At the other extreme we find behavioral technology in which, it must be presumed, belief in propositions about the world or experience play a minimal role. The relative ease with which behavioral techniques may be employed, however, is due to the fact that, like the shaman, the behaviorist can assume that his client will share the same world-view as he, since behaviorism depends upon the implementation of what for most of us is simply scientific "common sense."

Rieff is profoundly sympathetic to the Freudian technique, but his speculations concerning the creation of a therapeutic society do not stand or fall with that particular methodology. Since his emphasis is upon individual self-realization, he could not sensibly argue for the elevation of psychoanalysis to the status of the sole method of therapy. A plurality of therapeutic methods might better suit the conception of a decentralized social context. But this plurality should include therapies with strong mythical content. Evocative therapies would function to counter the trend toward the internalization of behavioral technology, and would at the same time enhance the self-creating, self-realizing activities associated with internal technique.

The plea for myth-laden therapies is based on the need to reverse a trend that has gone farther than it was destined to go. For the story of human cultural development told as the freeing of logos from *mythos*, which has been told in part throughout these pages, is but one chapter in the story of the civilizing of human experience. Technique in its externalized, material, and rational form is one theme of this chapter. Reason, untainted by myth, and free, therefore, from subjectivity, is its goal. And we see the promise of realization at hand. Rationality in its pure form is not to be found in the mind of some dispassionate philosopher or mathematician. Not there. The common failing of all histories of the human experience told in terms of increasing rationality is that they must presume the fulfillment of the process of rationalization in spite of overwhelming testimony of the sickeningly brutish behavior of many of our best and brightest minds. The assumption that reason emerges from out of myth and irrationality leads us to recognize in every reasoning being a taint of unreason still clinging, as a sign of its origins, to every rational activity.

Where is unsullied rationality to be found? Nowhere, if we insist upon remaining in the theoretical sphere. It is only as embodied in the technical processes of advanced technological society that we find reason at last fulfilled. Logos without *mythos* is actualized in efficiently organized technique. Objective reason is reason objectified; reason as an object in the world. Technology is scientific reasoning purged of its myth. And this is *science* as a set of practical factors in the world. The story of human development thus far has been that of, first, self-creation and then objectification. Objectification is the externalization of reason, which means, literally, the *precipitation* of reason into the Outside. And the story of the continued evolution of human beings can only be told with that fact in mind; the fact that, in some weird Kantian manner, reason has fulfilled itself in the practical sphere, in the sphere of external technology.

It would be too much of a good thing if we tried to internalize the objective structures of technology. To do so would be to create rational beings, but we must at some point recognize that the story of human experience is not the story of reason alone. In evolutionary terms it is the story of the realization of balanced intensity of experience. Reason has played its role to be sure. But in the narrow sense of rationality and technical reasoning, its function seems to be abating. Externalized technique can take over the rational activities of human beings, freeing the organism of the brain to integrate, co-ordinate, and enhance more complex and more intense types of experience. The internalization of behavioral technique would turn persons inside out, leaving no future internal possibilities.

The development of a therapeutic society containing a plurality of techniques capable of supporting individual self-realization and enhancing individual experience would seem desirable. The de-emphasis upon behavioral engineering as an ideological tool would be a prime requisite. That is to say, it would be necessary to realize that if behavioral technique is given dominance in a society, it is likely to subvert the aims of other therapeutic techniques, precisely because of its aversion to theory. We have much less to fear from a plurality of

dogmatic claims implicit in the theoretical or mythical underpinnings of conflicting therapeutic methods than from the
potential tyranny of a single technique that presumes that no
freedom, no subjectivity, no *Inside* exists.

Nicholas Kittrie, in *The Right to be Different*,[41] has
warned against the effects of politicizing the notion of therapy,
believing that the attempt to "cure" anti-social behavior,
rather than to punish it, cannot become the function of the
state without extremely detrimental consequences for the
entire social system. No doubt Kittrie is right in expressing
such fears, but, fortunately, they seem to be exaggerated.
Though our most enlightened courts and prison systems are
moving away from the narrow concept of punishment (although at present the movement is slow and more a matter
of rhetoric and principle than accomplished fact), it is not
the case that the belief in individual responsibility has been
given up. It is only in behavioral technique that the concept
of responsibility is absent. Even psychoanalysis, which is
grounded in a materialistic and deterministic view, expresses,
in its actual therapeutic procedures, a need for cooperation
and commitment largely if not completely absent from the
behavioral techniques. And for the last several years the use of
both behaviorist and Freudian methods has been declining in
our penal system. The latest developments in penal technology include an emphasis on techniques of self-actualization:
Transcendental Meditation, *T'ai Chi Ch'üan*, yoga, and so on.
And these therapies are aimed less at integrating the prisoner
back into society and more at improving his self-concept and
enhancing his abilities to cope with a demanding environment.[42]

Some of the difficulty we have in accepting the possibility
that we may, willy-nilly, move in the direction of a therapeutic
society, essentially free from political domination and pro-
gressively moving toward goals of individual self-realization, is
that the phase of technological development at the end of
which we find ourselves, the phase of objectification, was
predicated upon notions of understanding and control. Both
understanding and control suggest over-arching structures, be
they of knowledge or of practice. Understanding requires

rational principles and if understanding be a general cultural value, then the general acceptance of principles is required. Reason, in its earlier stages, sought truths to which all rational men must perforce give their assent. The institutional implementation of the truths that dominated given epochs of a society or culture—be they theological, philosophical, or scientific doctrines—established one phase of the organization of human experience longitudinally over time. The Marxian remonstrance against philosophers, that they should not be content with understanding the world, but should rather try to *change* it, signaled a general recognition of the fact that with the industrial revolution techniques of understanding had given way to techniques of control. But with the completion of the externalization phase, which consisted in the frustration of the aims of rational understanding and the final realization of reason in the objective structures of advanced technological society, technologies of understanding and of control are giving way to an *aesthetic* phase. Heretofore, we have been content to try to understand and to control the world. The point, however, is to *experience* it.

The conception of *techne* as therapy that is being forwarded from various points of view is perhaps a foreshadowing of a novel vision of the relations of art and nature. If we construe the concept of therapy in its original meaning as *therapeia*,[43] we can articulate meanings of the relation of art to nature that transcend the motives of understanding and control. The shift away from these motives to that of experiencing the world shifts the emphasis of technology away from the public to the private sphere of existence. As a result we require a conception of technology and of the relation of art to nature that does not merely emphasize motives of knowledge or power, and that does not construe the concept of pleasure in terms of a general set of principles derived from objective nature, a set of principles in terms of which the reduction of individual experience to general notions of pleasure and pain would be possible. *Techne* cannot be imitation, or sublimation, or transformation of nature in any of the senses discussed heretofore. A novel conception must be articulated.

The novel conception of the relations of art and nature

has already been adumbrated in previous chapters with the development of the philosophy of creativity from out of the philosophies of Whitehead and those of Chinese Buddhism and Taoism. The principal characteristic of this relationship is not that it is naturalistic, and to this extent parallels the Aristotelian vision, but that it is grounded on non-rational principles in the sense that it does not give to reasoning beings a privileged place in nature. The artist or technician has as his source the complex field of unknown and literally unknowable Nature. Nature is a field of reciprocally interfused centers of self-creativity. *Techne* is more than mere making; it is a *creating*. The basis of all making is the self-creative activities of the events constituting Nature. Art, or *techne*, is self-creativity.

The conception of art as self-creativity defines a relationship between art and nature distinctly different from that characterized by the terms *imitation, sublimation*, or *transformation*. As Whitehead says, "Art is the education of nature." This is the creationist sense of the relation of nature and art. The word "education" has two main roots. The Latin verb *ēdūcere* means "to draw out," "to lead forth." *Ēducāre* means "to bring up" in the sense of "to bring up a child." This latter sense of education has been most relevant to our cultural development. For another way to look at the conception of "bringing up" is to see it as "cultivation." Culture in its function as *techne* is a *cultivating process*. Cultivation presupposes the notion of ends or goals. One cultivates in order to achieve an end—the maturation of the object of cultivation. In this sense one of the fundamental principles of education has always been to cultivate the mind and spirit of the student so that he may achieve maturity. For the greater part of our cultural tradition, the aims or ideals that define maturity have been presumed known, and have served as the basic goals of a liberal education. Our situation has changed, however, and education has had to change along with it.

Though many are nostalgic for the old ways, and seek a return to fundamentals in education, the direction of our educational process is hardly to be found traditional in the broadest sense. To the extent that education has not capitulated completely to the vocational emphasis that for some time has constituted the only guarantee that one may remain true to the false God of Relevance, it has become increasingly personal, experimental and open-ended. We continually experience the move toward the sense of education as *ēdūcere*, the sense in which education must be an evocative event. Here there is less control, less predictability, associated with the educational process. In an age of relativity, education based upon the principle of evocation, of drawing out or leading forth, cannot yield guaranteed results. "Education by objectives" is, at present, an attempt to impose upon the educational process a set of artificial goals. When it becomes necessary to spell out the goals of an educational process it is because there is no common assumption concerning what those goals should be. When there is no longer a common assumption as to goals, it is because the culture from which such goals are derived has lost its unity. Without the unity of thought and effort that gives rise to a set of common values, explicit aims of education must be special pleadings.

If the relation between art and nature is defined in terms of *ēdūcere*, then we can characterize the proper direction of technological society (as the field of external as well as internal technique) in terms of the conception of *evocation*. Heretofore, culture has functioned as a means of cultivating; henceforth, what we have called "culture" must function, in the form of technological activity, as an evocative agency, one that educates not for pre-designed ends, but that promotes the evocation of intensity and spontaneity.

The conception of art as the education of nature entails the presumption that nature is educable. That presumption was encountered, in part, in the Aristotelian conception of imitation. There we saw that nature is educable in the *ēducāre* sense of the term. Thus, nature can be *cultivated*. The creationist construes education in its more radical meaning, however, and finds that nature is educable in the sense that it is the source of all elicited intensities. The aims of education and the aims of art are one and the same. But the aims of art, at least in the creationist sense of the term, are balanced intensity and contrast, the intense harmony that all "fine" art has continually sought to attain. Nature is educable, then, not only in the sense that it is possible to improve upon the activities of nature, but in the sense that it is possible to draw out of nature new possibilities of intensity and contrast only barely conceivable at the beginning of the process.

True novelty, spontaneously evoked, is the most desirable result of the educating process. The age-old question of the proper relevance of passion and decorum in the educational process is to be answered in terms of the element of *passion*. Nature as a field of self-creative events is primarily aesthetic. The act of self-creativity that is the fundamental aesthetic act is the primary activity of nature. Nature and art are related by the principle of *education*. But since the primary function of art is *self*-creativity, and the primary aesthetic act is the same, the conclusion can only be that nature educates itself. Nature educates itself, and one of the results of the self-education of nature has been the production of human culture as a means of promoting the aesthetic aim toward balanced intensity of experience. The cultural sphere served this aim well as long as there were novel variations on the principal themes of cultural activity possible. Cultural aims, such as Truth, or Beauty, were sought in terms of cultural interests such as science or art, each contributing something to the overall harmony of the cultural realm. But culture as the cultivation of experience is transcended when the maturation process is no longer relevant to the productions of novelty and spontaneity.

The spheres of nature and of culture are both defined by art, which aims at the production of the type of harmony resulting from intensity and contrast in experience. Once it came to be recognized that the study of nature was in fact a study of the ways in which nature had been construed, or what amounts to the same thing, a study of the relations between persons and nature, then it could, of course, no longer be maintained that there was a viable distinction between nature and culture. But it is not just that we could not heretofore have known nature apart from some cultural characterization of it; it is rather that we have come to recognize that culture itself is one of the aims of nature. The production of human culture, even the production of human beings capable of producing a culture, was but a strategy for the achievement of that balanced intensity that results from the free, self-creative activities of natural events. And it is at least possible that we have reached a point in the current aesthetic activities of natural events that culture as a strategy for the attainment of balanced intensity needs to be transcended.[44]

What lies beyond culture? Elsewhere, I have defined culture as "The complex of aims and interests that define and organize human social activity and its products."[45] The key to the recognition and characterization of a culture is the ability to discern certain defining characterizations of a culture and the media through which these characteristics are produced and maintained. Without a set of ideals or interests held in common at least by the cultural elites, and without a set of interests employed to produce and maintain these values or ideals, there can be no culture. Anarchists have no culture. And it is true, if somewhat paradoxical, that artists, in their most creative roles, have no culture. They may contribute to general culture, but in the intensity of their creative activities, they have no culture of their own. From the kaleidescopic chaos of artistic inspirations, a culture chooses those that serve its interest best, relegating the others to a state of limbo.

It is true with regard to the aesthetic activities of Nature, as in the realm of human culture, that the aim of art is art. Technological society as the externalization of the internal rational structures of *techne*, and as the techniques of individual self-realization, are the ends of art as practiced by the self-creative natural events defining our recognized cultural activities. But the realization of the aim of art is also the realization of the *end* of culture. Culture is possible only where art is a means to the achievement of ends other than the ends of art per se. Where individual self-creativity is the fundamental principle, no culture can exist. In its place there can only be a field of creative centers of aesthetic activity.

The aim of art at balanced intensity of experiencing is achieved when the conditions allowing for the ecstatic, enstatic, and constatic forms of experiencing are produced. Technological society can, in principle, constitute such a set of conditions. For such a society is patterned by a set of reciprocally interfused events. It is Teilhard's *noösphere*. But the interfusion of the elements of a technological society does not require that the individual give up his identity and merge with the social or technical order. The distinction between internal and external technologies ensures that technologies of control need not be exercised against human beings, but may be used to enhance the variety and intensity of individual experience.

Technological society can be the condition of constatic union, the objective form of nature as a field of interfused events allowing for the experience of the co-presence of the finite and the infinite in and through one another. Art as the education of nature gives rise to technology, which, when perfected in the condition of a technological society in which there is a harmony of internal and external technical activities, is recognized as Nature-itself. What becomes then of the distinction between art and nature? Nature is seen to consist in the art of self-creativity, and that art is best exemplified in the activities of a technological society. The conclusion of this process is the realization of art as nature and nature (*physis*) as *techne*, technology. But this must not be seen as a narrowing of the meanings of nature to the strictures of a single technical order. On the contrary, if the externalization of rational techniques frees individuals to practice internal technologies of self-creativity, then Nature as Cosmos, as the sum of all orders (i.e., Chaos) remains an infinite source of possibilities from which techniques, properly applied, can achieve novel and spontaneously created results.

The identification of nature and *techne*, which is contingent upon the progress toward the distinction and harmonious relationship of internal and external technology, does lead to some striking consequences, of course. The principal consequence is that the activities that go on in a technological society are now to be construed as natural activities in the truest sense of the word. Nature and culture are one, because culture has become nature. The limits of the natural environment are to be understood in terms of the limits of technique. The laws of nature are rules for technical organization and manipulation of one's ambience. And these laws are subject to repeal.

Obviously there are some limits to the ability of individuals to affect the dominant regularities of nature by recourse to other, less pronounced, more accidental phenomena. But we do not know what those limits are in fact. The limitations are set, in principle, by the capacities for *wu-wei*, *wu-chih* and *wu-yü* and the potentiality for the constatic experience of the reciprocal interfusion of events. Just as causal laws limit the possibilities for actions to those allowed by the linear, causal relations among events in nature, so the self-creative activities of events and the "laws" that emerge from them are limited by the sympathetic interfusion of each in every other event. The education of nature cannot consist in the imposition of rules or laws upon natural events; *education* must differ from *transformation*. The existentialist principle of power over nature presumes a separation of persons and nature that does not in fact exist in a technological society. It is necessary to substitute creativity for power as the principle upon which all activities are grounded.

Nature is *techne*. This is the first reinterpretation of the cultural paradigm initially presented in terms of the concepts of God, Nature, Passion, and Social Practice. And just as the concept of "God" determined the character of each of the other elements of the paradigm in traditional Anglo-European culture, so the concept of "Nature" as *techne* will provide the context within which the other elements can be construed. Nature is the field of reciprocally interfused events allowing for the experience of constasy, which, as a sense of balanced intensity, fulfills the aims of nature as *techne*. The relation of the individual to this context understood as "social" is determined by the *ecstatic* sense, as we shall see. Likewise, the relation of male to female is to be interpreted in terms of the sense of *enstasy*. The actual experience of constasy, as distinguished from the condition for that experiencing that is nature as *techne*, will be discussed in terms of the concept of deity, polytheistically interpreted.

NOTES

1. A valuable discussion of the actual influence of the Genesis myth on our scientific reasonings and practice may be found in Lynn White, Jr., *Machina ex Deo* (Cambridge: MIT Press, 1968), passim.

2. See Mazlich's "The Fourth Discontinuity," in *Technology and Culture: An Anthology*, edd. Melvin Kranzberg and William H. Davenport (New York: Schocken, 1972), p. 218.

3. I have not attempted to maintain a sharp distinction between what has come to be termed "technics" (referring to the tools, machines, and techniques of a culture), as opposed to "technology" (the study of technics), primarily because the distinction is so little employed in the literature. The purpose of this chapter is to uncover the logos of *techne*. The subject under consideration is the meaning of "making" insofar as that can be discussed as a public, institutionalized process. The various senses of "technology" as employed throughout the discussion must be understood in the light of this main purpose.

Needless to say the phenomenon of technology has received myriad and conflicting interpretations. We have not yet reached a point in our own social development that we shall be able to view the subject of technology either comprehensively or objectively. I certainly do not claim that I shall be able to do so in this chapter.

Besides the works cited in the text I have found the following discussions of technology illuminating: *Philosophy and Technology—Readings in the Philosophical Problems of Technology*, edd. Carl Mitcham and Robert Mackey (New York: Free Press, 1972); David and Ruth Elliot, *The Control of Technology* (New York: Springer-Verlag, 1976); Joseph Weizenbaum, *Computer Power and Human Reason* (San Francisco: Freeman, 1976); William Barrett, *The Illusion of Technique* (Garden City, N.Y.: Anchor Press / Doubleday, 1978); *Essays in Technology and Humanity*, edd. David Lovekin and Donald Verene (Dixon, Ill.: Sauk Valley College, 1978); Langdon Winner, *Autonomous Technology—Technics Out of Control as a Theme in Political Thought* (Cambridge: MIT Press, 1978); and Martin Heidegger, *The Question Concerning Technology and Other Essays*, trans. William Lovitt (New York: Harper and Row, 1977), and *The Computer Age: A Twenty Year View*, edd. Michael Dertouzos and Joel Moses (Cambridge: MIT Press, 1980).

4. See *One-Dimensional Man*, pp. 157ff.

5. See, for example, Marcuse's remarks on the development of philosophic thought in ibid., passim. He seems to believe that only "scientific" philosophy tends toward one-dimensionality. It has been the burden of my remarks throughout this work that Western cultural experience *in toto* is, ultimately, but a groaning and travailing in the service of technological rationality.

6. Trans. Joan Stambaugh (New York: Harper and Row, 1973), p. 93.

7. Ibid., p. 90.

8. Ibid., p. 86.

9. Ibid., p. 96.

10. I have, on occasion, participated in business seminars, discussing the subjects of "industry" and "technology." It has always been of interest to me to note that the students in these seminars, though not ill-disposed toward automation as such, become as critical of it as any machine laborer if it seems to threaten their managerial function. Our management seminars are faced with the paradox that they must try to teach the efficient exercise of managerial techniques to individuals who derive great satisfaction from the management of human beings through the personal exercise of power. The goal of efficiency in management often is in direct conflict with the intrinsic satisfactions of the job.

11. See *The Technological Society*, pp. 85–94. Cf. *The Technological System*, pp. 209–34.

12. Ibid., p. 89.

13. Lynn White has shown that, for example, the invention of the stirrup suggested the use of heavier armor and the invention of the pennon: the former because of the extra defense necessary due to the increased power of thrust permitted by the use of the stirrup; the latter, because without the pennon the lance might be irretrievably thrust into the victim. See "The Act of Invention: Causes, Contexts, Continuities and Consequences," in *Technology and Culture*, pp. 277–78.

14. English trans. *The Failure of Technology* (Hinsdale, Ill.: Regnery, 1956), p. 18.

15. The science-fiction novelist Ron Goulart has provided a satirical view of such a world of near social and political anarchy in which, nonetheless, the transportation and communication systems of advanced technological society are operative, and computers and android servo-mechanisms free the anarchist members of society to pursue advanced forms of leisure. See *After Things Fell Apart* (New York: Ace, 1970). Also see Anthony Burgess' *A Clockwork Orange* for a slightly more pessimistic version of this same foresight.

16. See *Myth and the Machine*, Chapters 2–4.

17. *The Technological Society*, p. xxv.

18. Ibid., p. 3.

19. Ibid., p. xxv.

20. *The Myth of the Machine*, p. 5.

21. José Arguëlles, in his *The Transformative Vision*, has recognized the value of art in the internal development of human experience and consciousness. See his chapter "Art as Internal Technology," pp. 277–87.

22. Quoted in Arthur Waley, *Three Ways of Thought in Ancient China* (Garden City, N.Y.: Doubleday, n.d.), p. 70.

23. *The Myth of the Machine*, pp. 180ff.

24. The behaviorist would deny this, of course, but only on the grounds that there is literally nothing internal: there is no "inside," only "outside," only *behaviors*.

25. Three now-classic works which carry this theme to its fascinating conclusion are Hanson's *Patterns of Discovery*, Thomas Kuhn's *The Structure of Scientific Revolutions*, and Paul Feyerabend's *Against Method*.

Read in sequence they form an increasingly radical critique of any absolutist notions in scientific understandings and practice.

26. This point is well made by the novelist Kurt Vonnegut in his satire *Player Piano*. The plot concerns a group of technicians at an electronics firm who, in effect, make war against the burgeoning control of the technical processes by the machines they themselves have created. After a devastating paramilitary assault that has left a factory in a shambles, the technicians celebrate their victory by immediately beginning to repair the machines they have destroyed. The point is not at all far-fetched. The now-that-we've-got-it-together-let's-take-it-apart-again form of behavior is inculcated in us from an early age by children's toys, by our first automobiles, chemistry sets, and so on.

27. (New York: Macmillan, 1948).

28. (New York: Knopf, 1971).

29. Quoted in R. M. Young, *Brain, Mind and Adaptation* (London: Oxford University Press, 1970), p. 253.

30. For an interesting theory of the grounding of the Ten Commandments in the necessities of biological survival, see Wolfgang Winkler's *The Biology of the Ten Commandments*, trans. David Smith (New York: McGraw-Hill, 1972). Peter Singer has provided a well-balanced critique of the concept of the biological origins of morality in *The Expanding Circle: Ethics and Sociobiology* (New York: Farrar, Straus and Giroux, 1981).

31. A good example of such a gain is found in the criticisms of Descartes' concept of "space" and its *ad hoc* rejection in favor of theoretically simpler concepts. See *The Nature of Physical Existence*, pp. 186–238, for an insightful summary of this development.

32. For an important discussion of alchemy by one within the gnostic tradition see Titus Burckhardt, *Alchemy: Science of the Cosmos, Science of the Soul* (Baltimore: Penguin, 1971).

33. See René Guénon, *The Reign of Quantity*, trans. Lord Northbourne (Baltimore: Penguin, 1972).

34. For a book of readings containing many examples of such cross-cultural researches, see *Altered States of Consciousness*, ed. Charles Tart (Garden City. N.Y.: Doubleday, 1969, 1972).

35. See *Nicomachean Ethics*, Bk VI, Ch. 4: 1140A 1–23 for this conception of art.

36. See *Physics*, Book II, Ch. 8: 199A 10–20.

37. See Marcuse's *Eros and Civilization*, and Brown's *Life Against Death*.

38. For a recent discussion of such techniques, see *Psychotechnology: Electronic Control of Mind and Behavior*, edd. Robert L. and Richard K. Schwitzgebel (New York: Holt, Rinehart and Winston, 1973).

39. For a collection of essays in transpersonal psychology, see *Transpersonal Psychologies*, ed. Charles Tart (New York: Harper and Row, 1975).

40. Op. cit.

41. *The Right to be Different: Deviance and Enforced Therapy* (Baltimore: Johns Hopkins University Press, 1971).

42. The assumption seems to be that if it is possible to provide the prisoner techniques for coping successfully with his environment, he will be able to employ these same techniques in meeting the demands of the free

social world. The stress is less upon integrating the individual into a "public" world, and more upon promoting a self-actualized, "private" personality that will not lead to sociopathic behavior.

43. See *Therapeia: Plato's Conception of Philosophy* (Chapel Hill: University of North Carolina Press, 1958) for a discussion of the concept of *therapeia*.

44. This possibility is not as far-fetched as it might seem. Already individuals are beginning to speculate on the need for a transcendence of culture. See Edward T. Hall's *Beyond Culture* (Garden City, N.Y.: Doubleday, 1975). Alvin Toffler's *The Third Wave* (New York: Morrow, 1980) provides numerous illustrations of the collapse of social, political, and cultural consensus in contemporary technological society (see esp. pp. 424 ff.). I have discussed the strictly philosophic implications of the transcendence of culture in my *Eros and Irony: A Prelude to Philosophical Anarchism* (Albany: State University of New York Press, 1982).

45. See *The Civilization of Experience*, p. 73.

7

A Eutopic Vision

BEYOND MALE AND FEMALE

OUR SPECULATIONS concerning the direction of technological society have led to the conclusion that the viability of human existence will increasingly depend upon the manner in which internal and external technologies are brought into a harmonious relationship. Nature as *techne* has both an "Inside" and an "Outside," and the polarity of inside and outside is the teleological notion in terms of which social existence must be characterized if we are to avoid the de-personalizing consequences of the internalization of external technique.

If technological society can serve as the matrix within which there can be an overcoming of the disjunction of persons and nature, then the process of the education of nature, which defines the proper employment of technology, can continue apace. Human beings at peace with their natural ambience can then set about to realize the possible resolution of the other disjunctions that threaten to truncate the process of self-actualization promised by the advance of internal technology.

The process of self-actualization, or self-creativity, depends upon the interpretation of nature-itself as fundamentally self-creative, and the aim of nature as the achievement of balanced intensity of experience. Such an aesthetic interpretation of experience requires that an adequate account of experiencing avoid any notion of a disjunction between the "subjective" and "objective" aspects of attending to the world. Experiencing must itself be an organic activity in which both "self" and "other" are relativized.

One major theme of contemporary philosophy, whether in its analytic, phenomenological, or speculative modes, has been the critique of experience, particularly perceptual experience, and the attempt to provide a non-disjunctive characterization of perceptual activity. In spite of the influence of alternative models such as the Hegelian dialectical analysis or the *coincidentia oppositorum* of the mystical tradition, our fundamental understandings of perceptual experience have tended to be disjunctive rather than polar. It is perhaps inevitable that this be so since the mode of consciousness best suited to both rational science and rationalized activity is the linear, causal form associated with object manipulation rather than the sensuous, spatial, holistic form related to aesthetic receptivity. Rational consciousness is born, after all, from out of the experience of contrast. As Whitehead has said, "Consciousness is the feeling of negation."[1] That is to say, consciousness involves "non-conformal" feelings. The experience of a portion of the perceptual field at the most primitive level is a sense of aesthetic immediacy, which is a receptive experience. A conscious perception involves not only the discrimination of figure and ground, but the stipulation of the perceived object by entertainment of a contrast. The perception of a blue object, therefore, involves not only the judgment, "blue-now," but also the more sophisticated judgment, "not-blue now." The most developed form of consciousness involves the employment of dialectical reasoning in which there is the conscious recognition of a proposition, "not-p," for every "p" that is entertained. Objectivity, then, is simply the recognition of objects. An object is something that *objects*. The objection of the object is a function of the employment of the negative judgment, which involves a conscious contrast between the recognized object and its oppositional possibility. The object objects because it is made to stand out through an act of negative judgment.

The press toward clarity in scientific understandings involves the assertion of contrasts as fundamentally contradictories, and contradictories as disjunctive rather than polar. The account of experience and nature that derives from the creationist perspective outlined throughout these pages demands that aesthetic rather than logical contrasts be held dominant. This means that conjoined perceptions, when propositionally entertained, may not be most fruitfully compared in terms of the characteristics of truth or falsity, but in terms of "interest" and "importance." This is but to say that *contrast* in any of its forms advertises the mutual relevance of the contrasted elements.

The aesthetic model of perception does not require the notion of disjunctive relations in order to interpret the phenomenon of conscious experience. Not only are propositional contrasts interpretable along aesthetic lines, but contrasting modes of perception, such as those mentioned in Chapter 5 in the discussion of "split-brain" research, are likewise to be interpreted aesthetically. Thus the contrasts between propositional and appositional, or digital and analogic, or active and receptive, modes of perception need not be viewed disjunctively. Contrasting modes of perception and consciousness form the basis of an integrated conception of the nature of personality, rather than alternative modes, one of which must dominate the other.

It is important to note that I am not suggesting that we substitute the so-called receptive mode of consciousness for the active mode. The necessity of thinking in such disjunctive terms is itself a consequence of the need to stress the dominance of the active mode in understanding nature and human personality. The vision of a new sensibility I am about to sketch is based on the balancing of the active and the receptive, the yang and the yin, forms of experiencing. Shifting the relative dominance to the receptive mode leads us to stress the necessary balance of each contrasting mode. Historical and cultural contingencies may well have determined that Anglo-European cultures have developed in accordance with an overemphasis upon disjunctive interpretations of experience and the consequent selection of only one of the polar elements defining experiencing as an organic whole. But changes in the form and character of technological society may be such as to provide the basis for a fuller realization of the aesthetic unity of experiencing.

The principal changes in the cultural context relevant to the search for a fuller conception of human personality have been those that challenge the agonal conception of human beings, whose "humanity" is measured in terms of struggle and the quest for greatness. The decreased importance of the public sphere as an arena for self-actualization through active engagement with the world has brought us to a situation wherein we may examine alternative models of personality. One of the most significant of these models is that which calls into question the concept of personality as a gender-related notion. The burgeoning interest in the question of "androgyny" in contemporary discussions of self-actualized individuals suggests that we are ready to attempt an integration of what has been traditionally thought to be essentially disjoined modes of existence.

It is, of course, Carl Jung among Western psychologists who has done most with the notion of the complementarity of the sexes within the single individual. According to the Jungian theory, there is an *anima*, or female counterpart, complementing every masculine *animus*. In the "normal" male the *anima* is unconscious and can be raised to the level of consciousness only with great difficulty, and then usually only late in life. The situation is the same for the female, whose conscious *anima* is contrasted with an unconscious *animus*. In heterosexual relationships, one's choice of mates is in large measure determined by the nature of one's unconscious contrasexual nature. Psychic integration, which at the level of sexual complementarity consists in raising to consciousness one's unconscious complement, results in a kind of autonomy in which one is no longer dependent upon the other sex. Conscious devotion replaces the blind passion that either is based in an unconscious eros driving one to pursue and win one's projected and externalized "other half," or else is grounded in the masochistic self-abnegation of a perverted agape. The realization of philia as a love among equals must await, therefore, the intrapsychic actualization of the masculine–feminine polarity. Equality, the presupposition of true individuality, depends upon the differential excellences grounded in the masculine and feminine experiences being actualized within the same personality structure.

I do not wish to indicate that the vision I am supporting must be interpreted in Jungian terms. The speculative notions I am employing are sufficiently broad and multi-valent to conform to several alternative theories of contrasexual polarity. All such theories receive their primary motivation and support by resort to the mythical substratum that attests the psychic importance of our androgynous beginnings. The principal myth of androgynous beginnings, as far as our own cultural heritage is concerned, is Aristophanes' myth, rehearsed in a previous chapter. It is but one of many that can be found by the most cursory examination of cosmogonic myths.

> Primeval man was held by the Babylonians to have been androgynous. Thus the *Gilgamesh Epic* gives Enkidu androgynous features. . . . The Hebrew tradition (a portion of which holds that Adam was originally created as an androgyne of Male and Female bodies joined back to back) evidently derives from Greek sources, because both terms used in a Tannaitic midrash to describe the bi-sexual Adam are Greek. . . . Philo of Alexandria, the Hellenistic philosopher and commentator on the Bible, contemporary with Jesus, held that man was first bisexual; so did the Gnostics.[2]

In the myths of androgynous beginnings, perfect humanity is conceived as a Wholeness in which both sexes are conjoined. Hesiod's *Theogony*, we may recall, tells of the creation of the world through the separation of Earth and Sky, female and male principles, respectively. The primordial totality contained all oppositional states within it. There is even the suggestion of this in the writings of St. Paul: "There is neither Jew nor Greek, there is neither bond nor free, there is neither male nor female: for you are all one in Christ Jesus" (Gal.

3:28). Though Paul could well here be referring to the *dissolution* of sexuality in the redeemed Christian, the Gnostic commentators contemporary with Paul explicitly favored the androgynous interpretation of perfected humanity. "Christ came to re-establish what was thus [divided] in the beginning and to reunite the two. Those who died because they were in separation he will restore to life by uniting them."[3] Such a reading of our mythical substratum would suggest a reinterpretation of the Genesis myth. Our new reading would require that we no longer identify the Fall with the eating of the fruit of the Tree of the Knowledge of Good and Evil, which led human beings to be punished by the twin curses of labor in the fields and pain in child-bearing. The Fall occurred, rather, when the Creator solved the problem of man's loneliness by the only expedient available to human existence: the making of an external *other*, as a means of completing the lonely man.

Always accompanying these myths of androgyny, there are significant rituals that have as their primary purpose the symbolic reintegration of opposites. Some of these rituals take place at the time of puberty; some are associated with shamanistic functions in which the shaman takes on both male and female characteristics. However performed, the function is to achieve "a ritual 'totalization,' a reintegration of opposites. . . . It is in fact, a symbolic restoration of 'Chaos,' of the undifferentiated unity that preceded the creation."[4] Here we meet the alternative conception of Chaos, that of undifferentiated homogeneity. And we meet it in those myths and rituals that stress the unification of opposites: the myths of polarity. We have stressed again and again throughout this work the radical distinction between those conceptions of chaos that stress overcoming through control, and those that seek a return to chaos through a complementary union of polar opposites that recalls the primordial homogeneity of the world "before" creation. The *coincidentia oppositorum*, celebrated as a mystical doctrine in Cusanus, a philosophical principle in Hegel, and a psychological concept in Jung, is grounded, *mythically*, in the primordial wish for self-fulfillment through the reintegration of opposites through contrasexual union.

The most sophisticated combination of the mythical,

spiritual, psychological, and philosophical techniques for the re-integration of sexual polarities is to be found in the tantric tradition developed in Tibet from the ninth to the mid-twentieth centuries.[5] The goal of tantric practices is to achieve a psychic and spiritual union of the masculine and feminine aspects of one's nature. Tantric practices have often been criticized for stressing overmuch the physical sexual union in ritualistic activity. But the testimony of the mystical and speculative wing of tantrism is clear: the union is symbolic of internal integration. Texts that speak of union with the female, for example, must interpret the term "female" as

> . . . all the elements which make up the female principles of our psycho-physical personality which, as the Buddha says, represents what is called "the world." To these principles correspond on the opposite side an equal number of male principles. . . . In other words, instead of seeking union with a woman outside ourselves, we have to seek it *within ourselves* . . . by the union of our male and female nature in the process of meditation.[6]

Expressed in the notion of the self-fulfillment of the human personality through contrasexual union is the fundamental possibility of resolving the dilemma associated with the element of passion in the history of our culture. For the female the element of passion has received its most acceptable, and most frequent, fulfillment in the process of *procreation*. Aesthetic creativity has substituted in males for the defect in procreative function. But that creativity has functioned under the guise of power since the productions of art have, insofar as they have found their place in the sphere of culture, been means for the achievement of greatness.

The status of our emerging technological society is such, however, that we may be in a position to bypass a number of heretofore immovable barriers on our way to self-fulfillment. That is to say many of the arguments that would lead us to believe in the necessity of the current division of *labor* among the sexes simply no longer carry any weight. The imminent collapse of the public sphere as the medium for the achievement of greatness will preclude the necessity for the promotion of singularly masculine (i.e., aggressive, agonal) behaviors. We have alluded to this fact at various points throughout these pages. Of interest here is the implication of advanced technology that the peculiarly feminine aspect of the procreative function will also be transcended.

One of the most striking consequences of our advancing technology is the fact that it is now possible, at least in principle, to free the female from the necessity to bear children. Pressures of population growth require that we stress some other than the procreative motive in sexual relations. But most of all, it is the possibility of extra-uterine procreation that frees both male and female from their well-defined sexual roles. The introduction of sperm and egg into a neutral environment removes the burden of childbearing from the female. Under such conditions the task of raising children now becomes one that can be performed cooperatively by males and females. The differences between male and female, once the childbearing function has been removed, largely reduces to differences in primary sexual characteristics and the emotional patterns these characteristics may involve. These differences are hardly as radical as they appear. And these differences can be adjusted by the procedure of hormonal therapies that exploit the inherent hormonal eco-systems in each individual to create the personality pattern most expressive of his or her propensities.

Even if it is shown that there are viable techniques for the production of children in extra-uterine fashion, there are, of course, still arguments that claim male–female sex-role differentiation is necessary if children are to have normal development. This kind of thinking is most often conjoined with two other assumptions—viz., that sex-role differentiation should be associated with the possession of primary physiological characteristics consistent with the sex-role identification (i.e., that ostensible males assume fathering roles and ostensible females assume mothering functions), and, second, that the mothering and fathering roles be played out within the context of the primary family unit.

There is a great deal of evidence that has been gathered of late that directly contradicts the claims that strong sex-role differentiation according to gender is a requisite for normal maturation processes. The Freudian claim that a normal out-working of the Oedipal situation requires the presence of both male and female figures within the home can, of course, be taken as true without convincing anyone of the importance of a successful outworking of the Oedipal situation. Indeed the existence of the Oedipal situation itself is due to the anteced-ent significance of the family unit. Given the results of Oedipal conflict in some instances, we might find reason to challenge the necessity of the family unit on these grounds alone! But there is some direct evidence that claims the healthiest social and interpersonal situation to be one in which the participants are possessed of a high degree of both masculine and feminine personality traits and attitudes.

Speculations concerning the notion of androgynous personality can be found among physiologists, psychologists, sociologists, and literary critics in addition to the mythologists and philosophers already cited.[7] The most significant of the conclusions drawn by these researches is that there are in-herent limitations to the attempt to correlate sex-roles with gender-identity. That is to say, traits identifiable as masculine and feminine should not be manifest according to specific gender, but each gender ought to possess *both* masculine and feminine characteristics and behaviors. The attitudinal or behavioral androgyne is apparently more successful in responding to the variable demands made by a pluralistic society.

One must be careful not to confuse the concept of an-drogyny with that of sexual non-differentiation. One of the consequences of the decreasing emphasis upon the specializa-tion of masculine and feminine roles according to gender could be that we will begin to see increasing numbers of individuals who are psychosexual neuters. Such individuals are to be found among the "super-cool" members of the current generation of college students who manifest the notoriously flat affect that is a symptom of a weakened sense of identity. Androgynous personality, on the other hand, is grounded in a sense of self that is capable of responding appropriately in situations demanding either classically masculine or feminine behavior.

It should not be in the least surprising that individuals who realize their contrasexual potentialities may in fact be more successful in adapting to the ambience of contemporary society. Nor should we be surprised at the intense interest in developing androgynous models of personality. The surprise, indeed the shock, many of us must feel when confronting the issue of sexuality in its contemporary context is due to the profound social and technical changes that have recently rendered even the most radical of our speculations so disturbingly relevant.

The androgynous unity celebrated in myth was, heretofore, not within the realm of possibility. It is now not only a psychological and behavioral possibility, but a physiological possibility as well. If we consider the recent developments in transsexual surgery and medicine, we shall see just how far we are capable of moving in the direction of the completely androgynous personality. Sex-change operations that alter ostensible male to ostensible female can now provide a functioning vagina, complete with clitoris (the surgically revised *glans penis* inserted and mounted within the "vagina"). Hormonal therapies support and sustain the primary psychological tendencies toward contra-sexual manifestation that normally functions as the reason for desiring the sex change. The problem of providing ostensible females who wish to alter their ostensible sexual character with an erectible penis has not, as yet, been satisfactorily resolved, but few researchers in this area would doubt that it is only a matter of time until the technical difficulties will be overcome.

The question of the birthing function presents the greatest difficulty, of course. The myth of androgynous beginnings as expressed by Aristophanes, however, includes the implication that "sexual generation is an accidental by-product of the absence of true harmony between men and women, who in their longing for each other seek to recapture the unity of the androgyne rather than an imperfect reduplication of their sundered selves in children. Sexual generation is thus the mark of imperfection in man's current nature."[8]

Prior to the splitting of the circle beings, sexual generation was achieved by the spilling of seed upon the ground. The return to the possibility of androgyny in advanced technological culture includes the possibility of realizing a special form of technical onanism in which the seeds of human generation are cast to the procreative machinery of the genetic engineers. There is no necessity to believe that such radical uses of external technologies are de-humanizing. It is quite possible that they might be employed as means of self-actualization. The crucial issue in such uses of technology is whether they are freely chosen or imposed by recourse to some external norm.

The resolution of the problem of the relation of male and female that has historically existed under the twin aspects of the curse of labor, provides the basis for the resolution of the fundamental distortions of aesthetic experience and expression that have plagued us from the beginning. Creativity and procreativity have been exercised by the male and female respectively in manners that have more often than not come directly in conflict with the desire for self-actualization. The goal of self-actualization has always eluded us because of the basic defect in us caused by our inherent sex-role differentiations reflected in, and in part a consequence of, the singularity of our sexual self-concept. The necessity to manifest sexual attitudes consonant with our ostensible sexual status as physiological beings has been tied to the inherent division of labor, and the consequent handling of the organization of the public and private spheres of existence. But the necessity for this specialization and organization is no longer felt in a society patterned by the ubiquity of *labor*-saving techniques.

The future psychological development of human beings as they attempt to remold their expressions of passion into an explicitly androgynous art need no longer be frustrated by the demands of procreativity as a substitute for aesthetic production, nor by creativity construed more after the fashion of exercises in affirmation that have as their goal stamping one's image upon the world. Platonic Eros, expressed either in the desire for children to carry one's image beyond the span of the parent's years, or as the artist's desires to remold and remake a part of the world after the fashion of one's own nature, may cease to define the nature of aesthetic activity in contemporary society.

The basic mode of aesthetic experience is what we have

before termed "enstatic." Enstasy is the manner in which meaning and significance is experienced *within*. It is the experience of oneself as the locus of intensity. The enstatic experience has not been possible to those incapable of attitudinal androgyny. Non-androgynous individuals have had to be content with the vicarious experience of either the procreative or the creative function. A functionally bisexual society is one in which the union of the sexes is experienced within a single individual and not between two individuals. The search for one's "other half" ceases when one looks within. The enstatic experience of bisexual integration is the paradigm for personal fulfillment in the future. And if we achieve the enstatic, bisexual, unity that is the pressing goal of human existence, we shall be prepared for the other two modalities of experience open to individuals in the future—viz., the ecstatic experience of otherness and the constatic experience of reciprocal interfusion.

The necessity of psychic and attitudinal androgyny is grounded in the concept of self-creativity as a praxis which is to be interpreted as *aisthesis*. When in a former discussion I identified *aisthesis* with the notion of preoccupation as a subjective form of feeling the world, I argued, by implication, for a fullness of potential forms of preoccupation. One of the principal conditions for such fullness is the achievement of contra-sexual integration. The attitudinal androgyne possesses the full range of aesthetic possibilities for preoccupation, by virtue of an integration of the fundamental polarities that characterize not only our modes of sexuality, but our modes of experiencing the world.

As long as one may justifiably claim that the distinction between ostensible male and ostensible female masks an important *functional* difference, then it will remain impossible to argue for the fullness of individual experiencing. The self-creative activity that defines nature must allow for the transcendence of the contrasexual "other" functioning as *arche*, or determining principle. If I can only experience my sexual *alter* vicariously, I must always be partly determined by her. Likewise, if I am forced, in principle, to experience my *alter* ecstatically, then I have not achieved ecstasy, but suffered alienation.[9]

The argument for androgynous models of personality has as its *least* essential consequence the more direct forms of sexual behavior. Bisexual activity manifest as hetero- and homosexual behaviors performed by the same individual is, though a possible implication of the arguments for functional androgyny, not in the least a requirement of the view I have been expressing. The fundamental consequence of the realization of androgyny will be found in the possibility of organic experiencing that transcends the dichotomy of self and other by providing a paradigm for active and passive, yang and yin, aspects of experience within the same personality structure. The possibility of the *blending* of experiences through ecstatic activity is grounded upon the possibility of *centered* experience, which can only be truly centered if it is the focus of a circle encompassing each of the fundamental elements characterizing the polarities of human experience.

The basic form of enstasy is expressed through *wu-yü*, that kind of feeling that is neither an emotion responding to an external stimulus nor an affective state serving as an agent conditioning external response. *Wu-yü* is *sui generis*, and is neither cause nor effect of conditions beyond itself. There can be no mutuality in the sense of inter-personal communion if there is not solitariness grounded in the enstatic sense of excellence. Such a sense is possible only if one's experiencing contains both the active and the receptive elements of experience within the same aesthetic event. The person as androgyne is nothing more nor less than the self-creative event that serves as the fundamental process in terms of which reality is to be understood.

At the close of the discussion on the conflict between the male and female in Chapter 3, I recalled that, as victims of the "further division" threatened by Zeus, the primary goal of sexuality had come to be expressed in terms of self-unification. Obviously such self-integration cannot be achieved if we depend upon the sociological and political modes of relationship that have characterized our classical understandings of eros. Nor can we accept psychological models such as the Freudian. Though we may still believe with Heraclitus that "character is fate," we are certainly no longer able to take seriously the notion that "anatomy is destiny." We are free to

alter our anatomy and physiology in order to suit our "character." And we are fated to do so. And what *is* our character
but that of the androgynous center of experiencing out of
which human existence emerged in order that it might play out
the divisive struggle of the active and the passive, the ruler
and the ruled, the masculine and the feminine, which has
constituted the interlude of *his*-story as a forced march toward
psychic integration?

ALIENATION AND ECSTASY

Perhaps the most significant consequence of the story of technological development as it is currently unfolding in contemporary Anglo-European societies is that it suggests a way of
realizing the full potentialities of individual existence. The
suggestion of androgynous personality as the basis for enstatic
experiencing, and as a model for the achievement of balanced
intensity, is but one way, however, of pluralizing and intensi-
fying the self-creative activity of individuals. In the potential
resolution of the conflict between the individual and his social
ambience we can discover yet another means of promoting
individual self-creativity.

Aristotle's poignant insight to the effect that "if shuttles
weaved of themselves" slavery would be unnecessary has
been more than vindicated through technological developments. Indeed, it is now possible to believe that in a society
patterned by the ubiquity of technical means, there may be the
increased freedom from forced dependence. Examining some
of the consequences for the understanding of individual existence of this relative increase in the freedom from unwilling
dependence will lead us into a consideration of the value of
ecstatic experiencing for the realization of self-creativity.

One of the most overused of the ideological catchwords
employed to characterize social existence in our industrial and
early technological period is the term "alienation." Philosophers, theologians, psychologists, sociologists, and historians have used the concept with a range of associations
derived from various sources: Marxist materialism, human-

istic existentialism, Hegelian idealism, and even from the pragmatism of James, Peirce, and Dewey. In terms of the arguments presented thus far in this work, the problem of healing the breach between individual and social existence may be most fruitfully posed in terms of the question, "How may we understand social existence in such a fashion as to articulate the possibility of moving from a mode of existence characterized by alienation in its various forms to a style of living patterned by ecstasy?" That this is an extremely felicitous manner of posing the problem may be seen from an examination of some of the historical connections between the concepts of alienation and ecstasy.[10]

In early neo-Platonic theology, the Latin term *alienatio* was used in the same sense as the Greek *ekstasis*. As Nathan Rotenstreich notes, Plotinus and his disciples had employed the term *ekstasis* in a manner consistent with Augustine's use of *alienatio*, as in phrases such as *alienatio mentis a corpore*. Both the Latin and the Greek terms indicate the condition associated with submergence of the human soul in the Divine.[11]

The separation of the meanings of alienation and ecstasy which today we take for granted, must be credited to Hegel, according to Rotenstreich. For Hegel, ecstasy is associated with the transcendence of only the emotional and imaginative aspects of thought. *Theoria*, which for Plotinus and his followers had meant the transcendent contemplation of the essences of things, is taken by Hegel to be realizable within the reasoning process itself. Or as Rotenstreich states: "Hegel understood ecstasy as the subsistence of thought by itself, whereas the ancients understood ecstasy as the alienating and elevating transcendence of thought."[12]

In this view alienation becomes a necessary stage on the way to final unity of the knower and the known. Alienation involves "the diffusion of the Spirit outside itself,"[13] which involves the creation of the structures of nature and history. Legitimate, as opposed to illegitimate, alienation involves the externalization of possessions that are not of the essence of the human subject. In this view, man's rationality, his essential self-determination, and so on, constitute inalienable aspects of his nature that cannot be legitimately alienated. Those forms of alienation that promoted the enrichment of rationality are viewed, therefore, as means toward the end of the ecstatic actualization of the unity of the knower and the known within the realm of what Hegel termed Absolute Spirit. For Hegel, then, "the transcendent realm of history and nature is created and . . . exists only as subservient to the return into himself of the creating subject." [14]

Feuerbach, as Rotenstreich notes, accepted the Hegelian view that transcendence was *created*, but for Feuerbach, this creation involves the projection of the essence of man and its hypostatization into an imaginary entity, "God." Alienation, then, involves the relationship of man to an imaginary essence. In this sense, alienation is seen to receive a critical assessment. Feuerbach's prediction that anthropology would eventually replace theology involved the claim that "self-knowing immanence [would] replace its own reflections in alienation." [15] It is this interpretation of alienation that is, perhaps, most influential in the existential tradition. [16] Inauthentic human existence leads to alienation because it involves the living of one's life in terms of an abstract essence or set of essences—from the grandest of Ideals to the most degrading of slogans—rather than in terms of the existential open-ended project that is life itself. Of course, the existentialists of the non-theistic variety went much further than Feuerbach by claiming that persons had no essence in the truest sense; they possessed only their own concrete existences construed as ambiences of open possibilities.

Marx's concept of alienation was grounded in the historical forms of domination or oppression that led to humans' being subjected to alien powers in the guise of other persons. When the products of one's hands and the relational structures of an economic order function as external sources of control, alienation exists as an intrinsic part of society. "Thus the circle is closed, and alienation qua relatedness to transcendence becomes alienation qua human creativity and creation, as perceived in a perverted manner." [17]

Modern thought has been patterned by the conceptions of alienation deriving from Marx and the existentialists. The former has stressed that Man is a product of society and social forces; the latter has stressed the internality of the notions of freedom and authenticity. To be free of alienation, according to the Marxist persuasion, one must alter the structure of society; from the existentialist point of view at least a change of consciousness and intention is involved. But for both of these modern views, alienation is certainly to be distinguished from the experience of ecstasy with which, in the contemplative tradition, it had once been identified.

My arguments concerning human existence in its relation to social order have derived from a semantic context at variance with each of the major philosophic alternatives dominating Anglo-European intellectual culture. The principal defect in accounts of individual and social existence, from the perspective of a philosophy of creativity, is the presupposition each of the dominant philosophical views contains concerning the *substantiality* of the individual. It is this assumption that precludes, oddly enough, the realization of true individuality, since the maintenance of some form of social order or public realm is necessary upon which individual personality is dependent for its generation and within which the individual realizes his principal goals as a substantial being.

The conception of self-creativity as the primary notion in terms of which individual existence is to be understood precludes the interpretation of individual existence in substantialist terms. The primary characteristics of any self-creative being—and we must suppose this holds pre-eminently for human beings—are freedom, transience, and novel purpose. Creativity as a reflexive concept guarantees that freedom will be realized in terms of self-actualization. But the fact that experiencing is construed in terms of the activity of intuition rather than that of reason requires that experiencing be fundamentally *process*. The denial of rationality as the primary character of experience and nature involves the denial of principles as external sources of order and thus entails the consequence that each aesthetic event will constitute its own source of order and novelty.

The necessity for identifying selfhood and *substans* was suggested by our discussions of the history of the disciplining

of chaos in Chapter 2. There we discovered a virtual consensus among thinkers such as Adkins, Snell, Dodds,
Cassirer, and Gouldner that the development of human personality in the Western context was a story of the transition
"from the many to the one." The psyche was originally a
loose bundle of transient states whose locus was the individual
whose deeds were subject to remembrance and narrative. The
individual was one who "stood out," and whose outstanding
character could be celebrated in story. The development of
consensual norms of greatness in art, morality, religion, and
the intellectual realm, which were then actualized in the social
and political arena, was the pre-condition for the realization of
a personality persisting through time.

The notion of the self as a loosely knit fabric of experiences has persisted in certain exotic views from the very
beginnings. Hume's vision of the self as but a "bundle of
perceptions," much celebrated but seldom taken seriously,
seems much less esoteric when placed in the context of
phenomena such as the increasing recognition of multiple
personalities existing in the "same" bodily organization, and
the increased credibility of the notion of reincarnation with its
assumption of the "same" spiritual identity existing through
various instantiations of bodily organization. Indeed, we do
not have to go to anywhere near such extreme views to recognize the viability of the process theory of selfhood.

One of the most straightforward presentations of this vision of personal identity has it that the self is less like a
substance persisting through time, and more like a "career" of
separate events.[18] What we normally call the self is in fact an
abstraction that names the class of all transient states linked
by sequential relations that define a set of genetically ordered
events. A person is known to be the same individual from one
point in time to another if the sequence of experiences that led
from the antecedent to the consequent moment can be traced.
And if the sequence of events cannot be traced? In such an
instance it makes little sense to insist that the person is identical with his presumptive former self.

The substance view of the self stresses the notion that
personal identity establishes a locus of responsibility. The

process view of selfhood allows for radical conversions that could completely transform the nature of the person from one moment to the next. It is easy to see how such a view would be little appreciated in societies that depend upon moral and legal obligations for their stability. It is the institutional commitments of the individual that guarantee that he will persist in essentially the same type of behavior from one day to the next. His acceptance of consensual values, a common language, continued membership in stable organizations, a permanent name, a social security number, and so on, ensures that he will be identifiably the same person from moment to moment and year to year.

It is hardly an accident that so many contemporary interpretations of human personality are drawing upon the process vision of the self. The notion that a person is fundamentally a *career*, rather than a substantial *thing*, recalls the sort of interpretation of human existence relevant to ancient and primitive societies and suggests, in fact, that we are returning to more "primitive" modes of social existence. Paradoxical only to some is the fact that technological society, with its stress upon functionality expressed in terms of its emphasis upon *use* over possession, *technical rules* over politically sanctioned laws, *ritualistic activity associated with the co-operation with technical processes* over rational decisions promoting public actions, de-substantializes human existence. The result is a movement "from the one to the many."

The process view of the self obviously has many implications for the relation between the individual and society, not the least of which is that the initial society to which an individual is related is that formed by the temporal sequence of events constituting the career that is the personal history of the individual in question. The fundamental form of social relationship in this case is that existing between the past occasion of the self and its immediate successor. That form of relatedness is "ecstatic" since the reference of the relationship is "outside," in the sense of *beyond*, one's immediate experience. Such relations are manifest in the sphere of the private as opposed to the public arena.

In a technological society of the type we have been

assuming, wherein the externalization of reason has reached its culmination, the end of the public sphere as a human sphere of communication will have been reached in principle. Whatever forms of public interchange still continue will have no specifically human or personal significance; they will receive their meaning from the technological apparatus they must, perforce, serve. The threat of alienation in a society of the type here presupposed derives from the extent to which the public realm, as an abstract consensual realm, determines a sphere of stipulated excellences serving as loci of experiencing for the individuals of a society. For alienation is nothing more than *forced ecstasy*.

In technological society it may be possible to see again the relationship between alienation and ecstasy. If it is the case that one is freed to be a career of selves strung out in time; if the open possibilities of existence are such that one does not have to be constrained to win for oneself but a single, solitary identity, it may be possible to live from moment to moment and to experience the joy of transcending oneself—this time not in terms of an *alienatio mentis a corpore*, but an *alienatio mentis a mente*! The change in the form of social relationships consequent upon the emergence of technological society can signal a change in consciousness which again raises the possibility of the positive experience of alienation as ecstasy.

We have but to recall the discussion of the development of the concept of selfhood and self-consciousness considered in Chapter 2 of this work in order to recognize the conceivability of human existence as patterned by process rather than substance forms of personality structure. The stage of technological growth into which we have so recently entered is one that shall emphasize the possibilities of the experience of the world in a direct, aesthetic fashion rather than through the theoretical or practical exercises we have employed for so long as the means of relating to our world. Theoretical knowledge and practical activities both require the pre-eminence of an objective, objectified world. The objects of knowledge and action have a separate existence and as such can be appropriated for one's knowledge or use.

The possibility of knowledge depends upon the existence of principles that, as the beginning points of thought, serve as the primary means of organizing our otherwise disconnected bits of information. The knowledge of principles, which is the mark of an educated man, constitutes the primary means whereby a constant and consistent idea of substantiality of self derives. We are not subject to the vagaries of disparate facts because we have principles that bring order into our understanding. But at the most fundamental level these principles are the foundations of the very possibility of knowing itself.

If we believed with Immanuel Kant that such structures were permanent and unchanging, we should have no problem affirming the substantiality of the psyche. But we have learned too much about the relativity of conceptual structures in the last two centuries to be able to accept that Kantian assumption in its strongest form. Indeed it is possible to go beyond the conceptual pragmatists who, in denying that a single set of categories of interpretation are necessary to define the possibilities of authentic understanding, made a firm step beyond the idealist interpretation of mind and its relation to the order of our understandings of the world. It is possible now to believe that the structures that once defined the possibility of knowledge have been poured into the world and that the theoretical understandings of human existence have been, or are in the process of being, realized in the self-augmenting developments in technology. Practice motivated by the desire for greatness has found its fulfillment in the structures of technological society. The theoretical interlude that defines the largest segment of human history was itself a product of these practical motives, and a necessary prerequisite to their realization.

With the advent of technological society we may well say that we have overcome the curse of labor placed upon human existence at its very beginning. The desire for greatness as a desire to rewin one's place in paradise has led to the re-creation of the garden of Eden; a kind of artificial paradise, of course, but paradise nonetheless. It may now be possible to *forget* what we learned by eating of the forbidden fruit. We can forget the knowledge of Good and Evil, and return to the primordial innocence that was once ours. Reason and moral inhibition are the sources (as well as the consequences) of the development of the substantial self. Rationality implies an objective, constant world to be known as well as the constancy of the self achieved through the structures (theoretical principles) comprising the possibility of knowledge. Moral inhibition entails the delimitation of the self in relation to norms defining what is and what is not permissible. The Return to the Garden involves the return to the innocence of primordial existence. Rationality and moral constraint have served us well. Technology, the product of the historical quest for greatness, patterned by the need first to survive and second to increase one's satisfactions, provides us with a new "nature" within which we may redefine our existence as human beings.

Techne is *physis*. Nature, as a constatic union of reciprocally interfused existences, is now to be understood solely in terms of its realization in and through technology. Technology is the education of nature. But, as we have already emphasized, the final understanding both of nature and of technology that leads to their identification is that *nature educates itself*. Man is no longer the measure of all things. Nature, as technological society, is the matrix of possibilities we have previously identified with the sum of all orders; it is the actualization of chaos. As such it is the *fundamentum* from which all construals are to be made. The necessity of upholding a firm conception of selfhood, along substantialist lines, would directly militate against the ability to exercise any number of options. The conception of *wu-chih*—unprincipled knowledge grounded in theorial rather than theoretical experience—presupposes the conception of *wu-wei*—that non-assertive activity that seeks to walk the ways of all things rather than to exercise power over them. And both *wu-chih* and *wu-wei* presuppose *wu-yü*, the fundamental form of the enstatic experience.

The possibility of realizing ecstasy and avoiding negative forms of alienation is grounded in the androgynous personality that makes enstasy possible. Ecstasy involves referring one's experience either *beyond* or *outside* one's present self. In the first instance the locus of experiencing is referred to a future self-creative experience. This is the experience of anticipated excellence. It is to be identified with the experience of the self-at-the-present-moment referred to a possible future experiencing of a member of the personal ordering of aesthetic events one understands as one's self-through-time. The second instance is associated with the present experiencing, which leads the individual to refer his experience to a locus of recognized excellence outside himself.

The intrinsic connection of alienation and ecstasy should now be quite obvious: Ecstasy is the experience in another (whether that other be another human being, a natural or "artificial" object, or oneself in the immediate future) of meaning and value, which can serve as the basis for thinking, acting, or feeling that freely takes the experience of that other into account. Alienation, on the other hand, is the forced or otherwise involuntary experience in and through another. Ecstasy is a free creative move beyond the self-at-the-moment; alienation involves other-determination. The constraint of external imposition, whether in the form of irrational violence or through the structures of law and sanctions, contravenes the possibility of the experience of ecstasy.

In this view, then, ecstasy is the form taken by experience leading to *wu-wei*, or action in accordance with the present natures of things. It is easy to understand how such a form of social activity has been impossible for most individuals throughout the greater part of history. *Wu-wei* requires that each individual be taken on its own terms; moreover, since each individual exists, as subject, only at the moment, each individual moment must involve new possibilities for experience and action. In a society that maintains a set of constant norms for human thought and action, *wu-wei*, *wu-chih*, and *wu-yü* are rarely possible. In a technically structured society in which the primary forms of publicly relevant order have been externalized, the likelihood of a variety of possible actions in response to the ecstatic experience of the other becomes possible. But, as should be obvious, this type of techno-structure can only be relevant in a society without a set of defining characteristics universally applicable to the members of the society. And if there is no generally applicable set of aims or interests that define human social thought and activity, and their products, then *there can be no culture*.

One of the main purposes of this book has been to chart those important developments in Anglo-European culture that have led to our present experience of the necessity to transcend the structures of our culture. We are now in a position to realize that the transcendence of our cultural forms is the transcendence of the very idea of culture. This should come as no great surprise, since, from the very first pages of this work we have been subjected to the view that it is the arbitrary, or at least *unnecessary*, presumption of the beginnings of our experience as requiring an encounter with chaos as confusion and disorder that has resulted in the cultural aims and interests that define not only our form of culture, but the very possibility of culture itself.

Culture will no longer be a viable concept in the future we have been envisioning, since the unit of social existence is no longer to be found in either substantive personalities or institutions stably existing through time, or in the ideas or actions that produce events or institutions recorded as paradigmatic for a society. Nor, for that matter, is the basic social unit to be any permanent or subsisting entity that determines the form of conglomerates of a society. With the realization of technology, culture has returned to nature. But the "nature" to which it has returned is one defined not in terms of atoms, or ideas, or organic patterns, or even by the volitional activities of its members. Nature, which in the projected future of advanced technological society will realize the fulfillment of cultural activity and preclude the necessity for the continuation of cultural existence, is the field of self-creative, reciprocally interfused, events of experience, which, as "the sum of all orders," is the ground of all harmony.

An individual conceived after the pattern of a sequence or career of experiences is capable of radical dissociation from his immediate past from moment to moment throughout his life. Unless there is a consensual realm characterized by cultural aims or ideals that are institutionalized in such manner as to direct, *in principle*, the interests and activities of individuals who are willy-nilly members of the society or culture so defined, there will be no necessity, perhaps no real possibility, of maintaining a substantial self through time.

The key questions concerning our interpretation of social existence as a process leading from alienation toward increasing possibilities of ecstasy are these: Is a consensual realm that as public world provides an objective characterization of the nature of human existence necessary to the survival and well-being of individuals? Second, is the realization of such a consensual realm a viable possibility for the present or immediate future? Third, we must ask a question that by its very nature suggests the manner in which the first two questions are to be answered: In the absence of a consensual realm, is there any means of maintaining individual existence as autonomous and self-creative?

The externalization of rational forms of technology, and the realization of the possibility of employing this technological substratum as a protective structure within which to begin the development of nascent forms of internal technologies aimed at self-creativity, provide the primary reasons for believing that a consensual realm as source of general principles defining social activity and its products will be increasingly unnecessary in the future. Moreover, the pluralization of intellectual culture and the realization of the conflicting norms and principles deriving from contradictory theoretical systems, phenomena advertised repeatedly throughout these pages, suggest that no consensus would even be possible. The hope for the promotion of individual self-creativity is based in the fact that rational technologies, as external products of reason, do not have intrinsic to them the aim of controlling or dominating, or otherwise construing the uniqueness and novelty that characterize human experience in its non-rational modes. The emptying of rationality into the world frees us from the constraints of reason while providing us with the comforts of its stabilizing and securing structures.

The process conception of selfhood is in agreement with Heraclitus' dictum, "One cannot step twice into the same river," stressing, however, the essential point that the self as well as the river "flows on." A substantial self facing our world of rapid change can only meet the future with anxiety and thereby suffer alienation. But to the person in process it is unnecessary to live against the future. Not *sub-stans*, but *ek-stasis* provides the sense of identity in a society at home with its technological developments.

A process-oriented society is *anarchistic* in the sense we have been employing the term in this work. No external principles construe individuals as centers of aesthetic activity; the individual is the only real *arche*. Such a view necessarily has striking, if not disturbing, consequences for the notion of moral responsibility. The ethical tradition from which Anglo-European culture has drawn is so pervaded by the presumption of the substantiality of the self that it is difficult to consider the question of moral responsibility from a process orientation without seeming to do violence to the very notion of our concepts of duty, obligation, and responsibility. Indeed, there is no exaggeration in saying that a complete understanding of the process vision of nature and society would preclude even raising the question of ethical norms and values in anything like the traditional manner. The reason for this, of course, is that a process view of the nature of things requires resort to an aesthetic model of understanding; and to put it as straightforwardly as possible: Goodness cannot be one of the aims of art. The balanced intensity that is the aim of experience is an aesthetic, not a moral, aim. This understanding of morality is, of course, not only radically contextual, but the context within which moral questions might emerge is one already conditioned by the aesthetic aim, which is that of self-creativity as the means of realizing balanced intensity of experiencing.

Contextual ethicists argue that the content of an ethical action or decision ought to derive from the specific context within which one finds oneself. Most contextualists, however, are not without a *formal* principle (usually characterized in terms of interpersonal love). But from the creationist perspective, there is lacking even a formal principle for the guidance of ethical conduct. It is precisely the personal character of human interrelationships that precludes the perpetuation of principles. Love, least of all, can be such a principle. For "love . . . is a little oblivious as to morals." [19]

The question of morality is never directly raised in the view we are presupposing largely because the conception of *wu-wei* previously considered precludes the necessity of moral norms. Interpreting experience in terms of enstatic, ecstatic, and constatic modes, which may be articulated in terms of the notions of *wu-yü, wu-wei,* and *wu-chih,* allows for the elaboration of an understanding of ethical action and sensibility grounded in the possibility of an individual's choosing the loci of excellences that will pattern his ambience, as well as the style of deference with which he will celebrate them. The presumption of a social context allowing for such an unprincipled existence is unquestionably the most radical aspect of the creationist social theory here adopted. It would, of course, be foolish to believe that we have reached a point in the development of technological society where we can consider individuals generally capable of living the kind of aesthetic existence we are currently considering. I merely hold that the kind of developments I am discussing may serve to inform our future if human beings come through the present crisis credited with more than mere survival.

A truly pluralistic society, possessed of myriad and fluctuating excellences, calling for ecstatic experiencing grounded not in an enforced consensus but in individual acts of deference, would decrease the incidence of alienation and free individuals, as temporal societies of self-creative events, to realize the aim of experience at balanced intensity. Before discounting this characterization of social existence altogether, it might be well to recall the discussion of functional androgyny we have just completed. The dramatic alterations in human physiology and psychology possible in contemporary society by virtue of technological developments are striking in their implications for our future. We might perhaps learn from that example to be somewhat patient with apparently utopian speculations.

MOMENTARY DEITIES

The principal notion defining the post-cultural sensibility promised by developments in technological society is "nature," construed as a constatic unity of self-creative events. We have thus far used this concept of nature as the medium through which to interpret the relations of male and female, and individual and society. The final interpretation will involve the relation of God and the world. When this is completed we will have re-visioned each of the elemental notions that formed our traditional cultural paradigm—viz., God, Nature, Passion, and Social Practice. With the completion of this task we will have realized the aim of this work, which is nothing more than to provide some means of articulating the character of our cultural present in order to understand our past and anticipate our future.

The functional identification of *physis* and *techne*, which leads to the interpretation of technology as "the education of nature" and to the understanding of education as self-articulation, constitutes the fundamental teleological notion in terms of which the character of present technological developments is being discussed. The traditional distinction between the processes of nature and those of *techne* is a conventional one. The grounds for this distinction are to be found in the fact that, as human organisms, we identify ourselves not only in terms of the character of our consciousness, but by the nature of our activities. The more conscious purpose enters into our actions, the greater do we consider the distinction between human and natural processes to be. The fact that traditional meanings of art have practically all emphasized the role of conscious purpose has necessitated that we recognize at least some difference between natural and cultural processes. Taoist conceptions of *wu-yü*, *wu-wei*, and *wu-chih*, realized through enstatic, ecstatic, and constatic senses, soften the distinction between the natural and the artificial significantly. Knowing, doing, and feeling in accordance with the natures of things leads to the realization of the ultimate arbitrariness of any separation of nature and culture.

The phenomenon of technology, particularly as "internal," is forcing us toward a new understanding of nature, one that identifies the process of *physis* and *techne*. If objects in nature are conceived as the termini of intuitions, and if *techne* is a process of creative self-realization that ultimately cannot be distinguished from the processes of nature, then nature as perceived (as the terminus of an act of intuition) and nature as content of perception, cannot be distinguished except for conventional purposes. What there is is process, and all process is self-creative. Acts of self-creation are both the perceivers and the perceived. Nature is a field of reciprocally interfused moments of self-creativity. The understanding of this field requires an appreciation of the various modes of intuiting nature.

Enstasy, ecstasy, and constasy define the primary ways of experiencing the world open to us. Experience and expression considered from these three perspectives will characterize the principal structure of our understandings of the world. The consequences of taking the mystical mode of consciousness as fundamental are not only to be seen in terms of religion—indeed, a reorganization of all cultural interests is required.

The first thing to notice about this reorganization is that there is no place for what is currently termed "science." The scientific mode of perception has been realized, in principle, in the external technology that constitutes our material environment. Technology, in its dominant sense, is "realized" science. Nature, as mechanistically interpreted, requires a form of scientific perception if it is to be known; nature, from a creationist perspective, on the other hand, can only be known and appreciated in the intuitive mode we have termed constasy. The constatic sense has replaced conscious sense perception in the scientific form as the means by which nature is known. In place of science as the principal mode of knowledge we have religious intuition.[20]

This implication for science is less radical than it seems. Classical science is "ecstatic" science. It finds its locus of excellence in nature construed as *objective*. The realization of such a scientific understanding is, of course, nothing more or less than the ubiquity of technologies we now see patterning our environment. Contemporary science, however, is not to be identified wholly with ecstatic science. As we have suggested at various points in this work, the transformations of scientific investigations along so-called instrumentalist and conventionalist lines lead to the increased concern for the character of the relationship between the individual and the phenomenon he is investigating. The "subjective" element is increasingly held to be an important aspect of scientific understanding. And the investigation of subjectivity in science is not undertaken in order to discover means of overcoming it. On the contrary, many contemporary researchers are finding that the human *participation* in nature suggests a reciprocal relationship that, understood as an intrinsic union, can only be investigated by recourse to what we have been calling the sense of constatic unity.[21]

It is not necessary that we seek to transform scientists into mystics and meditators. It is important, however, that we recognize the functions of ecstatic science in terms of technological developments of the external variety, and "enstatic" science in terms of techniques of spiritual self-actualization. Both internal and external technologies, properly harmonized, provide the means of transcending the distinction between self and other in order to experience the constatic unity of nature as a field of self-creative events.

Constasy has as its aim the intuition of nature. This intuition is the mystical sense, the foundation of the *philosophia perennis*. Science, religion, and philosophy are no longer construable as separate modes of endeavor; they are all grounded in the constatic sense, as are morality and art. Aesthetic and moral sensibilities are directed in accordance with the dynamics of the constatic sense. But in the case of what we are calling aesthetic and moral sensibilities, there is at least a qualified autonomy. The twin modes of the constatic sense, enstasy and ecstasy, are the bases of the aesthetic and moral senses, respectively. The enstatic sense is constituted by the immediate feeling of a datum as inseparable from the act of feeling. In the aesthetic sense there is no discrimination between feeler and felt, but the focus is upon the feeler. There is an internalization or incorporation of the datum in the feeling subject. The reference of the feeling is here-now and this-myself. In ecstasy one is "taken up," externalized, taken outside oneself. The reference of one's experience is outward. Thus ecstatic experiencing establishes the fundamental form

of moral relation, since morality is grounded in the sense of
the importance of one's immediate experience for experiencing beyond oneself. Science as the foundation of external technology is productive of the general moral context that is
technological society.

From the creationist point of view there are three modes
of being in the world, defined by the three modalities of the
mystical sense. The primary sense grounds the directly spiritual form of experiencing. The remaining two characterize the
form of aesthetic and moral experience. We have already
considered the nature of these latter types of intuition and
their manifestation in a technological context. It remains for
us to consider the relevance of the constatic mode of experience to human experience in our technological future.

The fate of a culture is intrinsically tied to the fate of its
religion. A corollary of this fact is that the expression of a
religion—its form—is in some significant sense an expression
of the dominant values of its culture. Religion is the source of
order and value that forms the background and foundation for
significant cultural expression. The reason for the pre-eminent
status of religion in a culture is that religious myths and rituals
have as their primary function the organization and schematization of the experience of absolute power. As such they are
both channels of power and defenses against the irrational and
unpredictable exercise of power. To see the way a specific
culture handles the experience and expression of undifferentiated power provides a most significant insight into the forms
of social and cultural organization of a society.

More than any other, it is the religious interest that has
suffered from the disjunction of experience, action, and idea
that has for so long, perhaps from the very beginning, characterized Anglo-European culture. Western understandings
and articulations of religious experience and expression have
proceeded almost exclusively along dogmatic and apologetic
lines. Consequently, we have viewed religion primarily in
terms of its doctrines and its cultural rationale—i.e., its *raison
d'être* as a cultural interest among other important interests
such as art, morality, science, and philosophy. So conceived,
the distinctly experiential aspects of religion have hardly

received their proper due. Doctrinal commitment aiming at the maintenance of orthodoxy, on the one hand, and intellectual respectability vis-à-vis complementary and contrasting cultural interests, on the other, have been the primary goals of religious activity in the Judaeo-Christian West.

The emphasis upon doctrinal commitment in religion has led to the wide-spread presumption that the fundamental religious belief is belief in God. The doctrine of God, central to the theological systems of Judaeo-Christian orthodoxy, has dominated theological discussions to such an extent that, for many, the discipline of philosophy of religion has come to be identified with philosophical theology construed as an articulation and defense of the doctrine of God. Proofs for the existence of God, rather than investigations of the nature of religious experience, dominate most works in the philosophy of religion. The emphasis upon rational argument is in large measure due to the apologetic flavor of most discussions of religion in a culture whose rules of interdisciplinary communication are dominated by scientific criteria of truth. Religious and theological discussions take the form of arguments for the intellectual respectability of belief in the primary religious object. Though it is understandable that the form of interdisciplinary communication will inevitably be suggested by the language and method of the principal cultural interest, we must not be blind to the consequences of such translations into alternative, and potentially alien, semantic contexts.

It is not merely the rational mode of discourse that has provided a context for the discussion of religious subjects. We have a strong tradition of voluntarism as well, particularly in certain of the Jewish and Protestant strains. *Revelation* as well as *reason* has constituted a source for theological discussion. But the revelation of religious truth is found not in private experiences of holiness, but in the objective, historical acts of God that constitute *Heilsgeschichte*, or the history of salvation.

Reason and *action* are the primary sources of religious truth in Western culture. But reason, dominated by scientific method, and action, the paradigmatic expression of which is found in the political sphere, are hardly unbiased sources for religious investigations. From such sources we can only expect what we in fact have received: a conception of an Omnipotent, Omniscient Being whose relations to the world are defined primarily in terms of knowledge and will.

The third source of religious and theological truth has not been accorded nearly the importance of the other two. The tradition of *philosophia perennis*, which stresses the mystical, directly experiential, character of religion has suffered at the hands of those who would characterize religion solely in "political" or "scientific" terms. Like the poets in Plato's *Republic*, the mystics have, for the most part, been condemned by *feigned* praise. The contribution of the mystical tradition has always been filtered through theological orthodoxy. Seldom has the influence been direct. In Western forms of Christianity, the statements and writings of mystics have always been subjected to the test of conformity with dogma and Scripture. When the experience of the mystic has conflicted with scriptural revelation or doctrinal propositions, it has been rejected as false, or reinterpreted along orthodox lines.

Suspicion of the mystical form of experiencing is due of course to the non-rational character of the experience. The rational unity of the elements of the psyche (thought, action, passion) and the principles of social order (justice, power, and love) have received their primary support from the rationally articulated conception of the modalities of Divine existence (Father, Son, Holy Spirit). The disciplining of chaos, rehearsed in an earlier chapter, constituted a difficult and presumably necessary stage in the development of human personality and society. We cannot expect that undisciplined experiences of the type encountered in unsupervised mysticism would be met in any other fashion than has in fact been the case as long as social order and harmony depend upon the maintenance of rational, principled behavior. But radical changes within the realm of theological reflection have recently signaled the possibility that such rationalized order may no longer be thought essential.

The death-of-God movement of some years ago set the problem for systematic theology of the future: How to char-

acterize the primary religious object or objects in such a way
as to render it compatible with our denial of absolutes. The
relativity experienced across our culture and expressed
throughout our cultural interests allows us little sympathy
with a God who is an exception to one of our most fundamental experiences. A finite and relative God is the only
acceptable religious object for those who would relate the
concept of the primary religious object to other areas of cultural experience. In an epoch the history of which has shown
the impossibility of discovering absolute truth, beauty, or
goodness, there is no credibility in the assumption of an
absolute source of holiness. The technological order, which
will determine the structure of society in the future, will
render increasingly impossible thoughts of absolutes and
permanences owing to its stress upon function, process, and
change. A society of the future will be less inclined toward a
God who is "from age to age the same" and more desirous of
a god or gods who can help make sense of the immediate flux
of experience.

The crucial point is that reason and action are no longer
the primary motivating forces they once were. They have been
immanently realized in the structure of advanced technological society. The religion, art, and morality of such a society
will conform to a new dynamic, one we may term *mystical*, if
by that word we name the three basic forms of intuition. If we
consider the meaning of religious experience and expression in
the context of a mystical interpretation, we soon recognize
how very little of our traditional understandings of religion
derive from such an experiential context and how much we
have been persuaded that reason and dogma are the sole
dependable sources of religious truth. Rational arguments are
infected with the tendency to envision the source or aim of
reason in terms of some absolute; revelation is infected by the
concept of power in the sense that it was the "mighty acts of
God" that determined the content of revealed doctrine. The
message of love is overshadowed by that of power in that
the person of Jesus must be construed as a "gift" from al-
mighty God, representing an action on the order of the *Deus ex
Machina*, aimed at the salvation of humankind.

Interpreting religious experience in intuitive terms would lead away from the stress upon absoluteness expressed in terms of omniscience and omnipotence. If religious experience is considered directly, then "God" is nothing more or less than a terminus of an act of intuition that serves as a means of sensing constatic unity. Such an interpretation of religious experience from a mystical standpoint has been suspect for a variety of reasons. All three intuitive modes have been variously employed to provide mystical interpretation of religion. In the Judaeo-Christian tradition, *ecstasy* is the primary means of characterizing mystical experience in its final stages for the simple reason that the concept of God as transcendent disposes one toward the interpretation of one's experience of unity as requiring a "standing-out"—a moving outward from oneself to God. Soul-mysticism is stressed in traditions such as the Hindu, which is not committed to a monotheistic doctrine. For the enstatic sense, which finds the locus of unity to be in the soul rather than in God, can easily lead to claims about the nature and power of one's soul that would be heretical within a strictly monotheistic context.

But the unitive experience as described by Eastern and Western mystics does not have to be construed in either an ecstatic or enstatic context. The constatic mode, which has so often been interpreted as "Nature-Mysticism," provides an interpretation requiring that neither the soul nor God be given absolute status in the experience. Constasy is a sense of all things standing together in an act of intuition. "God," if the term is to have any meaning at all, must be either the Totality as experienced, or the occasion for the experience of the Totality. The Identification of God with the Nirvana-concept, The Void, or the Totality of Nature, which, under the name of pantheism, has been widespread among so-called Nature Mystics, seems perfectly justifiable, except that in this manner all personality is denied God. That God is personal is a fundamental bias that is difficult to deny. An alternative course of action may be preferable, one in which gods, as holy objects, are the occasions, the means, or the media through which the constatic sense is attained. In this sense, gods are interpretations of religious experiences in the sense that they are the occasions of such experience and the medium through which its religious character is to be understood.

An added advantage of viewing the concept of god as the occasion for a mystical experience in the constatic mode is that it avoids the stress upon either knowledge or power in its absolutist sense. The sense of the holy as the basis of religious experience is ordinarily a focused, intense, and transitory experience. The identification of God as the occasion of such an experience invests the concept of diety with the characteristic of finitude. For if a god is to maintain the characteristic of personality, it cannot be identified with the ultimate religious experience from a mystical point of view since the testimony of the mystics is that unitive experience involves a loss of personality.

The Buddhists have, perhaps, best understood the difficulty of reconciling the concept of god as personality with a fundamentally mystical and therefore *experiential* set of religious practices. Buddhism, though essentially non-theistic in the traditional Western sense of the term, nonetheless recognizes a plethora of "gods" and "demons" that, though themselves without saving power, are capable of serving as the occasions of constatic experiences of the type that we have been discussing. Also, the mystical forms of the Bodhisattvas, or semi-divine beings who serve as means of the attainment of enlightenment, are directly experienced in meditative practices. These "deities" are employed as means for the realization of states of consciousness which have as their ultimate goal Enlightenment. Since, in the Buddhist tradition, enlightenment involves the realization of the "emptiness" (*sūnyatā*) of all things—i.e., their lack of "own-being," and their status as co-dependently originated aspects of reality— no finite aspect of nature or supra-nature could be allowed absolute status. Further, the understanding of emptiness involves the constatic sense of all things standing together, existing in and through one another.

This Buddhist understanding of the nature and function of divinities accords well with the concept of nature as a field of self-creative events we have taken as the basis of our speculations in this reinterpretation of our cultural paradigm. The plurality of religious experiencing allows for the experiencing of excellences against the background of the mutually articulating unity of reciprocally interfused events. The unity thereby achieved is not that of consensus in relation to some external source or criterion, but the *articulated* unity of self-creating individuals in the acts of enstatic and ecstatic experiences of excellence.

In this view of the nature of religious experiencing, "holiness" is experienced constatically. This interpretation of holiness is directly at odds with the traditional conception of holiness as grounded in an ecstatic experience. In the traditional view, God, as the source of the experience of holiness, transcends each of us who enjoys the experience. The sense of the holy as *mysterium tremendum et fascinans* stresses the extrinsic reference of the experience of holiness; its source is *beyond*. This vision of the character of the holy has led to one of the most significant confusions among cultural aims and interests in the history of Western culture. This is the confusion of morality and religion. The identification of an omnipotent, omniscient being as the source of the experience of holiness as well as moral guarantor and judge has required that an intrinsic connection between morality and religion be assumed. The ecstatic basis of religion and morality predisposes us toward the reduction of religion to the cultural interest of morality, since the value of social stability and order has always taken precedence over the transcendent claims of holiness.

The experiential basis of morality, as we have interpreted it, is to be found in the extrinsic reference of one's experience. The value of one's experience within the context of friends, family, peer-group, society, or nation can lead to questions of moral obligation involving *responsibility*. Responsibility involves issues relating to one's own self-actualization or to the obligations or duties that ought to be performed in relation to a finite selection of others, given certain aims, goals, or values to be realized. The moral sense is ecstatically based; it is a sense of the value of one's experience for relevant experiencing beyond oneself. The fact that such relevance might be established in accordance with criteria developed from a transcendent source such as we designate by the classical conception of God does not transform morality into religion, nor does it provide the least basis for those who would reduce religion to morality. In such an instance, it merely establishes a transcendent being as moral guarantor.

A principal consequence of our present characterization of religious experience is that it frees the experience of holiness from the aegis of morality. The constatic sense as a sense of the interrelatedness of all things precludes the necessity, or even the possibility of an absolute moral reference. There can be no rules or laws that establish a set of moral duties. The aim of religious experience is to participate in the chaotic, anarchic totality, which, as the sum of all orders, is non-restricted and non-restricting.

Freed from domination by the moral sense, religious experience is also freed from the concept of God as final, ultimate, transcendent reality. The experience of God in contemporary society no longer includes such an interpretation. The experience of God is closer to that of the functional, "momentary deities" described by commentators on the archaic Greek conception of *daimon*:

> These beings do not personify any force of nature, nor do they represent some special aspect of human life; no recurrent trait or value is retained in them and transformed into a mythico-religious image; it is something purely instantaneous, a fleeting, emerging and vanishing mental content, whose objectification and outward discharge produces the image of the "momentary deity." [22]

The *daimon* is, initially for the Greeks, "any perceptual content, any object, insofar as it arouses mythical-religious interest." [23] The later development of the concept of *daimon*, or *genius*, into an internalized principle that guides individual self-realization is a correlative of the development of the idea of selfhood traced in an earlier chapter. The fact that we here have recourse to a conception of religious experience that recalls a period in human experience prior to the firm realization of a focused self suggests something important about the characterization of selfhood or personality in advanced technological societies. The functional interpretation of experience from a religious point of view supports the view that personality itself will be de-substantialized and the functional, pluralistic, non-focused aspects of persons as routes of occasions of experience rather than as solid, permanent, personality structures will be emphasized.

The increasing interest in polytheistic theologies is a striking aspect of contemporary intellectual culture. In addition to the interest shown in Eastern forms of polytheism, such as the Buddhist and Hindu, there is a renewed interest in the active appropriation of the Greek gods as media through which to interpret contemporary religious experiences. David Miller's book *The New Polytheism: Rebirth of the Gods and Goddesses*[24] provides a playful, even mischievous, account of the relevance of polytheistic theology. Miller recognizes that such a theology has not only religious but psychological and cultural significance, and is in large measure a positive assessment of what has been inappropriately termed the "fragmentation" of social and cultural existence. According to Miller, we are not fragmented beings who ought to be in search of wholeness; we are rather beings capable of multivalent and metamorphic experiences who would do well to celebrate our manyness.

In his attempt to interpret contemporary culture along polytheistic lines, Miller correlates many of our intellectual, political, and aesthetic institutions with potencies or powers identified with the gods of the Greeks. The military–industrial complex is associated with Hera–Heracles–Hephaestus; Aphrodite emerges as the Playmate of the Month. The immanence of power and the conditions of its exercise, in the political, military, industrial, as well as the aesthetic and moral spheres, provide a rich resource for the discovery of quasi-religious activities. No doubt this kind of polytheistic interpretation of advanced technological society is quite esoteric and will not meet with an immediate responsive chord from the populace. But we must remember that theological activity, more than most activities within intellectual culture, is always elitist. Theologians have moved beyond the death of God to the proclamation of new gods at a time when the lay public is still patiently and inexorably telling its beads in the same manner as in the eleventh century.

For contemporary polytheists the world has again become the arena for interplay, if not the outright struggle, of benevolent and demonic forces that can in no way be constructively related to one God, Lord of all creation. Experiencing the world as a totality with shifting loci of excellences, we are more inclined to accept a plurality of gods as the termini of constatic experiences that provide a context for this or that aspect of our experience. We are as little patient with overarching, authoritative solutions to our religilous dilemmas as we have become impatient with such solutions to our political, scientific, moral, or aesthetic problems. Ours is, willy-nilly, a pluralistic age—an age of many answers to our many questions—and pluralism in religion is polytheism. It can be nothing else.

The assumptions of a pluralistic society and of a functional or process interpretation of the nature of personality provide primary supports for the concept of polytheism in our contemporary culture. "Polytheism corresponds better to the diversity of our tendencies and our impulses, which it offers the possibility of expressing, of manifesting; each of them being free to tend, according to its nature, toward the god who suits it at the moment."[25] The principal argument for polytheistic religion is that it provides a richer source of experiencing. Whereas "monotheism curbs our sensibility,"[26] polytheism broadens our possibilities for experiencing the myriad facets of our world.

One of the most significant of the recent attempts to provide a rationale for polytheism has come from the psychologist James Hillman, who believes that, "a renascence of psychology could only come about if the psyche is given a chance to find itself against the fullest of possible backgrounds. Psychic complexity requires all the Gods; our totality can only be adequately contained by a Pantheon."[27] We have in the polytheistic traditions of the past rich sources for the development of interpretations of the various modalities of psychic activity. Monotheism, which is based upon the need to overcome fragmentation and dissociation both in the self and in society, is no longer required by virtue of the fact that we live in a society that by its very diversity supports a personality structure capable of many-faceted responses to the events constituting its ambience. It is now open to us to recognize the manyness of our religious experiencing, the variety of ways we encounter the holy.

Our name is Legion . . . and our gods are many.

NOTES

1. *Process and Reality*, p. 245.
2. *Hebrew Myths: The Book of Genesis*, edd. Robert Graves and Raphael Patai (New York: McGraw-Hill, 1966), p. 67.
3. J. Doresse, *Les livres secrets des gnostiques d'Égypte*, II (Paris, 1959), 157, quoted in Mircea Eliade, "Mephistopheles and the Androgyne," Chapter Two of *The Two and the One* (New York: Harper and Row, 1965), p. 106.
4. Ibid., p. 114.
5. A number of worthwhile studies of the tantric tradition of Tibet have been written. The principal difficulty with learning about Tibetan Buddhism has consisted in the fact that there have not been sufficient numbers of tantric adepts who have mastered European languages and philosophies. As a result, a lot of nonsense has been produced by former Tibetan Lamas who, because of their ignorance of Western languages and culture, were unable to communicate their formidable learning to their Western audience. The Dharma Press and the Shambhala Press which together publish the works of such men as Lama Govinda, Chögyam Trungpa, and Tarthang Tulku, have significantly improved this situation. Introductions to the topic of Tibetan Buddhism include such valuable works as Lama Govinda's *The Way of the White Clouds* (Berkeley: Shambhala, 1970), and *Foundations of Tibetan Buddhism* (New York: Weiser, 1974). Perhaps the best recent work on Tantric Buddhism is Stephan Beyer's *The Cult of Tara: Magic and Ritual in Tibet* (Berkeley: The University of California Press, 1973).
6. Govinda, *Foundations*, p. 103. For a detailed account of the male–female polarity in Hindu Tantrism, see Agehananda Bharati, *The Tantric Tradition* (New York: Doubleday, 1970), pp. 199–227.
7. The best popular work on androgyny to date is June Singer's *Androgyny: Toward a New Theory of Sexuality*. For an interesting collection of essays on the subject of androgyny, see *Beyond Sex-role Stereotypes: Toward a Psychology of Androgyny*, edd. Alexandra Kaplan and Joan Bean (Boston: Little, Brown, 1976).
8. Stanley Rosen, *Plato's Symposium* (New Haven: Yale University Press, 1968), p. 139. I do not wish to appear to overstate my case. I have argued against the internalizing of external technologies. The surgical and pharmaceutical refashioning of human physiology and personality might seem to be a dramatic illustration of just such a misuse of technique. I do not believe so. Though my arguments are not dependent upon such radical procedures' receiving widespread employment, there is no contradiction involved in the use of such techniques if the aim is individual self-actualization. Technology employed to increase and to fulfill individual

potentialities is quite distinct from its use in limiting human possibilities. In no case, of course, are such techniques to be employed against the wishes of any one.

9. For a discussion of the relation between "alienation" and "ecstasy," see the following section.

10. See Nathan Rotenstreich's "Concept of Alienation and its Metamorphoses," Chapter Seven of *Basic Problems of Marx's Philosophy* (New York: Bobbs-Merrill, 1965), pp. 141–61. I am dependent on this work of Rotenstreich's for the suggestion of the historical relation between the concepts of alienation and ecstasy, though, of course, my subsequent applications of these terms to contemporary technological culture are by no means those of which Professor Rotenstreich would necessarily approve.

11. Ibid., p. 146.

12. Ibid., p. 150.

13. Ibid., p. 152.

14. Ibid., p. 155.

15. Ibid., p. 157.

16. For an illustration of Feuerbach's contemporary influence, see Martin Buber's *I and Thou*, trans. Walter Kaufman (New York: Scribner, 1970).

17. Rotenstreich, op. cit., p. 160.

18. The "career" concept of selfhood is discussed in Walter Maner's unpublished essay, "The Career Interpretation of Personal Identity," delivered to a symposium on philosophical psychology held at Boston University in the spring of 1970. This view is in essential agreement with earlier process interpretations of selfhood associated with the thought of Whitehead and Charles Hartshorne. The metaphysical foundations of this conception of the self are spelled out most completely in Whitehead's *Process and Reality*. For a brief interpretive summary of this conception see *The Civilization of Experience*, Chapter Three.

19. *Process and Reality*, pp. 520–21.

20. There are a surprising number of developments in contemporary science, particularly in microphysics, that call for interpretation in terms of aesthetic and mystical understandings. It is significant that those individuals promoting such understandings are inevitably drawn to Oriental thought. For a layman's account of these developments in theoretical physics, see Fritjof Capra's *The Tao of Physics* (Berkeley: Shambhala Press, 1975), and Gary Zukav's *The Dancing Wu Li Masters: An Overview of the New Physics* (New York: Morrow, 1979).

Also, see the interesting article "In Defense of Mystical Science," *Philosophy East and West*, 29, No. 1 (January 1979), 73–90. Two significant works concerning the contributions of the aesthetic sensibility to scientific understandings are *On Aesthetics in Science*, ed. Judith Wechsler (Cambridge: MIT Press, 1978), and Douglas R. Hofstadter's *Gödel, Escher, Bach* (New York: Vintage, 1979).

Recently the physicist David Bohm has been working out a novel conception of order relevant to the interpretation of quantum relativity. The intuition underlying this conception of order, as I understand it, is exactly that developed in this essay in relation to the concepts of "ecstasy," "enstasy," and "constasy." If this is so, or nearly so, then Bohm's intriguing interpretation of quantum relativity is dramatically supportive of the move toward "mystical science." See *Wholeness and the Implicate Order* (London: Routledge and Kegan Paul, 1980). See also the following articles by Bohm: "On Some Notions Concerning Locality and Nonlocality in Quantum Theory" (with A. Baracca, B. J. Hiley, and A. E. G. Stuart), *Il Nuovo Cimento*, 28B, No. 2 (1975), 453–66. "On the Intuitive Understanding of Nonlocality as Implied by Quantum Theory," *Foundations of Physics*, 5, No. 1 (1975), 93–109, and "Some Remarks on Sarfatti's Proposed Connection Between Quantum Phenomena and the Volitional Activity of the Observer-Participant," *Psychoenergetic Systems*, I (1976), 173–79.

21. For an interesting interpretation of what I am calling "constatic unity" in terms of the notion of "self-consistency," see Geoffery Chew, "'Bootstrap': A Scientific Idea?" *Science*, 161 (May 1968), 762–65, and "Impasse for the Elementary Particle Concept," *The Great Ideas Today*, 23 (Chicago: Benton, 1974).

22. Ernst Cassirer, *Language and Myth* (New York: Dover, 1946), pp. 17–18. Cassirer is here considering an idea originating with Hermann Usener's work *Götternamen: Versuch einer Lehre von der religiösen Begriffsbildung* (Bonn, 1896). This notion, however, receives widespread support from many sources including, of course, Adkin's *From the Many to the One*. See also Walter Otto's classic study, *The Homeric Gods: The Spiritual Significance of Greek Religion* (New York: Pantheon Books, 1954).

23. Cassirer, *Philosophy of Symbolic Forms*, II, 169.

24. (New York: Harper and Row, 1974).

25. E. M. Cioran, *The New Gods*, trans. Richard Howard (New York: Quadrangle / New York Times, 1974), p. 22.

26. Ibid.

27. *Revisioning Psychology* (New York: Harper and Row, 1975), p. 222.

The Uncertain Phoenix

ANDROGYNOUS PERSONALITIES? Persons as de-substantial-ized routes of experiencing events? Gods as transient media of constatic experiences? In themselves these notions seem bizarre in the extreme. When seen against the background of advancing technological society, which involves the external-ization of rational structures and functions and the increased concern for the development of techniques of self-realization, however, the vision we have sketched becomes almost believ-able. For the technical matrix within which we are currently enmeshed has both increased our powers and limited our choices. Even though we are able to suggest the skeletal struc-ture of a possible future, however, the flesh framed by these bones is beyond our descriptive powers.

More than any other discipline, perhaps, the philosophy of culture is burdened by uncertainty and confusion. But per-iods of crisis and transition compound our problems by requiring of the philosophical critic that—against his inclina-tions—he appear to take a stance not unlike that of the most tendentious of prophets. It is well, therefore, to recall at the close of this work that which we proclaimed at its beginning: the data for the contemporary philosopher of culture are limited to the ashes of uncertainty. In our present situation, a dogmatic prophet would serve no viable function, for all prophecies must stand as equals until, at some future harvest, the wheat is separated from the chaff.

Thus, contrary to the appearance of some of my speculations, this essay is not intended to be an exercise in utopian thinking. It is primarily an attempt at cultural self-understanding. I have tried to trace the emergence and decline of that cultural paradigm in terms of which not only have our ideas, actions, and feelings made sense to us, but we have in fact constituted ourselves as thinking, acting, and feeling creatures as such. And since in an age of decaying sensibilities self-understanding cannot simply be a function of knowing where we have been, I have sought to provide a "sensibility matrix" in terms of which we might envision a possible future. If my forecast seems less "realistic" than many others, as well it might, I can only say that we develop our sense of what is realistic from inertial habits of thinking that, more often than not, have a numbing effect upon our imaginations. In periods of crisis it is precisely our imaginations that are most essential to our survival and well-being.

I am certainly willing to grant that there are many more likely futures than the one I have outlined, the worst among them being the barbaric self-immolation of War, or political stalemate followed by the staleness of slow decay, or the cybernetic hedonism resulting from the internalizing of external technologies—to rehearse but a few. Surely there is a place, though, for the presentation of a less frightening vision of the future; we must, after all, be at least as prepared for the better as for the worse of our possible futures.

INDEX

Abraham, 87
Absolutes: belief in, 5–6
Abstraction: formal and selective, 47–48, 191–92
Action: and efficient cause, 284, 286–87; mode of consciousness, 281–84; as praxis, 236–37, 239; as sublimation of labor, 284
Acupuncture, 342
Adam, 86, 293
Adkins, A. W. H., 42, 92, 388; on individualization, 65–66
Adler, Mortimer, 39
Agape, 147–49, 375
Aisthesis: *see* Praxis
Alchemy: as gnostic science, 337, 340, 369; and synchronicity, 277
Alienation: and ecstasy, 384–97, 412; political, 153
Ananke, 343
Anarchism, 40, 287–88; and culture, 364; metaphysics of, 228; and society, 396
Anarchy: and chaos, 53; intellectual, 49; political, 368
Anaxagoras, 73; as a process philosopher, 174–75, 180
Anaximander, 73
Anaximenes, 73, 128
Androgyny, 165, 397, 411; attitudinal, 374–84; and sexual non-differentiation, 379
Anytus, 34
Aquinas, St. Thomas, 123, 178; on the Trinity, 79–80
Arendt, Hannah, 234, 288
Arguëlles, José, 41–42, 368
Aristophanes: on Chaos, 55–56; myth of the circle men, 143–46, 149, 375, 380–81
Aristotle, 58, 66, 78, 84, 87, 92, 102, 128, 129, 216, 217, 384; on "the acciden-

tal," 270–71; on the four causes, 15, 69; on imitation, 348–50; metatheory of, 15–17, 72–74; as a naturalist, 194; on the organization of knowledge, 68–69; on *philia*, 148–49; on praxis, 240–41; on Prime Matter, 215, 216; on science, 270; on *techne*, 239
Art: as a cultural interest, 84, 88, 127; as education, 361–66; and goodness, 396; as imitation, 347–51, 360; and passion, 150–52; and the public sphere, 162; and reductionism, 23; Renaissance, 257–58; as self-creativity, 361; as sublimation, 351–52, 360; Sung Dynasty, 257–58; and *techne*, 141, 239–40; and technology, 320; as transformation, 352–53, 360, 366
Augustine, St., 8, 20, 29, 30, 92, 118, 176; on evil, 177–78; on the Trinity, 77–78
Authority: political, 152–53, 156
Auto-eroticism, 150–52

Bacon, Francis, 232
Barret, William, 367
Baumgarten, Alexander, 242
Beatific Vision, the, 198
Beauty: as a cultural aim, 84
Beginning, the, 33, 45–46, 52–59; defined, 52; and principles, 52–53; and cosmogonic myths, 53–59
Behavioral technology, 136, 348–59
Behaviorism, 25, 133–37, 153, 233
Being: and becoming, 177, 193; and non-being, 116, 173, 176–77, 186
Belief, 37, 96–97
Berger, Peter, 92
Bergson, Henri, 32, 225, 243; as a process philosopher, 175, 180, 182, 192, 194, 196, 197, 199–200, 201
Beyer, Stephen, 411